UNITED NATIONS PUBLICATIONS
UNITED NATIONS, ROOM DC2-853,
NEW YORK, NEW YORK 10017 USA

UNITED NATIONS PUBLICATIONS
PALAIS DES NATIONS, 1211 GENEVA 10, SWITZERLAND

SALES NO. E.95.IV.4

ISBN 92-1-130165-3

COPYRIGHT © UNITED NATIONS 1996
ALL RIGHTS RESERVED
MANUFACTURED IN THE UNITED STATES OF AMERICA

Contents

Preface ... 4
1. Family Matters ... 7
2. Family: Forms and Functions ... 35
3. Family as an Environment: an Ecosystem Perspective on Family Life ... 61
4. Reinventing Fatherhood ... 81
5. The Intersection of Family, Gender and Economy in the Developing World ... 113
6. Family Enrichment: Programmes to Foster Healthy Family Development ... 149
7. Partnership Families ... 169
8. Family and Crime ... 207
9. The Family and Youth: Issues, Problems and Opportunities ... 229
10. The Elderly and the Family in Developing Countries ... 257
11. Families and Disability ... 289
12. Migration and the Family ... 335
13. Family Leave: Changing Needs of the World's Workers ... 379
14. The Concept of Family Health ... 395
15. Family: Agents and Beneficiaries of Socio-economic Development ... 419
Bibliography ... 439

Tables

2.1 Forms of families ... 42
12.1 Rate of urbanization, less developed regions by major areas, 1975-2025 ... 338
12.2 Person who made decision in first rural-urban migration by age at time of move, Philippines ... 345
12.3 Famine-coping strategies, Africa ... 349
12.4 Reasons for moving among owners and renters, United States, 1991 ... 363
12.5 Composition of families in the United States and Australia ... 364
12.6 Reasons for moving to current dwellings of persons living in private dwellings who had moved since reaching the age of 60, Adelaide and Melbourne, 1981 ... 368
14.1 Representative health indicators of family health by geographic region ... 408
14.2 Examples of indicators of families for capacity-building efforts ... 409

Figures

3.1 The Vanier Institute of the Family's working definition of family ... 64
3.2 Family as an environment in an environment ... 76
3.3 Family policy grid ... 78
12.1 Example of a recruitment network of prospective labour migrants (illegal) from east Java to Malaysia ... 353
12.2 Catagory of immigrants, 1976-1993, Australia ... 362
12.3 Persons aged 15+: proportion who changed usual residence in Australia, by reason for moving and type of move, year ending 31 May 1987 ... 363
12.4 Female labour-force participation rates by age at censuses conducted in Australia between 1947 and 1991 ... 365
12.5 Total fertility rates, Australia, 1921-1991 and United States, 1940-1989 ... 369

Preface

This collection of original papers was written to mark the International Year of the Family (IYF), 1994. First published separately in the IYF Occasional Papers Series between 1992 and 1995, the papers provide information on a wide range of family issues. They both report research findings of scholars and other specialists and reflect the opinions of the authors. The purpose of the book is to increase awareness of the importance and needs of today's families. Chapter subjects therefore are eclectic and far-reaching, as diversified in treatment and content as the topics they address. It is in this context that the key concerns of the family are identified.

Concern over the precarious situation of families was reflected in the General Assembly's proclamation of the International Year of the Family. The Year was conceived as an important first step in a long-term effort to support families. A partnership was thus established with Governments, the United Nations system and other intergovernmental organizations, plus the voluntary and private sectors.

The objectives of IYF were straightforward: to provide an impetus to supporting families as basic social units; to gain and promote an accurate understanding of family issues; to initiate activities to address them; and to create a climate and institutional capabilities, at various levels, conducive to these efforts.

For the first time in history, on 18 and 19 October 1994, the United Nations held a full-fledged debate, at a high political level, devoted exclusively to family issues. Forty-five delegations took the floor; many speakers were at the ministerial or equivalent level. The Conference demonstrated a remarkable maturation in political approach to family issues, including agreement that families must be a focus of development strategy at the highest levels and that the best interests of individuals and societies lies in promoting democratic families and family-friendly societies.

Great strides have been made in achieving the immediate goal of the Year: increasing awareness, both among policy makers and the general public, of the unique role of families and the need to address their concerns. A decisively positive approach evolved. Greater recognition of the importance of supporting families has emerged as an essential part of the efforts to achieve peace, human rights and sustainable development, along with lasting progress on behalf of women, children and other vulnerable members of society. Another important accomplishment is the recognition that the Year has been only the beginning of a long-term process of support for families.

In the opening chapter of this volume we have made an effort to capture the broad spectrum of the interest expressed in families and IYF. It is a testament, therefore, bearing witness to the concerns underlying the IYF. The text is drawn from various statements that I have delivered in my capacity as Coordinator for IYF, all over the world, mainly in the preparatory process for the Year. Like any record, it is lacking in some respects. Not all topics are amenable to this kind of treatment, nor have I had the privilege of participating in even a portion of the many gatherings assembled on issues related to the project. In addition, the statements themselves are neither definitive nor complete. The learning process is ongoing and, as the course of study and debate unfolds, so will the questions, and possibly their answers.

Some of the concepts recorded here have enjoyed remarkable consensus, while others have invited debate. What is important, what the problems might be and where solutions should be sought has stimulated a wealth of opinion. This diversity of opinion is one of the great resources of IYF, and indeed is reflected throughout the other chapters of this book. Some of the chapters had to be shortened in the interest of keeping the volume within a manageable length. In no case, though, has this changed the basic tone or ommitted any essential part of the various author's theses.

Families are and will remain a pivotal part of the human experience; this conviction is the one omnipresent feature before, during and after the IYF. Regardless of whether the views on the family are reformist or conservative, futuristic or nostalgic, or whether families are seen as part of the solution or part of the problem, people everywhere know that the family matters.

HENRYK J. SOKALSKI
United Nations Coordinator for the International Year of the Family

---

The views expressed in this book are those of the authors and do not necessarily reflect those of the United Nations Secretariat.
Mention of names of firms and commercial products does not imply the endorsement of the United Nations.

FAMILY Matters

The family: diversity and dynamism for unity

> "WE STAND AT A CROSSROADS BETWEEN THE CONCEPTION OF THE FAMILY WHICH PREVAILED IN THE PAST AND THAT OF THE FUTURE. WE MUST TAKE ACCOUNT OF THE PAST, WE MUST WORK IN THE PRESENT, AND WE MUST LOOK TOWARDS THE FUTURE."
>
> Catherine Lalumière

The family knows no frontiers

All over the world, families are as different and diversified as they are alike. Vital, productive families are essential to the world's future; they are the cradle of the generations to come. Their strengths and weaknesses largely reflect the societal fabric of every country. As the world's oldest form of expression of human relationship, the family has survived thousands of years, adapting itself constantly to changing socio-economic conditions and the progress of humanity.

In the modern world, society is made up of a complex set of relationships, among which the family is one. In fact, it should be conceived as a very special relationship; one of equity and reciprocity between genders and generations, based on biology, law, custom or choice, and often upon economics. Deriving from an etymology common to all cultures and traditions, the family knows no frontiers.

No simple view of the family exists, nor can there be a universally applicable definition. Throughout recorded history and in different parts of the world, many diverse types of families have existed displaying pronounced variations in their structures. In addition, new and divergent family forms are constantly evolving. So also are perceptions of the functions and roles of the family. The kinds of interpersonal relationships within the family differ both among and within national societies. This diversity and divergence is a faithful reflection of the cultural pluralism of the individuals that constitute societies.

More recently, new types of families have begun to emerge, such as the single-parent family, which do not fit the traditional characterizations of the family structure such as "nuclear" and "extended" families. Yet in most countries, legal systems and policy-making processes lag behind such changes, leading to a failure to support the needs of family members in a fully integrated, familial context. The increased prevalence of single-parent families, most of which are headed by women, pose important challenges for legal, social and governmental policy-makers.

The family must be viewed as a living, evolving institution, one affected by socio-economic factors as well as by the changes that shape its social environment. It has not escaped the impact of the complex problems brought about by the advancement of civilization. Change has also occurred in different places at different times, at different speeds and to different extents, creating even more variety in families. Families are undergoing constant change because of numerous factors. These include demographic trends; socio-cultural changes; economic recessions and depressions; wars; famine; unemployment; migration; technological innovation; the processes of industrialization and urbanization; the quest for equality between men and women; and widening opportunities for women.

In addition, shifts have occured in collective values, particularly those supporting individualism, where the worth of the individual can be seen as transcending that of the group and where a high value is placed on self-expression, self-realization, self-fulfilment, autonomy and the freedom of the individual. The impact of these factors, which vary greatly from region to region, is a driving force in the creation of new family structures, cultural values and socio-economic conditions.

The family: A central topic in social policy and development

Central to the purpose of any international effort on families is the need to encourage professionals and policy makers to find more effective ways of strengthening them. Action should proceed from three basic observations:

A The family is universally recognized as a basic unit of society. Many changes in society have altered their roles and functions, but families continue to provide the natural framework for the emotional and material support essential to the growth and well-being of their members. Additionally, families are a basic social unit of production and consumption and, as such, are at the heart of the economic process. Their needs must be intimately connected with the objectives of economic and social development, as a minimum standard of progress. In short, families are engines of the economic and social development process, and must be accounted for when establishing policies and priorities for economic and social development;

B The topic of the family is pivotal to a broad spectrum of social policy and developmental issues. Perhaps no other group lends itself better to a cross-sectoral and integrated approach in dealing with social progress; no other offers such a unique convergence of numerous issues. In the last two decades, the ever-increasing concern for the fundamental rights and well-being of individuals, particularly those who are disadvantaged, marginalized or discriminated against, as well as the efforts to improve their lot, concurrently has led to the rediscovery of the family. An important corollary of those activities has been the recognition of families as forming a crucial social safety net for improving the well-being of individual family members. Recently, this renewed interest in the family has accelerated in different parts of the world as the result of harsh economic realities and sweeping socio-political changes and shifts in traditional values;

c The family, as a living, evolving social institution, faces what may be its most difficult challenge in the history of the human species. Many societies are changing so rapidly that the speed of change alone is a major factor of stress in families. Never before in history have there been so many and so dramatic changes in such a short time. Human beings, however, often do not adapt as rapidly as changes occur. New attitudes and behaviours require time before they are learned and internalized. In many societies, old traditions of child-rearing or spousal relations have become outmoded while the new ones have yet to be launched or accepted, forming a kind of normative vacuum. At the same time, much of the societal change that challenges individual families originates and is promulgated at the familial level. Families are not just recipients of change: they also serve as its agents. Acknowledging the reflective interaction of society and families is basic to a thorough appreciation of the family as a fluid and dynamic social form.

In short, the challenges families face in the present-day world and the stress they undergo are numerous, largely depending upon the level of national socio-economic development and diversification. In performing functions vital to the well-being of its members and society, the family has responded to these changes in ways ranging from adaptation without significant dysfunction to total breakdown. Nevertheless, the struggle of families to respond successfully to change has been significant and deserves careful study. Therefore, IYF was an attempt to support families in their efforts to adapt and change as well as to support their pivotal role in social development.

Why have an IYF

"HAPPY FAMILIES ARE ALL ALIKE, EVERY UNHAPPY FAMILY IS UNHAPPY IN ITS OWN WAY."
Leo Tolstoy

Why not have an IYF?

A popular legend is of a philosophy professor who set a final exam consisting only of the question, "Why?", printed on a blank page. The student who attained the highest mark answered: "Why not?". While this may not offer much help to philosophy students studying for final exams it is, to a certain extent, instructive in the case of IYF. Families are, and have been, universally present, recognized in some form in all societies and fundamentally important to the structure and action of the societies of which they are part. Families are basic, foundational elements of the human social experience. Given the primordial significance of families, it is tempting to answer the question: "Why have an international year of the family?" in the words of the student, "Why not?". If, however, it can be accepted that the rationale for IYF is obvious, the question is really, "Why now?".

For five decades, the United Nations has been the major global presence in promoting, advocating and raising awareness of peace, security, economic and social development and higher standards of life in larger freedom. But promotion and advocacy are not ends in themselves. They are the first steps to action: real, concrete action, benefiting individuals, social groups and entire societies, as was the case with major United Nations events. The international years and decades of the 1970s and 1980s devoted to women, children, persons with disabilities, the elderly, youth and literacy have adequately proved that international years can successfully focus awareness, attention and the conscience of the world on important issues.

Those events, however, stressed a sectoral approach to social problems by concentrating primarily on selected aspects of human development. The subject of families offers a much more comprehensive and, at the same time, synthesizing approach, since the family represents the fullest reflection, at the grass-roots level, of the strengths and weaknesses of the social and developmental welfare environment. That is the first basic consideration in favour of an integrated approach to social progress and development through the family, and thereby is the strongest argument in favour of IYF.

IYF: An effort to support families

The proclamation of IYF was a direct result of the growing international concern over the precarious situation of families. It was conceived as a concerted effort of the international community, in harmony with a large number of crucial partners - Governments, the voluntary and private sectors, the United Nations system and other intergovernmental organizations - to support families as a basic social unit; to gain and promote an accurate understanding of family issues; to initiate and execute activities to address these issues, particularly at the local and national levels; and to create institutional capabilities for implementing changes at all levels that strengthen the family.

In comparison with similar earlier events, IYF was a unique undertaking. As the concerns of family apply to most social policy areas, it was within the scope of IYF to combine and synthesize several social issues, bringing them down to a common denominator of action. It offered an opportunity, as a noted expert on family policies put it, to bring together the threads of social life that previously had been treated separately and disjointedly.

Concerns and reservations

Initially, the idea of IYF provoked some questions, if not fears. Some of them were:

A That an emphasis on family life might undermine the national and international accomplishments in the struggle for the equal rights of men and women;

B That through IYF, an attempt would be made to impose a standard definition of the family and promote one specific family model;

C That the observance of IYF, by stressing the rights of families, might neglect to stress the important responsibilities of families.

However, after the initial phase of the debate on IYF, these concerns seem to have undergone a creative evolution. From the standpoint of the United Nations, IYF was intended to strengthen the cause of women's rights and equality between the sexes in all aspects of familial relationships; to respect the existing diversities; and to promote concepts based on family rights and responsibilities alike

IYF: A platform for action

IYF, like individual families, was not an undifferentiated, monochromatic formula. IYF was a dynamic process, involving individuals and groups at the grass-roots levels in preparing for the observance and follow-up to IYF in 1994. By focusing on action at the national and local levels, IYF has highlighted the many diverse strengths and weaknesses and problems and potentialities of families in different parts of the world. IYF served as a platform for the review, reform and improvement of policies, based on a principle of participation at the grass-roots level. It was therefore an important mechanism through which people could influence the policy-making process at the local, national and regional levels.

The words "family" and "families" are mentioned 63 times in the Declaration and Programme of Action of the World Summit for Social Development (Copenhagen, Denmark, 6-12 March 1995). As much as this may be an oversimplified criterion, the pervasive interest has been a result of, and a tribute to, the International Year of the Family. For indeed, the IYF has been responsible for a significant global awakening on family issues. Thanks to the Year, the world is and will be quite different in terms of its perception of families.

Furthermore, IYF was a platform for action because it called for the mobilization and empowerment of families. Despite the best efforts of the United Nations as an international body, and the combined efforts of major national and international non-governmental organizations, they will not succeed without the support and participation of families themselves. The biggest bloc of political influence and power with a vested interest in family policy are families. The principle of empowerment must be more than just an aspiration after IYF; it must be the modus operandi of its effective follow-up.

Changing families in changing societies

> "FREUDE MUSS LEID, LEID MUSS FREUDE HABEN."
> (JOY NEEDS WOE, WOE REQUIRES JOY.)
> Johann Wolfgang von Goethe

Change and evolution

Global concern for the family is not born out of a nostalgic desire for simpler times, when rules and roles were less clouded by ambiguity and the future was less uncertain. Indeed, the so-called uncomplicated world of yesterday was in many ways not the sort of society that people might want to live in tomorrow; notably, for example, in respect to the subjugation of women, the reprehensible exploitation of children or the neglect of the elderly and persons with disabilities. On the contrary, the concerns that spawned IYF were intensely contemporary issues, with real and substantial implications for the future.

The family, like the rest of society, has undergone a process of wholesale, transformative change. In this process, the family has been both the purveyor and the recipient of change; sometimes acting as its agent or, alternatively, being transformed by external forces. In some cases, the process has been adaptive, in others, destructive, threatening the survival of the family. Whatever the specific causes, many of the things nostalgically understood to constitute a family, for better or worse, are now lost to history. In addition, many of the stereotypes or conventions used to describe family life are often anachronistic and no longer borne out by reality.

Global transformation

Perhaps the most glaring example of change is the case of rural and urban families. In many parts of the world, urban centres increasingly consist of extended family units, drawn together as a survival strategy in the face of deteriorating economies and the lack of individual opportunity. Paradoxically, rural settings, once the province of extended families, are becoming increasingly nuclear, as the productive limits of subdivided land reduce the capacity of large families to support themselves. One reason why the family is so important at present is because increasingly less is known about what the family is in reality.

The global transformation of society has taken a number of forms, each with a unique set of opportunities and dangers for the family. For instance, geography has become less reliable as a predictor of culture than at any time in history. The place where one happens to be is more and more less important for determining who one is. For centuries the limits to mobility have been one form of ensuring cultural survival. This protection is vanishing rapidly as the world shrinks and the magic allure of economic globalization is on the lips of business people everywhere. In some cases, this transformation breeds positive change, releasing individuals, for example, from the cultural bounds of traditionally oppressive attitudes. In other cases, the shrinking world and its transnational economy have had problematic consequences.

Thousands upon thousands of migrant families, escaping scarcity and deprivation, wars or persecution are at present wandering the planet in search of security, a home and a better future. Such families are particularly vulnerable to the separation, and sometimes desertion, of their members. Often they have to shoulder the additional burden of cultural change, difficult processes of adjustment or assimilation, and rapidly transformed interpersonal relationships in the family.

At the same time, the migrant family is a powerful example of the family as a source of personal and group identity; as a place for intimacy, emotional and spiritual nourishment; and as a provider of mutual support in times of crisis and transition. The migrant unit is a general testimony to the importance of the family in the present-day world, and provides one more reason for turning attention to the family as a source of comfort and support on a planet where both are badly needed.

The relevance of the family is obviously not confined to changes in demography or geography nor to the emotional or economic support of its members. Families are affected by, and are a source of, change in the attitudes and values that lie at the very heart of social and global change.

Change as a provider of opportunity

The pace of change families are subjected to, both internally and externally, has never been so rapid. The rate of cultural, economic and political transformation in the world beggars description. Change incessantly pounding on their consciousness taxes the ability of people to understand, adapt or act thoughtfully in the world about them. Their capacity to cope with change through meaningful and productive action is constantly being challenged.

Families everywhere are in need of support to increase their capacity to adapt to and meet the demands of change. Environmental issues, the shrinking world of commerce and communication, massive political transformation and technological innovation all have profound impacts on families around the world. Environmental, economic and socio-political refugees are a fact of life on the planet. Poverty, displacement, hunger and violence are still ubiquitous, and can strike families with such dramatic rapidity and force that few, if any, options are available for positive adaptation. Revolution has always happened at a cost, and for some families this cost is too high. These families deserve protection by all entities acting in concert and under a social contract, in whatever form the latter may exist.

Rapid change is also a time of opportunity, when new and positive social forms can quickly replace those that are antiquated, inappropriate or unjust. History is full of examples of such positive change. Do not assume, however, that change will somehow independently generate benefits. The capacity for thoughtful human action is necessary for positive social change, and evidence of that thoughtfulness should be seen in the societies people build.

Changes in families

Forces of change have wrought immense transformations in society and have brought about equally profound changes in families themselves. Foremost among these changes, particularly in the developed world, are the sweeping accomplishments by and on behalf of women. Although this work is far from complete and much more is to be achieved, nothing can diminish the remarkable reforms that have already taken place, in families and human society, in response to the rising tide of feminist thought and collective action. What is most astounding is not so much the breadth and depth as the rate of this change.

The ability of medical technology to control or even to stimulate conception, the increasing numbers of elderly persons in families, the increased sensitivity to the rights and needs of children and persons with disabilities, and the rising rates of crime and substance abuse are additional factors generating internal change in families. Each are the subject of mediation through families, and reappear in the various stresses, changes and negotiations that surface in contemporary family life. As with rapid external change, changes internal to the family bring both opportunities and problems, benefits and costs, and certainties and risks.

Fundamental to the notion of family seems to be a dichotomy between the presence of the repressive, hierarchical structures of family life and the absence of a sense of moral obligation, awareness and solidarity concerning others' needs; the dichotomy between power and control, on the one hand, and the equal and inalienable rights of all family members, on the other. Historically, the family has too often been a refuge of patriarchal domination and served as a vehicle for the subjugation of women and children. In these situations, family life has been dominated by the invocation of exclusively male privilege, intimidation, coercion and threats, economic abuse, child abuse and child labour, and isolation or other forms of emotional abuse.

Positive growth

In singling out, therefore, the need for change to bring about positive growth in and progress for families and society, several crucial components can be conceived as constituting a true partnership in family life:

A   The establishment of procedures for sharing responsibility, including an equitable distribution of work, and for decisions on matters affecting the family to be made together as a family unit;

B   The creation of respect, trust and support, meaning being willing to listen to one another non-judgementally, valuing the opinions of all members, being emotionally affirming, supporting each other's goals in life, and respecting the rights of each person to have his or her own feelings, opinions and choices;

C   The use of non-threatening behaviour by family members in their relations with one another;

D   The practice of honesty and accountability, which means communicating openly and truthfully, admitting to mistakes and accepting

personal responsibility for feelings, thoughts and behaviour;
E The use of negotiation skills in an atmosphere of fairness, which implies seeking mutually satisfying resolutions to conflict, accepting change and being willing to compromise;
F The practice of economic partnership by making financial decisions together as a family and ensuring that all family members benefit;
G The use of responsible parenting practices, meaning sharing parental responsibilities and being a positive non-violent role model for other members of the family, including children, thereby providing the foundation for a partnership based on equal rights.

The sharing father

The twentieth century has introduced structural changes into the family and has created problems for many men in their identities as husbands and fathers, at least in the Western world. Fatherhood, however, is clearly both necessary and worthwhile and the problems of men must be addressed.

Three hundred years ago, William Penn complained that men are generally more concerned about the breed of their horses and dogs than about their children. Indeed, in many families, the role of the father has not evolved much beyond that of the principal or sole financial provider for the family. The increasing accomplishments of mothers as financial providers, and the effects of economic restructuring in some industrialized countries have done much to undermine men's predominantly breadwinner role. To a certain extent, social policy also has contributed to the latter's declining importance by providing income support and other types of financial programmes for families. Such programmes are and will continue to be necessary; however, the unfortunate result might be more fathers neglecting their responsibilities. From the point of view of social policy or legislative change, the challenge is to ensure that the financial responsibilities of fathers are recognized without strengthening the view that financial support is the exclusive province of fatherhood. Clearly, part of the solution lies in developing the non-financial dimensions of the father's role in the family, as an active nurturer, educator and emotional supporter of children.

For a variety of reasons, the role of the father provides a graphic and informative example of how an organic view of families is useful, and why such a view is so indispensable to understanding the relationships that make up families.

The case of fatherhood signals, first, the crucial interdependencies present in families and, second, the need for a comprehensive family policy accurately reflecting the complexity of familial relationships. Perhaps the most telling aspect is that the issue of fatherhood is most often referred to in relation to issues concerning the advancement of women. Specifically, the contemporary issue of the changed role of the father is largely the result of a changed understanding of the role of mothers.

Equality of the genders

The binding responsibilities engendered by a traditional patriarchal system continue to affect, through the medium of the family, the opportunities available to women. The classic example is the inequitable distribution of labour in the home. A simplistic but thoroughly desirable solution would be to have men assume equal responsibility for domestic work. This solution, however, can be meaningful only in the context of broader social changes, such as those that would ensure that the mother is able to capitalize on a reduced domestic workload by having unfettered access to equal pay for work outside the home. Families must not be penalized for attempting to incorporate fathers in meaningful non-financial ways of supporting mothers in non-traditional roles. Achieving a balance of roles and responsibilities in the home is inextricably entwined with achieving equality of the sexes in society generally.

In many important ways, progress in efforts towards equality of the sexes based on United Nations standards can be accomplished in the context of a harmonized organic view of the interdependencies that define families. The same structures that have limited the full participation of women in society also restrict the movement of men to non-traditional roles. The impact of both constraints combined restricts the ability of families to evolve and change in positive ways. Such challenges, however, were integral to the development of effective family policies and the support of families throughout IYF.

Social policy challenges

"WE MUST STRENGTHEN THE FAMILY - BECAUSE IT IS THE FAMILY THAT HAS A BEARING ON THE FUTURE."
George Bush

In proclaiming IYF[1], the General Assembly decided that the major activities for its observance should be concentrated at the local, regional and national levels and assisted by the United Nations and its system of

organizations, in cooperation with intergovernmental and non-governmental organizations, as well as interested national organizations. To assist in the identification of local and national priorities, the following categories of issues were proposed:
- A Strengthening the family's ability to meet its own needs;
- B Clarifying and understanding the balance between how the family can satisfy its own needs and what it can expect from public services;
- C Recognizing the effect of societal problems on family relationships and acknowledging that government policy intervention may be needed to counter any resulting negative effects or exploitation in the family.

The development of the State and civil society has produced a variety of institutions and structures sometimes competing with the traditional roles and functions of the family. Apart from the State and civil society, one finds the market-place, the church, the political party, the social association and various units of production and consumption. Even in traditional societies, some forms of individualism and personal consumption make their appearance and seem to question traditional family patterns. Although the great movements of present times have affected the nature of the family, its essence is here to stay, because there is no substitute for the primary solidarity that links, as well as envelops, the members of a family.

Community and equity: A special relationship

In spite of its transformation, the family continues to be the basic unit of what is called a community: it is, by itself, a community of people, a community of functions, a community of responsibilities and duties and a community of rights. As such, families perform a plethora of functions that no other element in society can or does.

The family remains a special kind of relationship: between genders and generations, and within civil society, the market, and the State. The special nature of this relationship, based on solidarity and reciprocity, calls for the special treatment of family issues, both from the material and psychosocial points of view.

In the decade to come, the family, remaining the crucial component of society, will be dominated by a concern with equity: within and between generations; in the allotment and use of resources; in the transfer of resources from one generation to the next, and within the newborn generation. In the family generational equity can flourish first; it has no functional equivalent.

Because of the changing nature of families, these basic units of society must play an increasing role in the resolution of social problems. In some cases, this role is merely implied; in others, it may be specifically and clearly defined. For example, equitablly sharing domestic work is seen as an important requirement for the advancement of women; active parental involvement is seen as important in the education of children; likewise, families are the most important source of preventative health care.

More and more, Governments are retreating from a leading role in providing social services, and are leaving (or returning) that responsibility to families. This movement finds expression at the highest policy levels as well as at the lowest level of field practice. Social workers, teachers, health-care workers and others routinely include the family among the resources available to solve the problems with which they deal. The move towards deinstitutionalization and community-based service is another sign of a growing trend to entrust families with the responsibility for meeting multifarious human needs. For diverse reasons, families are not always ready or able to take on these responsibilities; nor are they always sufficiently empowered to be effective.

IYF provided an opportunity for reflecting on this massive shift in the orientation of social-policy thinking, and for gaining a perspective on what is required to encourage families to take more responsibility in this process, another basic consideration in support of placing the family on the international agenda.

Reconciling the needs and responsibilities of families with those of the State reflects another balance that has to be struck: the balance between the rights of individual family members and the concomitant rights and responsibilities of the family as a group. Taken together, these also form a rationale for highlighting internationally the role of the family in society.

Resources: The need for appreciation

One of the social-policy principles most evident in those underlying IYF is that official support to families should empower them in the fulfilment of diverse roles and responsibilities. Such assistance should not replicate the functions of families, nor divorce them from the supportive, productive contribution they offer to society. If it is to be meaningful, however, this principle must be intelligently expressed in policy and practice and constructed in ways that do not distance families from the responsibilities they bear as part of a citizenship and community.

A legitimate concern raised in the context of families is the degree family resources are equitably distributed among family members. Another issue is who in the family should receive these resources and whether all the contributions of family members to the well-being of the family are accorded equal recognition by the State. Often, the familial resources created by earnings, for example, are recognized while those created by child-rearing and household management are not. In short, much of the thinking about family resources has been conditioned by particular and sometimes outmoded views of productivity in society and, in some cases, of families generally.

Challenging tasks

In years to come, families, as the unifying factor at the grass-roots of society, will have a special role to play. At least three factors will be present in the challenges ahead:

A   The perennial dichotomy between the individual and society, between individualism and collectivism, between the rights of the individual and those of the family as a collective social unit. Agreement has been growing in recent years that foremost in importance are the individual rights of family members and, particularly, the achievement of equality between men and women as well as between other family members. At the same time, however, society cannot fail to be concerned with economic and social phenomena and behaviour, the root causes of major social problems such as abject poverty, unemployment, famine, homeless and migratory families, child neglect and abuse, domestic violence, drug and alcohol abuse, poor care of the elderly or the lack of opportunities for persons with disabilities;

B   The social welfare process in most countries seems to be undergoing a reassessment of its own. The State is no longer willing to be at the centre of the picture as a powerful, all-encompassing social agent for families. The role of the family, therefore, as a provider of basic social services and an important resource base will have to grow;

C   The family-centred model and other related approaches will become increasingly important, particularly at a time of transition in many countries where the social safety net has disintegrated. The family will have to take over some functions of institutions that have not stood the test of time as effective providers of social services. Any future-oriented effort towards the creation of effective family support policies should not disregard the situation of families in developing countries.

Educational function of families

> "EDUCATION DOES NOT COMMENCE WITH THE ALPHABET; IT BEGINS WITH A MOTHER'S LOOK, WITH A FATHER'S NOD OF APPROBATION ... WITH HANDFULS OF FLOWERS IN GREEN DELLS, ON HILLS AND DAISY MEADOWS; WITH BIRDS' NESTS ADMIRED, BUT NOT TOUCHED; WITH CREEPING ANTS AND ALMOST IMPERCEPTIBLE EMMETS; WITH HUMMING BEES AND GLASS BEEHIVES; WITH PLEASANT WALKS IN SHADY LANES, AND WITH THOUGHTS DIRECTED IN SWEET AND KINDLY TONES ... TO BEAUTY, TO ACTS OF BENEVOLENCE, TO DEEDS OF VIRTUE, AND TO ALL THE SOURCES OF GOOD."
>
> *Anonymous*

Culture: The basis of humanity

Culture is much more than the content of the social inheritance; it is an actively produced and experienced way of life. Living culture implicates all its members as active participants in the creation of new ideas, modes of conduct and interpretations of the world. Culture is not a static form made up of formulae and immutable information. It is evolutionary and is progressively affected by the advance of human civilization, particularly in a modern context, by technological innovation and progress. Indeed, the organized knowledge of technology seems to be a prime and growing force for cultural change throughout the world. Culture is embodied in a rapid succession of new products and processes, and it is institutionalized in systems of thinking about practical problems. In today's shrinking world of communication technology, people are witnessing the birth of, and are participating in, an emerging world culture.

The information society has accelerated the process of socio-cultural change. Space and time do not insulate cultures as they once did. Communication, mobility and the global market-place have brought the diverse cultures of the world into the lives of individuals and families. The multiple sources of cultural information available to individuals around the world offers its peoples and families both an opportunity and a challenge.

On the one hand, cultural exchanges enrich lives, promote global understanding and are a foundation for a world at peace with itself. On the other hand, the current rate of change and the unprecedented growth in information place heavy demands on cultures and reduce their ability to provide direction, security and meaning. The family and education, however, offer important anchors for individuals, providing them with effective mechanisms for assembling and digesting the complex world of experience currently available.

In all societies, culture and education foster the harmonious integration of individuals and groups in the community. Economic and social development is determined largely by the prevailing world view of each society, a view influenced by the values transmitted through and implicit in educational systems. Education serves both as a repository of the cultural heritage and as a mechanism for cultural change. Similarly, families can anchor individuals in traditions and transmit the existing cultural heritage or, more importantly, they can also serve as agents of change, reform and cultural innovation. With families, as with education, it is important to recognize the potency of their effects on people's lives. This power can serve negative or positive ends and requires vigilant and caring stewardship. The alternatives are chilling, because there are also those who believe, as a twentieth century dictator did, that "education is a weapon, whose effects depend on who holds it in his hands and at whom it is aimed".

Becoming human

The development of culture depends upon continuity and on the human capacity to learn and transmit knowledge to succeeding generations. Education, as an intergenerational learning process, is not only schooling, but also an apprenticeship in life preparing young people to realize their potential and assume a useful role in society. Thus it regenerates and changes society by challenging accepted wisdoms, expanding knowledge and scrutinizing the functioning of existing institutions. The educational process is a comprehensive system that starts in the basic educational institution, the family, and reaches out from there to involve the entire society.

Each individual becomes a person, that is, an aware and social human being, through enculturation, through the process of learning how to live in the society where they are born. Each individual's life is shaped by the way culture is mediated for them by others, and each person, in turn, participates in shaping culture through interaction with others. The family is at the core of this process and bears the primary responsibility for the socialization of children. The initial learning for each individual takes place within the family, with all its echoing relationships, its reflections of a larger world and its responsiveness to the internal world of each of its members.

The process of enculturation in itself describes for individuals a way of thinking about the world. The teaching process, therefore, may contain the most important lesson, particularly in the modern information environment where the content of knowledge changes daily. Nowhere is the process of enculturation more important than in the family, where learning and living are so entwined as to be indistinguishable. Families are endowed with the first and most immediate capacity to shape the potentialities of the human person by means of their access to that most beautiful expression of humanity: the open, fresh, curiosity that is the mind of a child.

Families as educators

The World Conference on Education for All: Meeting Basic Learning Needs, held at Jomtien, Thailand, from 5 to 9 March 1990, endorsed the concept that "learning begins at birth". The period from birth to the age of six is critical in the formation of intelligence, personality and social behaviour, as is well established. The learning that occurs in the early months and years of life will either enhance or handicap learning throughout later life. Furthermore, this early development of a child occurs not in isolation but in the family milieu and is strongly affected by the family and the community. The family has, historically, performed a fundamental role in the process of socialization and, in modern societies, a critically supportive role in education. In cultures where education is valued highly, it has been observed that a stable family system is a major factor in encouraging children to acquire education. In contrast, the decline in educational attainment in some developed countries has been partly attributed to the decline of familial support systems.

Despite the growing support for the view that education is an essential right of all individuals, the decisions of society collectively and of parents individually still determine the amount and kind of education any child receives, either formally or informally. A number of factors play an important role in those decisions, including: the economic situation of parents, their social traditions and degree of exposure to the forces of modernization, and their level of appreciation of the importance of schooling, as well as their general attitudes toward the values that education should impart. Social priorities and economic conditions often limit or enhance the commitment of the State to education. The current financial crisis faced by many countries has shifted a larger part of the burden of education to parents, further taxing the ability of families to meet their needs at all levels and adapt to the mammoth changes required of them.

The tremendous transformations occurring in and around the family, combined with the early social maturation of children, their ability to earn incomes independently of the family, and the development of a youth culture in developed countries, have all diminished the influence of the family in the process of socialization in late childhood and early adulthood.

Single-parenthood, for example, has increased the responsibility of the sole parent to feed, shelter and educate children, often without the necessary support and collaboration of the other parent, or indeed the State. New communication technologies in education, particularly the introduction of computer science and computer-aided instruction into schools and universities, along with the increasing variety of video and audio equipment and programmes, are changing the socialization process during school years in largely unknown ways. These educative changes are often so rapid that parents are not able to identify with their children's educational experience. Consequently, as in so many other areas of daily life, families face severe challenges in their attempts to perform a supportive role in the education of their children in a changed and fluid educational environment.

Families and peace

> "SINCE WARS BEGIN IN THE MINDS OF MEN, IT IS IN THE MINDS OF MEN THAT THE DEFENCES OF PEACE MUST BE CONSTRUCTED."
> *Constitution of the United Nations Educational, Scientific and Cultural Organization*

Preparing for life in peace

The awareness of the constant need for peace and international security to be built concurrently into the practice of international relations and in the human mind has a long tradition and record of action. Unfortunately, as many writers, thinkers and politicians have long pointed out, humanity has developed more of an education for and mentality of war than of peace.

As the eminent Italian educator Maria Montessori put it, on a global scale, education for peace, in comparison with present-day armaments, has remained practically at the level of the bow and arrow. Following the explosion of the first atom bomb over Hiroshima, the renowned scientist Albert Einstein concluded that nuclear energy had changed everything except people's way of thinking, thus crisply putting his finger on the moral problem that confronted not just him alone: the immense and widening gap between the advances in technological civilization and the state of human consciousness.

The founding of the United Nations released new efforts to promote peace education. Despite the mounting tensions of the cold war period, a number of United Nations resolutions and declarations reflected a positive trend towards well-conceived education for peace. Equally important were numerous initiatives pursued by the United Nations Educational, Scientific and Cultural Organization (UNESCO) to found peace upon the intellectual and moral solidarity of human beings. All those efforts culminated in a major United Nations instrument: the Declaration on the Preparation of Societies for Life in Peace, adopted by the General Assembly in its resolution 33/73 of 15 December 1978.

Preparing societies for life in peace is a specific kind of education and is perhaps a more complex and somewhat different process than the one ordinarily meant by the classical term of education. While the latter seems slightly restrictive and one-directional, the former is meant to make all persons at the same time subjects and objects of one process, as students and teachers of the same process: both individually as persons, members of families and citizens of one earth; and collectively as States and members of the same family of nations. Preparation for peace also implies the inherent human right of every nation and of every person to a life in peace. Indeed, the haunting presence of war, conflict and tension are constant reminders of the importance of peace and of the need for peace education at all levels, including the basic one, that of the family.

Peace, however, is not merely a state in which war is absent. Peace is both a socially and politically constructed quality. Peace is a construction: something that takes at least two parties to create. The plans for this construction emanate from a vision of the world at peace: a vision that can be developed through peace education, particularly in the context of the family.

Learning to be peaceful

Peace must also be learned and this learning is pivotal to its achievement. Putting aside the long-standing dispute about whether the state of human nature is innately violent and competitive or peaceful, a personal experience of peace often suggests how a person should be living, while a personal experience of life often tells persons that they are not living as they should be. It is through learning and education that the activity of each human being can be conditioned to respect the collective need for peace, despite the long history of war and conflict.

Innumerable theories in the area of cognitive development are appropriate to the question of peace education. Of these, those that seek to integrate the individual and social dimensions of human development prompt the most interesting reflections. Peace is something that is understood as part of a person's relationship with people or with those elements of the planet that are external to the self. This is true of peace between nations;

of peace and harmony with nature; of peace within society; of peace between persons; or of peace in the family.

The family as the nucleus of peace education

A look at the challenge of educating for peace, and particularly at the investment in the education offered to the next generation, clearly shows that the family will figure prominently in the process. The most basic human education takes place long before institutional learning. In fact, such education takes place early in life, in the context of a finite and familiar set of relationships. The process of human learning begins in the family. The child, in contact with "significant others" such as siblings or parents, becomes aware of its self and of others. Sympathetic understanding is born in the family. First, it is born through imitation (of gestures, intonations, behavioural habits) and later through role-playing and role-taking, when the child perceives and constructs a limited but coherent view of the world and its place in it. From the cognitive and emotional point of view,"capturing" the concept of peace is not possible unless the individual is first able to understand the view of others and can assimilate information from different perspectives in meaningful and self-affirming ways.

The most basic methodology for peace education are the patterns and styles of social interaction in the family. Numerous studies have established a relationship between parental styles and child development. Although this literature covers the spectrum of parent and child relationships, the issue of violence in households offers particular insights into the issue of peace education in families.

The intergenerational transmission of violent behaviour in families is an established, albeit dismal, fact of social life. Children who witness or are the victims of violence are more likely to be violent in adult life. An abused child is more likely to grow up to abuse his or her own children.

As learning begins and is established in families, clearly family life provides more than a model for behaviour. Family life intimately, directly and intensely affects the very structure of each person's understanding of others, of the self, and of his or her relationship with the external world. A family that lives in peace, offers not only a model of domestic tranquillity, but also an entire vocabulary for understanding the world of children, adults and, ultimately, the world of nations.

The entire repertoire of each person's modes of behaviour, especially those that constitute daily routines, are deeply embedded in the history of his or her family relationships. These learned modes are more than gestures, external expressions and single attitudes but complete sets of responses to social situations. The kind of learning that takes place in families teaches a person more than words; it implants in him or her the structure of social language.

A familial pedagogy for peace

The pedagogy for peace is a living and inspiring science. The earliest education a person receives teaches him or her how to think; namely, how to organize and make sense of the world of physical and social experience. At this level every family faces choices such as deciding what motives can be imputed to others, how conflict can be understood or peaceful resolution valued. In families, a person learns (or does not learn) how to recognize fear, insecurity or malice in others.

The symptoms and causes of a non-peaceful world surround each person daily. For all persons, and particularly children, this daily exposure can breed complacency, acceptance and insensitivity. The world of everyday life is composed, to a large extent, of non-reflective and time-honoured routines that are taken for granted. The decision to refuse the intrusion of non-peaceful behaviour into those routines must be the conscious act of a vigilant will. The methodology of peace education in families requires reflection, discussion and adopting the practice of having second thoughts as primary social instincts. Too often children learn the horrible logic of "an eye for an eye" in the casual advice of a parent, in the practice of discipline in the home or in the cruel pecking order of the local playground.

As with many simple truths, peace is more difficult to put into practice than to espouse; it is much harder to do than to believe. Peace in the family requires opportunities for reflection and discussion, where new and peaceful understandings can be cultivated and nurtured. Similar to all routines, non-peaceful interpretations of the world are often supported by the weight of established culture. Only in the family, and in families everywhere, can one hope to engender the kind of self-assurance, will, durability and personal courage required to be reflective and committed to the cause of peace, despite pressures or conveniences to the contrary.

The boundaries of family have served negative purposes, such as hiding the atrocities of child abuse or the subjugation of women. In the positive case, the boundaries of family should provide a sanctuary from the forces of society, where new and constructive ideologies can be nurtured and practiced. A familial pedagogy for peace is a lived and active process, involving choices and conscious decision-making. Teaching peace also involves encouraging and maintaining an environment where questioning the established order of things is accepted and routine. In the final analysis, it means providing, in all its symbolic richness, a sanctuary for reflection and peacefulness.

Lessons of the family for the world

A living peace between family members holds the promise of creating a lived tradition of peace in society generally. Clearly, the family that lives by principles such as mutual respect, empathy and kindness will cultivate a sense of the rights of others that can be transported to society. Family relationships between men and women can and should reflect a full and equal partnership such as would be aspired to in society at large. The proliferation of peace in and by families can also help to build broader stability, as the backbone of the happiness of the family and indeed of secure societies, where social peace is basic to progress and development.

The family at peace exposes its members to the living principles of a peaceful world. These living principles include reciprocity, respect for the rights of others, sharing of responsibilities, sympathetic understanding, self-affirmation in the face of personal differences, tolerance, freedom from fear, security and love. As these principles are expressed in the daily life of a family, through familial interaction, fundamentally important perspectives on the rights and needs of people are embedded in the world view of its members. The literature on families, and the problems of families, are often analogous to the problems of nation States. A case in point is the issue of conflict management in families. Families differ markedly in the way conflicts are resolved (or not resolved). Approaches range from avoidance or physical punishment to negotiation and concession. With families as with nations, choices on the approach to be adopted must be made.

Clearly, with families as with nations, all non-peaceful forms of conflict resolution should be considered as a failure or as a lack of commitment to the consistent and peaceful conflict resolution of conflicts. With the planet, as with families, conflicts and disagreements cannot be expected to simply go away. Children no longer rely on their parents, and often reject parental protection as controlling, unfair and unnecessary. As adult partners grow, develop and change in the course of relationships, they need to learn interpersonal skills that promote ongoing negotiations and discussion in an atmosphere of mutual respect. Consequently, peace in families is not an established fact of life. Peace is not a state of being: it is a learned process. Family is not a static form: it is an evolving entity.

No world progress seems to be achievable unless led by enlightened and peaceful-minded contributors, be it at the grass-roots, national or global levels. Pope Paul VI once said that there would be no disarmament of weapons if there was no disarmament of hearts. Recent years have amply shown how much can be accomplished, in a peaceful way, if leaders or whole populations are committed to the peaceful resolution of conflict. Indeed, the new face of the globe and the considerable progress in disarmament can be attributed to the disarmament of hearts. Despite the turbulence experienced in many parts of the world, a new environment is in the making, an ecology of more peaceful thinking and inner commitment to peace, which has its roots in, and derives its nourishment from, the family.

The future of the family

> "THE WORTH OF THE STATE, IN THE LONG RUN, IS THE WORTH OF THE INDIVIDUALS COMPOSING IT."
> *John Stuart Mill*

The principle of subsidiarity

The dynamic diversity of families offers each person a remarkable opportunity to make a fundamental impact on the future of the planet, in the cause of peace and social justice, and on his or her own life. Families are integral to the global structure of subsidiarity which, in the human quest for a better world, seeks out solutions to problems at the lowest possible level of the societal structure.

As a link in the total system of subsidiarity, from an individual to the planet, the family has demonstrated itself to be the most universally resilient, durable and flexible social form known. The family will persevere under constant change, and probably it will survive. This is the lesson of history, which also provided the reason why, given such a record of survival, IYF was needed or desirable for the support and protection of families.

The unknown family

One of the difficulties plaguing the efforts of Governments to deal with the question of families in social policy is the lack of a clear understanding of what families are. This difficulty has been complicated by the many changes rapidly unfolding in family structures and the diversity of forms found within and between national societies.

One of the great paradoxes surrounding families in the context of social policy is that, despite the fact that Governments are turning to families for solutions, there is a significant lack of official information on families. In short, much about families is not known.

Often what one claims to know about families is founded more on stereotypes, intuition, anecdote and experience than on a rigorous and systematically constructed understanding of what families are. Furthermore, the family has undergone such profound changes recently that the view of families held by many policy makers, scholars and others may not be an accurate reflection of families as they currently are. Nor is it clear that the existing legal and policy frameworks for families reflect the contemporary realities of family life. Given the increasing reliance of social policy on families, the efforts to rediscover the family through strengthened research activity is an important objective of IYF.

Families in need

Despite the critical need to undertake research, a significant body of literature and knowledge exists that must be brought to the attention of legislators and policy bodies in order to inform and provoke them to take constructive action. Such knowledge must include some of those things that are known but that people are hesitant even to recognize. Societies exist, for instance, where girl children are left to starve because they are considered of no use; where twins are abandoned because they are considered a manifestation of evil; and where children are being sold into slavery or prostitution.

Human beings display their ignorance and indifference towards and within families in many ways. These include the selfishness of an adult; child abuse and neglect; inequality between family members expressed, inter alia, by the abuse and exploitation of women; the insensitive cruelty with which human beings sometimes act, or don't act. Such ignorance and indifference is also seen in the hypocrisy with which human beings do something, because it is easy or visible, and shut their minds to the needs of others. Finally, the harbouring of racist, sexist or other intolerant attitudes represents some of the most persistent forms of ignorance.

Families of the world are under sustained and heavy stress. Economic and political transformations in many parts of the world, environmental problems, disease, war, poverty, famine and other such forces are taxing them, often beyond their ability to cope. These pressures are clearly not confined to the developing world; witness the pressures generated in families by unemployment, drugs, crime, and the scourge of the acquired immunodeficiency syndrome (AIDS). Families are often left to mediate these pressures by themselves and many will need help if they are to be successful.

Major tools for action

With its primary focus on action at the local and national levels, supported by regional and international action, IYF had the following aims: strengthen national institutions, enabling them to formulate, implement and monitor policies; enhance the effectiveness of local, regional and national efforts to carry out specific programmes; stimulate efforts to respond to problems affecting, and affected by, the situation of families; improve collaboration between national and international non-governmental organizations in support of multisectoral activities and, last but not least, build upon the results of international activities on social issues of direct concern to many organizations of the United Nations system and outside of it. In the search for the strongest and most viable family environment to help rekindle the flame of family solidarity, IYF was a step in the right direction.

The guiding principles of IYF envisaged that its activities should lead to the equal and full enjoyment of individual rights, both within the context of the family and throughout society. IYF did contribute to developing and strengthening perceptions and perspectives regarding the family and intra-familial relationships that were consistent with basic human rights, fundamental freedoms, and internationally accepted social policy standards and principles. Important elements promoted the implementation of the Nairobi Forward-looking Strategies for the Advancement of Women,[1] the Convention on the Elimination of All Forms of Discrimination against Women,[2] the Convention on the Rights of the Child[3] and the World Declaration on the Survival, Protection and Development of Children and the Plan of Action for Implementing the World Declaration on the Survival, Protection and Development of Children in the 1990s,[4] as well as United Nations global plans and programmes of action in the field of ageing, disability, youth and crime prevention.

Challenges to meet

A distinctive feature of United Nations efforts to meet current social policy challenges is the necessity for Governments in all countries, irrespective of the level of material development or the socio-cultural context, to be fully aware that their political and economic objectives can be achieved only if they give their fullest attention to social aims as well. Without wanting to belittle the precarious economic situation in many regions of the world, two perceptions are still prevalent and must be overcome if a better world is to be achieved for families. They are the following:

    A   That there is a dichotomy between "economic" needs and "social" needs, and that the latter are subordinate to the former. The allocation of resources still appears to be inhibited by the persistence of such orthodox thinking; however, what is "economic" and what is "social" are but two perceptions of a single reality;

B That social development is concerned with marginal sections of society and is of no great relevance to the central issues of economic and political development. Social development, however, concerns entire populations as well as their disadvantaged sections and is central to the problems of productivity, growth, welfare and stability.

Social policy must seek to overcome these limited perceptions if the human condition is to improve, the eradication of poverty is to be a realistic goal and society is to be based upon the principle of distributive justice. As the Human Development Report 1991[5] in its opening sentence concluded: "the lack of political commitment, not of financial resources, is often the real cause of human neglect".

IYF is not a house that is already built, where people can look for the room that suits them: it is a process of construction, requiring the energy, input and commitment of those who will live in it. This distinction is basic to an understanding of IYF, and to the vision of 1994. The opportunity and challenge beckon, the door is open and the time is ripe.

References

[1] *Report of the World Conference to Review and Appraise the Achievements of the United Nations Decade for Women: Equality, Development and Peace, Nairobi, 15-26 July 1985* (United Nations publication, Sales No. E.85.IV.10), chap. I, sect. A.

[2] General Assembly resolution 34/180, annex, of 18 December 1979.

[3] General Assembly resolution 44/25 of 20 November 1989.

[4] "Ceremony for the presentation of the Declaration and Plan of Action adopted by world leaders at the World Summit for Children: Note by the Secretary-General" (A/45/625, annex).

[5] United Nations Development Programme, *Human Development Report 1991* (New York, Oxford University Press, 1991).

FAMILY
Forms and Functions

Introduction: towards a conceptualization of families[*]

Families represent a wide variety of styles, structures and functions; they have been different across societies and throughout history. Instead of speaking of the family always in the singular, it might be more appropriate often to speak of "families", since the forms vary within regions and through history, in accordance with changes in social, political and economic circumstances.

Families are psychological as well as socio-economic units. They form the basis of every society, since every individual has a family of origin and most people live within a family context for their whole life. The human infant needs the shelter of family during the time it requires for its development through childhood and adolescence into adulthood.

While families are of pivotal importance to interpersonal life and to the greater societies, they are also undergoing rapid transformations. Formalized marriage is losing its status, especially in European countries, where cohabitation without marriage has increased, at least before children are born. The number of divorces has been rising in almost all countries where divorce is attainable[5]. An estimated one third of all families are now single-parent families headed by a female[6].

The number of single-person households is rising in big cities. At the same time, however, and more often than ever before, people are living together either as married partners or cohabitants, for at least a part of their adult life[7]. In spite of the increase in divorces, the average length of marriage does not differ from that of marriages at the beginning of the century, owing mainly to longer life expectancy.

These changes can be seen in families as a sign of decline, of course, but despite the pressures and challenges it has faced, the institution of the family has shown remarkable vitality and resilience. Rather than indicating an erosion of the worth of the family, new forms of family life are developing to meet the challenges of the modern world and, in so doing, are struggling to find more effective ways of balancing individual rights and social responsibilities.

---

[*] The chapter was prepared by the IYF secretariat with editorial guidance from three senior consultants to the secretariat, Sirpa Taskinen, Barry K. Weinhold and Janae B. Weinhold. It is based largely on four essays prepared for the Second Ad Hoc Inter-Agency Meeting on the International Year of the Family of the United Nations organizations and specialized agencies, held 5-6 March 1992 at Vienna.

The essays were written by four eminent scholars: Laszlo Cseh-Szombathy[1], Wilfred Dumon[2], Don Edgar[3] and Luis Leñero Otero[4]. Their essays stand as individual statements, each complete in its own right. Although the essays have been frequently quoted, this chapter does not attempt to exhaust all the views and ideas expressed in them.

The IYF secretariat wishes to thank the four scholars for their innovative and thought-provoking works.

FAMILY Forms and Functions

Families are constantly evolving. Changes occur both through external factors and the relationship of families to the society and through internal factors, as the family and its members pass through different stages of their development. A family changes when it gets new members or when they grow up, move away, die or go through other life stages or events. A family can be regarded as a system wherein each individual member affects and influences the others. Thus, the well-being or pain of one member concerns the others, too. If one family member defines his or her role in a new way, it may change the whole family system.

The relative strength of a nation or a society depends largely on the strength of its families. What occurs in families affects the whole of society, and vice versa. There is a complicated relationship between the two. Many family conflicts are related to the problems families encounter in their relationship with the macro-society and to external economic and social conditions. Families have been greatly affected by urbanization, industrialization, ecological disasters, wars and famines and by political, economic or social changes in the structure of their countries. In most countries, social policies or family policies have been able to support families only minimally to compensate for these unintended stresses. Most countries still rely on the family to provide the basic safety net to care for its members.

Regarding the problems encountered by families, or their solutions, as resting solely in the society or solely in the family would be too simplistic. Society may be too easily inclined to see the circumstances in a particular family (e.g., divorce or teenage pregnancy) as an individualized problem rather than as a problem connected to more basic conditions in the whole society.

Every family has its problems. Since development most often occurs through crises and difficulties, many situations need to be seen merely as a sign of an ongoing process and not necessarily as a disaster. The situation may require outside intervention only if the problems are acute and cannot be resolved by the family members themselves.

The ongoing process of family change and readjustment has always been a sensitive point from one generation to another. By its nature, the (multigenerational) family necessarily produces new family members with attitudes that incorporate not only past traditions but also new and not always well-formed values[4]. This invariably causes some measure of conflict between parents and their children.

Families can serve as agents of, or as obstacles to, change and development, notably in respect to social values. If families actually were "the smallest democracies at the heart of society", the whole world would be different. Today, this is not the case in very many families. Severe inequalities in the division of labour and in the distribution of power exist within many families[1]. The discussion of children as equal democratic partners in their own affairs has only begun. Egalitarian possibilities for both genders are but words in most families.

Despite this, there have been signs of improvement. In many parts of the world, opening up options for women, either through market work outside the home or social security payments, has challenged the power balance within family life.

Two questions now arise: How can the diverse forms, functions and needs of families be better understand? How can better ways be developed to support and strengthen families so they can actually become "the smallest democracies at the heart of society"? The complexion of the future world will depend on the answers to these important questions.

Structures and typologies of families

Precisely defining the family is dificult because there are so many different types of families. It has been defined, inter alia, as "any group of persons which cares for a child" and as "a group of persons ... regarded as a family under the legislation and practice of a State" (United Nations Committee on Civil and Political Rights)[9]. However, these definitions, like many similar ones, do not include all families. For social and historical reasons, a type of family that may be quite acceptable in one society may not be condoned in another.

In this chapter, families are defined in their broadest sense. Ties exist between individuals who are related through birth, mating or adoption. The description that follows is intended to provide a background for the subsequent substantial discussion on the functions performed by the various types of families.

Distinguishing a family from a household is not always easy, and many would prefer the latter term. Although usually overlapping, these concepts differ in several important ways. The "household" is a concrete unit of people usually living under one roof. The "family" is a more abstract concept that is not tied strictly to one location or time. Families only rarely live together over their whole life cycle: children move out, spouses may separate and so forth. A person can live in one household but have some of his or her family members living in another household. Children departing and forming their own households do not lose their status in their family of origin. In spite of the external changes in life, families usually feel as if they belong together. Even when family members die, they may still be considered as belonging to the family.

What differentiates families from other social groups are the emotional, sociocultural and legal relationships between the various members:
- Spouses
- Parents and children
- Siblings
- Relative

Usually in speaking of a family, reference is made to the existence of one or several of these relationships, which can also be defined as subsystems of the family, e.g., spousal or parental subsystems. Usually, these relationships are both genetic and social, but most societies have made provision for social parenthood even when the biological father or mother or both are not present, not identified or have ceased child-rearing activities for some reason.

Nuclear families

Nuclear families can be described as having two important forms: one biological, the other social. The biological element, the family "molecule", consists of the two parents and a child. An infant is born of a woman and has a genetic father. These two adults may or may not live together, but the child's biological nuclear family is defined by their union.

The social nuclear family is not necessarily the same and is created when two people establish a relationship, by marriage or by cohabitation. Many countries recognize this as a nuclear family whether biological children are present or not.

Modern Western families tend to create the biological nuclear family, where two generations, parents and dependent children, live together. Even if the children move out, the "empty nest" is still considered a social nuclear family. Statistics show that both forms of nuclear family, social and biological, are more common in countries where the life expectancy of people is high. They are well suited for urbanized societies, since they can easily move and do not need large dwellings. While the nuclear family offers a number of possible advantages in some societies, the limited number of family members makes it quite vulnerable to internal and external pressures.

If the parents divorce and remarry or cohabitate with another partner, one can also speak of a reorganized nuclear family structure. These so-called step-families can be considered nuclear families containing a mixture of biological and non-biological children.

The biological nuclear family has additional variations. The most common variation is the one-parent family, consisting of a mother or a father and one child or several children. Single-parent families are formed through the death of one spouse, divorce, migration, separation, desertion or a decision by the partners not to live together. The various single-parent families differ greatly in their socio-economic conditions but often have more limited resources than two-parent families. Usually, widows are economically more advantaged than divorced or single mothers. Most one-parent families are female-headed, but the number of male-headed nuclear families seems to be rising in the Western world. They have, in general, a better economic position than female-headed units.

Another variation of the nuclear family is the adoptive family, particularly evident in societies where adopted children get the same rights and legal status as biological children. Families with children conceived through in vitro fertilization are usually considered as nuclear families, even if the social father or mother is not the biological parent.

The legal recognition of same-gender relations, as expressed in laws (Denmark) and court decisions (North America/Europe) on inheritance and other issues, is based on the growing social recognition and acceptance of such relationships[2]. This form of family also exists in many countries where it is not recognized in law.

Extended families

The "family" means a combination of several biologically related family "molecules" in many parts of the world. An extended family need not be big; it would, for instance, be small in the case of a grandparent and a grandchild living together. Usually, however, the extended family refers to numerous people either living together or otherwise having frequent, intimate interaction. In many cases, it is not easy to tell the difference between an extended family and a household.

A common form of extended family is the three-generation family, where grandparents, parents and children live together. Cultures that value respect and care for the elderly may be predisposed to the three-generation family as the most desirable form of the family. Such a family often exists in circumstances where the division of land and other property would diminish the economic possibilities of all family members. Thus the three-generation form is more prevalent in rural areas. With the growing shortage of housing in urban areas, many young couples have no choice but to live together with their parents. In such cases, the tendency is to view a household as containing two nuclear families, which break up when separate dwellings become possible. This situation is also encouraged by the tendency for urban dwellings to be designed around the needs of smaller, nuclear units. As life expectancies continue to lengthen, the four-generation family will likely become increasingly common.

Kinship families usually consist of even larger units than a three-generation family. In addition to three (or more) generations, other relatives may belong to the same household and be regarded as members of the family. The kinship family may disintegrate when siblings come into conflict and, above all, when there is a breakdown in relations between the father and children. The disintegration of the kinship family is less marked when married couples break up or when one partner dies.

Tribal families are usually built on a social rather than a biological basis. Responsibility for the care of a child may be taken up by several people. The biological mother's sisters may be called mothers, and the biological father's brothers, or in some cases even the mother's brothers, may also be responsible for fathering the child. All cousins, in the Western sense, are often called sisters and brothers. This type of family rarely leaves orphaned children, because there is an abundance of parents.

In some polygamous families, all of the wives (or, more rarely, the husbands) may or may not live with their spouse; in others, they do not all live together. Nor is the residence of the biological family necessarily the residence of the children. Sometimes several allied family units are under the same head.

Reorganized families

In all the forms of families, reorganizations can occur through the marriage, remarriage or cohabitation of persons having children by their former partners.

There are several forms of remarriage, or living together under common law, after one or several earlier relationships. One spouse or both spouses may have a child or children who may or may not live with them. The spouses may or may not have children together, either biological or adopted. In this way, children can have several half-sisters and half-brothers, "half- grandparents" and other non-biological relatives. These can be seen as new resources for the child. The interrelationships are even more complex if there are several chained remarriages, or if remarriage occurs in an extended family.

Instead of formally marrying, people sometimes choose to live in a mutual support community, where several nuclear families and/or single persons might live together. There are also household configurations of couples or small groups of women who care for the children of one or more of them. In some cases, it is difficult to differentiate these forms of families from a household. Also, some children's institutions having a house-mother and, possibly, a house-father, consider themselves to be extended families.

The different family forms are listed in table 2.1.

TABLE 2.1. FORMS OF FAMILIES

Nuclear	Extended	Reorganized
Biological	Three-generation	Remarried[a]
Social	Kinship	Community living
One-parent	Tribal	Same-gender[b]
Adoptive[c]	Polygamous[b]	
In vitro[b]		

a Divorce is accepted in most countries.
b Legal status presently strengthened in only a limited number of countries.
c In countries where legal adoption is recognized.

Basic functions of families

Many different functions can be ascribed to the family, depending on how it is viewed. In this chapter, which takes the view that the most prominent feature in all kinds of families is the interrelationships between the family members, the family's functions are identified as follows:

A Establishment of emotional, social and economic bonds between the spouses;
B Procreation and sexual relations between the spouses;
C Giving name and status, especially to the children;
D Basic care of the children and, in many cultures, of the elderly and relatives with disabilities;

E   Socialization and education of the children and even of the parents;
F   Protection of the family members;
G   Emotional care and recreation of the family members;
H   Exchange of goods and services.

The functions are listed here in no order of priority, because they vary greatly from one culture to another. In Western nuclear families, for instance, the affective functions, interaction between family members and mutual love are usually emphasized. The extended family is "... based on the principle of respect and loyalty for consanguineous bonds. Marriage is subject to such bonds and not the other way around. The role of everybody and each of the members is governed by their commitment with those of the same blood. There is nothing higher than this except God and the fatherland" ([4], p. 16).

The priority assigned to particular functions varies over the life-cycle of a family, according to the stage or turning point it has reached, such as courtship, marriage or cohabitation, the birth of the first child, the departure of the last child from the parental home, the end of the economic activity of the ageing partners, possible divorce and the death of family members.

Establishment of bonds between spouses

The first step in forming a family is often marked by the commitment of two adults to join their lives. Depending on the part of the world, this can be done by traditional rituals, by legally formalized marriage or by cohabitation.

Socially recognized relationships between spouses, as well as mutual emotions, form the basis for family life. The main responsibility for establishing these functions is vested, of course, with the families themselves, since the relationships are to a great extent psychosocial.

In addition to emotional bonds, marriage establishes social bonds between relatives of the partners. Legal and informal economic bonds may emerge as well, and marriages have been used throughout history to establish and reinforce wealth and power.

The laws and norms concerning marriage and divorce, spousal relations and the economic rights and responsibilities of family members are of major concern to any society. In common-law marriages, the absence of such rules may pose a problem, especially when the relationship is dissolved.

Only 22 countries to date, most of them in the industrialized world, have granted equal rights to both sexes in matters of marriage, divorce and family property [4]. In other words, inequality between the sexes is still institutionalized in most of the world.

Most countries have laws establishing a minimum legal age for marriage to protect children from the problems of early matrimony. However, in some countries the legal age of marriage for females is still as low as 12 or 14 years, and the minimum legal ages are not always enforced. There are millions of child brides each year all over the world [6].

In some cultural traditions, partners are chosen by the family. This does not constitute a problem if the marriage is celebrated with the free and full consent of the future spouses, but such is not always the case. Attempts by the parents to arrange or induce the marriage of their children, in order to continue the tradition of alliances with suitable families, are now frequently rejected because they infringe upon the personal freedom of the individual. On the other hand, in modern societies, where no help or service is available for mate selection, youth might benefit from some guidance in selecting their spouse. Informal training for family life takes place primarily in families. In response to the need for more formal training, programmes in family life education are being offered by schools, churches and social agencies in some countries.

Marriage and its equivalents give the two partners their first roles in the new family: that of spouses. Over the years, both partners need to make constant efforts to develop a warm and well-functioning spousal relationship, regardless of the way it was established.

At times of marital dissatisfaction, people are generally willing to turn to advisors or mediators for help in making decisions that are in the best interests of their children and themselves. If the relationship between the spouses has become a burden for one or both parties, divorce or separation are a recognized alternative in most countries. Divorce almost always places an emotional strain on the family. Some experts have suggested that as the turning points of life are usually strengthened by rituals, at the time of divorce there should be counter-ritual to that of a wedding to effectively dissolve the spousal relationship.

Procreation and sexual relationships between spouses

Marriage and, in some parts of the world, cohabitation are the ways to socially legitimate sexual relationships. In areas where the use of contraceptives is accepted, sexuality is seen as distinct from procreation. Still, it has its biological basis and serves a vital function as a connecting link between the spouses. Sexual regulators such as incest taboos, courtship rituals and religious and civil marriage laws are in fact social mechanisms for the control of sexual behaviour, and human history is rich with a variety of mechanisms for controlling sex[3].

Population renewal is crucial to the survival of any society. In many parts of the globe, programmes have been formulated and established to enable families to exercise the right to freely and responsibly determine the number and spacing of their children. Access to family planning information and programmes is vital to the health of families. In addition, information on reproduction is needed for youth to prevent unintended teenage pregnancies.

Technological progress in maternal health care has dramatically increased the survival rates of babies and their mothers. Health workers and maternal health clinics have been major contributors to this increase. Research has shown that the health of both women and children can be significantly improved by spacing births at least two years apart, avoiding pregnancies before the age of 18 and limiting the total number of pregnancies to four[10].

Promoting prenatal, maternal and infant health care can be done in many ways. One way is to encourage regular contacts with health workers or attendance at maternal health clinics, where available. For example, many countries have granted financial support or greater benefits for a born baby if the mother regularly attended a maternity health programme.

A severe problem of discrimination exists in some countries where boys are more valued than girls. This is often reflected in infant mortality rates, which are considerably higher for girls than for boys in some parts of the world.

Pregnancy is an appropriate time to support the whole family. Parenthood is a new phase in the life cycle of the family and requires new ways of behaviour. It is essential to see to it that the adults are able to perform their dual roles in the family, as spouses and as parents. These roles differ crucially, and in order to preserve the basic relationship between the spouses, they should be kept separate. Besides being a mother, the woman continues to be a wife, and the man is both a husband and a father. In relation to their children, the parents should keep their adult care-giver roles and not burden young children as care-givers for their parents, as sometimes happens.

Parent training for both sexes provides skills and information to inexperienced mothers and fathers. Through counselling programmes or family resource centres, vital information concerning pregnancy, delivery, care of the child and the role of the parents can be disseminated. Culturally sensitive programmes for responsible fatherhood, in particular, are in demand all over the world. In societies where fathers assist in child delivery and undergo parental training, they usually develop close and warm relationships with their children. Studies show that all those present at the birth of a child are more bonded to that child. When the mother, father and other significant members of a family (grandparents and siblings) are bonded to a child, abuse of the child by family members is less likely.

In addition, the birth of a child entails economic burdens for a family and creates day-care problems for working parents, particularly in nuclear units. Since families are the institutions taking care of reproduction, in numerous countries their contribution is often acknowledged in the form of subsidies for the care of children. In many industrialized countries, a pregnant woman has the right to maternal leave with compensation and the right to return to her job after the leave. Parental leave is also available to the father in some countries. In other countries, parents may be eligible to receive a tax deduction and a child allowance until the child is self-supporting.

Giving name and status to family members

According to the Convention on the Rights of the Child (General Assembly resolution 44/25, annex), every child has the right from birth to a name and to acquire a nationality. Indeed, children born to married parents usually automatically assume the name of the family and enjoy certain legal entitlements, e.g., they can inherit family property. Unfortunately, these legal entitlements are not universally available to females. For children born to unwed parents and for orphans and abandoned or adopted children, name and status often become a special concern. Children born to unwed parents should have the same rights as other children, and adoption laws should give adopted children rights equal to those of biological children.

In many countries, all children have legal rights to financial support from their biological father, even if they are born out of wedlock or from unmarried cohabitants. These rights are usually equal for girls and boys and include being eligible for inheritance from the father. If the child is born out of wedlock, the father may have to pay an allowance for someone to care for the child. In the absence of financial support from the father, the State may provide for the care of the child. In a case where the father is unknown or is contesting the child's paternity, a legal officer is usually appointed to examine the matter and establish (or not) paternity by a court decision.

The joint custodial care of children after separation or divorce is possible in many countries; this arrangement gives both parents the right to take part in decisions concerning the care of their child or children.

Basic care of children and relatives

Meeting the basic needs of children and other family members is a crucial function of the family. In many societies, the care of disabled or aged relatives is left to families. Without the support provided by the family, many sick, disabled and elderly persons would not be cared for. Even in advanced social policy situations, family members may be actively involved in gaining access to existing services.

Caring for children remains the most generally recognized basic responsibility of families, because the human infant needs a great deal of care to survive. Human development requires emotional involvement and interaction with the child as well as physical care. Parenting is important even after the pre-school age, during childhood, adolescence and beyond. Without adequate training and support, this responsibility can be too heavy a burden for many parents, particularly those who are separated from the support systems of extended family or kin. About 100 million children are physically abandoned each year by their families, many of them condemned to spend their lives on the streets engaged in hard labour or crime[11].

The old traditions of child care are no longer practised in many cultures. Moreover, owing to the absence of an extended family structure, the older relatives are not able to transfer their knowledge or offer support to younger generations. Parental education is therefore most urgently needed when children are small and when they are teenagers, since the end of childhood is often difficult for both the children and parents. In the teenage years, conflicts with parents are almost inevitable; indeed, they are a part of the socialization process. These conflicts, if handled properly, can help the child develop his or her own values and beliefs. Unfortunately, because many parents lack the skills or the understanding to properly handle these conflicts, many teenagers end up rejecting their parents as consultants and turn to peers or other adults outside the family for support and guidance.

As the employment of both parents and the number of single-parent families are increasing, day care for young children has acquired a special importance. Non-parental care for young children is nothing new, however. In most societies there have always been forms of day care for children, by grandmothers, siblings and other relatives, to provide the parents with time for survival and production tasks. What is new, however, is the demand for secure, controlled and professional day-care arrangements. While parents generally like public day-care systems, many would prefer flexible work arrangements that would allow them to be more involved with their children. Nurseries and kindergartens may also be needed for children in the evening, if the parents work at night.

In some countries, one of the parents has the right to stay at home while the child is young, without being threatened by the loss of his or her job. The family may also have the option to place the child in a community-owned nursery at a reduced price or to receive a so-called home-care benefit. When the child is ill, one parent may be entitled to a paid leave from work. A child-care allowance for each child is also paid by Governments in many countries.

State-supplied social and economic benefits to help meet the basic needs of families may not always support marital bonds, although this is often unintentional. Opinions differ as to whether the benefits awarded married couples and families, including tax reductions and other subsidies, should be the same for single persons and cohabitants.

Caring about and for dependants traditionally has been sex-based. The care of children, the elderly, and physically or mentally disabled family members has been undertaken typically by women. Generally the distribution of family work must be the more equitable, but when women take on additional responsibilities, such as working outside the home or caring for the aged or disabled, this need is even greater.

If there are many children and disabled or aged persons, or if the providers of the family are ill, welfare support services need to be designed to help the family in its household tasks, for instance by providing home helpers. In some countries, when the family is caring for an older relative at home, it is paid an allowance or compensated for the extra costs of this care.

Socialization and education of children

Families have a challenging task in educating and socializing their children. Even in times of financial difficulty, reducing these efforts would be shortsighted, because education is the main way to build up the future of the child and the society. In addition, some argue that society would not function well without the contribution of children to the production of knowledge, through their work at school[12]. Especially in education, equal rights for both sexes should be emphasized. For example, the level of education of the mother has been found to have a direct correlation with the health of the family, its size, the spacing of the children and the family's economic well-being.

The degree of responsibility of the family as the educator of children varies from one culture to another. Everywhere, the socialization of children is considered so important that societies have undertaken, in varying degrees, to formalize the educational process. Children are obliged to attend school for a certain number of years in most parts of the world, but the quality of the schools and of the education varies enormously. In many countries, institutional education is free and children are provided with the equipment and materials needed. In others, the family has to pay considerable amounts of money for the basic education of its children. Also, education has not always been seen as a right of the child, especially of disabled children. An estimated 120 million children in the world between the ages of 6 and 11 do not attend school. In many developing countries, one pupil out of seven drops out before reaching second grade[11]. This has a great psychological and economic impact on the family of origin as well as on the family he or she may eventually create themselves.

In addition to formal education, the family has to take care of the emotional and social upbringing of its children. The child's basic self-understanding and self-esteem are developed in the family. The family is also responsible for transmitting social and cultural values. Traditions are learned and enriched in families; they are also altered by the everyday life of family members. For future families, the learned roles of mother and father, as well as husband and wife, are crucial. When children become parents they tend to repeat the behaviour of their own parents in child-rearing. Parental behaviours and traditions are very much part of the inheritance passed between generations.

In the socialization of family members, the role of siblings and other children is considerable. For example, the presence of siblings can diminish the influences of peer groups in day-care centres, schools and various free-time settings. Outside the family, the emotional and social development of the child can be promoted through specialized programmes, adventure camps, clubs, art, sports, care of animals and plants, pen-friends and other friendship programmes.

The impact of a child's behaviour on his or her parents' personalities should not be forgotten. Children socialize their parents from the first moment. Parents learn from their children about child development, peer and sibling relationships, school, fashion and changes in society. In particular, immigrant and refugee parents often learn their new country's language and customs from their children. Similarly, parents often report that the care and nurturing of children is personally and emotionally enriching, despite the attendant stresses and problems.

Protection of family members

One of the major functions of families is the protection of its members, especially those who are vulnerable, against all kinds of violence, psychological, physical, sexual or social. Unfortunately, violence and abuse do occur inside families, and at times family members have to be protected from one another.

In some ancient traditions, the father one had the right to decide if a newborn child was allowed to live. The paterfamilias used his power over his wife, children and slaves. While signs of this extreme form of paternalism still exist all over the world, males can also be objects of child abuse and family violence. The problem can be compounded across generations; too often the perpetrators of family violence have learned this behaviour when they themselves were the victims of family violence.

Family violence has long been largely hidden; only recently has it begun to be dealt with more openly. It includes beating and other types of assault on family members, the burning of women in dowry-related disputes, murders, conjugal rape, female circumcision and the widespread sexual abuse of children. Emotional abuse and threats of violence also leave hidden scars on family members.

Modern studies show that most often violence in the family is directed at wives, and the most likely perpetrator is the husband. However, children are battered by both fathers and mothers. Additionally, elderly family members, particularly elderly women, are vulnerable to their grown-up children. Sick or disabled family members are more often the objects of violence than other members. In polygamous families, one co-wife may assault another, and in other extended families, female members are often at risk from both male and female relatives[13].

Criminal laws have been rewritten in some countries to include various forms of domestic violence, rape in marriage and the physical punishment of children. However, examples of the awakening sensitivity to the misuse of power within families are still rare. Only five countries currently have outlawed the use of corporal punishment on children by parents: Austria, Denmark, Finland, Norway and Sweden. The law has been in effect for over 10 years in Sweden and has greatly reduced the incidence of physical child abuse[14].

Besides the more aggressive types of violence, there is also so-called passive violence. For instance, more children are neglected than abused. The rising number of abandoned and runaway children on the streets is a sign of families lack of capacity to take care of their children as well as the inability or unwillingness of society to create an effective social safety net.

Numerous programmes are emerging in the prevention of domestic violence and child protection. Violence is an abuse of power and emerges from the desire to dominate, possess and control. In the long run, the promotion of human rights, better education and an improvement in the status of women are needed, as well as public education to change attitudes towards the domination or humiliation of other human beings. Studies have shown that adult abusers were usually abused or neglected as children. The treatment of an adult abusers must include, therefore, counselling that promotes awareness of the abuse and neglect patterns inherited from the abuser's own childhood experience and that helps him or her handle more problems effectively.

For families at risk, the most promising prevention programmes emphasize and promote the strength and healthy development of individuals and families. Programmes offering immediate protection and short-term or remedial assistance include shelters, children's legal centres, telephone hot lines and therapy programmes.

Emotional care and recreation of family members

Families may be differentiated from other integrating groups by the emotional attachment of their members. For many people, home is the main place for emotional care, intimacy, understanding and support, but the emotions are not always positive. If relations are permanently hostile, overly possessive or otherwise tense, severe problems are the predictable outcome.

The emotional atmosphere of families is greatly affected by the sex roles and behavioural models in the wider society. Several myths are being strengthened constantly by the mass media. They are about motherhood and fatherhood and the roles of women, men and children. These written or implied norms have an enormous impact on the real behaviour of people. As circumstances and families change, such norms should change accordingly. Unless openly discussed and studied, they can become a barrier to healthy emotional development.

Even today, when a large number of women work outside the home as mothers, wives or partners, they are still the primary managers of tension levels within the family. A woman tries to provide a nurturing haven for her husband and to give soothing reassurance to her children in the face of problems they experience at school or in peer groups. Working women are exposed to confrontations of their own outside the family; they bring them home as their own set of tensions that need soothing. This is certainly true also of women working in the home. When the emotional needs of women are not met and their burden of emotional care is neither shared nor recognized, they may come to deeply resent the emotional reliance of other family members. Some respond by withholding the nurturing care they previously supplied. Men are not always willing or equipped to provide nurturing, emotional support to family members. The sex-based division of labour in the emotional care of family members, like the division of physical domestic work, is a problem that must be addressed.

If the family has aged or disabled members, yet another level of tension is present for the women to manage. In families with little extended family support or in single- parent families, women find that their tension-management function stretches them to levels that imperil their health and the equilibrium of the family. All members need to share this function within the family by paying attention to the problems of the other family members and giving them reassurance when stressful things happen[1].

In only a small minority of families are family members curently able to share this function. What typically happens in families where this emotional nursing function is not shared is that disinterest in and resentment of the problems of others eventually develop. This process is known as devitalization[15]. In devitalization, the tensions are not effectively managed, creating even more tensions for the family members, which can lead to a break-up of the family.

Sometimes the support of the family, relatives or friends is not enough to promote healthy emotional relationships. There are, however, other ways to do this. In many cultures, representatives of religious institutions, health personnel, counsellors, social workers, teachers or others are involved and helpful. In some countries, services such as family resource centres help families and distribute information on more satisfying and appropriate modes of family life. Both women and men need to develop effective communication skills to facilitate equal partnerships with families.

Exchange of goods and services

Some have argued that families have shifted from being units of production to units of consumption as the labour force has moved outside the family and members have taken up paid employment. Especially in times of economic strain, however, many families still retain their ability to act as units of production.

For most people, the family is the main provider of many basic services, e.g. cooking, cleaning and care of clothing, and of economic resources for daily living, education and recreation. These material resources, including shelter and housing, are vital to the maintenance of the family and its living standards.

As more and more women work outside the home, their contribution to family income is greatly increasing. At the same time, the problem of division of labour within the family usually has to be addressed. Otherwise household work can, and often does, become a double burden for women, who are left to cope with it alone.

Time-use statistics on paid and unpaid economic activity and unpaid housework reveal that women still spend more of their time working than men in all developed and developing regions except North America and Australia, where the hours are almost equal[16]. According to egalitarian principles, men and women equitably sharing domestic, parental and family responsibilities is an essential aspect of progress. To achieve this progress, schools may need to offer boys as well as girls training in the skills necessary for domestic tasks and in rudimentary household management. For families at risk and needing help with their domestic work, services such as home helpers, health visitors and respite care are in great demand.

In many countries, programmes are called for that would make it easier to reconcile and combine employment and family life. Remuneration, working conditions, hours of work and parental and other forms of leave all enable or disable families in their economic survival and child-care functions. The changing proportion of the time spent on work and that spent on leisure also changes the activity patterns of families.

The role of children in sharing household tasks and contributing to family income is a problem in many ways. In developing countries, children may enter the labour force at an early age, or they may have to do heavy domestic service. Over 50 million children are part of the labour force. They are often subjected to unsafe working conditions and deprived of basic education and a normal family life[11]. In industrialized countries, teenagers tend to work after school to earn money for their own consumption and to leave the household tasks to the adults. Within bounds, some participation of children in family maintenance tasks is not only helpful but can also be instructive. Alternatively, no family should measure the value of its children in terms of their contribution, in finances or labour, to family maintenance. A balance between the rights and responsibilities of children sometimes seems difficult to find, but it is critical. In many instances, the imbalances are extreme.

Family life is also dramatically affected by the back-up resources available to the family unit. Changes in national economies, unemployment and housing shortages, among other things, have greatly affected families all over the world. Some countries have had to develop economic counselling services for families who are struggling with debt. Separation and divorce have large impacts on family resources, notably the impoverishment of women and children. Public support for single parents and the enforcement of child maintenance laws often lessen adverse impacts on the living standards of single parents.

Having access to extended kinship networks is also important in many societies. The decreasing size of the family all over the world means fewer people on whom to depend within the family. However, greater longevity often means access to three generations of potential support. Even when they live away from the common dwellings, family members may continue to be provided with financial resources. Income transfers between generations may flow in both directions; a household may have no children present but may be supporting offspring living, studying or working elsewhere. For example, a single-person or couple-only household may appear to have few family obligations yet may be supporting aged parents or other family members living separately.

In defining the goals of social policies, societies often consider the family as the provider of resources and services for its members. Governmental policies differ greatly with respect to the distribution of public funds to individuals and families. The fewer social benefits and public services available, the more individual welfare depends on the resources of the family, making it vulnerable to forces beyond its control.

A good example of how families have maintained a strong economic function was seen in eastern Europe. In the 1960s, when Governments eased the rigidity of the command economy and allowed villagers to farm small plots, families reacted immediately and started to produce agricultural products not only for home consumption but also for sale. In some countries, such as Hungary and Poland, private production on family farms quickly surpassed State-cooperative farm production in activities such as pig breeding. This private production was largely attributable to the participation of all family members in the farm work. In countries attempting to reconstruct a market economy, small family enterprises are emerging in all fields of work and are the driving power behind this transformation.

General observations on creating a family-friendly society

All over the world, families are undergoing great changes. Although these changes differ from region to region, there are commonalities: smaller nuclear families, an increase in divorces, the greater longevity of family members and the transformation of relationships due to changes in values and industrial and post-industrial economics. Also, changes in the roles of men, women and the family itself are of great interest and importance everywhere in the world.

This chapter focuses on some general recommendations that can help create a more friendly society for all families. Obviously the reasons for family problems do not lie solely in families. Neither are the solutions to these problems solely in their hands. Families at risk should not be viewed as "risky families" but as "families in risky situations".

In response to the diversity of needs, Governments must develop effective legislation and family policies, services and benefits to strengthen those family functions needing the most support. This will entail forms of support that meet the particular needs of the country.

Knowing the level of family functioning

As a general requirement, policy makers must be aware of the state of family functioning in their national societies. Families, no matter what form they take, are called upon to perform basic functions in every society. Their ability, or inability, to perform these functions is one pragmatic and thus valuable approach to identifying unmet needs and isolating specific targets for policy intervention. This approach requires research and data collection to determine the level of family functioning in key areas and to identify appropriate supports and barriers. Possibly methodologies and measurement instruments can be evolved that would provide a standard for cross-national comparisons in this area, including the quality and impact of existing supports. A cross-national comparative study on family functioning, modelled on the cross-national studies in the Human Development Report, published every year by Oxford University Press for the United Nations Development Programme, would facilitate exchange and provide Governments with objective measures of progress in family policy and benchmarks for setting national priorities and goals.

The fusion of economic and social policy

The experience of families, and ultimately their well-being, is mediated by a complex interplay of social and economic factors. Family policies must be formulated without making an artificial distinction between the "economic" and the "social".

When treated as a "social" issue, family concerns are too often isolated from the economic policy arena, where critical decisions taken have profound impacts on family life and functioning. Moreover, such a compartmentalization does not reflect the role of families as the basic units of production and consumption or their pivotal importance to the process of economic development.

Building on the strengths of families

Families, in their functioning, display remarkable adaptability, resilience and inherent strength. Family policies should reflect these strengths and the capacity of families to meet their own needs. Consistent with this view, the levels of empowerment and consultation are standards against which family policies can be judged.

Families are expert in their own affairs and should be enabled, through participatory approaches and other forms of consultation and feedback, to be full and active partners in decision-making, policy formulation and the design and evaluation of services. It is important to remember that few family units have ever survived on their own without some public, external support. This is the moral obligation that most societies regard as necessary for maintaining a civil culture. In different parts of the world and in different countries, the amount of intervention will vary considerably.

Families can and do function to the benefit of their members. Empowering social policy and participatory approaches extend that range of functioning, and family policy becomes another family resource. Public services that support and strengthen the family in the performance of its functions need a strong preventative focus, building on strengths rather than reacting to weaknesses.

Being aware of the diversity of family forms

Families come in many shapes and varieties, and there is change over the life cycle of individual families. A family-friendly society is one that recognizes the diversity of family forms and respects the unique conditions, benefits and disadvantages each experiences in the execution of its functions. The relationship between form and function is as elusive in families as it is in art and deserves the attention of policy makers and legislators everywhere.

Concluding statement

Clearly much remains to be done to strengthen families and to find effective ways to support their main functions. To strengthen families, the combined effort of researchers, policy makers and families themselves is needed. The situation and needs of different families must be assessed, and existing services, laws and benefits must be evaluated.

A functionalist view of families is but one perspective on this complex and vital part of the human experience. From the point of view of policy, however, and within the purview of the International Year of the Family, such a perspective may offer much. First, it strives to identify commonalities between families, across forms, cultures and time. These commonalities are, defined, furthermore, around what families do, as part of the lived experience of family life. Moreover, a functionalist perspective focuses on that aspect of the family that is most significant for policy - its irreplaceable function of providing for the multiplex and changing needs of family members. A functionalist yet dynamic view of families seems to capture much of what is meant when it is said that family is the basic unit of every society.

- "Strenghtening the Family: Guidelines for the Design of Relevant Programmes" (1987), *The Family* (No. 4). United Nations office at Vienna, Center for Social Development and Humanitarian Affairs. E.87.IV.4. New York: United Nations. (Also available in French and in Spanish).
- "The Role of the Family in the Development Process" (1986), *The Family* (No. 2). United Nations office at Vienna, Center for Social Development and Humanitarian Affairs. E.86.IV.7. New York: United Nations. (Also available in French and in Spanish).
- Trost, J. (1990), "Do we mean the same by the concept of family?" *Communication Research*, Vol. 17, No. 4, 431-443.
- UNICEF, WHO, UNESCO (sine anno), *Facts for Life*, Oxfordshire, U.K.: P&LA.
- UNESCO (1991), *International Directory on the Young Child and the Family Environment*. The Young Child and the Family Environment Project 1990-1995, Paris.

References

[1] L. Cseh-Szombathy, "The family at the end of the twentieth century", Paper presented to the Second Ad Hoc Inter-Agency Meeting on the International Year of the Family, Vienna, 5-6 March 1992.

[2] W. Dumon, "What is family?" Paper presented to the Second Ad Hoc Inter-Agency Meeting on the International Year of the Family, Vienna, 5-6 March 1992.

[3] D. Edgar, "Conceptualising family life and family policies", Paper presented to the Second Ad Hoc Inter-Agency Meeting on the International Year of the Family, Vienna, 5-6 March 1992.

[4] L. Otero, "Conceptualization, typologies, structures and functions relating to the familiar family", Paper presented to the Second Ad Hoc Inter-Agency Meeting on the International Year of the Family, Vienna, 5-6 March 1992.

[5] See, for instance, W. Lutz, A. B. Wils and M. Nieminen, "The demographic dimensions of divorce: the case of Finland", in *Population Studies*, vol. 45, 1991, p. 437, or A. Riazantsev, S. Sandor and O. Labetsky, *Child Welfare and the Socialist Experiment: Social and Economic Trends in the USSR, 1960-1990*, Innocenti Occasional Papers, Economic Policy Series, No. 24, Special subseries: Child Poverty in Industrialized Countries (Florence, United Nations Children' Fund, International Child Development Centre, 1992) or "Vingtième rapport sur la situation démographique de la France", *Population*, No. 5, 1991, p. 1091.

[6] *Women: Challenges to the Year 2000* (United Nations publication, Sales No. E.91.I.21).

[7] See, for instance, "Vingtième rapport sur la situation démographique de la France", *Population*, No. 5, 1991, p. 1081, and *Canadian Families in Transition: The Implications and Challenges of Change* (Ottawa, Vanier Institute of the Family, 1991).

[8] V. M. Moghadam, "Approaching the family: gender, development, and equity", Paper presented to the Second Ad Hoc Inter-Agency Meeting on the International Year of the Family, Vienna, 5-6 March 1992.

[9] Cited in *International Directory on the Young Child and the Family Environment Project 1990-1995* (Paris, United Nations Educational, Scientific and Cultural Organization, 1991).

[10] UNICEF, WHO, UNESCO, *Facts for Life: A Communication Challenge* (Benson, Oxfordshire, United Kingdom, P&LA).

[11] "Convention on the Rights of the Child", *United Nations Focus* (DPI/1016-41219).

[12] Jens Qvortup, "Childhood as a social phenomenon - an introduction to a series of national reports", *Eurosocial Report*, vol. 36, 1991.

[13] *Violence against Women in the Family* (United Nations publication, Sales No. E.89.IV.5).

[14] A. Miller, *Breaking Down the Walls of Silence* (New York, Dutton, 1991).

[15] J. Cuber and P. Harroff, *The Significant Americans* (New York, Appleton-Century-Crofts, 1965).

[16] *The World's Women 1970-1990: Trends and Statistics* (United Nations publication, Sales No. E.90.XVII.3).

Bibliography

Ariés, P. Centuries of childhood; a social history of family life. New York, Knopf, 1962.

Canadian families in transition; the implications and challenges of change. Ottawa, Vanier Institute of the Family, 1991.

Cseh-Szombathy, L. The family at the end of the twentieth century. Paper presented to the Second ad Hoc Inter-Agency meeting on the International Year of the Family, Vienna, 5-6 March 1992.

The demographic dimension in Indonesian development. By C. J. Hugo *and others, eds.*Singapore, Oxford University Press, 1987.

Deutsches Jugendinstitut. Wie geht's der Familie? Ein Handbuch zur Situation der Familien heute. By K. Leube *and others, eds.* München, Kösel, 1988.

Dumon, W. What is family? Paper presented to the Second Ad Hoc Inter-Agency Meeting on the International Year of the Family, Vienna, 5-6 March 1992.

Edgar, D. Conceptualising family life and family policies. Paper presented to the Second Ad Hoc Inter-Agency Meeting on the International Year of the Family, Vienna, 5-6 March 1992.

Eroles, C., ed. Cuestiones actuales de familia. Comisión Nacional de Politicas Familiares y de Poblacion. Ministerio de Salud y Acción Social de la Nación. Argentina, Secretaria de Desarrollo Humano y Familia, 1989.

Les familles d'aujourd'hui. Colloque de Genève, 17-20 Septembre 1984. Paris, Association internationale des démographes de langue française, 1986.

Fleiner-Gerster, T., P. Gilliland *and* K. Lüscher, Eds. Familie in der Schweiz, Familles en Suisse; Famiglie nella Svissera. Freiburg, Universitätsverlag, 1991.

Kain, E. L. The myth of family decline; understanding families in a world of rapid social change. Massachusetts, Lexington Books, 1990.

Kamerman, S. B. and A. J. Kahn, eds. Family policy; government and families in fourteen countries. New York, Columbia University Press, 1978.

Lauras-Lecoh, T. Family trends and demographic transition in Africa. *International social science journal* : *Changing family patterns* (Oxford) 126:475-492, 1990.

Levin, J. How to define family. *Family reports*, 17:7-18, 1990.

Lutz, W., A. B. Wils *and* M. Nieminen. The demographic dimensions of divorce: the case of Finland. *Population studies: a journal of demography* (London) 45:437-453, 1991.

Medina, B.T.G. The Filipino family. Quezon City, University of the Philippines Press, 1991.

Nave-Herz, R. *and* M. Markefka. Handbuch der Familien- und Jugendforschung. Band 1: Familienforschung. Neuwield, Luchterhand, 1989.

Otero, L. Conceptualization, typologies, structures and functions relating to the familiar family; nature, plurality and future of the family phenomenon. Paper presented to the Second Ad hoc Inter-Agency Meeting on the International Year of the Family, Vienna, 5-6 March 1992.

Parsons, T. *and* R. F. Bales. Family, socialization and interaction process. Glencoe, Illinois, Free Press, 1955.

Quah, S. R., ed. The family as an asset; an international perspective on marriage, parenthood and social policy. Singapore, Times Academic Press, 1990.

Riazantsev, Alexandr, Sipos Sandor *and* Oleg Labetsky. Child welfare and the socialist experiment: social and economic trends in the USSR, 1960-1990. Innocenti Occasional Papers. Florence, UNICEF International Child Development Centre, 1992. (Economic Policy Series, No. 24. Special subseries: child poverty in industrialized countries)

Skolnick, A. Embattled paradise. The American family in an age of uncertainty. New York, Basic Books, 1991.

Srinivasan, K. and S. Mukerji. Dynamics of population and family welfare: 1987. Bombay, Himalaya Publishing, 1988.

Trost, J. Do we mean the same by the concept of family? *Communication research*, 17:4:431-443, 1990.

United Nations. Models for providing comprehensive services for family and child welfare. *Family*, No. 1, 1984. Sales no.: E.84.IV.2. Also available in French and in Spanish.

National family policies: their relationship to the role of the family in the development process. *Family*, No. 3, 1987. Sales no.: E.87.IV.2.

Also available in French and in Spanish.

The role of the family in the development process. Family, No. 2, 1986. Sales no.: E.86.IV.7. Also available in French and in Spanish.

Strengthening the family: guidelines for the design of relevant programmes. Family, No. 4, 1987. Sales no.: E.87.IV.4. Also available in French and in Spanish.

Violence against women in the family. Sales no.: E.89.IV.5.

Women: challenges to the year 2000. Sales no.: E.91.I.21.

Economic Commission for Latin America and the Caribbean. Latin American Demographic Centre. Familia, desarrollo y dinámica de población en America Latina y el Caribe. 1994 Año Internacional de la Familia. Taller de Trabajo, Santiago de Chile, 27-29 Noviembre 1991.

Statistical Office. Statistics and indicators on women in Africa 1986; statistiques et indicateurs sur les femmes en Afrique 1986. (Social Statistics and Indicators, Series K, No. 7) Sales no.: E/F.89.XVII.11.

United Nations Children's Fund, World Health Organization and United Nations Educational, Scientific and Cultural Organization. Facts for life. Benson, Oxfordshire, United Kingdom, P&LA [n.d.].

United Nations Educational, Scientific and Cultural Organization. International directory on the young child and the family environment. Paris, The Young Child and the Family Environment Project 1990-1995, 1991.

Vingtième rapport sur la situation démographique de la France. *Population* (Paris) 5:1081-1160, 1991.

FAMILY as an Environment: an Ecosystem Perspective on Family Life

Introduction*

In the introduction to its recently published brochure entitled Canadian Families in Transition: The Implications and Challenges of Change, the Vanier Institute of the Family had the following to say:

"We all have been and most of us are still members of families that provide some degree of mutual caring and sharing, that transmit knowledge, values and material benefits from generation to generation. As infants and small children we learn from our families the patterns of behaviour that affect all our later relationships both with other individuals and with society as a whole. Families continue to be society's most basic and pervasive organization, bridging the gap between the individual and the larger context of group activities such as jobs, communities, recreational activities and all the many social and economic organizations within which we interact"[1].

The family is placed within a larger social context, an environment within which its members are shaped for functioning in the larger society. Persons and institutions interested in families, such as the Vanier Institute of the Family, consider the family the basic social unit in any society. It is accepted as an unquestioned given. This chapter suggests a way of defining and looking at the family that enables the reader to contemplate change in family structure and function without necessarily arguing that family, as traditionally understood, is heading for extinction. The chapter develops a concept of family that helps one understand the claims made in the name of the family and to understand better why families differ in their ability to live up to those claims.

All too often one hears the family spoken of as if it were a static structure or form that could be labelled and contained by a universal prescription. Coupled with this belief is the feeling that family problems and social problems are the result of failure to follow the prescription. No doubt divorce, single-parent families, blended families, violence between and against family members, rape and incest point towards a great degree of family dysfunction. Many want to be reaffirmed in the belief that the ills of society, including growing violence and the abuse of alcohol and drugs, are a result of changes that have taken place in that fundamental unit of society called the family, which is thereby invested with a kind of institutional value that ignores the changes that have taken place in the lives of the individuals who create families and in the society of which families are a part. There is an ongoing search for family tradition and a routine, rem-

---

* Paper prepared for the IYF secretariat by Doris R. Badir, University of Alberta, Canada.

iniscent of the "good old days", that will be stable in a world of constant change. The fact that some of this tradition has been invented is often either forgotten or not understood. The very word family evokes an emotional response. The word is immediately personalised, with the hearer thinking of his or her own family and imposing his or her own value system on the word. Other families are judged by one's own experience in a family.

Contemporary social historians such as Philip Aries[2] or Witold Rybczynski[3] put nostalgia in its place. To blame family for societal problems or to blame society for familial problems is to fail to understand the relationship between individuals and the society they live in or to comprehend how changes in society affect how people relate to one another in families. There is a symbiosis about these interrelationships that must be understood if the meaning of family is to be correctly interpreted and understood.

Defining family

Defining the family may help people reinforce their own particular value systems, but definitions also tend to create models or patterns that freeze the family into static molds. Attempts are made to define family in terms of its structure, e.g. how many people and of what age and sex. The reality is that today's families come in a variety of packages: extended, nuclear, single-parent, adults of the same sex, foster families, teenage families, ageing families and families in the "sandwich generation". What happens to families that don't fit the norm of the nuclear family with its two parents, its single wage-earner and its 1.5 children? Are they dismissed as irrelevant? Are they accepted into the way of thinking about families? Are they seen as dysfunctional? Who fits into families: people living in the same house? people living in the same compound? people living in the same geographic area? two generations living together? several generations living together? How far back and sideways does one go in defining family? There is no universal size or appearance of the family today. Visualizing families as particular structures does not take into account the interrelationships formed between and among the persons characterising themselves as a family group.

The Vanier Institute of the Family has produced a working definition of the family (figure 3.1). This definition illustrates how comprehensive and diverse the various conceptualizations of families are[4]. Family, here, is more than just a structure made up of a set number of people. It is a way of living together intimately and sharing economic, social and emotional responsibilities. It is a way of interacting to make the decisions required for everyday life. Here the family is described in terms of structure, relationships and functions. This definition does not prescribe the size or the age of family members. It does not prescribe job functions for family members. It suggests merely that one or all or any combination of the functions listed are performed by persons living in familial relationships. The important thing to note is that those who define themselves as family take responsibility for the functions they define for themselves and agree to accept.

FIGURE 3.1.
THE VANIER INSTITUTE OF THE FAMILY'S WORKING DEFINITION OF FAMILY

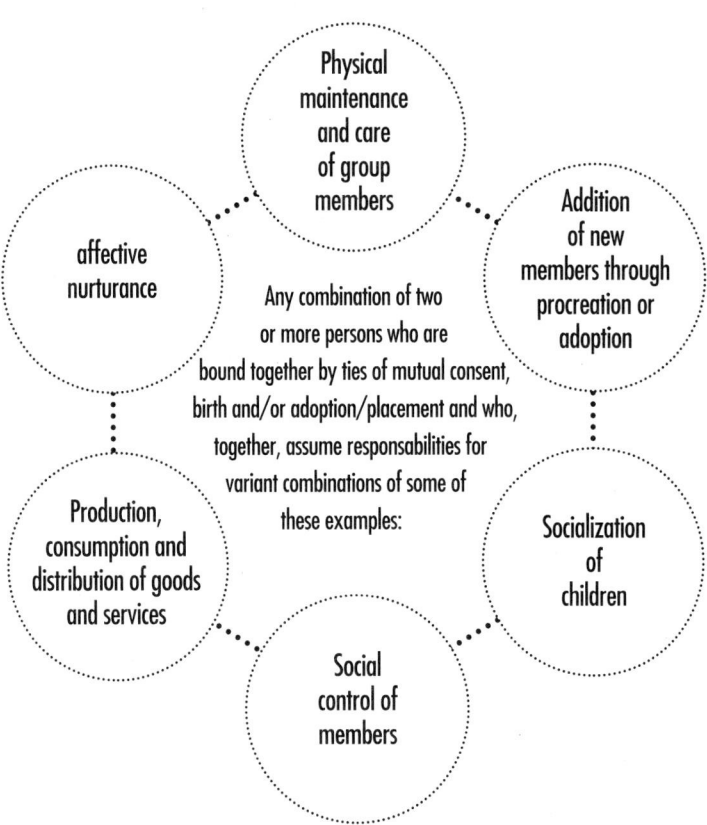

Source: Vanier Institute of the Family, "Definitions of family: what's it to me?", Transition, March 1992.

Defining family as a cultural construction

Family is a cultural construct consisting of traditional, social, religious and political values acted out by individuals. The ways families are formed, the ways the members relate, or are expected to relate, to one another, the political and religious sentiments involved in the formation of families - all of these are established by the cultural milieu. The value system of individuals in the society that forms the basis of familial and social relationships is culturally determined. Families, therefore, are not uniform around the globe. The environment called family is framed by the society within which it is nurtured. Moreover, within families, and over generations of families, a particular or even unique culture is formed. The dictates of the larger social system are interpreted and/or modified by families as they experience life together. The cultural construct of a particular family is made up of a patchwork of rules of family formation, patterns of relating to individual members, family traditions, rituals and celebrations and ways of spending family time. David Reiss suggests that family ritual and routine act as guidelines for how things should be done in families and they help families acquire a view of themselves and of how they function in their social world[5].

Glossop describes some of the ways Canadian families live the culture of their society:

"Each family has its own history, its own set of interwoven biographies. Families mature, grow old and die as the places of one generation are assumed by the members of the next. If we pay attention to all the little, mundane and even silly rituals, celebrations and traditions unique to our families, we see that what these rituals do is acknowledge change, development and growth. Birthdays, anniversaries, tooth fairies, Bar Mitzvahs and confirmations, piano recitals, driver's licences, graduations - all are acknowledgements of change.

"Each family demarcates the passage of time by embroidering these culturally-prescribed rituals and making them their own. These family traditions become the stuff of memories of our times together and of our membership in a family. The same box of Christmas decorations gets brought out year after year. A year has passed, but the box brings our recollections of Christmasses past and reconfirms that our lives are lives lived with others, that our experiences are shared and important to others and are part of the lives of others"[6].

These traditions, celebrations, family times and routines help to buffer the negative impact of change and/or unexpected life events for families[7]. Formed by the underlying culture and by family experiences and nurtured by family tradition, they are strengths that not only mark change but provide a stability to family life.

In the process of meeting the emotional needs of their members and renewing the society through procreation, families, structured by the cultural systems prevalent in a society, develop patterns for interacting with one another, patterns that determine the internal culture of family life, the ways they will go about satisfying their daily needs; patterns of loving and caring and hating and harming one another. A constant process of change is taking place whereby the larger sociocultural context determines how families form and provides expectations for family members. However, as families experience life together, they re-form culture and change society. Thus, while the familial environment is in many ways formed by cultural tradition, at the same time it re-forms that tradition.

Defining family as a set of relationships

Family is also characterized by relationships between individuals, and these relationships change along with the experiences of the individuals. Family is a way of living together, of meeting emotional needs through interaction. The loving, the hating, the fun and the violence all provide an emotional environment where individuals learn the skills that will determine their interactions with others in the world around them. It will determine their abilities to learn in the educational system, their abilities to function in the work environment, their feelings of self-worth and their concern for others. It is the milieu within which people interact to deal with the emotional and physical needs of the family's members. In this milieu children learn the process of making decisions and the techniques for handling situations such as the loss of a job, infidelity, the introduction of new members into the household, limited financial resources and the abuse of alcohol and/or drugs by one of its members. In the milieu members learn to handle emotional issues like anger and love and independence, to abide by the law or to break it and to cheat or not on the payment of income tax. It is here that the basics of human interaction, consideration for others and responsibility for one's own actions, are learned and practised. Ideas and values are exchanged and learned in this intimate environment.

Take, for instance, a woman living in poverty who gives birth to a child every year. She is worn out from childbirth and unable to look after her many children, but is her need for the child understood? That totally dependent, tiny human being who responds to the care and warmth of mothering for such a short time may be the only real experience of loving for the woman. In fact mothering may be the only thing that she feels she does well. Her inadequacies in providing for her growing children are only too obvious to her. The new child provides her with meaning.

Another woman may remain in an abusive relationship because she believes she deserves the abuse: if only she were a better wife and a better mother she would not have to suffer the abuse. Where did these women learn such values or the patterns of behaviour that follow from them? These are examples of the effect that an inadequate familial environment can have on individuals.

Often the emphasis is placed on the weaknesses and dysfunction of family life. McCubbin and others, however, emphasize the strengths and capabilities of families: "Family transitions over the life span predictably create stress and often move the family unit to a state of crisis. How well families negotiate and navigate their way through these critical normative and non-normative transitions has and will continue to be a major concern of family scholars, counsellors, family life educators, and policy makers"[8].

The authors emphasize the resilience of families in their ability to adapt and regenerate after a crisis. The time family members spend together, whether engaged in family routines or in working out solutions to family problems, makes a positive contribution to the strength of the family bond[9].

Children learn definitions of self and skills for getting along with one another by example and by interaction with their parents. Emotions are acted out in the family milieu. To a certain extent, it is the safe place to practice the handling of joy, of anger, of disappointment and of failure or success. It is safe if the child is in an intimate environment made up of people who care. It is unsafe if the skills are inadequately learned in an environment where people do not care. Unconditional love granted by each member of the familial unit to every other member of it is a further resource that carries the family unit over the rough spots and through the years. In short, the emotional needs of people are looked after (or neglected) within a familial environment.

Defining family as an economic construct

In every society, family is an economic construct, an institution charged with the functions of production and consumption. The material needs of people are, for the most part, considered the responsibility of their families. In some societies all members of the family work together to provide food, clothing and shelter. In these societies the larger economy is more or less informal and operates at a subsistence level. As technological advances allow many of the material needs of families to be mass-produced, the economy becomes based on a monetary system. People no longer work to produce their needs; instead they work for a wage, used in turn to purchase the needs formerly produced within the household. The family in many ways changes from a production unit to a consumption unit. This is, however, a simplistic way of looking at familial activity. Even in a monetary economy, the family produces much of its own material needs. Food, purchased raw, must be transformed into food for the table. The health and wellbeing of children must be looked after. Ageing members of the family must be cared for. Household chores have to be done and repairs carried out to maintain the family living space. In other words, the family is an important part of the economic well-being of a society. Its effective use of the resources available to it can be an important element in a country's economy.

For most people, the family is the unit that provides food, clothing and shelter for its members. It is the environment where the physical wants of its individual members are attended to (or left unattended). The concepts of family as cultural context and family as set of relationships can be extended by considering the family need for space. A family is most often circumscribed by a sheltered space where the interaction and the problem-solving take place. Whether it is a flat, a mansion, a modest house in a new suburb, a tenement in the inner city, a farmhouse, a rondavel on a grassy plain in Africa, a thatched hut in the Malaysian country-side or some pieces of cardboard pulled together under a motorway overpass, this shelter is the immediate physical environment where families live out their lives. Lucy Ngige describes what it was like to grow up in a round house in rural Kenya:

"As I recalled living in a round house, I felt a powerful affection for my parents and siblings. Our close knit lives in the 1960s in that small hut birthed the unity that is maintained in that household to this day. Even after we got married, we continued to visit our parents on National days, and in turn they are welcome to visit our homes and stay with us. We owe our deep purpose in life and smooth running of our homes to the way of life they shaped for us. They would go hungry during famine so that we could be fed, and thereby taught us the value of sacrificing for our loved ones. There is something unique about my family of origin: I think it was the simplicity of everyday life that was then characteristic of indigenous Africans. I look back with longing to those days"[5].

Caution is needed when judgements are made about the adequacy of family space. For many, the crowded quarters of the house Ms. Ngige grew up in would be inadequate, but for her it provided the environment that established the values and warmth that now characterize her life in her new family. From the cultural, economic and familial standpoint, the space satisfied her needs and those of her family.

Similar criteria can be applied to the satisfaction of other physical needs, such as nourishment and clothing. Paolucci argues that the options exercised by families every day about meeting their material needs provide a kind of security within which the autonomy of the individual is fostered and developed: "Life is autonomy in action, it provides freedom to choose coupled with responsibilities. The family is a basic setting for exercising this autonomy"[11]. The interaction required to solve the problems of daily living can be a positive experience for family members.

An important consideration for the economic welfare of a family is the division of the labour required to support the family's members. That division is undergoing a slow but relentless change. Just as women are finding satisfaction in using their talents in the public sphere and in contributing to the economic well-being of their families, men are discovering the satisfactions of contributing to family well-being through household work and care of the children. Traditional familial roles are changing, and in the process new work patterns are opening up for both men and women. It becomes less difficult for a woman to take time out from the workforce for child-bearing as men see some benefits in taking time out to assist with child-rearing. Now that so much has to be purchased in the marketplace (child care, care of the elderly, prepared foods and ready-made clothing), household work is recognized as a productive activity.

A number of attempts have been made to bring the productive work of the household, traditionally performed by women, to the fore and to recognize it by monetizing it. There are dangers in this exercise, unless it is carefully conceived. The income family members earn tends to be given more weight than the daily, taken-for-granted activities that go on in households and families and for which no money is exchanged. In a real way, society undervalues the things done for members of families out of love, affection and caring. Placing a monetary value on tasks that enhance relationships may undermine the emotional importance of the relationship itself. Recognition of the financial value of the work involved in family and household activity has to come in ways that do not destroy intimate familial relationships.

The economic activity of the household directly affects the larger economy. The relationship between the consumption patterns of families and the industrial economy is obvious. Less obvious is the relationship between income earned and the money available to Governments from taxes on those earnings that allow them to provide family support systems. Together, familial productivity in the household and on the job and familial consumption keep a national economy active. The national economy, in turn, provides the income and support systems that maintain families and sustain their welfare. Thus, like their emotional needs, the physical and material needs of people are looked after (or neglected) within the family, and the economic well-being of a society depends to a large extent on the effective economic functioning of its families.

Family as an ecosystem

Family as an environment

Family can be seen as an environment made up of people and their immediate physical surroundings. Individuals who are members of a family interact on a daily basis. They are the human elements of their environment. They are a part of a system directed towards the goal of human survival. In other words, family is a structure, that is, a set of relationships and a space, that creates an environment where the social, psychological, physical and economic needs of individuals are constantly interacting. It is an environment in which individuals relate to one another in a variety of capacities and in which the problems of everyday life are worked out. The solutions to the problems, and the skills needed to arrive at them, ultimately form the quality of life for each family, and the totality of those solutions determines the quality of life for all the individuals and societies in the "global village".

Family in an environment

Family is imbued with a whole set of attitudes and ideas that are a part of a cultural, social and economic tradition. It is an environment situated within the larger environment of a society, and the two environments interact constantly, affecting one another. The interaction creates change in both environments. For the individuals involved, the interactions can promote maturity, health and personal satisfaction or they can promote violence, discontinuity, disorientation and poor health. The need is to be aware of, sensitive to and in touch with the environment of family life as families around the world are living it.

Family as part of a human ecosystem

In the preceding attempt to define family, the recurring emphasis was on the reciprocal relationship between family and the larger society. The family was perceived as an environment in which family members constantly interacted with one another in the environment of the larger society. Every member of every family lives each day differently. When all the interactions come together at the end of the day, it is a different group of people who are interacting. In other words, the individuals who make up the environment must constantly adapt and change. The interactions experienced by one member of the family after a day away from home at work or at school or shopping for the groceries can affect the whole family. As an example, the single mother on welfare may in one day have dealt with a social worker; been summoned to school to speak with a teacher about a child who has trouble concentrating; shopped for groceries, only to find that the welfare cheque would not cover the weekly needs of her family; or have had words with her ex-partner, the father of her children, who has been granted joint custody of children. She is not the same mother who said good-bye to her children and sent them off to school in the morning.

Meanwhile, the children were facing challenges from classmates at school because their clothes were not the latest fashion, their lunch was not adequate or they did not have the latest video game at home; they may also have seen their father, who criticized their mother for not providing them with pocket money. They are not the same children who left home that morning. The potential for conflict is great when that family comes together again in the evening. The challenges presented to families with limited material and emotional resources have the potential to lead to dysfunctional familial relationships. Delinquency, child abuse and homeless children are all too often the result of inadequate support for overburdened families. The need is to understand the way experiences outside the family environment can affect the interactions between the individuals within it.

Yet another example is the overburdened career woman who after a hard day at work must come home to deal not only with family members who may also have had difficulties in their day but also with household tasks that are still considered, in her culture and by her family, as "women's work". The overexpenditure of emotional energy and the accompanying loss of physical energy lay the groundwork for difficult, if not unhappy, family interaction. The interplay between the time spent in the labour force and the time required to carry out the tasks related to basic survival affects in particular the family with two income earners. Maternal employment has resulted in a whole new set of values being introduced into family life. The restructuring of power within the family is one important way families have changed with women's entry into the labour force. This power shift has profoundly changed how family members interact with one another. The adaptation of the individual and of society to these new circumstances and the recognition of their impact on the individuals who make up the family is of great concern to those who understand the family as an emotional environment within which its members interact. Physical and emotional burdens based on an outmoded concept can destroy the familial environment.

The world has become conscious of the delicacy of the relationship between people and the physical environment in which they live. People are beginning to take seriously the earth's ecosystem and the dangers that threaten when they exploit some aspect of that environment to the point of extinction. By seeing themselves as a central part of the global ecosystem, "families can learn to be efficient stewards, not just manipulators, of their environments, understanding that a reverence for life is dependent upon a concomitant reverence for its conditions"[12]. Moreover, as people become more aware of the functions of societies and Governments around the world and of the conditions they themselves live under, they have begun to recognize the threat to the ecological balance. The family becomes responsible for protecting that balance, for responsible parenthood and the responsible use of resources. Both physical and social systems must be balanced if life as it is known on this planet is to be maintained.

Melson explains the family ecosystem approach as follows: "The concept of the family as an ecosystem reflects the belief that family life and its immediate environment - its space, food, clothing and artefacts - form a complex, dynamic, living system of which family members are a part. By viewing the family as an ecosystem, one can begin to understand how family life may be both the product of environmental forces and a significant creative force itself"[13]. Paolucci, Hall and Axinn caution, however: "The options the family exercises in shaping everyday activities can result in the most disquieting of human actions and emotions or the opportunity for the most reassuring of human experiences"[14]. They go on to say that the use of "an ecological approach that places the emphasis on viewing the family and environment holistically, allows one to note the interdependence of people to people, families to one another and to other social systems, and, especially, the interdependence of families to the natural environment"[15]. Skills in problem-solving, from the identification of the problem through the analysis of alternatives, the selection of the solution and its subsequent evaluation, are important for the effective functioning of the family "as an environment" and "in an environment".

Change and a family ecosystem approach

Looking at the family "as an environment" and "in an environment" helps to put change in context. It makes clear the inevitability of change because it enables understanding about how the interaction between and among people in the domestic environment is similar to that between elements in the external environment and the resultant changes there. Living things create change simply by living in an interactive mode with other living beings and things. Change is a constant and inevitable part of human interaction. As individuals add experiences to their lives, they change. As their changed members interact with one another, families change. Families change in structure - children leave, seniors come to live with adult children, family members die - and with each of these occurrences comes a change in the family environment. Great emotional stress and inability to cope with it comes with separation or divorce or when teenage children leave home because of what they feel is an unhappy environment. None of these changes take place without adjustment. The family environment is not static. It is just like the physical environment: today it is cloudy or rainy but tomorrow will be sunny. The vagaries of nature bring hurricanes, cyclones, earthquakes and floods. The leaves change colour on the trees. Spring brings renewed hope. So, too, does the environment of the family change. People learn to live with the physical environment by appreciating its beauty and warmth, by accepting its troubles and by preserving it for others to enjoy. They learn to live in the family environment by reacting to and adapting to the changes that affect it. Just as with the physical environment, understanding the environment of the family and the complexity of its tasks and relationships will help to protect it, and a lack of understanding can destroy it.

Family problem-solving: an ecosystem perspective

Acknowledging the changing aspect of the familial environment and viewing family as having cultural, economic and relational components raises the question of how these components, together with the individuals who make up the family, are managed to bring about an effective familial environment. A number of authors have devised problem-solving frameworks to explore the multifaceted issues families face[16, 17, 18, 19]. Kieren says: "Problem solving researchers have avoided viewing family problems negatively. For example, families are deemed more rather than less effective when they continue to define situations as problematic and therefore ones they should act upon"[20].

The issues faced daily that require decisions and solutions should be dealt with immediately rather than allowed to accumulate to crisis proportions. According to Klein[18], problems should be looked at as routine and expectable disruptions and dislocations of family life. Problem-solving becomes a continuous process requiring communication and management skills. Routine problems arise many times during a day, a week, a month or a year. Not all of them require the full problem-solving process be put into effect. Some are never fully solved because new issues emerge to complicate their resolution. Others, most often those arising out of emergencies or in highly emotional situations, are dealt with quickly, without recourse to a rational process. In every instance, however, the resources that the individuals and the family collectively possess are brought into play. When the family is viewed as an environmental system interacting with other systems in the larger social, economic and physical milieu, problem-solving is seen as a non-confrontational, rational approach to the changes constantly confronting families.

Managing the household economy effectively is a familial task requiring problem-solving skills. Families are responsible for making the decisions that determine how they will meet their basic needs for food, clothing and shelter. Dividing up the responsibilities for income generation, household work, child care, consumer behaviour and recreative activity requires decisions. Working out the number and spacing of children and child-rearing policies needs thoughtful inter-action. A cooperative approach to problem-solving requires that the power structure in a family be relatively flat, with all members being given the chance to contribute according to their ability and understanding of the issues involved. "The family ecological perspective, which focuses attention on family members and their environments allows one to better understand problems and arrive at solutions because it forces one to look at each part of the ecosystem (each family member) and the relationships among them"[12]. Regardless of the cultural background, needs are satisfied within a familial construction and a pattern for doing this is passed on from one generation to the next.

Experiencing family: an environmental view

There is a universality to the family experience. All societies view the formation, continuation and breakdown of family as a basic life experience. Melson suggests that "each family appears in a special relationship to its environment. The life of the family often seems to be organically part of its setting, to have grown up out of its nurturing soil. At the same time, the family exercises all the power and creativity in its grasp to fashion an environment that will reflect its aspirations, values and means"[13].

Families may have different experiences: try to imagine the family from the viewpoint of a daughter of a Muslim servant in a Christian, Egyptian middle-class home in Cairo. She knows no home but the bedroom she shares with her mother in the employer's home. She knows no father; her idea of a father is what she sees when she watches her mother's employer interacting with his two sons. She has no brothers or sisters; her only experience of persons her own age is that of the sons of her mother's employer. She does not, however, have the freedom of the household. She is confined to the kitchen and her mother's bedroom. She is definitely a servant, but the mistress of the house assists in her upbringing. She is sent to school, although not all girls of her class would have such as opportunity. She even is given the opportunity to study teacher education and she becomes a teacher in the elementary school system in Cairo. What does she call family? Who are her family members? What fabric of family life does she hold on to and pass on to her children? Her experience in this family, limited though it may have been, and her observation of the family in action will likely influence patterns of behaviour of this young woman when she forms her own family.

Those involved in promoting family life must recognize they have their own perspective of everyday life. They must understand the difference between viewing a family from the outside and from the inside, i.e., being a member of it. Many would view Ms. Ngige's childhood, for example, as having been deprived, yet she describes it as warm and loving and says it gave her a whole set of values to live by. Often families are seen to be caring and loving because that is what they wish to show, but the interactions that take place behind the closed doors of many a mansion may be physically and emotionally abusive in ways that destroy people rather than empower them. Looking at the family as an environment allows the environment experienced personally to be distinguished from the environment observed by a visitor. Unless the outside observer wholly participates in a family and knows all about the milieu that influences it, he or she can only observe, not judge. The intimate, human environment of the family is so dependent on the subtleties of everyday interaction that what is seen through the eyes of an observer is very different from what is felt as a participant in the situation. The objective (or outsider) view tells something about the family as a social institution. The subjective (or insider) view tells about the family as an environment for personal growth and development [21].

Family policy within an ecosystem perspective

Using the concept of family as an environment in an environment (figure 3.2) and thereby acknowledging the changes that take place as a result of the interplay between individuals in that environment, as well as the changes that take place when those individuals interact with environments beyond the family space, is a useful mechanism for helping family counsellors, welfare workers and politicians address the issues that face families. Once a dynamic approach is applied, which recognizes the constant formation and reformation of individuals and their environments, it provides a whole new perspective from which to view family.

FIGURE 3.2. FAMILY AS AN ENVIRONMENT IN AN ENVIRONMENT

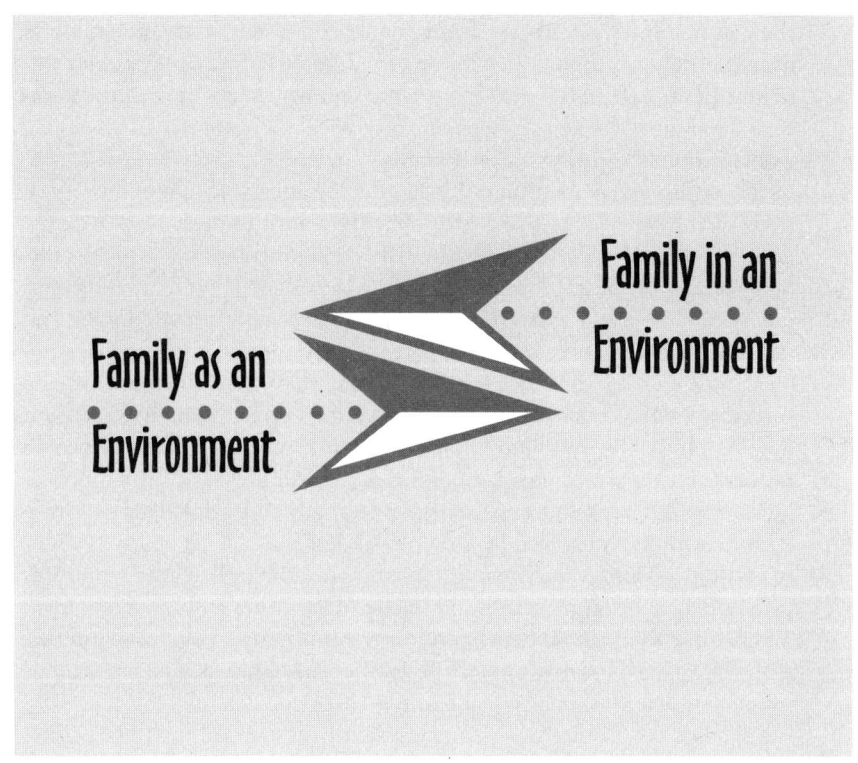

Conflict and abuse are often the result of frustrations experienced in dealing with new situations. People who have not been given the power to examine their problems and to seek insight into their source are people who become frustrated and angry. Effective problem-solving is the basis of a healthy familial environment. Helping people develop ways of loving and caring for the familial environment and of passing its values on to future generations is the concern of everyone. Resources must be available to families to assist them in the management of their daily lives: the provision of basic needs, the development of family relationships and the skills for effective problem-solving. Developing support systems and training and counselling families are needed to deal with the changes that are inevitable whenever people come together in intimate relationships while at the same time experiencing interactions with the larger world.

Not all families have the ability or resources to look after their own members. Yet everywhere human beings are recognized as having the right to health and happiness. It therefore becomes the responsibility of institutions and Governments to develop policies that provide health and security for everyone. Since individuals form Governments through the vote and taxes, the families they are members of become important units, with responsibility not only for their own welfare but also for the welfare of the society as a whole.

The policies of Governments and of non-governmental organizations are often developed in isolation from the real problems of families. They view the family from the outside, seeing it as falling short of what it "should" be. A basic question is how to ensure familial environments that will shape family relationships in ways that promote maturity, health and personal satisfaction. Beginning with an understanding of the constant change that is a part of the lives of families, policy makers and implementers must have some basis for judging the effects of their decisions.

Concerned about family policy, the provincial government of Alberta, in Canada, has produced a document entitled "The family policy grid". It is meant to be a "standard by which laws, policies, programmes and administrative procedures can be assessed"[22]. The significant question whenever policy is being discussed or implemented is, Will this policy, law or programme be fair, supportive and encouraging to Alberta families? The stated purpose of the grid (figure 3.3) is to heighten awareness of the ways the Government affects families; to facilitate a review of existing and proposed policies and programmes; to address the consequences of policies for families; to facilitate agreement on the objectives of policies and programmes for families; to facilitate a coherent policy approach to families; and to increase sensitivity at all levels of the Government to the importance of supporting and strengthening families in all governmental actions.

Beginning with the assumption that policies lead to legislation, legislation leads to the development of programmes and programmes lead to procedures for delivery, the grid lists a number of aspects of familial interaction that could be affected by policy and subsequent actions. Questions can therefore be raised with respect to the effect of policy, legislation, programmes or procedures on family well-being, family roles, family diversity, family support, family ties, family commitment/responsibility, family interests and partnerships. The list could be different, and it could be shorter or longer, but the very notion that policy decisions can be judged as to their effect on interaction within the familial environment is what makes it important. This grid, or one similar to it, could be a useful tool for government agencies, as well as for promoters and critics of family policy, to measure their proposed policy. Rather than assuming that legislators or professionals know what is best for families, a model can be used to analyse the effect of a policy or programme on the family.

FIGURE 3.3. FAMILY POLICY GRID

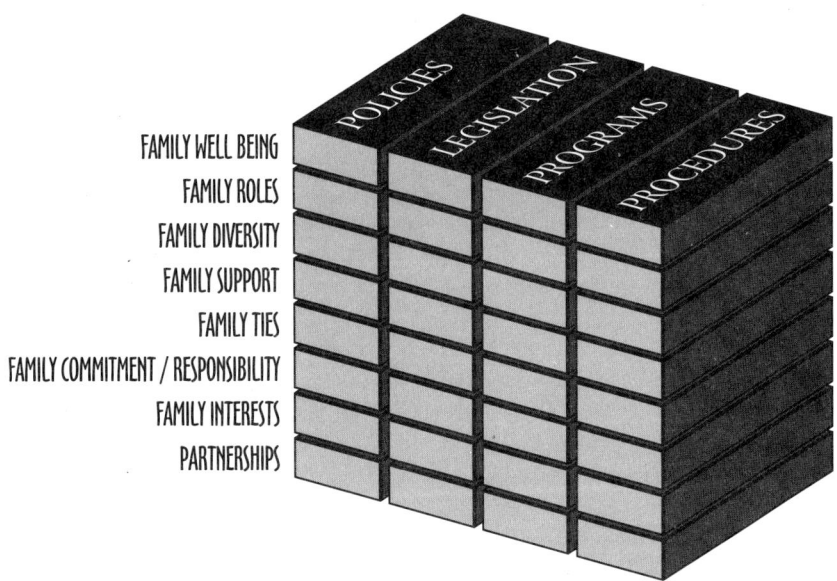

Source: Canada, Government of Alberta, Premier's Council in Support of Alberta Families, *Family Policy Grid* (Edmonton, 1992).

Summary and conclusions

Family is defined as an environment within which individuals interact while solving the problems of daily living. Using an ecosystem approach, family becomes a system made up of individuals operating within the larger system of the society in which it is embedded. In such a framework, the family interacts with other systems, often on a daily basis. The framework is dynamic and suggests that change to both the family environment and the larger environment it is situated in is constant and inevitable. It is useful, moreover, for recommending, developing, implementing and critiquing family policy.

To think of family as an environment within an environment helps in understanding the many complexities of the interplay between culture, emotions, needs and economics when individuals get together in families. All people are shaped by the familial relationships in which they grow from childhood and which they forge for themselves throughout their lives. People may select a vocation, career or job, join a political party, even emigrate to a new society, but their parents, siblings and ancestors are a given, and they remain a potent shaping force throughout life. Even in an individualistic society, the influence of families cannot be shrugged off: their very existence tells us of our origins. When people think of what families have given them, they are forced to consider what they wish to keep, change, discard or improve both within their own lifetimes and for the benefit of their descendants[1].

People and their Goverments must respond to problems of poverty, child support, care of the elderly and health care by instituting family support systems in the form of guaranteed incomes, child care centres, health care systems, family life education programmes and family planning initiatives. Seeing the family as an environment where people interact in various ways, traditional, ritual or routine, to solve the everyday problems of human survival; recognizing that the family is embedded in a larger social, cultural, economic and physical environment that it depends upon for the satisfaction of those needs; accepting the interdependency of these environments and acknowledging the responsibilities it places upon the society for the decisions made: all these should enable the family to influence policy, so it is truly able to build "the smallest democracy at the heart of society", which became an unofficial motto for the International Year of the Family.

References

1. Vanier Institute of the Family, Canadian Families in Transition: The Implications and Challenges of Change (Ottawa, 1992), p. 1.
2. P. Aries, *Centuries of Childhood* (New York, Vintage Books, 1962).
3. W. Rybczynski, *Home: The History of an Idea* (London, Penguin Books, 1987).
4. R. Glossop, "Family definitions: what's it to me?", *Transition*, vol. 22, No. 1 (1992), pp. 5-8.
5. D. Reiss, *The Family's Construction of Reality* (Cambridge, Massachusetts, Harvard University Press, 1981).
6. R. Glossop, "Today's families: continuity, change and challenge", *Transition*, vol. 20, No. 3 (1990), p. 5.
7. H. McCubbin and others, *Family Types and Strengths: A: Life Cycle and Ecological Per-spective* (Edina, Minnesota, Burgess International Group, 1988).
8. Ibid., p. 25.
9. Ibid., p. 75.
10. E. Vaines and L. Ngige, "A family perspective on everyday life", *People and Practice: International Issues for Home Economists*, vol. 3, No. 2 (1992), p. 9.
11. B. Paolucci, O. A. Hall and N. Axinn, *Family Decision Making: An Ecosystem Approach* (New York, John Wiley, 1977), p. 13.
12. Ibid., p. 25.
13. G. Melson, *Family and Environment: An Ecosystem Perspective* (Minneapolis, Minnesota, Burgess, 1980), p. 1.
14. Paolucci, op. cit., p. 13.
15. Paolucci, op. cit., p. 184.
16. D. Kieren, J. Henton and R. Marotz, His & Hers (Hinsdale, Illinois, Dryden Press, 1975).
17. D. Kieren, E. Vaines and D. Badir, *The Home Economist as a Helping Professional* (Kingston, Ontario, Canada, Frye Press, 1982).
18. D. Klein, "Family problem solving and family stress", *Marriage and Family Review*, vol. 6, 1983, pp. 85-112.
19. D. Kieren, "Adolescent diabetic management and home economics practice", *People and Practice: International Issues for Home Economists*, vol. 1, No. 2 (1988).
20. Ibid., p. 3.
21. Vaines and Ngige, op. cit.
22. Canada, Government of Alberta, The Premiers' Council in Support of Alberta Families, *Family Policy Grid* (Edmonton, 1992).

FAMILY
Reinventing Fatherhood

Introduction

These are times when fatherhood is moving in two contradictory directions. The rise in fatherlessness is happening at the very time when fatherhood itself is being redefined by many men and women.

Fathering has never been easy for any generation. Most Western cultures barely have a language to describe fatherhood. Among citations on parenting in the library of the University of California, references to motherhood outnumber mentions of fatherhood by five to one. During the 1970s and 1980s, the phrases most commonly used to describe good fathers in the United States of America were "Mr. Mom" and the "new father", who were said to be far more nurturing than the "old fathers" of the 1950s. The new standard was overblown; for one thing, those 1950s fathers were likely to be around more, even if they were not necessarily so nurturing. "Mr. Mom", a term used for fathers who stay home with the children, or who are at least responsible for most of the housework and child care, is, in a sense, a diminishing term: it suggests that such a father is a second-class mother. The new father aims at androgyny, says fatherhood expert David Blankenhorn, President of the Institute for American Values. The term: "Suggests that good men are those who eschew many historically masculine traits (such as protecting and providing for wife and children) and cultivate historically feminine traits (such as emotional sensitivity and the nurturance of young children)." Blankenhorn and others see merit in the ideal of the sensitive new father "as a corrective to an older norm." But as a new definition of masculinity, he suspects "that most men, and perhaps most women, find it lacking."[1]

Many experts believe that fathers do parent differently; for example, men tend to play rougher and more adventurously with their children and, if only because of upper body strength, offer a distinctive discipline to adolescents. Nonetheless, experts often expressed ambivalence about assigning precise roles to parents based on their gender. They expressed a sense that the role of fathers is changing in Western society, and that this change represents both a threat and an opportunity.[2]

The rise in fatherlessness and new family forms

In much of the world, it is premature or irrelevant to talk of a newfa-

---

* The present paper has been prepared for the IYF secretariat by Richard Louv, a journalist and writer, San Diego, California, United States of America.

therhood based on shared parenting. "Although different societies have very different views about what qualities are masculine, such qualities are invariably more highly valued than those thought to be feminine", writes Jo Boyden, in her book Families: *Celebration and hope in a world of change*.

"In many societies, men have considerable authority over women. It is the male's family that a bride usually joins. In extreme cases, women lay down their own lives at the death of their husbands. In modern industrial society many old customs have vanished, but signs of them remain: at marriage the father gives the bride away; the husband chooses her hand."[3]

She points out that women comprise about half the world's population, perform about two thirds of its work, receive only one tenth of its income and own less than one hundredth of its assets. The price is high:

"Although women live longer than men ... in many countries of Asia and the Pacific there are fewer than 95 women for every 100 men. The reason for this, the UN has shown, is that there are higher death rates for women in poor countries. They generally receive inferior nutrition, health care, and education."[4]

According to the World Health Organization, contraceptive use worldwide is three times greater among women than men, yet female contraceptive methods present higher risks. Most sexually transmitted diseases also have graver medical consequences for women than men.[5]

Even as the concepts of shared parenting and shared breadwinning gain currency in Western media, the reality of emotional and physical fatherlessness grows. Boyden cites a study of four-year-olds in 10 countries that discovered that the average daily time fathers spent alone with their children was less than one hour, ranging from 6 minutes per day in Hong Kong and 12 minutes in Thailand to 54 minutes in China and 48 minutes in Finland. When the average time spent by both parents with their children was added to these amounts, the number of hours that fathers were present with their children ranged from 1 hour and 36 minutes per day in the United States to 3 hours and 42 minutes in Belgium. "These findings suggest that even when fathers are present as an active member of a family their direct involvement in child care can be very limited."[6]

Father hunger, or awareness of it, is especially acute in the United States. Some observers believe that the United States is in danger of becoming, in effect, a fatherless society, shorn of its male parents not by war or disease, but by choice. A look at the statistics of family life suggests that this is not an exaggeration. One American study suggests that two years after a divorce, more than 80 per cent of the non-custodial parents, most of them fathers, have little or no steady pattern of visitation with the children. A second reason for fatherlessness is the rise in out-of-wedlock births. In 1990, 27 per cent of all births, more than one in four, were to unmarried women, a fivefold increase in 30 years, according to the Census Bureau. (The rate peaked in the 1970s and has dropped slightly.)[7] The percentage of white children born to single parents has nearly doubled over the last decade, to almost 20 per cent and is a much faster growth rate than found among African Americans.

New family forms

Another way of looking at the rise of fatherlessness is that it represents a worldwide movement away from marriage, towards new forms of families and a wider choice of living and parenting arrangements. Alternative family forms are increasing in number and variety. Cohabiting couples, for example, have increased from half a million in 1970 to 2.5 million in 1988.[8] The proportion of births to those living out of wedlock has increased significantly in countries in all regions, according to Boyden. The proportion of women bearing children without a partner is also growing. In both Belize and Sweden about half of all births are to unmarried women. The majority of Western men and women are married by the age of 30, according to Boyden:

"Half the women in Africa, 40 per cent in Asia, and 30 per cent in Latin America are married by the age of eighteen. In recent years, however, global statistics show that the proportion of married people has fallen, indicating the trend toward later marriage - and an overall decline in marriage in the developed regions. Even if marriage is less common, this does not mean a movement away from life as a couple. Many people in developed regions, Latin America, and the Caribbean live together -often recognized as married in law."[3]

Families today include nuclear families, unmarried heterosexual and homosexual couples, single-parent families, step-families, foster and adoptive families, childless couples and multiple-adult households. In the United States, and perhaps in other countries, single-father families are growing at a faster rate than the multitude of other family types. Still, single fathers constitute a demographic blip on the screen. The vast majority of single parents are still mothers.

This shift is having a profound impact on how children grow up. In the United States, one in four American children live in single-parent, usually female-headed, households. More than half can expect to live in such households before they turn 18. About 40 per cent of the children who live in fatherless households have not seen their fathers for at least a year.

Of the remaining 60 per cent, only one in five of these children sleeps even one night a month in their father's home. Only one in six sees his or her father an average of once or more a week, according to a study by Frank F. Furstenberg Jr. and Kathleen Mullan Harris, both of the University of Pennsylvania. More than half the children whose fathers do not live with them have never been in the paternal home.

The price of fatherlessness

While many single mothers are clearly able to raise effective, healthy children, the odds are against them, at least in the United States, given current economic and social realities. The following studies show the importance of having more than one parent in the household:

- Most single mothers work full time, but earn no more than $20,000 and receive little child support. A child in a female-headed household is six times more likely to be poor than a child in a two-parent family. The median per capita income for children in single-parent families is less than one third of the median per capita income of those from two-parent families. Two thirds of single-parent children will fall into poverty before they reach the age of 18, compared with 20 per cent of those from two-parent families. After divorce, children are twice as likely to be poor, according to a Census Bureau study.[9]
- Most research on infant health has focused on the behaviour of the expectant mother, according to Dr. Louis W. Sullivan, a former Secretary of Health and Human Services in the United States: "We are beginning to realize, however, that the behavior of the expectant father is also very important. Having the support of a husband may play a larger role in infant health care than factors such as maternal income and educational attainment. For example, the mortality rate of infants born to college educated but unmarried mothers is higher than for infants born to married high school drop-outs."[10]
- The most reliable predictor of crime and teenage pregnancy is not income or race, but family structure. Seventy per cent of imprisoned United States minors have spent at least part of their lives without fathers. Gangs feed on fatherless sons, as Nina J. Easton reported in the *Los Angeles Times Magazine*: "Father Greg Boyle of Dolores Mission Church in East Los Angeles once listed the names of the first 100 gang members that came to mind and then jotted a family history next to each. All but five were no longer living with their biological fathers - if they ever had."[11]
- The proportion of single-parent households in a community predicts

its rates of violent crime and burglary, according to a study of researchers Robert Sampson and W. Byron Groves published in the Journal of Research in Crime and Delinquency: "Two-parent households provide increased supervision and guardianship not only for their own children and household property, but also for general activities in the community. From this perspective, the supervision of peer-group and gang activity is not simply dependent on one child's family, but on a network of collective family control."[12]

The relationship between crime and fatherlessness is seen in all segments of society, but it is most pronounced in inner cities, where murder is the leading killer of young men. According to Mercer Sullivan, a research associate at the New School for Social Research in New York, where he has been studying the inner city for the last 30 years: "It's not just the absence of a stable adult male figure from a single household that does so much damage in these communities. At the neighbourhood level, when you have lots of households where fathers are not present, the whole social order breaks down. Teenagers take over the streets."[13]

- Children with fathers at home tend to do better at school, are less prone to depression and are more successful in relationships. Children of single-parent families are about 50 per cent more likely to have learning disabilities. Children from divorced families, especially boys, on average score lower on reading and mathematics tests. Single-parent children are twice as likely to drop out of high school as two-parent children.[14]
- Other long-range studies have shown that elementary schoolchildren from divorced families (who usually live with their mothers) are absent more, are more anxious, hostile and withdrawn, and are less popular with their peers than their classmates from intact families.[14]
- Children from one-parent families (again, usually mothers) achieve less and get into more trouble than children from two-parent homes, according to a study of 18,000 students sponsored by the National Association of Elementary School Principals in the United States. In fact, children from low-income two-parent families outperformed students from high-income single-parent homes.[15] Almost twice as many high-achievers come from two-parent homes as one-parent homes.[16]
- Children from single-parent homes are as much as 200 per cent more likely than children from two-parent families to suffer emotional and behavioural problems, according to a study by the National Center for Health Statistics in the United States. Over 80 per cent of the adolescents admitted to hospitals for psychiatric reasons come from

single-parent families[14] What about children with step-parents? The financial conditions of these children improve, but they are at least as likely as children from single-parent families to have learning disabilities and emotional and behavioural problems[14]
- The cycle continues: adults who grew up in divorced homes are more likely to be unhappy, in poor health, and dissatisfied with their lives, and more likely to become single parents themselves.
- Compared with adults who have grown up in two-parent households, men from divorced families are 35 per cent more likely, and women 60 per cent more likely, to get divorced or separated. Psychologist Judith Wallerstein, co-author of *Second Chances: Men, Women, & Children A Decade After Divorce*, followed the progress of 130 children of divorced parents 15 years after the divorce. Many of the boys experienced learning and behavioural trouble in school. In their early years, the girls did much better emotionally in school than the boys. (In fact, as other studies have shown, they did even better than girls from intact families.) But Wallerstein found that by the time they became young adults, girls and boys were experiencing equal difficulty in forming loving relationships. The girls were fearful of being alone, fearful that men would abandon or betray them. Many of the girls jumped from male to male, married early and divorced at a high rate. The boys, as they grew up, resisted relationships with girls[14]

The father-friendly workplace

Many observers believe that a new fatherhood is finally becoming a reality because of changes in the workplace brought about by new technologies, changes in the labour market, and the influence of women working outside the home. Some studies show that fathers feel more conflict between their jobs and their families than many of them will admit to their spouses or their bosses or even to themselves. Work/Family Directions, a consulting, management and research organization, based in Boston, Massachusetts, reports that men feel an increasing desire (and pressure from their spouses) to share housework and spend time with their children. Male employees experienced a doubling, from 1985 to 1988, of work-family conflicts; for example, the difficulty of finding child care during overtime hours.

"It's fair to ask whether society supports active parenting by women or men", writes Dr. Robert Glossop, director of programmes for the Vanier Institute for Family, and Ish Theilheimer, editor of *Transition* magazine. Peggy Nash, Director of Women's Programs, Canadian Auto Workers, sees:

"Growing economic pressures on families that make it tough for parents to do their jobs. Global trade and industrial transformation are making workers insecure while, at the same time, social programs are being cut back. The free market, left to its own devices, usually won't create the social support to allow families to survive."[17]

Yet despite the odds, change is coming in the way many men view work and family, and gradual change is taking place in the workplace.

Pressure from below

Some fathers decide to put their careers on hold. *American Health* reports that at one large Minneapolis company about 60 per cent of the fathers under the age of 35 say they are not currently aggressively seeking promotions or transfers for family reasons.[18] The trouble is that implicit in the Daddy track is still the message that parents, fathers, are second-class employees. Many men will choose a less ambitious work path, but paring back their careers (which has long-term economic implications for families and children) can be minimized if companies adopt flexible, family-friendly policies for all employees. Men will inevitably push back. One reason is demographic. Although still few in number proportionally, single fathers comprise the fastest growing type of households with working parents and children, according to statistics from the Bureau of Labor, United States, even though single working mothers still outnumber single fathers by four to one. Of men in the workplace, single fathers are more likely to feel a sense of urgency in creating family-friendly policies.[19] A second, and more important reason why change is inevitable: women are pushing companies to adjust their policies towards families. And, while fathers may not be rushing to take advantage of paternity leave, many of them are rearranging their priorities.

"Business used to think of employees as employees period", says Marie Tellier, Assistant Vice-President, Employment Equity, with Canadian National in Montreal. "They weren't parents or children of elderly people. They were just people who were supposed to come into work." According to Glossop and Theilheimer,[17] Tellier sees big changes in attitude and life styles among Canadian National's employees, with executives in three-piece suits bottle-feeding infants in the company's on-site day-care facilities and fathers saying they cannot work late because they have to pick up their children. Besides day care, Canadian National offers counselling on all kinds of family matters, flexible work options, and time off for family duties. "I wouldn't say the work environment is absolutely open to parents," says Tellier, but "there is a little more acceptance."[20]

Examples of change

Company acceptance and accommodation of fathers varies widely, depending on culture, social class, and workplace. However some companies and countries are responding. The *Wall Street Journal* reports that nearly half of the 200 large-company United States executives surveyed by Robert Half International say that managers are not as willing to work long hours as they were five years ago. In 1991, the *Monthly Labor Review* surveyed two agencies of the federal Government that allowed flex-time. Almost half of the fathers chose this option, electing to come to work earlier so that they could leave earlier to spend more time with their families.[21] Johnson & Johnson now offers flex-time schedules. When Apple Computers announced its new family policy in 1991, the company devoted an entire page of its in-house newsletter to fathers, sending the message that the company's family policies applied to men, and not only to women. The article described the double standard towards fathers and mothers: women are expected by the typical corporate culture to balance work and family, but men are not. Apple announced that this would no longer be the acceptable norm within the company.

Proponents of such programmes often argue for them on the basis of presumed increases in company productivity. According to a report by the Families and Work Institute, with headquarters in New York:

"There is, however, very little research to back up such sweeping claims. Gradually these programs are being subjected to greater scrutiny by business management and the press. Managers have begun to question the effectiveness of work-family initiatives ... and the press has begun to question whether companies with high-profile, family-friendly initiatives actually practice what they preach."

In 1991, the Families and Work Institute asked the Fortune 1000 companies what family-supportive policies they offered. Johnson & Johnson has the most comprehensive policies in its Balancing the Work and Family Program. Among the impressive benefits offered: child-care resource and referral, on-site, child-development centres, family-care leave, time off for short-term emergency care, adoption benefits, School Match (a resource and referral service that assists parents in choosing public or private schools), elder-care resource and referral, and relocation planning. The company also provides training in work-family issues for managers. The study's results, released in April 1994, were encouraging. Among the findings were the following:

- From 1990 to 1992, there was a sharp increase in the proportion of employees who agreed strongly that their immediate supervisors were

helpful with routine family or personal matters.
- Employees have become more open to telling the truth about family issues. (For example, they no longer call in to say they are sick when they need to stay at home with a sick child.)
- The proportion of employees who felt they paid a price for using flexible time and leave has decreased significantly.
- Employees affected by the family-supportive programmes are more loyal to the company, more satisfied with their jobs and more likely to recommend Johnson & Johnson as a place to work.

One of the more interesting findings was that some elements of the programme appeared to affect men and women differently. Mothers at Johnson & Johnson reported spending less time worrying about the welfare of their children with day care within walking distance. But fathers reported more distraction. Probably, that is because it is still something of a novelty for men to assume any responsibility for child care, and the fact that their children are within walking distance presents a distraction. Nevertheless, men who use on-site child care were significantly more likely to want to stay at Johnson & Johnson.[22]

Resistance

Several men have told the present writer that, as employees, they were afraid to take paternity leave or to even acknowledge their devotion to their family. They fear that, like women who end up on the second-tier Mommy track, they will be treated from that point on by the boss or by fellow workers as second-class employees. Even when paternity leave is offered, few men take it. Two out of five companies in the United States that grant family leave admit that they frown on men who apply for it, according to Catalyst, a research organization based in New York City.

Sweden leads the world in parental-leave policies, child care and women's labour force participation. Still, men take paternity leave so much less frequently than women do that the Swedish Government has sponsored advertising campaigns targeted at men. In the first year in which these policies were instituted, in 1974, only 3 per cent of eligible fathers actually took leave, according to a study conducted in 1991 by Linda Haas, a sociologist at Indiana University. By 1989, 44 per cent were doing so. In the Haas study, those fathers who took the leave took an average of 53 days, compared with 225 days for mothers.[23] Haas maintains that there are four categories of factors that prevent Swedish fathers from taking more paternal leave: biological factors, social-psychological factors, lack of social support, and economics. According to researchers Janet

Shibley Hyde, Marilyn J. Essex and Francine Horton:

"Regarding biological factors, it was traditionally assumed in Sweden that mothers were better able to meet their infants' needs. Furthermore, 90 per cent of Swedish mothers breast-feed for 5 months or more, again favouring women over men in taking leave. It is rare for Swedish fathers to take leave before the baby is 5 months old. Social-psychological factors include men's beliefs that they should be the primary breadwinner and the men's own lack of exposure to role models of men caring for infants. Lack of social support is a factor in that fathers may fear that people will form negative opinions of them for taking paternity leave; indeed, the majority of fathers in the Haas study did not receive positive support for taking parental leave from their friends and parents. The less likely the fathers were to receive support, the less likely they were to take leave. Economic factors are involved, too. The system of pay reimbursement favors leave taking by the lower-paid parent, usually the mother."[24]

Beyond the company: inventing new work/family systems

The rising economic and social pressure for shared parenting is having an impact on employees, particularly at companies without family-friendly work policies. "They used to say that as women entered the work force and there were more dual-earner families, that women would become more like men", according to Linda Duxbury, an associate professor of business at Carleton University in Ottawa, part of a team that conducted a national Canadian study on balancing work and family. "We've observed exactly the opposite. Men are becoming more like women: stressed out, suffering the same kinds of overload, the same kind of interference patterns between work and family as women traditionally have."20 Sociologist Judith Stacey encountered some real surprises while researching for her book *Brave New Families*. She writes, "In a typical middle-class family, the man really does have higher career status and higher pay, and he doesn't really have much time to devote to his kids, even if he had the interest. In working class households, the structure of work is very different." Men are more likely to be laid off or to work shifts than women. At Levi Strauss & Co. (Canada) Inc., Julie White, manager of community affairs, sees attitudes changing among working-class men. She describes an employee who eavesdropped on a male-only Friday night poker game: "They spent the first two hours of the evening talking about toilet training."[20]

Some men are refusing to wait for their companies to change. Along with their wives, they are coming up with new ways to structure two-career households. Joe Dicks, 35, and Linda Workman, 31, were married in 1986 and graduated from law school the same year. Joe was immediately offered a job with the biggest law firm in San Diego, and Linda went to work for another powerful local firm. Linda and Joe wanted to have children. "Joe and I couldn't wait for the world to become family-friendly, something had to give."

Usually, in a situation like this, the wife decides to stay home after a child is born, but Joe and Linda were convinced they had another option. "My firm had a slower career track for lawyers who wanted a slower pace", says Joe. "But it was a Mommy Track. No man I knew at the firm had ever taken paternity leave, let alone chosen the slower track. To be honest, I don't think I could have taken that track and watched my colleagues pass me." So, Joe and Linda created their own family track. In anticipation of becoming a parent, Joe left the firm. In July 1992, their first child, Spencer, was born. Then Linda left her job. They opened separate law practices, and each of them cut the work week to four days. Their offices are on different floors of the same building. Linda takes Friday off to be with her son; Joe takes Monday. A part-time nanny helps out on the days when both of them are working. On weekends, they share the duties and joys of parenthood equally. "Our son has never gone through a stage where he preferred me over Joe", says Linda. Their income has dropped, but Joe believes that, over the long haul, they may earn more than some of their fellow attorneys "because we're less likely to burn out".[25]

Although the number of full-time at-home fathers is still proportionately small, they report that life at home can be surprisingly fulfilling, though sometimes frustrating. Many of them wear their role as a badge of honour. At-home father, Ted Bzdega, 38, of Des Moines, Iowa, says:

"My wife is a physician, and makes a good living working many hours. We live out on a 70 acre farm, so I don't have a life much beyond the kids. I'm always there. The tough thing is your day doesn't have as much structure to it. But I sort of feel guilty that I'm having so much fun with my kids when my wife is going out to work."

When forced to loosen their grip on breadwinning as their primary identity, some men discover deeper dimensions of their fatherhood, and their manhood.

In Rifle, Colorado, an out-of-work construction worker, says:

"I love my kids, and I want to take care of them the best way I know how. In order to do that, I've got to be that kind of a person, gentle. When I was growing up, I was a pretty hard-core person myself. I was kind of the bully of the crowd I ran around with. Me and my wife share on everything. When I was working all the time, I'd come home, help with the cooking, the dishes, the cleaning, raising of the children. I was hurt on the job; I ruptured three disks in my back. I've been laid up for a little more than a year and a half. I'm getting ready to retrain to go to school, to learn a new trade. Now that I'm disabled and I'm home a lot, I take care of the kids at home while she's at work. When she gets home, she helps me. It's been real hard on me, being laid up, and real hard on my wife. I'm used to getting up at six in the morning, going to work all day, working till 5 or 6:00 at night and coming home. Now (my wife) gets up and goes to work, and I stay at home with the kids. I've learned that there's a lot more to home life, to raising the kids, than I really realized. In a way, hanging sheet rock was easier on me because I could take my frustrations out on the work. I would never hit my kids, it's one of my strong beliefs. When I was working, I only saw them at night. There's a closer bond now than there was before. When the baby - he's only a year old - was first born, he was always going to his mom. He was kind of a momma's boy. And now, when he gets hurt or something, he comes running to dad. He's becoming a daddy's boy. It's a neat feeling; I don't know how to describe it."[26]

Dr. Kyle Pruett, a clinical professor of psychiatry at the Child Study Center, Yale School of Medicine, conducted a five-year study of stay-at-home fathers and their children:

"They were less defensively macho. Caring for another human being changes us all, men and women. It humanizes us ... The fathers become more considerate of their friends and families, find themselves more interested in human relationships, and are less competitive. But they don't lose their business sense or their edge. One father who kept at his real estate business said he became more efficient at negotiation because he learned to read people better."[27]

Mothers are often surprised at the changes they see in men as they become more intimately involved in fathering. Holly Rigby, of Burleson, Texas, tells how her husband was laid off eight months ago. She says:

"I went back to work. This has been a very hard transition for him. I have been watching him change every day. His interaction with the children has changed beyond belief. I have taken time away in another room during dinner time and have listened to him and the children. If you had asked me three months ago if I ever thought he could be so much fun, so loving and caring with the kids I would have said no. Well, I was wrong. He has become the best father I know of."[28]

Some men, linked to their offices or clients by computer, modem and fax machine, are discovering a kind of fatherhood their great-great-grandparents might have recognized. Some men now work in what might be called a "virtual blacksmith shop". In their home office, they work at their computer while their sons, a few feet away, do their projects on their own computer. Such an arrangement is a relatively rare but growing result of the increase in home offices.

A more involved role at home

More attention is needed on the father's role at home, as worker and nurturer, by social scientists, psychologists and paediatricians. Most past research on child care and development has focused on infant-mother attachment. Among psychologists, the generally accepted theory is that children with a secure attachment to their mothers, especially during infancy, are more likely to feel confident, have good relationships with teachers and peers, and are more likely to be problem-solvers. But, until very recently, the father's role as a nurturer has been viewed by many researchers and media as being secondary to the mother's.

In an early edition of his famous guide to child rearing, Dr. Benjamin Spock advised fathers: "A man can be a warm father and a real man at the same time ... Of course, I don't mean that the father has to give just as many bottles or change just as many diapers as the mother. But it's fine for him to do these things occasionally. He might make the formula on Sunday." Times change. Today, the revised edition says:

"I think that a father with a full-time job - even where a mother is staying home - will do best by his children, by his wife, and himself if he takes on half or more of the management of the children (and also participates in the housework when he gets home from work and on weekends)."[29]

The father as a nurturer at home is gaining cachet, but not without some serious revisions in parenting advice, and resistance from economies, institutions and parents.

The second shift

For the most part, however, women continue to assume most of the responsibility for child care, even as they pursue careers. In Japan, married career women are rare. Jo Boyden reports that: "A married woman is likely to be a sengyo-shufu - full-time housewife - or a kengyo-shufu - a housewife who works part-time."[3] At the same time, businessmen typically put in six days a week at the office. Some women work part time outside the home. Known as *kengyo-shufu* a married woman is expected to look after her children full-time until they are about to complete their schooling. She is then free to seek a job but finds that few are open to her, and usually ends up doing manual work with poor pay and little security. When some Japanese women rise in the business world, they are expected to work as obsessively as men. "Until male working hours are reduced and child care services provided, Japanese women will continue having to choose between family and career."³ Boyden continues: "Women everywhere work more than men - on the average, twice as many hours a day in the developing world. The burden of family life falls mostly on women, and their role in producing the goods on which families depend for their survival is often ignored. In many parts of sub-Saharan Africa, for example, women undertake the arduous and heavy agricultural work, in addition to the bearing and caring of children, and running the home and family life. Yet it is men who control the resources of production."³⁰

Arlie Hochschild states that the questions of who does what and what needs doing can become the sources of deep tension in a marriage. Among the American families Hochschild studied over an eight-year period, the fact that wives worked outside the home did not account for why some marriages were happy and others were not; what contributed to happiness was the husband's willingness to share the work at home. Whether traditional or more egalitarian, couples were happier when the men did a sizeable share of housework and child care. She points out that in one study of 600 couples filing for divorce, the second most common reason women cited for wanting to divorce, after "mental cruelty", was their husbands' neglect of home or children. Women mentioned this reason more than finances, physical abuse, drinking or infidelity. Hochschild's study found that, when hours of work outside and inside the home were added up, women in the 1960s and 1970s worked roughly 15 more hours each week than men. Over a year, they worked an extra month of 24-hour days. Over a dozen years, they worked an extra year of 24-hour days. Most women, according to Hochschild, work one shift at the office or factory and a second shift at home. She came to believe that:

"Those husbands who helped very little at home were often just as deeply affected as their wives - through the resentment their wives felt toward them and through their own need to steel themselves against that resentment ... Even when husbands happily shared the work, their wives felt more responsible for home and children. More women than men kept track of doctor's appointments and arranged for kids' playmates to come over."

Also, she found, when men do participate in the care of their children, they choose more of the fun jobs, for example, taking their kids to the park while the wife does the dishes.³¹

Towards shared parenting in the home

The home front, however, may be improving. *American Demographics* magazine reports that research carried out from the mid-1960s to the mid-1980s shows that men have been doing a gradually greater share of housework since 1965. Between 1965 and 1985, men have gone from 5 to 20 hours of housework a week.[32]

The thousands of fathers who responded to the fatherhood poll conducted by Parents in 1993 showed that fathers have come a long way in the 10 years since the previous fatherhood poll was carried out in 1984. In 1993, on almost every front, from household chores to daily child care, men have moved closer to parity with women. This is particularly true for families whose mothers work full time outside the home. Increasingly, many fathers have become involved in their children's lives in areas in which their own fathers were excluded. For example, fathers are now likely to be present in the delivery room, an experience their fathers never had. This experience, increasing in frequency, often has a profound influence on a father and his children. "The joy of seeing a child born is indescribable, and having delivered many during medical school did not prepare me for the excitement of my son's first cry", says Tennessee physician Jerry L. Roberts.[33] One study found that of 20 deeply involved fathers, all but one had witnessed their children's births[18] This is one of the most positive changes about fathering today.

The *American Demographics* and *Parents* magazine reports seem to suggest an impressive increase, except men still do only one fifth of the cooking, cleaning, and laundry[32] If men continue at the rate of progress reported by *Parents* magazine, they will be doing as many child-related chores as women in the year 2118. "We're in the midst of an evolution", says James Levine, director of the Fatherhood Project, quoted in *American Health*, "not a revolution"[18]

"It's still difficult for the man and for society", says Dr. Kyle Pruett. "Most men find themselves explaining what they're doing with the child at the supermarket week after week. The first response they get is, Isn't that lovely - you're babysitting! But when it keeps happening, most men get pretty perturbed."[27] However, men are less and less likely to let such comments go unchallenged. "Since I do the shopping I take Kayle with me when I can", says William Partenheimer of Stone Mountain, Georgia. "We went to the store the other day and saw a lady I work with. Her response was, Oh, I see you are babysitting today. Well I do not consider that babysitting. I am her father and she is just as much my responsibility as she is my wife's."[34]

Resistance in the family

James Levine argues that, within families, cultural resistance to fatherhood, especially the new father, must be identified and challenged, not only the father's resistance but that of other members of the nuclear and extended family. For example, when a man does take family leave or decide to be a part- or full-time at-home father, he may encounter subtle or not-so-subtle messages from his in-laws, such as: Aren't you working? Don't you have a job yet? A mother can also communicate conflicting messages about the father's involvement, even undermining it by assuming that her way of doing the laundry is better than his. Most women (and men) grew up being told that child rearing was primarily a woman's job. Such a sense of responsibility is difficult to share, particularly if the man is also sending out mixed messages; he may say he wants to do more at home, but he may also find that his wife's subtle resistance is a useful excuse to dodge his own responsibilities.[35]

"The mother is the gatekeeper to fatherhood", says Dr. Michael Diamond, associate clinical professor of psychiatry at the University of California (Los Angeles). "She may allow it or obstruct"[21]. Linda Haas suggests that the working women who most welcome the father's help share three traits: They do not feel guilty about their jobs; their own fathers helped to raise them; and their husbands have flexible hours. One mother told the present writer:

"Something happened when our first daughter was six months old, we were suffering through colic. I was crying, she was crying, and my husband took her from me. I said, No, I need to take care of her; I need to do this. And he looked at me, and he was really startled, and he said, *She's my daughter too*, and just because it's your way doesn't mean it's the right way. I just assumed that I was the mom, I was the nurturer, I was doing it the right way. And damned if that child didn't stop crying anyway, just to spite me." (She laughed). "It really was a wake-up call to me, that he has instincts toward his children, and he acts on them, and it's not like when my father used to come in the door and my mother would say You kids go back in your room and I'll call you when dinner's ready. She protected our father from us."[36]

"For many women, it's apparently better to maintain responsibility for parenthood, even at the cost of what we might call role overload, rather than yield some of that status and responsibility to a partner", says Michael Lamb, a psychologist with the National Institute of Child Health and Human Development in Bethesda, Maryland.[37]

The more educated a woman is, the more this sense of competitiveness seems to increase. A Boston University study showed that the older a mother was, and the higher her educational level and previous job status were, the more she monopolized parenting. "If women were as truthful as possible, they'd admit it's difficult both to ask husbands for help and to give over some of the responsibility", says sociologist Judith Auerbach, former director of the Institute for the Study of Women and Men at the University of Southern California. "Women feel that they're supposed to want to be involved, and if they're not, then there's something wrong with them."[18]

Dr. Ronald Levant, a Harvard Medical School psychologist who calls the home "the next frontier for men", suggests a father can be more of a partner in the home and less of an employee of the wife, if he assumes total responsibility for a certain aspect of housework or child care; for example, he might get the children ready for school, and she might get them ready for bed.

Dr. Kyle Pruett, advises mothers to expect such territorial feelings, and not to squash them. "Talk about it. Humor is the best way to cope." He suggests that fathers should not rise to the competition. "If you learn some secret about your baby, don't keep it from the mother."[18]

Dr. Michael Diamond says fathers should not turn themselves into "junior mothers", and children do not need two competing mothers, but parents who help each other.

"The father's role is to serve as a structuring presence. He should be challenging. Pushing his child ahead. Leading the child to the outer world. Mentoring. One way the father introduces the child to the world is through play."

Indeed, some pioneering research at the University of California (Davis) found that, in addition to being good babysitters, adult male rhesus monkeys play more with baby monkeys than do mother monkeys. Ape fathers and human fathers, says Diamond, evoke play. "And play is a way to achieve mastery. It encourages mastery in the sense of being able to deal with phenomena. They don't control you; you control them. You're the rider on the horse; you aren't simply dragged along by it. The father gives you the sense of riding the horse. Of riding life."[21] One cautionary note: Fathers who try hard to connect with their children, to be superfathers, sometimes lose touch with their wives. Levine advises the men enrolled in his fathering sessions to schedule dates with their wives. He says, "Dating your wife has a dramatic effect on being able to connect with your kids. After all, you are a family."[21]

Fathers in the community

One frontier of the new fatherhood is the father's role as a nurturer beyond his home, as a community builder. After men joined the Industrial

Revolution, women became the lasting glue that held together the web of social connections in the schools and neighbourhoods and towns. These women have been the community builders, the school volunteers, who, more than men, raised money for community centres, and made sure the parks were safe and well equipped. Nowadays, many women, too, have moved into the workplace and away from the neighbourhood. In recent decades, men have withdrawn from their roles as neighbourhood protectors; many value community less than their fathers and grandfathers did. According to a Massachusetts Mutual Life Insurance study[44], per cent of Americans believe that present-day fathers are not doing as well as in the past at the most basic element of community-building: showing respect for others.

Yet, many men yearn for something beyond today's limited definition of the father as breadwinner or even nurturer. Some are discovering the powerful community role fathers once had. Some men are beginning to reclaim their stake in the neighbourhood, the school, the preschool, and they're finding it to be surprisingly fulfilling. The reasons for this reawakening range from the fact that so many men are feeling lonely to the fact that men are, often, no longer the sole or main breadwinners within their families; in order to express themselves, to feel potent, they may reach beyond work, beyond their house, in ways they may find surprisingly fulfilling and oddly familiar. The father connection can occur in a soccer league or father-child church programmes or parent-teacher activities.

In the United States an increasing number of fathers enjoy such programmes as Y-Indian Guides, originated by the Young Men's Christian Association in the 1920s for fathers and their sons aged between 5 and 8. This programme is experiencing a boom in membership. It focuses on strengthening the bond between parent and child while teaching children about native American culture. Unlike the Boy Scouts, fathers are required to attend every meeting and camp out with their children. Fathers comment that such community activities not only force them to carve out time for their children, but also to bond with other fathers. At schools and in neighbourhoods around the United States, father patrols are cutting back bushes in vacant plots of land and creating school security teams. Fathers of students at Arlington High in Indianapolis created Security Dads. They ride buses to and from sporting events or on field trips and students say they prefer having the fathers around instead of security guards.[38] Fathers are also potent figures in the classroom, as volunteer aides or speakers

Facing father fear

Although this is an era of increasing fatherlessness when male role models are desperately needed, it is also a time of fear, when men who are involved with children are somehow suspect. This may be particularly true in the United States. Consciously or unconsciously, many childhood education professionals shy away from hiring male workers or encouraging male involvement in the classroom.

"The way to deal with this fear is not by curtailing the involvement of men with kids but by creating safety zones where men can care for children without fear or without creating fear", says Levine. Some organizations have demonstrated that safe zones, or at least safer zones, can be created. During the 1980s, for example, the Boy Scouts of America adopted a "two-deep leadership" policy, which requires that at least two adult leaders be present at all Boy Scout and Cub Scout activities. Yet the question is whether the only kind of male involvement to be sanctioned by the culture should be organized, public activities such as scouting, soccer or Big Brothers? Informal community connections between children and adults are just as important. Perhaps more important.

Some suggestions for creating safer neighbourhood zones for children and for adults are given below:

- Devise household and neighbourhood plans that prevent abuse and false accusations. The sexual abuse of children is an uncomfortable topic for many adults to discuss, so it should be addressed as part of a larger agenda of safety, including how to protect the children on the block from being injured in a traffic accident.
- Parents should know who lives where, which child belongs in which house. Each neighbour should accept the idea that he or she is responsible for all the children on the block. Parents should get to know any adult with whom children have a relationship. One warning sign: Does the adult interact on a social level mostly or entirely with children? While not a definitive sign of a child abuser, it is one that should cause parents to be extra cautious.
- When neighbourhood children are present in your home, adopt an open-door policy, whether they are with other children or adults. Invite the other parents to stop by. Whenever possible, rather than calling on the phone, walk over to your neighbour's house to retrieve your child in person.
- If you are going to offer activities for neighbourhood children, make sure the adults know about it and are, at some level, involved.

Only so much can be accomplished by institutional or neighbourhood safeguards. The most important preventive measures take place between parent and child. Arm your children with knowledge about child abuse, and arm them with self-esteem. "A child who has good self-esteem, self-confidence, a close relationship with the parents, is much less likely to be victimized", says David Finklehor, co-director of the Family Research Laboratory at the University of New Hampshire. "Our studies show that predators sense that these are the kids who will tell, who can't be fooled or conned."

However, children who come from troubled households, who lack-self esteem, are the ones most in need of positive adult contact.

Changing institutional attitudes

In the years to come, institutions must reinvent their relationship with fathers. Levine believes that media should pay more attention to those companies that are father-friendly. For example, many magazines have published articles describing great companies for working mothers; few have focused on good companies for working fathers. He also believes that companies, schools and religious institutions must create ways for fathers to mentor, encourage and train other fathers. Levine offers a structured way to encourage male involvement. His book, *Getting Men Involved*, recently published by Scholastic Inc., which also publishes the magazine Early Childhood Today, shows how men can be more a part of early childhood education and how schools can help them do it.

"The book is designed for education professionals", says Levine, "but also for parents who want their children's school to be father friendly".

Several success stories are reported by Levine. A Head Start programme in Dayton, Ohio, recruits men from churches, businesses and other professions located in the area to volunteer to spend time in classrooms, where they assist in reading stories, help with computer projects and talk about their work and hobbies. In Minneapolis, nearly[40] per cent of the parents participating in Parents in Community (a programme designed to increase parental involvement in education) events are men. The programme attributes its success to the redefined role of the school bus drivers. Treated as full members of the educational team, drivers spend one hour a day in the classroom, go on all field trips and attend staff meetings and parent-teacher conferences. The male drivers involved then recruit other men as volunteers.

In calling for greater male involvement in early childhood education, Levine is not suggesting women are not doing or cannot do a good job. But as he writes:

"The stereotype that women alone should care for children, or that they alone are capable of caring for children, limits the opportunities and talents of both sexes. It leads women disproportionately into the caring professions without exploring a broader set of career options, and it keeps men from broadening their career options to the caring professions, despite their interests and abilities ... It also ... perpetuates the devaluation of women and children, linking them together in a feminine world that is deemed less serious and important than the world of masculine activities."[39]

Other institutions that involve parents or children are beginning to examine how their assumptions and language exclude or excuse men from participation. For example, in Colorado, the director of a community centre for parents told them why the name of the centre had been changed:

"For eight years, we were called The Mother Center. We changed it to The Parent's Center. Right away we had dads with their toddlers taking part in the support groups. We had dads writing editorials for us. We had dads on the board. One guy showed up at a potluck with this contraption that looked like a steam engine; it was a barbecue smoker and he smoked all this meat for everybody. He was the provider of the meat. That's the first time he came, and he kept on coming."[40]

Teaching fatherhood

The rise in fatherlessness has lead to the creation of some programmes specifically focused on teenage fathers. One example, Responsive Fathers Program at the Philadelphia Children's Network, teaches young unmarried men to become better fathers and spouses by receiving counselling services and job search assistance. The participants, who range in age from 16 to 26 years, meet in group sessions once a week and discuss child rearing, male-female relationships, the job market and self-esteem. According to the Program's director, Thomas J. Henry, the social welfare system discourages fathers from family involvement, but he believes this can be reversed: "You have many fathers declared absent when they are actually present. People think they're just making babies and don't have any feelings attached to that act. Everyone says, We want you to be a responsible father, but we give them nothing to be responsible with."[41]

Interest is also growing in the public and private sectors in programmes designed to nurture nurturing fathers. In Barcelona, Spain, Joan Mestres is project director of the Casa de Colors, where men learn to relate to their children in new ways. Despite Spanish society's image of the father as a figure of authority, she believes some fathers are changing. She cites a recent encounter with a father who attended a storytelling workshop. "The father told me that to him telling stories was like starting a new sport. In the beginning it hurts because you get pain in your muscles; then after some practice, you find you can do it easily. Day after day, as you practise, you enjoy it more."[42]

A number of programmes have sprung up around the United States to help men explore the deeper dimensions of fatherhood. Paul Lewis started the Family University in San Diego several years ago; part of his curriculum is called the College of Fathering, or Dad's University. He started the programme, and accompanying newsletter, after having had lunch with a friend and discussing the divorce of a couple no one had suspected would split up. "We began to wonder why we wouldn't be next", he says. "We didn't want to be next. Then we got to thinking about why we didn't do more planning to be fathers." In 1978, they launched a newsletter entitled *Dads Only*:

"The focus of it has been to put in the hands of busy guys ways to interact with their kids, how to keep their marriage fresh. The idea is to be preventive rather than remedial. My conviction is that a lot of men care deeply about their families, but their careers are on the fast track, and small parenting problems become big ones before they know it."

One rite-of-manhood model is Avance (Get Ahead), a church-based, Government- and corporate-funded retreat in San Antonio, Texas, where young Latino men participate in traditional American Indian ceremonies and take vows of non-violence and responsible fatherhood. As Nina Easton reported in the *Los Angeles Times Magazine*, Avance founder Gloria Rodriquez originally taught only women. "But she quickly sensed that their newfound skills and confidence threatened their husbands and boyfriends. Rather than risk breaking up families, Avance opened its doors to men, who attend regular classes on child development and parenting techniques."[11]

Before boys inseminate

A more difficult problem is how to prepare young men for fatherhood before they become fathers. When the topic of fatherhood is broached in State schools, or even in most church youth programmes for that matter, it is almost always associated exclusively with sex, as if insemination (and how to avoid it) is the only aspect of fathering worth discussing. In American high schools offering pregnant-minor programmes, the young women who participate in them are required to attend child-development and parenting courses in these same schools. Young men, some of whom have fathered the children of these girls, are not required to take any kind of parenting course. Ultimately, the double standard shapes government policy. In Nashville, Tennessee, in 1993, Vice President Al Gore moderated a national conference entitled, "Reinventing family policy". During

10 hours of discussion by 40 panellists, the subject of fatherhood was barely mentioned. (Partly as a result, Gore organized a national fatherhood conference in 1994.) However, a handful of pioneering programmes have suggested that poverty and violence, especially violence towards women and children, can be decreased if society begins to find ways of teaching young men, directly and by example, in families, schools and religious institutions, about fatherhood before they become fathers. This objective might be achieved by requiring State-school students to take a child development or parenting eduction course; or it might be achievable by creating a "community curriculum" in parenting as an educational requirement but to be provided by religious, business and government programmes representing a diversity of cultures and family values.[43] In a recent interview, Vice President Al Gore said that such a course, either directly or as part of a community curriculum, "ought to be required in every school as a condition of graduation".[44]

Facing other inequities

Ultimately, the reinvention of fatherhood will demand not only programmes, but also a fundamental realignment of economic and social power between men and women.

"The biggest roadblocks to active participation by fathers in child care still are socio-cultural in terms of how fathers see themselves", says Professor Donna Lero of the University of Guelph in Ontario, and director of the National Child Care Study, which surveyed 22,000 families across Canada.[45]

Jack Levine, of Tallahassee, Florida, is frustrated with his fellow men, and with good reason. Over the past few years, Levine, a former high-school English teacher, has organized one of the most potent political efforts on behalf of children in the United States. As director of the Florida Center for Children & Youth, a private non-profit citizens' organization, he and his fellow activists launched the Florida Children's Campaign, a non-partisan political organizing effort. Among his coups, Jack Levine has not only led a massive voter registration drive of parents, but has arranged for child-care centres to stay open two extra hours on voting days: a practical way of obtaining the usually paltry parent vote. But Jack Levine does not overlook the fact that he is a rare creature in the world of child advocacy: a man. He says:

"It's still the odd guy who fully shares responsibility in the home, and outside the home it's the same proportion. Last night, I spoke at a PTA meeting about the politics of childhood. We had a fantastic turnout. Every seat was filled. We had about 150 people. Of those, 35 kids and nine were guys. The rest were women."

Not only do men not show up for the meetings, they also do not join the advocacy groups (Jack Levine estimates that of his group's membership of 2,000 Floridians, 75 per cent are women). They are much less likely than women to write letters to the editor on behalf of children's issues and they are, according to many polls, less likely than women to vote in support of education or for government programmes for children.

One reason why women act more forcefully than men on children's issues is because they carry a greater burden of child-rearing duties and custody. Jack Levine says:

"In Florida, 87 out of 100 custodies are held by women. One reason is that, in my state, 53 percent over a four year period of marriages end in divorce. (Though if these marriages survive the first five years the rate of success is high.) My point is that if a high proportion of marriages dissolve and upon dissolution, 90 percent of the children go to the mother it's the mom who's going to be carrying the primary responsibility."

As long as women carry the bulk of the responsibility for children, in intact marriages as well as among divorced couples, men will continue to be presumed to be less responsible.

To some extent, fatherlessness is the result of legal processes that, supported by societal attitudes and the recent historical non-nurturant role of men, have tended overwhelming to favour women in custodial decisions. One way of addressing that inequity would be to reform custody laws that discriminate against men, and there is some movement in this direction. But this approach will not be successful without concurrent progress on several other fronts. Marriage must be encouraged; divorce laws must be reformed, and mediation should be widely available. Nowadays, dissolving either a business contract or a business partner is much more difficult in the United States than dissolving a marriage. No other contract may be breached as easily. During the past two decades, reform in American divorce law has not only offered mutually agreed-upon, no-fault divorce, but has also created a right of unilateral divorce. This unilateral feature is prompting calls for reform. The National Council for Children's Rights, an organization of non-custodial parents, argues that courts should provide mediation in divorce proceedings, in an effort to keep both parents as involved as possible in their children's lives after the divorce. Associated with this question is the issue of fathers' post-separation/divorce responsibilities usually being described in terms of material support (e.g., implicitly reinforcing the breadwinner role in addition to presenting real obligations).

Currently, in the United States and other countries, there is a widespread movement towards toughening child-support laws and collection techniques. The approach adopted in the United Kingdom of Great Britain and Northern Ireland, and overhauled in 1993, is emerging as one of the world's toughest. To ensure compliance, the enforcing agency has been given broad powers to track wayward fathers by examining their tax and employment records, and when necessary, to dun them. The agency will also seek the arrest of a parent who does not pay. Such a movement towards the tougher enforcement of child support laws, though sometimes overly harsh, is generally overdue. A broader approach is emerging in the United States, one more appropriate for men who are not affluent. During the mid-1980s, the conventional wisdom among American reformers was that the way to get child support payments out of fathers was by garnishing their wages. However, if the father changes jobs frequently, or cannot find work, or does not want to work, this approach does not work. So several States now require fathers to join job-search programmes: In Grand Rapids, Michigan, such a programme found jobs for 432 of 1,077 men. As a result, child-support payments increased by more than 300 per cent in eight months.[46]

Extensive social and economic rebalancing, a new gender contract, must take place if society is to make the transition successfully into a less gender-weighted view of parenthood. As long as men, women and institutions allow mothers to monopolize parenthood, by choice or by default, men will find it difficult to become more active in nurturance. The feminization of caring limits positive growth for both men and women. Gender inequalities favouring men (e.g., higher wages) dent the opportunities for men to become more active parents. Reducing wage inequalities between men and women would reduce the disincentives to families of working men assuming more caring responsibilities. The actions of abusive, violent men will also continue to affect all men; society must put as much effort into the educational or retraining needs of men as it puts into their incarceration. As in the early days of the feminist movement, men may have to undergo a peer-supported redefinition process that creates enough awareness to sponsor societal change. Reinventing fatherhood requires a redefinition of maleness as well as a reassessment of motherhood.

The advantages

If men and women ever come to see the role of fatherhood differently, and give it more value in the home and in institutions, the results could be impressive. Despite the paucity of studies on fatherhood, considerable evidence exists of the power of nurturing father love. For example:

- Children with involved fathers are more nurturing and generative, according to Dr. Kyle Pruett. He says these children are much more likely than other kids to raise pets: "My guess is these kids will find it easier to nurture their own children." This good outcome may be due to something intrinsic about fatherhood as a male occupation, or it may simply be, as Pruett puts it, because two active parents are better than "one and a lump".[18]
- Fathers who spend more time with their young children appear to have an important influence on how compassionate they will be as adults. A study extending over 26 years, the first study of empathy that tracked young children into adulthood, shows that paternal involvement was the single strongest, parent-related factor in adult empathy. The father's influence "was quite astonishing", says psychologist Richard Koestner, McGill University, Montreal. Fathers who spend time alone with children more than twice a week, giving baths, meals and basic care, reared the most compassionate adults.[47] Among the explanations for the father-empathy link: fathers who spend more time with their children *model* empathy by being there long enough to care for their children's needs, or perhaps fathers who are willing to spend a lot of time with their children are more empathetic themselves. "My hypothesis is that these children do better not because their fathers are more involved, but because their parents as a pair both feel happier with this arrangement", says Michael Lamb. "Father involvement allows both parents to feel that they are achieving and fulfilling themselves."[48]
- Boys with strong, warm, nurturing fathers are more socially competent, more persistent at solving problems and more self-directed, according to Norma Radin, a professor at the School of *Social* Work at the University of Michigan in Ann Arbor, writing in the periodical entitled *Social Work in Education*. Among her findings: boys as young as five months who had more contact with their fathers were friendlier with adult strangers than were those who had less. Two psychologists, John W. Santrock and R. A. Warshak, from Dallas, Texas, report that boys who lived with their fathers after divorce were warmer, had a higher degree of self-esteem and were more mature and independent than boys who lived with their mothers. However, when the father is not present physically or emotionally, boys tend to be more aggressive and less compliant, and they have greater problems in preschool with peer relationships.[49]
- Girls with supportive fathers are more likely to be successful in their careers.

My father loved me unconditionally", says Elisa Sanchez, who directs Trade and Economic Development for Transborder Affairs for San Diego County, California. She recalls that even when her parents divorced, her father was a strong presence in her life. He continued to support her and her sisters, remembered their birthdays, and made a point of seeing and talking with them as much as possible. Says Veronica Collazo, Director of the Office of Training Systems for the United States Postal Service: "My father was a tremendous source of encouragement, always so supportive of my activities, whether they were traditional or non-traditional." Both women, who also had strong mothers, attribute much of their success in their careers to their father's nurturance.[50]

- Fathers are also the primary influence regarding sex roles for sons and daughters. A father who is powerful, nurturing and available is usually seen as a role model by a son; a weak father is less likely to be imitated. A growing body of research shows that boys as young as three years old are searching for masculine models for their sense of self, but, as Samuel Osherson writes, "the urge to identify with father creates the crucial dilemma for boys. Boys have to give up mother for father but, who is father?"[51]

Men growing up without a good gender model grow up with an inflated, hypermasculine view of manhood and are therefore more prone to violence. Ken Canfield's National Center for Fathering investigated the images of fatherhood held by 100 Minnesota prison inmates. They were asked to describe men whom they considered father figures. Less than 12 per cent even put their own father on the list; 52 per cent named sports or entertainment heroes as their father figures. "I work with a number of people who work with juvenile delinquent kids. I've never had a single case worker who has ever had a kid report a healthy relationship with their dad. Not one out of hundreds", says Paul Lewis. He and other researchers are also convinced that the father's role is as important, and possibly more important, than the mother's in giving the son or the daughter confidence in sexual identity. "I'm convinced by the available research, and after working with thousands of families, that when fathers withdraw from their adolescent daughters, because of discomfort with their daughter's sexuality, that this sets the stage for the daughter's sexual experimentation or promiscuity; the daughters are looking for the closeness that has been withdrawn by their fathers." A daughter looks to her father to confirm her attractiveness; when that is withheld, she looks elsewhere, often with a sense of desperation.

Walking tall: a new paradigm

Considering the continued poor conditions of women in much of the world, and the rise of fatherlessness, it is difficult to see how a new fatherhood could be spreading. Indeed, the new fatherhood may be no closer than when it has been announced in times past. Robert Griswold of the University of Oklahoma, and author of *Fatherhood in America: A History*, looks at "the invention of the new fatherhood". Articles in popular magazines "from the '20s, '30s, '40s, and '50s don't look very different from what we're seeing today. Stories about fathers not spending enough time with their children or how-to articles teaching dads how to interact with their kids have been around for decades. It's amazing how similar they are to what's appearing now". Griswold is skeptical, but he does not rule out a paradigm shift.[17] Yet evidence for something close to a paradigm shift does exist.

Thirty years ago it was rare to see men changing babies' nappies or dropping children off at the day-care centre or school. Nowadays it is far more common, and nearly everyone knows some man who has chosen to or had to stay at home to look after young children. Active fathering, however, is still far from being the norm.[52]

Is a new fatherhood finally here? Or is society simply returning to an older, much earlier model? Is shared breadwinning and shared parenting in humanity's bones?

In October 1994, anthropologists announced the discovery in Ethiopia of *Australopithecus ramidus*, the so-called missing link, a diminutive creature positioned between humans and apes. While scientists have not yet determined whether this oldest known direct human ancestor walked upright, two bones suggests it did. This discovery could overturn the conventional wisdom that humankind's ancestors learned to walk upright only after they had left the forests for the savannahs. *Ramidus*, who lived in a forest filled with carnivores, had little to gain by standing upright, except one thing. Females may have sought mates who could help care for offspring, the ones who walked upright, using their hands to carry foods and infants, according to anatomist Owen Lovejoy of Kent State University. "If further finds confirm that our oldest direct ancestor learned to walk in the primeval forest", *Newsweek reports*, "it will push to center stage a very '90s notion: the crucial spur toward becoming human was changing from a tooth-baring aggressive ape to one that carried home dinner and helped raise the kids."[53]

Indeed, for much of humankind's history, men and women hunted or gathered, or tended the fields together, with their children nearby. "Tribal families are usually built on a social rather than biological basis".

According to an occasional paper published by the IYF secretariat of the United Nations Secretariat, "The biological mother's sisters may be called mothers, and the biological father's brothers, or in some cases even the mother's brothers, may also be responsible for fathering the child ... This type of family rarely leaves orphaned children, because there is an abundance of parents."[54] In tribal families, the sexes are not exactly equal, but they are complementary. In her book *Families: Celebration and hope in a world of change*, Jo Boyden writes that among the Mbuti men of northeast Zaire, a man has minimal contact with his child until it is two years' old. But then the mother brings the child to him and holds it to his breast. The baby tries to suck, often crying *ema!* (mother!), and then the father gives his child its first solid food, teaching it to say *eba* (father). The anthropologist Colin Turnbull says that Mbuti men are first perceived by their children as "another kind of mother - one who cannot give milk but does provide other kinds of food".[6] In colonial America, men were expected to fulfil well-defined, important domestic roles in the lives of their children. Fathers were responsible not only for their children's moral and spiritual upbringing but also for their children's education beyond the home. They introduced their children (the emphasis was, unfortunately, too much on boys) into the world of work and adults. Children often worked and played in close proximity to their working fathers, on farms or in shops. Such intimacy was swept away by the Industrial Revolution. Men trudged off to the factories and the mines far from home. By the end of the nineteenth century, men were stereotyped as wage-earners and women as housewives, separate and unequal.

The industrial age family may have been something of a historical anomaly. Society is now in the middle of a painful transition to post-industrial parenting; painful most of all for children whose parents are caught between two eras. But change is coming. Fax machines, computers, modems and other technological advances make it easier for mothers and fathers to work part- time or full-time from home, rediscovering some of the attributes of the family farm and village. The transformation may seem glacial, but seen in the light of history or evolution, it is an overnight event. Maybe modern man is remembering why he stood up in the first place.

REFERENCES

1. David Blankenhorn, "The vanishing father", *Atlanta Journal-Atlanta Constitution*, 4 November 1990, p. G-1.
2. Richard Louv, *Fatherlove: What We Need; What We Seek; What We Must Create* (New York, Pocket Books, 1993).
3. Jo Boyden, *Families: Celebration and Hope in a World of Change.* (London, Gaia Books, 1993), p. 68.
4. Ibid., p. 70.
5. Ibid., p. 72.
6. Ibid., p. 74.
7. Louv, op. cit., p. 35.
8. "The revolution in family life", *The Futurist*, September/October 1990, pp. 53-54.
9. Myron Magnet, "The American family, 1992", *Fortune*, 10 August 1992, p. 43; Paul Taylor, "Two faces of fatherhood: Dads become more domesticated, more distant", *Washington Post*, 16 June 1991, p. A-1.
10. Remarks made by Dr. Louis W. Sullivan at the Institute for American Values Council on families in America, New York City, 9 January 1992.
11. Nina J. Easton, "Life without father", *Los Angeles Times Magazine*, 14 June 1992, p. 15.
12. Charles Donovan, "Why children need both their parents", *San Diego Union Tribune*, 2 August 1992, p. C-4.
13. Taylor, loc. cit.
14. Magnet, loc. cit., p. 44.
15. John Leo, "A pox on Dan and Murphy", *U.S. News & World Report*, 1 June 1992, p. 19.
16. Judy Mann, "Murphy, where's my Pa?", *Washington Post*, 15 May 1992, p. E-3.
17. Dr. Robert Glossop and Ish Theilheimer, "Does society support involved fathering?", *Transition*, March 1994, p. 11.
18. Lisa Schroepfer, "Dad: new & improved", *American Health*, June 1991, p. 64.
19. Sue Shellenbarger, "Work & family", *Wall Street Journal*, 27 May 1992, p. B-1.
20. Glossop and Theilheimer, loc. cit., p. 9.
21. Aaron Latham, "Fathering the nest", M., May 1992, pp. 66-75.
22. Richard Louv, "Data lacking on success of work-family programs", *San Diego Union Tribune*, 14 August 1994.
23. Linda Haas, "Equal parenthood and social policy: Lessons from a study in Sweden", in Parental Leave and Child Care: Setting Research and Policy Agenda, J. S. Hyde and M. J. Essex, eds. (Philadelphia, Pennsylvania, Temple University Press, 1991), pp. 325-405.
24. Janet Shibley Hyde, Marilyn J. Essex and Francine Horton, "Fathers and parental leave: attitudes and experiences", *Journal of Family Issues*, vol. 14, No. 4 (1993), pp. 617-618.
25. "Couple makes a case for sharing load", *San Diego Union Tribune*, 23 October 1993.
26. Louv, op. cit., p. 103.
27. Randall Beach, "Househusbands", *Utne Reader*, March/April 1990, pp. 79-82.
28. Richard Louv, "Absent fathers: remaking fatherhood", *Parents*, December 1994, pp. 180-182.
29. Louv, op. cit., p. 88.
30. Boyden, op. cit., p. 69-70.
31. Arlie Hochschild, "The second shift: Employed women are putting in another day of work at home", *Utne Reader*, March/April 1990, pp. 66-73.
32. John P. Robinson, "The hard facts about hard work", *Utne Reader*, March/April 1990, p. 70.
33. Richard Louv, "How fathers feel ...", *Parents*, December 1993, p. 228.
34. Ibid., p. 232.
35. Louv, op. cit., p. 254.

[36] Ibid., p. 108.
[37] "The new father: part reality, part media hype, says psychologist", *Stanford News Release*, 22 February 1989.
[38] Hank Whittemore, "Security dads", *Parade*, 27 September 1992, pp. 20-22.
[39] Richard Louv, "Let's send men back to school - to help", *San Diego Union Tribune*, 8 January 1994.
[40] Louv, op. cit., p. 153.
[41] Sophfronia Scott Gregory, "Teaching young fathers the ropes", *Time*, 10 August 1992, p. 49.
[42] Boyden, op. cit., p. 76.
[43] Louv, op. cit., p. 221.
[44] Richard Louv, "Gores want more respect for fathering", *San Diego Union Tribune*, 16 July 1994.
[45] Glossop and Theilheimer, Loc. cit., p. 8.
[46] Steven Waldman, "Seeking new solutions", *Newsweek*, 4 May 1992, p. 49.
[47] Marilyn Elias, "Dad's role crucial to careing kids", *USA today*, 30 May 1990.
[48] "The new father: part reality, part media hype, says psychologist", *Stanford News* Release, 22 February 1989.
[49] Paul Ciotti, "How fathers figure", *Los Angeles Times Magazine*, 18 June 1989, p. 10.
[50] Elvira Valenzuela Crocker, "Today, a fitting recipe for fathers of Latina daughters", *San Diego Union Tribune*, 21 June 1992, p. C-8.
[51] Samuel Osherson, "Finding our fathers", *Utne Reader*, April/May 1986, pp. 36-42.
[52] Glossop and Theilheimer, pp. 8-9.
[53] Sharon Begley, "Out of Africa, a missing link", *Newsweek*, 3 October 1994, pp. 40-41.
[54] United Nations, "Family: forms and functions", *Occasional Papers Series*, No.2, 1992.

FAMILY
Gender and Economy in the Developing world

Introduction[*]

An upsurge of interest in the family has taken place among the major development agencies during the 1990s. For the United Nations, 1994 was the International Year of the Family (IYF). The present chapter is a contribution of the International Research and Training Institute for the Advancement of Women to IYF, linking the themes of family, gender and economic development. In addition, the United States Agency for International Development (USAID) launched its own family and development initiative in December 1990, to "strengthen and increase the participation of families in the development process".[**]

The present paper applauds these emphases on the family as a vehicle for development, but it makes a case for the importance of viewing the family as a flexible institution rather than a monolithic black box.[**] It is time to break open that box and examine its contents.

Myth of the monolithic family versus the reality of the flexible family

Both principal paradigms of development - the mainstream, modernization model and the left-of-centre dependency/world systems/neo-Marxist approach - share the same view of the household and family[***] as a monolithic black box, indeed, as the basic unit of analysis. From this perspective, it does not matter who does the work, who receives the information (e.g. on agricultural extension), or who earns the income, because the co-resident family/household is a unit that pools resources. In fact, most mainstream development efforts follow Becker in describing this unit by a single production function[9].

---

[*] The present paper has been prepared for the IYF secretariat with the cooperation of the International Research and Training Institute for the Advancement of Women. It was written by Rae Lesser Blumberg, with the assistance of Kathryne Pethan, University of California, San Diego, United States of America.

[*] The initiative's purpose is "to use the family ... as a starting point for analysis of what people need, how they use the resources they have, and as an organizing principle for mobilizing the energy of people to create progress" ([80 and 136] summarize the major thrusts of the initiative).

[**] Three caveats are noteworthy: in the present paper, the terms "monolithic" and "black box" family/household are used interchangeably or in combination as "monolithic black box". This monolithic black-box model implicitly assumes both a male household head and economic isolation from extended kin whereas the flexible family model proposed in the present paper subsumes both the external economy of the household (section III) and female-headed families (section IV).

[***] Despite decades of anthropological and sociological writings on the sometimes subtle differences between household and family (Jaquette[80] gives a recent summary), the development literature has generally conflated the two. Accordingly, although the present paper emphasizes family units, defined in terms of kinship as well as residence, it treats co-residential households and families interchangeably (unless the blood tie vs. dwelling-unit distinction is the focus of a particular discussion).

Since the mid-1980s, however, a growing group of gender or women-in-development (WID) researchers have proposed an alternative view to this black-box family or household. Their approach focuses on the internal economy of the household, differentiated along axes of gender and age, and characterized by relations of competition as well as cooperation[20, 24, 35, 60 and 67].

The internal economy perspective maintains that it does matter how development-assistance-linked information and economic and welfare resources are distributed to male and female and to senior and junior family members. Moreover, this view insists that the targeting of development aid to the family needs to be sensitive as to how income - as well as time, labour and calories - are divided among family members.

In the present chapter, selected hypotheses are reviewed from Blumberg's theories of gender stratification[20 and 22] and gender and development[19, 20, 24 and 39], which illuminate the triple intersection of family, gender and economy. The hypotheses are used to focus the discussion on why it is important to take the perspective of gender and the internal economy of the family into account. Then, the propositions are linked to concrete outcomes that affect the wealth and well-being of both families and developing countries. Dealing with families in planned development efforts is important, but the basic model of the family or household must change from the monolithic black box to the flexible family.

This flexible-family model assumes that male-headed families are arrayed on a continuum based on the nature of their internal economies. The continuum ranges from the (empirically rare) single-production-function unit with no internal differentiation at one end to the "separate-purses" family at the other. At the separate-purse end, income streams and expenditures tend to be distinct for men and women - his, hers and (a little) theirs - and individualistic, bargaining strategies pre-dominate[100, 101].

Four points concerning the flexible-family model should be previewed here. First, empirically, the separate-purse end of the continuum is most prevalent in sub-Saharan Africa. Second, for reasons linked to poverty, the majority of the world's families tend to be closer to the separate-purse end than the single-production-function or monolithic-black-box end of the continuum. Third, the significant boundary of the family may not coincide with the walls of its residence: the external economy of the family and larger kinship patterns must also be looked at. Fourth, the flexible-family model incorporates not only husband-wife units, but also the growing legions of female-headed households as well.

A proposed continuum of the internal economy of the family

Families around the world may generate income, intimacy and children but handle them in many different ways. Nevertheless, Blumberg posits that it is relative control of income by women versus men that has the biggest impact on both gender stratification and family welfare[20, 22 and 39]. Some propositions concerning the internal economy of the family[20] are given as follows:

A   It is proposed that worldwide, there is a continuum of the extent families or households are unitary, common-pot entities as opposed to having at least partially separate purses for male and female, senior and junior, members;

  I   Gender and age can vary independently within the internal economy of the family. Husbands, wives and different children (e.g. eldest vs. younger sons; boys vs. girls) may be favoured or penalized to differing degrees[20, 133]. Here the focus is more on gender - men versus women - than age, especially children versus adults;

  II There is a worldwide continuum of the extent wives (legal or consensual) get to keep or control the resources or income they have generated. Although it ranges from controlling all earnings to controlling none, empirically, few wives surrender control of all - or even most - of their income[34, 90];

  III There is also a worldwide continuum of the extent women have provider obligations towards their children (and extended kin). Overall, however, as men migrate, families fracture and economic crisis exacerbates poverty for many, women's provider obligations are rising. The percentage of women earning income also is rising[25, 125], but women's provider obligations may be rising faster than their earnings;

B   The internal economy of the family varies greatly by geographic region, class and ethnicity;

C   Geographically, the internal economy is strongest in much of sub-Saharan Africa. Often (especially where polygyny remains common and marriages are unstable), husbands and wives maintain separate purses for most income streams and expenditures[66, 67, 72, 73 and 128]. Frequently, African women have strong obligations as providers, especially towards their own children. Most women are economically active, predominantly in low-resource farming and market trade, although this often is not recorded in national accounts data on the measured labour force[6, 16, 58, 59 and 145]. Nevertheless, according to recent studies, African women grow up to 80 per cent of locally produced food[116];*

D Worldwide, the central tendency of this posited internal economy of the family continuum is closer to the separate-purse end than to the common-pot or single-production-function end;

E The main reason** that most families are closer to the separate-purse end is social class: the majority of the world is poor and the relationship between social class and women's economic contributions is usually inverse:

   I   The lower the social class, the higher the proportion of women who are economically active;
   II The lower the social class, the higher the proportion of household subsistence that women contribute;
   III The lower the social class, the higher the proportion of female-headed households[28, 30 and 47];

F The main exception to (E) above, the inverse relation between social class and women's economic contributions, is by ethnicity. Highlands Ecuadorian Indians, for example, are much more gender egalitarian than neighbouring mestizos. Women in better-off versus worse-off Indian families are equally likely to generate much of the household food and income, and female-headed households are equally rare among richer and poorer families[5, 31, 36 and 109]. Among mestizos, the propositions of (E) (I), (II) and (III) above prevail and the ideal woman is economically inactive.

These propositions and the proposed continuum model of the internal economy of the family focus attention on the home as an arena of competition and conflict, as well as cooperation. Despite considerable regional and cultural variations, most families or households in developing coun-

---

* In male-headed households, where women have few or no opportunities to earn own-account income, the internal economy may be reduced to the single-production-function model with respect to a family's adult men and women. This is not too common worldwide, and decreasingly prevalent. For example, such a situation exists in rural areas of Yemen, where half the young men typically work in the Persian Gulf, sending remittances home to the senior male of their families, while the women act as unpaid family labour in agriculture[49, 79]. It also occurs in a number of remote colonization projects in tropical lowlands, mainly in South America[31, 119]. It more frequently occurs among South Asian and Middle Eastern groups where women producers in a family enterprise are treated strictly as labour and all income is channel-led only to men (e.g. among the Indian lacemakers studied by Mies[97]). But even in the Arab world, micro-level studies show much higher rates of women's income generation than are recorded in national accounts. For example, Nassif[102,131] found that some 40 per cent of the women in a Tunisian village earned income, though only 13.2 per cent of rural women were officially counted as being economically active.

** See, for example, Mencher on India[96], Roldan on Mexico[111], Blumberg[23], Blumberg and Okoro[26], Matlon[95] and Norman, Simmons and Hays[104] on Nigeria; and Deere[55] on Peru.

tries are not monolithic entities in which all members subordinate their individual advantage and pool their resources to assure a family survival strategy masterminded by the (male) household head. The extent to which anything is shared varies widely. A few dimensions* (other than income) that may or may not be equally shared, but which are important to family wealth and well-being, include labour, information and food.

Labour power. Time-budget studies invariably find that women work longer total hours (because of the double day of productive and reproductive tasks), although the amount varies greatly (see, e.g. Carr and Sandhu[51]).

Information. Numerous studies find that technical advice given to the husband about farming tasks carried out by the wife is often not shared with, or incorrectly transmitted to, her. These include cases of Cameroon[86], Ecuador[13], Thailand[11] and the United Republic of Tanzania[70].

In the Thai case, because men who were not full-time farmers were trained for operations done by their wives, "crops were planted incorrectly and did not grow, the power tillers provided by the project could not be used, and a nitrogen-fixing crop intended to fertilize rice did not get planted. Even when the husband was present, advice on crop production was incorrectly transmitted from husband to wife" (Carloni[50]).

Food. Even calories have been found to be unequally distributed by gender and age within families (i.e., not in proportion to individual size and energy requirements). Sometimes, this merely results in the malnutrition of disadvantaged members, as in Senauer's studies in the Philippines[124]. In the extreme case, where females are devalued and income prospects for adult women are grim, the death rates of girl infants are higher[113,121]; lower access to calories and health care contributes to this outcome.

Indeed, in the case of Bangladesh, China, India, Pakistan and west Asia, Sen[122] argues that some "100 million women are missing"; i.e., there are fewer than the 102 to 106 women per 100 men that characterize regions such as Africa or Europe. Yet even in these female-deficit countries, there is internal variance. In Kerala State, India, for example, he notes, surviving traditions of matrilineal descent and inheritance buttress a contemporary situation where large proportions of working women are in jobs that command respect, and literacy is high for both sexes; demographically, there is no female deficit either. There are 104 women for

---

* Other dimensions not treated here unequaly distributed by gender and technology (boserup 40:men has greater access) and, even more fundamentally, property (women usually have less but not always; see Blumberg 14 and 22, and Blanc-Szanton, Viveros- Long and Suphanchainat 11.

every 100 men, compared with an all-India rate of only 93 women per 100 men, and a deficit of 37 million women[123]. Analogously, Rosenzweig and Schultz[113] found a lower female infant mortality rate in areas of India where adult women had higher earnings.

In short, the internal economy of the family can extend literally to matters of life and death. These studies on female survival show that where adult women are income producers, their daughters are not sacrificed. Even when the stakes are lower than life itself, the extent women generate and control income affects family welfare. This is because of the different ways men and women spend the income they control.

Income under female versus male control

A few relevant propositions from Blumberg's theories of gender stratification and gender and development about the gendered control of income and its consequences are given below. Male/female control of income is proposed as the most important dimension of the internal economy of the family in determining the distribution of family power and well-being.

In fact, the main hypotheses of Blumberg's stratification theory are:

A Women's economic power relative to men (defined as control of key economic resources such as income, property and other means of production) is posited as the most important and achievable* (though certainly not the sole) independent variable affecting gender stratification at a variety of nested micro and macro levels ranging from the couple to the State[22];

B Unless she is a household head, a woman may not, however, get a dollar's worth of economic power for every dollar she brings into the family because of what are termed discount factors[20, 22, 33 and 39]. Discount factors may operate at both the macro level (e.g., the State) and the micro level of family and community, and subtract or

---

* Empirically, of the four major sources of power discussed by Lenski[92] - economic, political-hierarchical, force and (slightly less importantly) ideological - women have fared best with respect to economic power. There are many societies where women have an equal or larger share of economic power at the micro level of the family and sometimes the community. These include a number of hunting-gathering and horticultural peoples and a few more complex societies, ranging from ancient Crete[62] to contemporary north-east Thailand[11, 14 and 106]. Actually, women's share of relative economic power varies from near-zero (as among the Azande of Sudan) to near-total (as among the Iroquois of colonial North America; see Brown[42], where women controlled virtually the entire economy). But in no other type of power do women get beyond the 50-50 mark: there are a few societies that proclaim an ideology of gender equality but none that hold women superior; nor is any society known in which women have even an equal share of political power. Moreover, women fare worst with the power of force, where men's one-third to one-half greater upper body strength and disproportionate control of weapons give them almost universal sway over women.

add pennies to that hypothetical dollar, depending on whether they are negative or positive;

I   At the macro level, the greater the level of gender inequality (i.e. the more the political, economic, legal, religious and ideological systems are a disadvantage to women), the greater the negative discount rate, and the less leverage a woman gets from each dollar;

II At the micro level, discount rates may be negative or positive:

A   These include the gender ideology of each partner, as well as the prevailing gender ideologies of their class and ethnic group at the community level. If the ideology says that a woman should be an economic dependant, it will nibble away many cents of the potential leverage she gets from each dollar, since she never should have earned it in the first place;

B   They also include the relative commitment of each partner (the less committed one has more leverage by the principle of least interest), the relative attractiveness of each partner, the extent of their perceived need for the other's income, and even their relative assertiveness;*

C   Additionally, one gets more power out of controlling and allocating surplus than bare subsistence. Blatantly denying food to hungry children is rarely an option within the family, and may be why poor women do not get more leverage from the often high proportion of resources they provide. But for both genders, the more surplus controlled, the greater the economic power;

D   Adjusting a woman's overall economic power by these macro- and micro-level discount factors and the surplus versus subsistence income distinction shows her net economic power, posited as the best predictor of a variety of consequences:

I   The greater a woman's net control of income, the greater her increase in self-esteem and self-confidence[20, 25, 34, 90 and 110];

II The greater a woman's net control of income, the greater her leverage in fertility decisions, i.e. the more these reflect her own utilities versus those of her husband, the extended family and the State[24, 25, 34, 39 and 110];

III The greater a woman's net control of income, the greater her leverage in both family economic and welfare decisions. This means the greater her voice and vote in such economic decisions as buying or selling land, animals or other property. It also means

---

* Most females are not socialized to bargain hard to realize economic leverage in intimate relationships[52 and 63].

more say in domestic welfare decisions, such as which children are sent to school for how long; the appropriate level of health-care spending for each member and illness, as well as other expenditures on items of well-being ranging from shelter to shoes. It also means the greater her voice and vote (power) in the marital relationship (see references in Blumberg[20, 24, 25] and Blumberg et al[148]).

E Mere work in economic activities (or even ownership of economic resources) does not translate into economic leverage in the family if the person derives no control of economic resources from that work[2, 3, 4, 20 and 24];

F Women who lose income lose domestic power more quickly and sharply than they gain it when income rises[20, 34 and 39];

G Men tend to spend income under their control differently from women who have provider responsibilities (even as providers of the last resort), with women focusing more on children's well-being and family subsistence. Specifically:

  I   It is the mother's, rather than the father's, income or food production that tends to be more closely related to children's nutrition (see Blumbern[20, 24 and 25] for a review of the literature);

  II Women tend to contribute a higher proportion of their income to family subsistence, holding back less for personal consumptio[20, 24, 25 and 96];

H Women tend to allocate labour towards activities that put income (and/or food if they have provider obligations) under their control and, to the extent culturally feasible, away from activities that do not - even if these are somewhat more profitable for the husband[20, 24, 25, 39 and 87].

Presenting data on all these propositions is beyond the space limitations of the present chapter, so only those most relevant to the intersection of family, gender and economy are discussed. These are the hypotheses that link a woman's income control to her say in fertility and family welfare decisions, and her spending patterns to family well-being.

When wives control and spend income: selected consequences

The greater a woman's net control of income, the greater her leverage in fertility decisions (hypothesis (D) (II) above).

It can be argued that for a woman, controlling her own fertility in accordance with her own wishes is the most basic dependent variable that flows from her increased economic power.* A woman's life chances are enormously different if she starts having children every two-plus years from her mid-teens on, versus, for example, starting her fertility career several years into her twenties, and having fewer, more widely spaced offspring.

Perhaps this is why two Latin American studies, a generation apart, found that initiating contraception is an early priority of women who begin earning significant income. Weller's study[146] in Puerto Rico found that when women entered the labour market, their household decision-making power rose, and beginning to use contraception was one of the first ways they exercised their greater control. In summer 1993, the author of the present chapter studied the impact of potable water systems in 14 com-munities in rural Ecuador[27]. In two of these com-munities, following a focus group interview on the impact of the water, she was besieged by women who wanted help to put them in touch with some organization through which they could gain access to contraception. As it turned out, these were precisely the two villages where the women had reaped the greatest economic profit from recently installed water systems.

The first community, Bella Vista, is a poor, heavily eroded Quichua Indian community with a spectacular view of the 21,500 foot-high Mount Chimborazo. There, the water made it possible for the women to buy garlic, wash and peel it, and sell it at a value-added price. Cachiguzo, the second, is a mixed mestizo community in the southern Andes where 68 women and one man (the sales manager) formed a sweater production group. The women used the water to wash and dye the wool, using imported colour-fast tints. They knitted and sold a minimum of 100 sweaters a week, earning a substantial income.

In three of the other 14 villages in the sample, women had managed to use the water to increase their incomes slightly; in the rest, the water had not yet made an economic impact. In all 14 villages, the same (single) question about fertility was asked: how many children each focus group member had. But only in the two villages where women had most increased their income from the water was the author queried - urgently - about how to get access to family planning.

Two more examples also come from Latin America.

In Mexico City, Roldan[110, 111] studied 140 poor women who did garment or other industry piecework in their homes; 53 households were fol-

---

* Although in most parts of the world, women with increased leverage opt for lower fertility, there are exceptions. The most notable is sub-Saharan Africa, where women tend to want - and seemingly need - many children to help them. Especially in the rural areas, increased environmental degradation, male migration, and children's school attendance all have increased women farmers' labour burdens. Children fetch water, and increasingly scarce fuelwood and fodder, help in cultivation, tend babies and animals, and, as adults, help with crisis and old-age support. Under these circumstances, women may prefer more children than their husbands[23] and have enough autonomous control of income to realize their own preferences.

lowed up intensively. In 33 poor households where both husbands and wives contributed to a common pool, there was a clear relationship between the proportion contributed by the woman and her say in fertility decisions. For example, the decision to have more children was one made by the woman alone in 50 per cent of the cases where wives contributed 40 per cent or more of the total income; in contrast, it was the woman's sole decision among only 20 per cent of the cases where wives provided less than 40 per cent of the income, and where husbands were the main providers.

In Guatemala, in 1985, Blumberg followed up a 1980 study by Kusterer et al.[90] of the impact of an agribusiness enterprise on the lives of three villages of poor, largely Indian contract growers and the Ladina (mestiza) women who worked in its processing plant[34 and 35]. The villagers grew broccoli, cauliflower and snowpeas for the wholly owned subsidiary of a transnational corporation based in the United States of America, and the women processing-plant workers froze and packed the vegetables for export to the United States. The company paid these women the minimum wage. During the eight-to-nine-month high season, shifts of 12-16 hours a day, six days a week, were not uncommon. The result was a wage level as high as that of an urban, male blue-collar worker: enough to transform the women's lives. The women kept control of their earnings, and by 1985, the fertility impact was unmistakable.

Among 15 of the 1980 veterans in the 1985 sample (median age of 32.5 years), only 13 babies had been born between 1980 and 1985. These women averaged only 2.2 children each and had taken control of their fertility: seven said that they would not have any more babies (at median age of 37 years, mean rate of 2.3 children). In contrast, in 1985, 20 women from the only contract-grower village with a substantial Ladina population (Patzicia) averaged 5.2 children at a median age of 33.5 years. Even though about half these women helped their husbands in the fields, the company's cheque was made out solely to the husband. When asked about further fertility, the Patzicia wife's frequent response was: "Well, I don't want any more but my husband does, so I'll have to continue."

A final example comes from Thailand. In the north-east, women have an exceptional degree of economic power, based on the traditional control of all money entering the household, regardless of who earned it, and a kinship system that gives them strong structural leverage. Kinship involves matrilineal descent and matrilocal residence; that is, kinship is reckoned through the female line and the young couple goes to live near the bride's female kin. Until the present generation, the inheritance of rice land also was matrilineal, from mother to daughters; now, in the wake of deforestation, drought and population pressure, sons as well as daughters are beginning to inherit a share of the land[11, 14 and 106]. Since the youngest daughter continues to inherit the house and the household spirits stay with the house, women also have some "spiritual power".

What many consider to be the world's most effective family-planning programme has brought fertility down to two to three children per woman in a single generation[132]. It is suggested, however that, in addition to the aggressive family-planning effort, two other factors seemed to have played a role in the drop in fertility. The first is a visible need for reducing fertility (the deforestation of much of the north-east during the Viet Nam war resulted in intensified drought, and other negative environmental consequences increased pressures on a land already over-crowded). The second and, it is proposed, key factor is that women have the (economically based) power to control their bodies. In research conducted in 1993 in four north-east Thai villages, both men and women farmers told the author of the present chapter that the couple discusses family planning but the wife has the final say. In addition, more women are opting for sterilization after two children, even if those children are two girls[14].

In northern Thailand, which is richer and wetter than the north-east, kinship is also matri-lineal and matrilocal. However, there is more socio-economic stratification, more influence from the more patriarchal Chinese, and, in addition, men outearn women and have more power in family decision-making. In one lowland village, the author was told that the final decision on family planning was joint, not the woman's[14].

The research also involved four villages of the Karen ethnic group, one of the six main hill tribes of northern Thailand. Traditionally, all villages practise slash-and-burn horticulture on the steep, forested slopes; formerly they cultivated opium poppies to varying degrees. The Karen are matrilineal and matrilocal, but men outearn women. Even so, according to Care International workers, Karen women have more power and much higher rates of contraception than the neighbouring Hmong women. The Hmong are patrilineal and patrilocal and women are highly subjugated. In the Hmong village in question, men have already cut down their remaining forest and currently earn considerable income from intensive vegetable farming.* These men want many children to help them farm, and therefore veto family planning.

The greater a woman's net control of income, the greater her leverage in family domestic welfare decisions, including those promoting children's education (hypothesis (D) (III) above).

Specifically, it is hypothesized, income-controlling women will not only promote education, but will also tend to be more even-handed about educating girls as well as boys.**

In a recent study, Blumberg et al.[148] tested this hypothesis with random sample data from a household survey undertaken in Santiago, Chile. The actual hypothesis proposed that where women have purse power, either by outearning their husbands or heading their households, favouritism towards boys in secondary education is eliminated. The hypothesis received empirical support: although in male-headed households, boys were significantly more likely to receive secondary education, this was not the case if the woman earned more than her spouse, or was a household head.

Women who lose income lose domestic power more quickly and sharply than they gain it when income rises (hypothesis (F) above).

Two examples of this rapid decline in female power with loss of income emerged in the study of the Guatemalan ALCOSA agribusiness project[34, 35, 38 and 39]. First, in the village of Patzicia, one interviewee was a woman who had moved there recently when her husband inherited a plot of land from his father shortly after losing his job in Guatemala City as a surveyor. In the city, she had always worked and marital decisions were joint. They decided to raise broccoli on contract for ALCOSA, the agribusiness firm. Since ALCOSA pays by cheque made out to the husband alone and she has no independent source of income, she is now completely dependent. The joint decision to take the contract was the last in which she had a say. Now she works harder than ever but he makes the decisions such as how much to spend on food, clothes and school expenses, and even whether she should have more children.

Second, in the Mayan Indian village of Santiago Sacatepequez, there was a thriving cooperative, and it had negotiated a master contract with ALCOSA for raising broccoli and cauliflower. In research conducted in 1980[90], women worked three days a week farming contract and other crops; the husband or wife could deliver the ALCOSA crops and collect cash from the cooperative. Women also earned income from selling in the market in Guatemala City three days a week. But in 1984, the cooperative switched to paying by cheque to the legal member, who was always the

---

* According to Care International workers, these vegetable farming techniques will probably lead to considerable land erosion if continued, but for the present they make money.

** Where the returns on girls' education are drastically lower than those of boys, and/or where women's livelihoods depend on their daughters' help, they may not push for their education. An example of this can be found among Muslim Hausa women in northern Nigeria who live in strict seclusion, but who run various microenterprises from inside their compounds. They rely on their non-secluded pre-adolescent daughters to hawk their wares and have resisted sending their girls to school[23 and 117].

husband if he was alive, even though the women were by then working up to four days on the contract crops (and had less time to sell in the market). Their power fell sharply. In 1985, a purposive sample of 17 women complained that they had less voice in all decisions, from how much to plant of which crops to buying food. The cooperative social staff noticed the decline in women's autonomy and leverage. They noted that even though many husbands were earning enough to buy vehicles and land, there was no corresponding rise in spending on children's welfare, including nutrition. Women's income and status were so diminished that a number were unable to attend home economics meetings arranged by the cooperative social staff: their husbands wouldn't let them.*

In contrast, the trajectory is not as smooth or fast when women's economic power increases. Women may feel greater self-confidence but take a slow and cautious route to asserting themselves more. One reason may be to avoid battering. When a woman's relative income rises, especially if this happens while her husband's income falls, there is a possibility of increased domestic violence. The more he feels threatened by her relatively enhanced economic position, the more likely he is to retaliate with the male trump card: physical force (see Roldan[110, 111] on outworkers in Mexico City). But as the author of the present chapter found in a study of 61 pre-industrial societies, once women's greater economic power is consolidated, they are less subject to male violence[29, 33].

It is the mother's, rather than the father's, income or food production that tends to be more closely related to children's nutrition (hypothesis (G) (I) above).

Kumar's 1978 study[89] undertaken in Kerala, India, found that mothers with resources under their control, kitchen gardens and/or income, had better-nourished children. The study involved a random sample of 48 landless or near-landless families (72 per cent owned under one tenth of an acre). No increase in child nutrition was found as paternal income rose, although child nutrition was enhanced by increasing maternal income. This research was the first to document empirically the stronger relation of child nutrition to women's income than to men's.

Since then, Kumar's results have been replicated around the world. Another early study by Stavrakis and Marshall[129] on the effect of the introduction of commercial sugar cane in a Belize village was less quantitative and used a purposive, not a random, sample. Yet it, too, found that increas-

---

* Other studies also have found that women with little or no income have less freedom to participate in project activities (e.g. Blumberg[18]); conversely, with increased income, they may become more involved in project and/or community activities[13].

ing the income under male control (in this case, from sugar) did not translate to better nutrition for children. While the consumption of fruit, meat and fish declined, "consumption of soft drinks and frozen koolaid increased by 255 per cent"[129, p. 161].

Senauer's research in the Philippines[124] also found that the father's (increasing) wage had a negative impact on his children's nutritional status in the long run, whereas the mother's income had a positive effect. Kennedy and Cogill's[85] work in south-western Kenya found a similar improvement in children's nutrition from income controlled by the mother. Tripp's research[134] in a drought-prone and poor area of northern Ghana discovered that of all the variables examined, it was the mother's trading income (which she completely controlled) that had the most significant association with the child's nutritional status.*

Additionally, Johnson and Rogers[81] found the same pattern for a national sample of families in the Dominican Republic; the effect proved most pronounced in the lowest income quartile.

The most spectacular findings on the differential impact of female-controlled versus male-controlled income within the household on child nutrition come from Engle's study[64, 65] of a random sample of 294 children and their families from two Guatemalan industrial towns. There, the higher the percentage of total family income that the mother earned, the better the child's nutrition; whereas, for fathers, the proportion of income contributed proved the best predictor. Bruce and Lloyd[44] recast Engle's regressions in more dramatic terms, noting that the attainment of an additional half a standard deviation of height for a child (a standard measure of child nutrition) would require $11.40 a month if earned by the mother and $166.00 a month if earned by the father.** Engle's study highlights the difference between earnings and contributions, which reflects another relevant hypothesis.

Women tend to contribute a higher proportion of their income to family subsistence, holding back less for personal consumption (hypothesis (G) (II) above).

Clear-cut evidence of this hypothesis is available from Roldan's study of home workers in Mexico City[110, 111], where women in the 33 poor households that pooled income claimed to put in 100 per cent, whereas men held back 25 per cent or more as a personal allowance.* Even clearer evidence comes from Mencher's random sample data on 20 villages in south India[96],

---

* All these studies are summarized in more detail in Blumberg[24 and 25].

** The mother's income also is related to increased spending on children's health, but space limits preclude the inclusion of these data in the present paper.

where she found that women invariably contributed a higher proportion of their income to family subsistence. Wives earned a mean of only 56 per cent of their husbands' income, but by contributing a mean of 97 per cent of it versus men's mean of 76 per cent, wives ended up contributing a mean of 94 per cent as much as their generally higher-earning husbands.

Why should women contribute a higher proportion of income towards family subsistence? Some have argued that since women earn less than men, their behaviour merely illustrates Engel's law. Formulated by the German economist in 1857, it states that the lower the income, the higher the proportion spent on life's basic necessities[78]. However, the one study that compared the patterns of men and women earning identical incomes found that women still put in more. Mencher[96] found that in one of her 20 villages (Alleppey 1, in Kerala, India), males and females earned the same. Women contributed 92 per cent of their 752 rupees earned, whereas men put in only 76 per cent of their 748 rupees.

These findings have obvious policy consequences. Where income from a development project is channelled only to men as heads of families, many of the benefits to the family's well-being of women's more welfare-focused spending patterns are lost.

There is a final hypothesis and set of data to be examined in this section, and they provide the strongest indication that the monolithic black-box family of shared efforts towards maximizing income is not a sufficiently accurate description of many families' empirical reality.

Women tend to allocate labour towards activities that put income (and/or food) under their control and, to the extent culturally feasible, away from activities that do not - even if these are somewhat more profitable for the husband (hypothesis (H) above).

Jones's econometric study[82] of an irrigated rice project in Cameroon bore out this hypothesis. Although swamp rice traditionally was a crop that women grew and controlled the income from, a new irrigated rice project gave the returns only to the husbands. Everyone still expected the women to continue to cultivate rice.

Jones found the project in economic difficulty because only 3,228 hectares of the project's 5,400 pump-irrigated hectares were being cultivated, despite a 45 per cent increase in rice prices. Moreover, husbands did compensate wives, and at more than their opportunity costs. The reason for the shortfall was that, although women did cultivate one plot of rice as a marital obligation (the local people were patrilineal and patrilocal), only

---

* A number of studies summarized in Blumberg[20, 24 and 25] show this, including Guyer[72, 73].

widows who cultivated on their own account, or wives who were compensated well above the average, cultivated two plots.

As it happened, transplanting rice conflicted with the planting and first weeding of sorghum. Everyone - men and women - grew sorghum, a low-return staple that women also used to brew beer, but the sorghum that the women grew was their own. Jones's regressions showed a 1:1 trade-off of days worked on sorghum versus days worked on rice, and most women chose to grow sorghum under their own control, despite its lower return, once they had transplanted just one field of rice for their husbands. While they could, in theory, earn more from what their husbands gave them from that rice, and the family's income would be considerably higher, there was a risk: they were dependent on their husband's mood or financial situation when his rice cheque came. So women reallocated much of their labour towards a less lucrative food crop whose income they controlled and the project suffered.

The external economy of the family

Although it is hypothesized that relative male/female control of income and other economic resources is more important than kinship in explaining women's family power and impact on family well-being, the nature of the kinship system also is proposed to have an effect.

Parameters of the kinship system: descent, residence and inheritance

Ceteris paribus, with respect to descent, women fare better in groups with matrilineal than patrilineal patterns; bilateral kinship systems (which characterize most of the West) tend to be intermediate. Yet descent proves less important than marital residence in boosting women's power from the external economy of the family. When the young couple goes to live with the female kin (matrilocality) of the wife, she has access to nearby allies of her own family and gender. They can provide not only economic resources but also political and emotional back-up. Patrilocal residence tends to be the least favourable to women, unless the inmarrying wives organize. For example, Igbo women of south-east Nigeria band together in village wives' associations. These provide a counterweight to the patrilineage's hegemony[23]. Neo-local residence tends to be intermediate. Finally, the greater women's inheritance rights, the greater their economic power, and the favourableness of the external economy of the family. Full matrilineal inheritance (mother to daughter) is increasingly rare, but on the other side of the coin, legal reforms in various countries are giving more women some rights of inheritance, at least on paper. Worldwide, few groups retain matrilineality and matrilocality. Patri-oriented kin institutions remain the most common in sub- Saharan Africa, as well as in north Africa, the Middle East and west, south and east - but not South-East - Asia. In South-East Asia, kin arrangements tend to be matri-oriented or bilateral. Bilateral kinship characterizes Europe and its former territories in North America, Latin America and the Caribbean; however, women have tended to promote economic and service exchange relations with extended kin, even when the formal kinship system revolves around males.

Kin-based sharing networks

Women may depend more on the external economy of the family than do their husbands. Bruce and Lloyd[44] suggest that defining families or households as bounded economic units is more descriptive of male than female reality. For many poor developing country women, extended kin form a network of support that keeps them afloat. Among African patrilineal or patrilocal peoples, for example, one of the reasons women need their own income (and separate purses) is so they can maintain their obligations or exchanges with natal extended kin. If things go wrong in the marriage, the woman has a place to return to; if she runs out of food or money, she has people to turn to. As an illustration, Guyer[72] studied the patrilineal Beti in Cameroon and found that transfers from people other than a woman's husband (mostly her kin) accounted for 34.4 per cent of her transfer income and 15 per cent of her total cash income. Such largesse must be reciprocated. Thus, when income under a woman's control drops, so may her ability to maintain kin ties, to both her family's and her own detriment. Two more examples are given below.

Belize. Stavrakis and Marshall's study[129] found an exchange network among female kin, although the larger kinship system was bilateral. The network redistributed corn for past favours and provided food and aid to women whose husbands had had a bad crop year, which provided a valuable insurance function for both genders as well as serving as a main basis for female power. But corn production dropped as the men turned to newly introduced sugar cane. Women not only lost the chief staple for in-kind help, but they also lost their main source of income from raising pigs. Women had fed to their pigs 40 per cent of the corn that was not good enough to sell. Thus the drop in both corn production and women's independent income from pig sales dealt a double blow to "kin insurance".

Burkina Faso. Conti[54] found that women who were hurt economically when a resettlement project caused at least a 50 per cent drop in their own-account commercial activities were much less able to continue in extended family exchange networks. Their plight arose because the project did not give women the personal plots they had cultivated in their previous location. Instead, they were expected to work on the staple of the project, cotton. The cotton required 15-hour workdays but the profits were given to the women's husbands. Bereft of time, economic independence and the means of maintaining their ties to their natal kin, i.e. the external economy of the family, the women mounted numerous protests.

In general, sharing or exchange networks with kin (or kin-like close friends) are most common where there are unpredictable fluctuations of sometimes scarce resources. This has long been demonstrated in the literature on hunters and gatherers (Lee and DeVore[91] and Sahlins[115] provide early overviews). Moreover, the resource fluctuations and sharing networks also have long been found among various marginal groups both in the United States[93, 126, 127, 137 and 138] and around the world (e.g. Calley[48] on Australian part-Aboriginals; Brown[43] on the Dominican Republic; Peattie[107] on Venezuela). Most of these studies looked at the gender of those most involved in kin-based sharing networks and found that it was women, even in bilateral systems.

Lombardi[93] showed mathematically how such redistribution smooths out fluctuations in the net available resources: it spreads risks.* He also demonstrated empirically, through an input-output analysis, that sharing was what prevented one welfare family in the United States from going below his zero point three times in a single month. (Zero meant no money, no food in the house and nothing to pawn.) In this example, too, the sharing was largely between women.

In sum, regardless of the formal structure of the kinship system, poor women seem more likely than their husbands to buttress their position in the internal economy of the family by exchanging resources with an informal kin-based network; namely, relying more on an external economy of the family. Some of the studies indicate that these external relations are most important to female-headed households, the next topic of the present chapter.

The political economy of the mother-child family

When the author of the present chapter first explored this topic[28, 32], the literature still stressed the disproportionate prevalence of woman-

---

* He used the same equation, for the damping of a sine curve, that actuaries use in their calculations of expected losses, which set the basis for insurance rates.

headed families among blacks in the United States and the Caribbean. Instead, the author argued that the mother-child family was structurally or economically based and widely distributed around the world, rather than a phenomenon linked to being "ethnically Negro", as alleged by Murdock and Wilson[99]. The author also formulated five structural or economic conditions under which mother-headed units might emerge, become prevalent and persist.

Nowadays, there is more awareness that such units are increasing in both developing and developed countries[44, 46, 68, 69 and 112], and among diverse ethnic groups in Africa, the Caribbean, Europe, Latin America, the United States and parts of South-East Asia.[*] Data even show that although woman-headed units are most frequently encountered among the poor, not all are poorer than male-headed counterparts[71].

The first four of the five conditions for mother-child families have recently been reassessed after 15 years[30]; they seem to have fared well in predicting the prevalence of such units. After briefly reviewing the conditions, the section below focuses on the consequences of mother-headed versus father-headed families because they provide a clear test of how gendered control of income affects family welfare: it is assumed that in a female-headed unit, the woman actually controls any income she brings in.

Four conditions for the rise and prevalence of woman-child families

The four conditions for the rise and prevalence of woman-child families are:

A That the unit of labour, the unit of compensation and the unit of property accumulation be the individual, independent of gender;

B That women have independent access to subsistence opportunities. This is a function of, first, the existence of viable economic opportunities open to women through: (I) their own work; (II) their economically productive children to whose labour or compensation they have access; (III) inheritance; and/or (IV) State-provided welfare; and, second, women being permitted, and able, to head a separate residence and control property;

C That subsistence opportunities open to women can be reconciled with their child-care responsibilities. If women's work can be carried on simultaneously with child-care responsibilities, the condition is satisfied. If not, paid child care might be used, or the formation of

---

[*] Such units are not prevalent in the Muslim crescent running from North Africa to Pakistan[1] or South Asia (see Buvinic, Youssef and Von Elm[47] and Folbre[69] for data on geographic prevalence).

the mother-headed unit might be postponed until young children can be cared for by a sibling old enough to do so and/or some other child-care agent, or until no young children are left, and/or until the woman can arrange to receive sufficient income from a working child, property, inheritance, and/or State welfare to permit her to stay home;

D That a woman's subsistence opportunities from all sources in the absence of a male head of household not be drastically less than those of the men of her class.

As discussed in Blumberg[30], condition (A) above is almost everywhere more prevalent than 15 years ago: female headship has been facilitated by the rise in economic individualism. With respect to condition (B) above, more and more women are earning income. Their participation in the formal labour force has increased at twice the rate of men's since 1950[125, p. 12], and even faster in the burgeoning informal labour force[10, 15 and 18]. It is now known, also, that income-earning children in a number of countries are more likely to turn over money to the mother than the father (Blumberg[17] on Ecuador; Segalen[120] on England; Blumberg[34] and Kusterer et al.[90] on Guatemala; Wolf[47] on Java). On balance, women's higher rates of economic activity have meant more fulfilment of condition (B) above.

Condition (C) above is the weakest of the four conditions, since economic factors generally outweigh child-care considerations in the formation of mother-child families. In extremis, a woman may leave even tiny children alone in a shack while she tries to earn enough to feed them. Nevertheless, there are options. Women heads of household tend to go into informal sector occupations more compatible with simultaneous child care, and are more likely to have co-resident extended kin in their home than are male heads of household: part of the reason may be for child care. Alternatively, women may postpone starting such a unit until children are older; almost everywhere, women heads of household are older than men heads of household.

Two points are germane concerning condition (D) above: that female-headed families rise when a woman's total subsistence potential is not drastically less than those of the men of her class. On the one hand, the data indicate that the male-female wage gap has shrunk little in most parts of the world in the last 15 years. On the other hand, more and more developing-country women are earning an absolute level of income that enables them to become female heads of household, especially if aided by an extended kin-based sharing network and, perhaps, children's earnings. For these women, this combination of their own or their children's earnings and the kin-based exchange network may not add up to as much as a counterpart male's income, but it may be enough for them to make it on their own, without absolute penury, thus fulfilling condition (D) above. In affluent countries (e.g. the United States and northern Europe), despite the persisting wage gap, increasing numbers of women earn enough to choose single motherhood without economic help from either kin or State, and the proportion of female-headed units has risen explosively. Moreover, all over the world, men may be less hesitant to leave if they know their wives can earn enough to keep their children from starvation.

The evidence given above on the four conditions for the rise of female-headed families is illustrative and no substitute for rigorous study, but the fact remains that woman-headed families are increasing in large areas of the globe, and almost everywhere the four conditions seem more likely to be fulfilled now than they were 15 years ago. This reality makes it even more important to replace the monolithic black-box-household model with a more flexible one, since the former is unable to account for the growing legions of woman-headed families.

The impact of gender of family head on family well-being

The main dimension of the internal economy of the family treated in the present chapter has been relative male/female control and spending of economic resources. Women heads of household are widely acknowledged to control their own income, even by people who are sceptical that wives do so. Therefore, if the same (or stronger) patterns of enhanced children's and family well-being are found in income-earning woman-headed families that were found by comparing income-earning wives versus husbands, the case for proposing a more flexible, less monolithic, model of the family is strengthened. Accordingly, three of the hypotheses that were discussed previously are re-examined, but this time comparing the performance of male and female heads of household vis-à-vis: (A) children's education (by adapting hypothesis (D) (III) above); (B) children's nutrition (by adapting hypothesis (G) (i) above); and (C) proportion of earnings contributed to family subsistence (by adapting hypothesis (G) (ii) above).

Gender of family head and impact on children's education (hypothesis (d) (iii) above)

Much evidence is not yet available, but three studies found that women heads of household highly prioritized education and emphasized the education of girls as well as boys. First, Chant's study of Mexican shanty-town dwellers found that "in female-headed families, there tended to be less discrimination ... toward ... girls, [who] were given opportunities equal to those of boys. In fact, female heads stressed the need for girls to have education, should they be deserted by their future husbands"[53, p. 646]. Second, Koussoudji and Mueller[87] found that children in female-headed families in Botswana received more education than those in male-headed units, but Botswana is one of perhaps three countries in the world where women have a higher educational attainment than men* [125, 148].

The third study is the quantitative analysis by Blumberg et al.[148] of random sample survey data from Santiago, Chile. The subsample analysed involved households containing teenagers of 13-19 years, which is the usual high-school age range (N = 2,519). Some 21.6 per cent (543) of these teenagers lived in woman-headed households. As in most other studies, these Santiago female heads of household proved a little older and less educated than male heads of household (48.4 vs. 45.7 years old; 7.65 vs. 9.42 years of education), and they were more likely to live with extended kin than were male heads of household (43.6 per cent vs. 33.6 per cent). However, these differences paled beside the income gap: the women heads of household earned only half the income, 12,200 pesos versus 24,000 pesos for men heads of household.

In the male-headed Santiago households with at least one teenager, boys proved significantly more likely to go to secondary school (83.6 per cent) than girls (79.0 per cent). Although female-headed units earned only half the income, 72.9 per cent of their boys and 76.7 per cent of their girls went to secondary school. Moreover, it was clear that women heads of household prioritized education highly to come so close to male-headed households' rates of attendance on only half the earnings.

Gender of head of household and impact on family/children's food and nutrition (hypothesis (g) (i) above)

First, in a random sample survey conducted in Malawi that included some fairly well-off de facto female-headed units receiving absent husbands' remittances, Peters and Herrera[108] found that women heads of household spent a higher proportion of income on food (i.e. a pattern that cannot be accounted for by Engel's law alone). Second, two studies in Jamaica found that women-headed families ate foods of higher nutritional quality[77 and 94]. Third, Engle's study of 302 urban mothers in Guatemala[64] controlled them for income level - unusual but important since most woman-headed families are poorer - and found that female-headed units spent a greater percentage of income on food for children.

---
* The reasons involve less male interest in education: poorer males either begin herding cattle at an early age (around 10 years) or migrate to South African mines and other jobs.

Fourth, turning to nutrition, in Rwanda, when male- and female-headed units were compared, holding income constant, woman-headed units consumed 377 more calories per adult equivalent per day[140]. Furthermore, von Braun and Pandya-Lorch[142] presented four case-studies: in two, children were less likely to be malnourished in female-headed units (von Braun and Wiegand-Jahn[141] in Rwanda; Vosti and Witcover[144] in Brazil). In the other two case-studies, children's nutrition was no worse than in male-headed units, even though female-headed ones were poorer (Edirisinghe[61] in Sri Lanka; Kumar[88] in Bangladesh). In addition, Kennedy's extensive literature review[83] found that the studies for Africa and some of the research in Latin America and the Caribbean showed that the children in female-headed units were better nourished. She does not clarify, however, whether the Latin American and Caribbean studies that revealed contrary findings controlled for level of income, for it is control of income that is pivotal.

For example, Kennedy and Peters' research in Kenya and Malawi[84] found that the proportion of income controlled by women, in both male- and female-headed households, had a significant positive impact on caloric intake and on lowering child malnutrition. Even in the United States, a national study of the WIC programme (a food subsidy programme for low-income women and children under three years of age) found that when males were present, children's height for age was lower[114].

Finally, women's control of food (not just income) also enhances nutrition: in Gambia, the share of cereal production controlled by women added 322 more calories per adult equivalent per day[143].

Gender of head and impact on proportion of income contributed to family subsistence (hypothesis (g) (ii) above)

First, Chant found that, whereas just over half (12) of the male heads of household in her in-depth sample in Mexico held back up to 50 per cent of their income for personal use, "female heads, alternatively, seem to contribute all their wages to family welfare"[53, p. 642]. Second, various studies show that women heads of household are much less likely to spend on alcohol: in Malawi, women heads of household spent 25-50 per cent less [84 and 108] and in Jamaica, they spent significantly less[94]. In Côte d'Ivoire, Hoddinott and Haddad [76] found that doubling female-controlled income would mean much less spending on alcohol (-26 per cent) and cigarettes (-14 per cent).

These findings are significant for development efforts, yet these data would never have been examined under the monolithic black-box-household model. Ignoring the varied contents of this black-box can result, and has resulted, in erroneous assumptions and ill-conceived development efforts. Nowhere has this been more the case than in Africa.

The black-box model, the African food crisis, excessive fertility and some concluding policy recommendations

First, erroneous assumptions and actions with respect to gender have been found to have negative consequences for the development projects that make them. The major finding of the largest-scale evaluation to date of WID efforts (involving USAID-funded projects) is that:

"Mainstream projects that ensure women's participation in proportion to their roles and responsibilities within the project's baseline situation are more likely to achieve their immediate purposes and their broader socioeconomic goals than are projects that do not"[50, xiv].

There is a long list of African development projects that failed to do this and ended up as relative failures while hurting women and families (see Blumberg[12 and 25] for an overview; also, Apthorpe[7], Broch-Due[41] and Hanger and Moris[74] on different projects in Kenya; Dey[56] and[57] on the Gambia; and Jones[82] on Cameroon).

Even without factoring in the problems caused by ignoring gender and holding to an inappropriate model of the family, Africa is currently in deep trouble. The debt crisis has forced 32 countries to adopt structural adjustment austerity measures mandated by the International Monetary Fund[105] or the World Bank. Between 1980 and 1987, the gross national product (GNP) stagnated, population growth rates rose sky-high to 3.1 per cent a year (up from 2.6 per cent in 1965-1973), and GNP per capita shrank 2.8 per cent per year, as fast as it had grown in 1965-1973 [149, pp. 221-222 and p. 269; and 105, table 2]. Worse, currently, food production is lagging ever further behind the world's highest population growth rates.

Yet aside from the gender or WID specialists, few people are analysing these problems in terms of the neglect of the people who grow up to 80 per cent of the locally produced food [116 and 125, pp. 5 and 17] and have 100 per cent of the babies: African women. Despite increasing lip service and the occasional programme recognizing the importance of African women farmers, most crop development assistance still is targeted to men, whether or not they are full-time farmers[12].

Why? The first culprit or reason, it is suggested, is the black-box model of the monolithic household. It obscures the reality that, in Africa, men and women maintain largely separate purses, often carry out different farming activities and typically control the income from different crops and animals; thus, they have different incentives.

The black-box model also shuts out the external economy of the family and the reasons for those separate purses. Kinship is overwhelmingly patrilineal and patrilocal, so wives farm their husband's kin group's land, and have only use rights to their plots. Moreover, women continue to be the predominant cultivators (according to Bryson[45] and Murdock[98], men are the principal farmers in only around one fifth of sub-Saharan African ethnic or tribal groups). Additionally, in patrilineal/patrilocal groups, women farmers have a marital obligation to farm at least one plot for their husbands, who typically also get a share of the harvest even of women-owned crops[45, p. 36]. This means that a man with more than one wife prospers. So polygyny remains quite common (for example, it ranges from 30 per cent to 47 per cent in most of the nine sub-Saharan countries included in the World Fertility Study sample[135, p. 324]. Furthermore, women's natal families charge a bride-price to the bridegroom, since he is gaining a valuable producer. Yet the black-box model gives short shrift to the unique regional, cultural and kinship factors that affect men's versus women's incentives; hence, it harms development projects that adopt it.

A second reason for the fact that so little agricultural extension training, credit and input (such as fertilizer and pesticides) are targeted to women farmers is that most development policy makers and practitioners were trained in Western countries where cultivation is rain-fed plough-based agriculture, rather than the hoe-based slash-and-burn horticulture prevalent in sub-Saharan Africa. Since much of tropical Africa has poor, acidic, easily leached soils too thin to take the plough, this is unfortunate. Even worse, rain-fed plough agriculture tends to be a male farming system, whereas shifting horticulture has long been known to be, overwhelmingly, a female farming system[8 and 40]. Even when some of these development experts acknowledge that women do work in farming, it does not stop them from automatically targeting agricultural advice and resources to men and home economics to women, just as in the American Midwest. After all, they reason, it is all one family: the information and resources will be shared. Besides, almost all agricultural agents are men (93 per cent at the latest count[12 and 130, p. 57]. Furthermore, it is presumed, often mistakenly, that male extension agents are more comfortable dealing with men[26].

So in attributing blame for the increasing shortfall of food in Africa, the development experts emphasize the "four Ds" of the environment: drought, degradation, deforestation and desertifi-cation. They also blame war and civil strife. Many also blame the sins of the State; for instance, bloated bureaucracies, overvalued currencies, and prices that favour urban residents over rural farmers and grant privileges to heavily subsidized import substitution manufacturers over export industries[12]. The shortcomings of the monolithic black-box model - and the neglect of women farmers - are almost never mentioned as factors.

Yet surely it is no accident that the food shortfall and birthrates are rising together. African women farmers get plots with poorer soils from their patri-kin to begin with[103], and now with increasing male migration and individualization of land tenure, they have to keep those plots in production too long.* The women farmers cannot afford to let the plots lie fallow and regenerate because they might not get a replacement plot from their husbands or patri-kin and the young men who used to do most of the heavy bush clearing are in the cities. Moreover, as the environment further degrades, and deforestation brings drought, it takes longer to fetch fuelwood, fodder and water (especially in the dry season). These last three tasks are almost always women's responsibility but children typically help, even if only when they are not in school. In fact, before the eldest is 12 years old, the children of a woman may be doing the work equivalent of one adult. Furthermore, women have the traditional obligation to feed their children, as well as the urgent need to keep up their traditional obligations to natal kin so they will have someone to turn to in times of trouble. Little wonder, then, that African women tell interviewers they want and need such large families, and the birthrate keeps rising.

In Africa, breaking into the black box - which nowhere else is a worse fit with empirical reality - may help to alleviate the two crises of underproduction of food and overproduction of babies. If women were recognized as primary farmers with their own set of income incentives and targeted accordingly, their returns from farming could increase, as would their ability to spend for their families' welfare. Their yields also presumably would increase so that it would no longer be necessary for their countries to spend scarce foreign exchange on food imports, or prepare for another round of famine. Furthermore, if development assistance were targeted to help their farming and cut the time they spend in unnecessary drudgery (including 4-5 hours a day just collecting water and wood), their need for children also should drop. This, in turn, should lead to a drop in the birthrate.

Finally, as Hess[75] has convincingly demonstrated in a major econometric study, as fertility falls in the developing countries, national income grows. In short, helping women so that they need fewer children helps

---

* Slash-and-burn horticulture typically involves farming a plot for 1-3 years and then letting it lie fallow for at least 5-6 years to regenerate; shortening this period lowers the yields and degrades the land.

the countries in which these women live. This starts with breaking into the black box.

Conclusions and policy recommendations

The present chapter has attempted to make the case that the prevalent model of the family or household, which treats it as a monolithic entity, is inappropriate, and that it should be replaced by a new model of the flexible family. This new model recognizes the internal economy of the family, in which gender and age affect the distribution of everything from work to income to information to calories. The flexible-family model also can deal with the fact that men and women, and younger and older members, may have different resources, incentives and priorities, and they may have different degrees of interaction with the external economy of the family: a kin-based sharing and exchange network. Moreover, the flexible-family model can deal with female-headed households, as well as account for their increasing prevalence.

The present chapter has emphasized gendered control of income as the most important aspect of the internal economy of the family, because it affects relative male/female power, and, in turn, women's degree of say in fertility, as well as in household decisions on allocating family resources to economic and welfare goals. In addition, men and women with provider obligations spend income under their control rather differently, with women devoting theirs more single-mindedly towards children's nutrition, education and other measures of well-being. Therefore, one outcome of replacing the old black-box model of the family with the new flexible, internal economy model should be an intensified concern for targeting development assistance resources and income to women as well as men. In conclusion the following four policy recommendations are proposed:

A   For any new development project or programme, instead of assuming a single- production-function household, a rapid appraisal methodology should be used to specify the internal economy of the family for target groups. This should measure the division by gender and age of labour, time, resources and income for the various socio-economic and racial/ethnic sub-groups affected by the project;

B   It then should be ascertained empirically that project information and resources are targeted to the right people within the family: those who do the work and those who reap the benefits;

C   Wherever possible, women should be explicitly targeted for activities leading to increased income, since female-controlled income helps not only family wealth but also family well-being.

The intersection of **FAMILY** Gender and Economy in the Developing World

Furthermore, it is important to target not only wives but also women heads of household;

D Project delivery systems (e.g. timing, cost and location of activities and benefits) should be reviewed to ascertain that they are appropriate for all the groups targeted; otherwise, they should be adapted to overcome any built-in constraints that diminish the access to, and retention of, benefits by any subgroup of beneficiaries, such as landless women.

References

[1] Abu-Lughod, Janet. Review of Eames and Goode (1973). *Contemporary sociology* (Washington, D.C.) 4:448, 1975.

[2] Acharya, Meena and Lynn Bennett. The rural women of Nepal: An aggregate analysis and summary of eight village studies, Vol. 2, part 9. Kathmandu, Nepal, Centre for Economic Development and Administration, Tribhuvan University, 1981.

[3] Women and the subsistence sector: Economic participation in household decision-making in Nepal. Working Paper No. 526. Washington, D.C., World Bank, 1983.

[4] Women's status in Nepal: A summary of findings and implications. Washington, D.C., United States Agency for International Development, Office of Women in Development, 1982. Mimeographed.

[5] Alberti, Amalia. Gender, ethnicity, and resource control in the Andean highlands of Ecuador. Ph.D. thesis. Stanford, California, Stanford University, 1986.

[6] Anker, Richard. Female labour force participation in developing countries: A critique of current definitions and data collection methods. *International labour review* (Geneva) 122:6, November-December 1983.

[7] Apthorpe, Raymond. Some evaluation problems for cooperative studies, with special reference to primary cooperatives in highland Kenya. In Two blades of grass: Rural cooperatives in agricultural modernization. Peter Worsely, ed. Manchester, Manchester University Press, 1971.

[8] Baumann, Hermann. The division of work according to sex in African hoe culture. *Africa*, vol. 1, 1928.

[9] Becker, Gary. A treatise on the family. Boston, Massachusetts, Harvard University Press, 1981.

[10] Berger, Marguerite. The woman in the informal sector. In The informal sector, microenterprise and women's work in Latin America. Marguerite Berger and Myra Buvinic, eds. Washington, D.C., International Center for Research on Women, 1980.

[11] Blanc-Szanton, Christina, Ana Maria Viveros-Long and Nongluck Suphanchainat. Northeast rainfed agricultural development project in Thailand. In Women in development: A.I.D.'s experience, 1973-1985. Vol. II. Ten field studies. Paula O. Goddard, ed. Washington, D.C., United States Agency for International Development, 1989.

[12] Blumberg, Rae Lesser. African women in agriculture: Farmers, students, extension agents, chiefs. Development Studies Paper Series. Morrilton, Alabama Winrock International, 1992.

[13] Cash, cows and coffee: Gender and technology adoption in rural Ecuador. Quito, United States Agency for International Development/Ecuador. Report on rapid rural appraisal of a FUNDAGRO/AID agriculture project. 1992.

[14] Enduring echoes of equality: Evidence from Ecuador and Thailand. Presented at the International Conference on Engendering Wealth and Well-being, University of California, San Diego, 17-20 February 1993. (Revision forthcoming in *Sociological perspectives*.)

[15] Entrepreneurship, credit, and gender in the informal sector of the Dominican Republic: the ADEMI Story. In Women in development: A.I.D.'s experience, 1973-1985. Vol. II. Ten field studies. Paula O. Goddard, *ed.* Washington, D.C., United States Agency for International Development, 1989.

[16] Females, farming and food: Rural development and women's participation in agri-cultural production systems. *In* Invisible farmers: Women and the crisis in agriculture. Barbara Lewis, *ed.* Washington, D.C., United States Agency for International Development, Office of Women in Development, 1981.

[17] Gender and Ecuador's new export sectors: A rapid rural appraisal study. Washington, D.C., United States Agency for International Development, Office of Women in Development/GENESYS, 1992.

[18] Gender and microenterprise in Ecuador. *In* Ecuador micro-enterprise sector assess-ment: Key characteristics of the micro-enterprise sector. Chap. 2. Washington, D.C./ Bethesda, Maryland, United States Agency for International Development. GEMINI Technical Report No. 12, 1990.

[19] Gender, control of income and planned development: 20 hypotheses. Washington, D.C., United States Agency for International Development/GENESYS, 1990.

[20] *ed.* Gender, family, and economy: The triple overlap. Newbury Park, California, Sage, 1991.

[21] Gender, microenterprise, performance and power: Case studies from the Dominican Republic, Ecuador, Guatemala and Swaziland. *In* Women in the development process in Latin America: From structural subordination to empowerment. Christine Bose, *ed.* Philadelphia, Pennysylvania, Temple University Press, forthcoming.

[22] A general theory of gender stratification. *In* Sociological theory 1984. Randall Collins, *ed.* San Francisco, Jossey-Bass, 1984.

[23] The half-hidden economic roles of rural Nigerian women and national development. Washington, D.C., The World Bank, Women in Development Division, 1988. Draft.

[24] Income under female vs. male control: Hypotheses from a theory of gender stratifica-tion and data from the third world. *Journal of family issues* (Newbury Park, Calif.) 9:1:51-84, 1988.

[25] Making the case for the gender variable: Women and the wealth and well-being of nations. Washington, D.C.,United States Agency for International development, Office of Women in Development, 1989.

[26] *and* Eme Okoro. Pioneer's progress: A case study of innovations to help women farmers in the Imo State, Nigeria agricultural develop-ment project. Washington, D.C., The World Bank/Population and Human Research Series, prepared for the African women farmers' pro-ductivity project. Katrine Saito, *ed.* 1992.

[27] Piped water in the house: A rapid appraisal of its impact on the well-being of women, children and men users in four Ecuadorian provinces. Quito, United States Agency for International Development/Ecuador and Management Systems International, 1993.

[28] *with* Maria Pilar Garcia. The political economy of the mother-child family: A cross-societal view. *In* Beyond the nuclear family model. Luis Lenero-Otero, ed. London and Beverly Hills, Sage, 1977.

[29] The political economy of the mother-child family revisited. *In* Family and kinship in Middle America and the Caribbean. Arnaud F. Marks *and* Rene A. Romer, *eds.* Curaçao and Leiden, Netherlands. Co-publication of the Institute of Higher Studies in Curaçao, Netherland Antilles, and the Department of Caribbean Studies at the Royal Institute of Linguistics and Anthropology at Leiden, Netherlands, 1978.

[30] Poverty versus "purse power": The political economy of the mother-child family III. *In* Where did all the men go? Female-headed/female-supported households in cross-cultural perspective. Joan P. Mencher *and* Anne Okongwu, *eds.* Boulder, Colorado, Westview, 1993.

[31] *and* Dale Colyer. Social institutions, gender and rural living conditions. *In* Agriculture and economic survival: The role of agriculture in Ecuador's development. Morris Whitaker *and* Dale Colyer, *eds.* Boulder, Colorado, Westview, 1990.

[32] Stratification: Socioeconomic and sexual inequality. Dubuque, Iowa, William C. Brown, 1978.

[33] *and* Marion Tolbert Coleman. A theoretical look at the gender balance of power in the American couple. *Journal of family issues* (Newbury Park, Calif.) 10:2:225-250, 1989.

[34] Toward a feminist theory of development: From the African food crisis to the Israeli kibbutz. *In* Feminism and sociological theory. Ruth A. Wallace, *ed.* Beverly Hills, California, Sage, 1989.

[35] A walk on the "WID" side: Summary of field research on "women in development" in the Dominican Republic and Guatemala. United States Agency for International Development. Presented at the International Conference on Gender and Farming Systems, Gainesville, Florida, April 1986. Draft. 1985.

[36] Women and the wealth and well-being of nations: *In* Macro-micro interrelationships. In Macro-micro linkages in sociology, American Sociological Association Presidential Volume. Joan Huber, *ed.* 1989 President, Newbury Park, California, Sage, 1991.

[37] Women, development and the wealth of nations: Making the case for the gender variable. Boulder, Colorado, Westview, forthcoming.

[38] Women's work, income and family survival strategy: Guatemala's ALCOSA agribusiness project in 1980 and 1985. *In* Women, the family and policy: A global perspective. Esther Ngan-Ling Chow *and* Catherine White Berheide, *eds.* Albany, New York, Suny Press, forthcoming.

[39] Work, wealth, and a women in development "Natural experiment" in Guatemala: The ALCOSA Agribusiness Project in 1980 and 1985. In Women in development: A.I.D.'s experience, 1973-1985. Vol. II. Ten field studies. Paula O. Goddard, *ed.* Washington, D.C., United States Agency for International Development, 1989.

[40] Boserup, Ester. Woman's role in economic development. New York, St. Martin's, 1970.

[41] Broch-Due, Vigdis. Women at the backstage of development: The negative impact on project realization by neglecting the crucial roles of Turkana women as producers and providers. Rome, Food and Agriculture Organization of the United Nations, 1983.

[42] Brown, Judith. Iroquois women: An ethnohistoric note. In Toward an anthropology of women. Rayna R. Reiter, *ed.* New York, Monthly Review Press, 1975.

[43] Brown, Susan. Love unites them and hunger separates them: Poor women in the Dominican Republic. In Toward an anthropology of women. Rayna R. Reiter, *ed.* New York, Monthly Review Press, 1975.

[44] Bruce, Judith *and* Cynthia Lloyd. Beyond female headship: Family research and policy issues for the 1990s. Presented at the Workshop on Intrahousehold Resource Allocation: Policy Issues and Research Methods. 12-14 February 1992, International Food Policy Research Institute, Washington, D.C., 1992. Draft.

[45] Bryson, Judy C. Women and agriculture in sub-Saharan Africa: Implications for development (an exploratory study). *The journal of development studies* (London) 17:3:29-46, 1981.

[46] Buvinic, Myra. The vulnerability of women-headed households: Policy questions and options for Latin America and the Caribbean. Paper prepared under the auspices of The Population Council/International Center for Research on Women Seminar series of determinants and consequences of female-headed households, 1990.

[47] Nadia Youssef *and* Barbara Von Elm. Women headed households: The ignoredfactor in development planning. Washington, D.C., International Center for Research on Women, 1978.

[48] Calley, M. Economic life of mixed-blood communities in northern New South Wales. *Oceania* (Sydney) 26:200-13, 1956.

[49] Carloni, Alice Stewart. Personal communication. 1988.

[50] Women in development: A.I.D.'s experience, 1973-1985, vol. 1. Synthesis paper. Washington, D.C., United States Agency for International Development. A.I.D. Program Evaluation Report No. 18, 1987.

[51] Carr, Marilyn *and* Ruby Sandhu. Women, development and rural productivity: An analysis of the impact of time and energy saving technologies on women. New York, UNIFEM Occasional Paper, 1988.

[52] Chafetz, Janet Saltzman. The gender division of labor and the reproduction of female disadvantage: Toward an integrated theory. In Gender, family, and economy: The triple overlap. Rae Lesser Blumberg, *ed.* Newbury Park, California, Sage, 1991.

[53] Chant, Sylvia. Single parent families: Choice or constraint? The formation of female-headed households in Mexican shantytowns. *Development and change* (London) 16:4:635-656, 1985.

[54] Conti, Anna. Capitalist organization of production through non-capitalist relations: Women's role in a pilot resettlement in Upper Volta. *Review of African political economy* (Sheffield) 15/16:75-91, 1979.

[55] Deere, Carmen Diana. The social relations of production and Peruvian peasant women's work. *Latin American perspectives* (Newbury Park, California) vol. 4, Nos. 1 and 2, 1977.

[56] Dey, Jennie. Development planning in the Gambia: The gap between planners' and farmers' perceptions, expectations and objectives. *World development* (New York) 10:5:377-396, 1982.

[57] Gambian women: Unequal partners in rice development projects? In African women in the development process. Nici Nelson, *ed.* London, Frank Cass, 1981.

[58] Dixon, Ruth. Women in agriculture: Counting the labor force in developing countries. *Population and development review* (New York) 8:3:539-566, 1982.

[59] Dixon-Mueller, Ruth. Women's work in third world agriculture. Geneva, International Labour Organisation, 1985.

[60] Dwyer, Daisy *and* Judith Bruce *eds.* A home divided: Women and income in the third world. Palo Alto, Calif., Stanford University Press, 1988.

[61] Edirisinghe, Neville. Income and employment sources of the malnourished rural poor in Kandy District, Sri Lanka. In Income sources of malnourished people in rural areas: Microlevel information and policy implications. Joachim von Braun *and* Rajul Pandya-Lorch *eds.* Working

Papers on Commercialization of Agriculture and Nutrition, No. 5. Washington, D.C., International Food Policy Research Institute, 1991.

[62] Eisler, Riane. The chalice and the blade. New York, Harper, 1987.

[63] England, Paula and Barbara Stanek Kilbourne. Markets, marriages and other mates: The problem of power. Paper presented at the Conference on Economy and Society, University of California, Santa Barbara, 1988.

[64] Engle, Patrice. Influences of mother's and father's income on children's nutritional status in Guatemala. *Social science and medicine* (Elmsford, N.Y.) 37:1:1303-1312, 1993.

[65] Mothers' and fathers' income control and effect on children in Guatemala. *In* Effects of selected policies and programs on women's health and nutritional status. Eileen Kennedy *and* M. Garcia, *eds.* Washington, D.C., International Food Policy Research Institute Report, 1993.

[66] Fapohunda, Eleanor. The nonpooling household: A challenge to theory. In A home divided: Women and income in the third world. Daisy Dwyer *and* Judith Bruce, *eds.* Palo Alto, Calif., Stanford University Press, 1988.

[67] Folbre, Nancy. The black four of hearts: Toward a new paradigm of household econo-mics. *In* A home divided: Women and income in the third world. Daisy Dwyer *and* Judith Bruce, *eds.* Palo Alto, Calif., Stanford University Press, 1988.

[68] Mothers on their own: Policy issues for developing countries. New York/ Washington, D.C., The Population Council/International Center for Research on Women, 1991.

[69] Women on their own: Global patterns of female headship. *In* The women and inter-national development annual. Vol. 2. Rita S. Gallin *and* Anne Ferguson, *eds.* Boulder, Colorado, Westview Press, 1991.

[70] Fortmann, Louise. Women's work in a communal setting: The Tanzanian policy of Ujaama. *In* Women and work in Africa. Edna G. Bay, *ed.* Boulder, Colorado, Westview Press, 1982.

[71] Gupta, Geeta. Female-headed households, poverty and child welfare. Paper presented at the Population Council/International Center for Research on Women seminar series on determinants and consequences of female-headed households. New York, April 1989.

[72] Guyer, Jane. Dynamic approaches to domestic budgeting. Cases and methods from Africa. *In* A home divided: Women and income in the third world. Daisy Dwyer *and* Judith Bruce, *eds.* Palo Alto, California, Stanford University Press, 1988.

[73] Household budgets and women's incomes. Working Paper No. 28. Boston, African Studies Center, Boston University, 1980.

[74] Hanger, Jane *and* Jon Moris. Women and the household economy. *In* Mwea: An irrigated rice settlement in Kenya. Robert Chambers *and* Jon Moris, *eds.* Munich, Weltforum Verlag, 1973.

[75] Hess, Peter. Population growth and socio-economic progress in less developed countries: determinants of fertility transition. New York, Praeger, 1988.

[76] Hoddinott, John *and* Lawrence Haddad. Household expenditures, child anthropometric status and the intrahousehold division of income: Evidence from the Côte d'Ivoire. Washington, D.C., International Food Policy Research Institute, 1991.

[77] Horton, Susan *and* Barbara D. Miller. The effect of gender of household head on food expenditures: Evidence from low-income households in Jamaica. Paper presented at the Yale Conference on Family, Gender Differences and Development, 1989.

[78] Houtthaker, H. S. An international comparison of household expenditure patterns, com-memorating the centenary of Engel's law. *Econometrica* (Oxford) 25:532-551, 1957.

[79] Howe, Gary Nigel. The present and potential contribution of women to economic develop-ment: Elements of methodology and analysis of the Yemen Arab Republic. Washington, D.C., report prepared for the United States Agency for International Development/ Office of Women in Development, 1985.

[80] Jaquette, Jane. The family as a development issue. *In* Women at the center: Development issues and practices for the 1990s. Gay Young, Vidyamali Samarasinghe *and* Ken Kusterer, *eds.* West Hartford, Connecticut, Kumarian Press, 1993.

[81] Johnson, F. C. *and* B. L. Rogers. Nutritional status in female-headed households in the Dominican Republic. Paper presented at the International Conference on Women, Development and Health, Michigan State University, 21-23 October 1988.

[82] Jones, Christine. The impact of the SEMRY I irrigated rice production project on the organization of production and consumption at the intrahousehold level. Washington, D.C. Report prepared for the United States Agency for International Development, Bureau for Program and Policy Coordination, 1983.

[83] Kennedy, Eileen T. Effects of gender of head of household on women's and children's nutritional status. Paper presented at the Workshop

on the Effect of Policies and Programs on Women. Washington, D.C., International Food Policy Research Institute, 1992.

[84] and Pauline Peters. Household food security and child nutrition: The intersection of income and gender of household head. *World Development* (Elmsford, New York) 20:8:1077-1085, 1992.

[85] and Bruce Cogill. Income and nutritional effects of the commercialization of agriculture in southwestern Kenya. Washington, D.C., International Food Policy Research Institute. Research Report No. 63, 1987.

[86] Koons, Adam Surla. Reaching rural women in the northwest province: A presentation of more ways in which women are not men. Paper prepared for the Conference on Development and Cameroon: The Role of Food and Agriculture. University of Florida, Gainesville, Florida, 7-9 April 1988.

[87] Koussoudji, Sherrie *and* Eva Mueller. The economic and demographic status of female-headed households in rural Botswana. *Economic Development and Cultural Change* (Chicago) 31:4:831-859, 1983.

[88] Kumar, Shubh K. *In* Income sources of the malnourished poor in Bangladesh. In Income sources of malnourished people in rural areas: Microlevel information and policy implications. Working Papers on Commercialization of Agriculture and Nutrition No. 5. Washington, D.C., International Food Policy Research Institute, 1991.

[89] Role of the household economy in child nutrition at low incomes: A case study in Kerala. Occasional Paper No. 95. Ithaca, Department of Agricultural Economics, Cornell University, 1978.

[90] Kusterer, Ken, Maria Regina Estrada de Batres *and* Josefina Xuya Cuxil. The social impact of agribusiness: A case study of ALCOSA in Guatemala. Washington, D.C., United States Agency for International Development, A.I.D. Evaluation Special Study No. 4, 1981.

[91] Lee, Richard D. *and* Irven DeVore. Man the hunter. Chicago, Illinois, Aldine, 1968.

[92] Lenski, Gerhard. Power and privilege. New York, McGraw-Hill Books, 1966.

[93] Lombardi, John R. Exchange and survival. Paper presented at the meetings of the American Anthropological Association, New Orleans, Louisiana, November 1973.

[94] Louat, Frederic, Margaret Grosh *and* Jacques van der Gaag. Welfare implications of female-headship in Jamaican households. Washington, D.C., The World Bank, 1991.

[95] Matlon, Peter J. Income distribution among farmers in northern Nigeria: Empirical results and policy implications. Washington, D.C., United States Agency for International Development/Michigan State University, 1979.

[96] Mencher, Joan. Women's work and poverty: Women's contribution to household maintenance in two regions of South India. In A home divided: Women and income in the third world. Daisy Dwyer and Judith Bruce, eds. Palo Alto, California, Stanford University Press, 1988.

[97] Mies, Maria. Lacemakers in Narsapur: Indian housewives produce for the world market. London, Zed Press, 1982.

[98] Murdock, George P. Ethnographic atlas: A summary. *Ethnology* (Pittsburgh) 6:109-236, 1967.

[99] *and* Suzanne F. Wilson. Settlement patterns and community organization: Cross-cultural codes 3. *Ethnology* (Pittsburgh) 11:254-95, 1972.

[100] Nash, John F. The bargaining problem. *Econometrica* (Oxford) 18:155-62, 1950.

[101] Two-person cooperative games. *Econometrica* (Oxford) 21:1:128-40, 1953.

[102] Nassif, Hind. Women's economic roles in developing Tunisia. Paper presented at meetings of the Association of Arab-American University Grads/Middle East Studies Association, 1976.

[103] Norem, Rosalie. Personal communication, 1988.

[104] Norman, David W., Emmy B. Simmons *and* Henry M. Hays, *eds.* Farming systems in the Nigerian savanna: Research strategies for development. Boulder, Colorado, Westview, 1982.

[105] O'Brien, Stephen. Structural adjustment and structural transformation in sub-Saharan Africa. *In* Structural adjustment and African women farmers. Christina H. Gladwin, *ed.* Gainesville, Florida, University of Florida Press, 1991.

[106] Palmer, Ingrid, Sukaesinee Subhadhira *and* Wilaiwat Grisanaputi. The northeast rainfed agricultural development project in Thailand: A baseline survey of women's roles and household resource allocation for a farming systems approach. New York, The Population Council, 1983.

[107] Peattie, Lisa. The view from the barrio. Ann Arbor, Michigan, University of Michigan Press, 1968.

[108] Peters, Pauline *and* G. Herrera, *with* Thomas Randolph. Cash cropping, food security and nutrition: The effects of agricultural commer-

cialization among smallholders in Malawi. Cambridge, Massachusetts/Washington, D.C., United States Agency for International Development, 1989.

[109] Poeschel, Ursula. La mujer salasaca, 2. ed. Quito, Ediciones Abya-Yala, 1988.

[110] Roldan, Martha. Intrahousehold patterns of money allocation and women's subordination: A case study of domestic outworkers in Mexico City. Prepared for Women, income and policy seminar. New York, Population Council, March 1988.

[111] Renegotiating the marital contract: Intrahousehold patterns of money allocation and women's subordination among domestic outworkers in Mexico City. *In* A home divided: Women and income in the third world. Daisy Dwyer *and* Judith Bruce, *eds.* Palo Alto, California, Stanford University Press, 1988.

[112] Rosenhouse, Sandra. Identifying the poor: Is "headship" a useful concept? Living Standards Measurement Study Working Paper 58. Washington, D.C., The World Bank, 1989.

[113] Rozenzweig, Mark R. *and* Paul T. Schultz. Market opportunity, genetic endowment, and intrafamily resource distribution: Child survival in rural India. *American Economic Review* (Nashville, Tennessee) 72:4:803-815, 1982.

[114] Rush, David, Daniel G. Horvitz *and* W. Burleigh Seaver. The national WIC evaluation: An evaluation of the special supplemental food program for infants, women and children. Vol. 5, Instrumentation. Raleigh-Durham, North Carolina, Research Triangle Institute, 1986.

[115] Sahlins, Marshall. On the sociology of primitive exchange. *In* The relevance of models for social anthropology. Michael Banton, ed. A.S.A. monograph I. London, Tavistock Publications; New York, Praeger, 1965.

[116] Saito, Katrine *and* Jean Weidemann. Agricultural extension for women farmers in Africa. Washington, D.C., The World Bank. Policy, Research and External Affairs Working Papers. 1990.

[117, 118] Schultz, T. Paul. The relationship between local family planning expenditures and fertility in Thailand, 1976-1981. Yale University, 1988. Draft.

[119] Scudder, Thayer. Evaluatory report on mission to Sri Lankan settlement projects: A discus-sion of some basic issues. Washington, D.C., United States Agency for International Development, Asia Bureau, 1979.

[120] Segalen, Martine. Historical anthropology of the family. Cambridge, University of Cambridge Press, 1986.

[121] Sen, Amartya. Gender and cooperative conflicts. *In* Persistent inequalities: Women and world development. Irene Tinker, *ed.* New York, Oxford University Press, 1990.

[122] 100 million women are missing. *New York Times,* 5 November 1991.

[123] The economics of life and death. *Scientific American* (New York) May:40-47, 1993.

[124] Senauer, Benjamin. The impact of the value of women's time on food and nutrition. Department of Agricultural and Applied Economics, University of Minnesota. 1988. Mimeographed.

[125] Sivard, Ruth. Women - A world survey. Washington, D.C., World Priorities, 1985.

[126] Stack, Carol. The kindred of Viola Jackson: Residence and family organization of an urban black American family. In Afro-American anthropology: Contemporary perspectives. Norman E. Whitten, Jr. and John F. Szwed, eds. New York, Free Press, 1970.

[127] All our kin: Strategies for survival in a black community. New York, Harper & Row, 1974.

[128] Staudt, Kathleen. Uncaptured or unmotivated? Women and the food crisis in Africa. *Rural Sociology* (Bozeman, Massachusetts) 52:1:37-55, 1987.

[129] Stavrakis, Olga *and* Marion Louise Marshall. Women, agriculture and development in the Maya lowlands: Profit or progress? Paper presented at the International Conference on Women and Food, Tucson, 1978.

[130] Swanson, Burton E., B. J. Farner *and* R. Bahal. The current status of extension worldwide. Rome, Food and Agriculture Organization of the United Nations, 1990.

[131] *and* Jaffer Rassi. International directory of national extension systems. Champaign, Illinois, University of Illinois, Bureau of Educational Research, 1981.

[132] Tipprapa, Somjit. Interview with Director, Community-Based Integrated Rural Development Bureau, Population and Community Development Association of Thailand on documen-tation of declining fertility in Thailand, especially the north-east. Bangkok, Thailand, January 1993.

[133] Treas, Judith. The common pot or separate purses? A transaction cost interpretation. *In* Gender, family, and economy: The triple overlap. Rae Lesser Blumberg, ed. Newbury Park, California, Sage, 1991.

[134] Tripp, Robert B. Farmers and traders: Some economic determinants of nutritional status in northern Ghana. *Journal of Tropical Pediatrics* (Oxford) 27:15-22, 1981.

[135] United Nations. Department of International Economic and Social Affairs. Fertility behaviours in the context of development: evidence from the World Fertility Survey. 1987 (ST/ESA/SER.A/100).

[136] United States Agency for International Development. The family and development initiative. Washington, D.C., 1990.

[137] Valentine, Charles. Blackston: Progress report on a community study in urban Afro-America. St. Louis, Washington University, 1970. Mimeographed.

[138] Culture and poverty: Critique and counterproposals. Chicago, Illinois, University of Chicago Press, 1968.

[139] van Dusen, Roxann. A. Integrating women into national economies: Programming considerations with special reference to the Middle East. Washington, D.C., United States Agency for International Development, Office of Technical Support, Near East Bureau, 1977.

[140] von Braun, Joachim, Hartwig de Haen *and* Juergen B. Lanken. Commercialization of agriculture under population pressure: Effects on production, consumption and nutrition in Rwanda. Research Report No. 85. Washington, D.C., International Food Policy Research Institute, 1990.

[141] *and* Graciela Wiegand-Jahn. Income sources and income uses of the malnourished poor in northwest Rwanda. In Income sources of malnourished people in rural areas: Microlevel information and policy implications. Working Papers on Commercialization of Agriculture and Nutrition No. 5. Washington, D.C., International Food Policy Research Institute, 1991.

[142] *and* Rajul Pandya-Lorch. Income sources of malnourished people in rural areas:Microlevel information and policy implications. Working Papers on Commercialization of Agriculture and Nutrition No. 5. Washington, D.C., International Food Policy Research Institute, 1991.

[143] ..., Detlez Puetz *and* Patrick Webb. Irrigation technology and commercialization of rice in the Gambia: Effects on income and nutrition. Research Report No. 75. Washington, D.C., International Food Policy Research Institute, 1989.

[144] Vosti, Stephen A. *and* Julie Witcover. *In* Income sources of the rural poor: The case of the Zona de Mata, Minas Gerais, Brazil. In Income sources of malnourished people in rural areas: Microlevel information and policy implications. Working Papers on Commercialization of Agriculture and Nutrition No. 5. Washington, D.C., International Food Policy Research Institute, 1991.

[145] Wainerman, Catalina H. and Zulma Recchini de Lattes. El trabajo feminino en el banquillo de los acusados: la medición censal en América Latina. Mexico, The Population Council, 1981.

[146] Weller, Robert H. The employment of wives, dominance and fertility. *Journal of Marriage and the Family* (Minneapolis, Minnesota) 30:437-442, 1968.

[147] Wolf, Diane. Female autonomy, the family, and industrialization in Java. *In* Gender, family, and economy: The triple overlap. Rae Lesser Blumberg, ed. Newbury Park, California, Sage, 1991.

[148] "Women's 'purse power' in the household: Reducing favoritism toward boy's schooling in Santiago, Chile". By Rae Lesser Blumberg *and others*. Paper presented at the annual meetings of the American Sociological Association, Pittsburgh, United States of America, 1992.

[149] World Bank. Sub-Saharan Africa: From crisis to sustainable growth. Washington, D.C., 1989.

FAMILY Enrichment: Programmes to Foster Healthy Family Development

Introduction*

Throughout history, strong marriages and families have been the foundation of well-being. Nicholas Stinnett wrote:

"As we look back in history we see that the quality of family life is important to the strength of nations. There is a pattern in the rise and fall of great societies ... . When these societies were at the peak of their power and prosperity, the family was strong and highly valued. When family life became weak in these societies, when the family was not valued - when goals became extremely individualistic - the society began to deteriorate and eventually fell."[1]

History is a lesson that the continuance of the family must be safeguarded and strengthened in the world today.

Why are families needed? Unlike other forms of life, human children have to be nurtured and cared for over an extended period or they will die. The continued existence of the human race is a primary function of families.[2,3]

Family patterns have changed and adapted through cultural development over the ages and continue to change. The primary need to love and nurture the human child esists so that the generations may continue despite the ongoing changes in the world.

The need for the family in human society is as great as ever and may be even greater because of the increasing complexity of life. The functions and opportunities of the family are not limited to individual self-contained units: they have ever-increasing possibilities of expanding. The healthier and stronger a family unit, the more likely that such units may constitute a strong nation and, in turn, strong nations make a stronger world.

With the recurrence of profound changes, families are facing difficult challenges. Families are at risk. With such realities as poverty, war, mass migration, changes in the workforce, domestic violence, drug addiction and crime, the need is for programmes focused on families ranging from the educational and preventive to therapeutic. This spectrum can be graphically demonstrated as follows:

Education/prevention . . . .*Intervention/therapeutic*
(Strength-centred) . . . .*(Problem-centred)*

Prevention programmes are described in terms such as "enrichment", "wellness" and "self- improvement". Since the family is the basic social unit and thus affects the direction of societies, helping families meet their

---

* Chapter prepared for the IYF secretariat by Claudia S. Arp, David H. Arp and Vera Mace.

own needs is critical. Family enrichment programmes can provide competencies to enable families to be appropriately self-sufficient. Enrichment programmes empower individuals within families and the family as a unit; this enables families to contribute to the communities and nations they live in, strengthening governmental and non-governmental organizations.

Proactive services give priority to the prevention of serious trouble rather than to meeting remedial needs. Catalano and Dooley define proactive services as those that prevent the occurrence of risk factors, and reactive services as those that improve the responses to risk factors.[4] There are several reasons to emphasize prevention programmes. For instance, prevention is cheaper. Widespread family wellness programmes could reduce the economic burdens of some nations. Prevention is broad-based. In recent years an increase of skill-oriented prevention programmes have overlapped with remedial programmes, reaching many of those people who were overlooked in the past. Prevention is also easier. Working with families who are basically healthy is not as complicated as working with unhealthy (dysfunctional) families. Working with families before they are in crises conserves energy and time that can be used to promote growth. By increasing prevention-oriented services, disruptive and destructive patterns can be changed and constructive help offered to families.[5]

To leave a legacy of family wellness to future generations, the concept of family enrichment must be emphasized and taught. Strengthening family life needs to be a top priority. It is time to emphasize prevention, to reorder values and to make a commitment to family life and human relationships in the way time and energy are spent. To do this, developing national and international priorities for family wellness will be necessary. Countries need to match remedial programmes with prevention and enrichment programmes. Prevention may be seen as the equivalent of the prenatal care of future families and immunization and vaccination against disease.

Present marriages need to be strengthened and couples must be prepared for healthy marriages to improve family life in the future. Abuse prevention, family planning and preparation-for- parenthood programmes can help bring needed change in future families. Family-life education programmes can help families raise emotionally healthy children who are well prepared to be partners and parents in the twenty-first century.

In a press release, the President of the Carnegie Corporation considered the transformed American family, "largely unprepared to meet the challenges of raising a child".[6] He asked the Government, health-care institutions, schools and voluntary organizations to cooperate in providing a network of supportive health, educational and social services that would be available to families with children and adolescents in all communities. Among the family services he termed essential were family support organizations serving some of the same functions as the traditional extended family: augmenting parents' knowledge of and skill in child-rearing; helping them to deal with the problems of adolescents; enriching families' skills in coping with stress; affording families access to services; facilitating the development of information support networks; and helping families organize to counteract dangerous trends in the community.

One recurring theme in the research on early intervention, conducted by the Carnegie Corporation in 1991, was the potential value of teaching young parents to deal with their own children effectively. As children grow, parents can be helped by programmes that promote positive verbal interactions among family members and the verbal responsiveness of adults to children. The great challenge is to devise family-centred interventions that will enhance children's cognitive development and emotional resiliency in situations of chronic poverty and relative social isolation.

Professor Small of the Carnegie Council on Adolescent Development described the need for parent support as a problem requiring inter-parental communication. Parents need a way of obtaining social support from other parents by sharing experiences, pooling information and exchanging coping strategies. A mutual-aid ethic among parents who have a common concern for the well-being of their developing adolescents and yet who bring diverse experiences to parenting their adolescents can be helpful.

The Minnesota Council on Family Relations included the following statement in a Position Statement on Strengthening Families:

"We believe that in every person there is potential for growth and change, that too often this potential is unrecognized, untapped or under-utilized ... . We further believe that one of the most significant forces for growth and change in persons can be a supportive, nurturing group. Through interaction with persons whom we trust, we are able to explore better ways of doing things ... . And we believe that the family is a group that more than any other group determines the kind of people we are."[7]

Basic elements of functional families

"A FUNCTIONAL FAMILY IS THE HEALTHY SOIL OUT OF WHICH INDIVIDUALS CAN BECOME MATURE HUMAN BEINGS."[8]

Family enrichment or wellness programmes can best be developed and implemented if the functions of families are used as a foundation. The primary functions of families might be summarized as set out below.

The first function of the family is to pass on human values from generation to generation. Some civilizations believed that people gained immortality by passing on their essential selves to their children. But a child is not merely the propagation of parental personality. Children do not belong to parents. They are a sacred trust, the most sacred trust that men and women can receive. The task of parents is to accept children for who they are; to love them; to care for them; and to strive to surround them with wholesome and positive influences. In this way, positive human values such as honesty, caring and tolerance will be passed on to the next generation.[9]

The second function of the family is to provide a place for all its members, from birth to death. To fulfil this function, skills for achieving and maintaining human relationships must be learned. Human relationships need to be based upon an acceptance of the commonalities of all while valuing diversity within the family, which includes respect for each family member's unique personality. Extending this concept beyond the individual family can lead to improved relations between races, faiths and nations.

The third function of the family is to provide a place where its members can learn how to achieve and maintain human relationships and how to work together for the common good. Ultimately, this includes working for world peace.

The fourth function of the family is to find ways of sharing and passing on the message of a better world so that all persons will want it and will work for it. Families are the primary vehicle for the preparation of ideas and human goals across generations.

These are noble family functions that can be better fulfilled through family enrichment.

Qualities of strong families

Much of what has been written about families has focused on what is wrong with the family. From an enrichment-oriented preventive focus, the emphasis has been upon pathology. It is critical, however, to build upon what is right about families and to provide tools for families to be strengthened. Research on family strengths provides, therefore, a valuable point of beginning for family enrichment programmes.[10]

Stinnett's research project spanned more than a decade and included over 3,000 families in every State of the United States of America and 20 other countries in Africa, Europe and Latin America. The top six qualities of strong families identified through Stinnett's research[11,12] are summarized below.

Appreciation

Every individual has a basic need to be appreciated. Strong families have the habit of looking for each other's good qualities and expressing their appreciation. Every person has strengths and positive qualities; the family is the primary place where the affirmation of strengths should occur. Healthy families concentrate on the positive.

Spending time together

Strong families genuinely enjoy being together. This requires pre-planning and structure. Time together doesn't just happen; strong families make it happen. One interesting pattern emerged from Stinnett's research: there was a high frequency of families participating in outdoor activities. A possible explanation is that when families are together outdoors, distractions are fewer and they can concentrate on each other. Also physical exercise (especially outdoors) contributes to health and to personal feelings of well-being; both can strengthen the family.

Commitment

Strong families are deeply committed to the family group and to promoting each other's happiness and welfare. While there has been little research on family commitment, Yankelovich observed that society was in the process of leaving behind an excessive self-centred orientation and of moving towards a new ethic of commitment emphasizing new rules of living that supported self-fulfilment through deeper personal relationships.[13] Mac[14] writes that commitment produces behavioural change. When life becomes overwhelming and family members are pulled in many different directions, strong families take the initiative in restructuring their lifestyle. They may eliminate the discretionary activities that do not benefit the family. Such families also set realistic family goals that will enhance the quality of their family relationships.[15]

Good communication patterns

Strong families demonstrate good communication patterns. This quality is closely related to the previous ones. Good communication requires an investment of time.[14]

Not only do strong families talk to each other, but they also listen well, thus communicating a mutual respect for one another. They are also willing to deal with conflict and are committed to finding solutions that are best for everyone. They are able to express their feelings and do so in non-combative, constructive ways. They are able to make creative use of conflict. This kind of broad-based communication is integral to the life of strong families.

High degree of religious orientation

Strong families tend to have a high degree of religious orientation. The research undertaken during the past 40 years shows a positive relationship of religion to marital happiness and family well-being. Mace[14] and Stinnett1 point out that this quality of strong families goes beyond attending the church, synagogue or mosque, or participating in religious activities. Stinnett found that an awareness of a higher power gave many families a sense of purpose and strength. This awareness also helped them to be more patient with each other, more forgiving, quicker to get over anger, more positive and more supportive in their relationships.[16]

Ability to deal with crises in a positive manner

Strong families are able to deal with crises in a constructive way. They are able to deal with problems while remaining supportive of one another. They have problem-solving skills and are able to see some positive elements even in the darkest of situations. They are able to identify the crisis and to attack the problem and not each other.[17]

These characteristics of strong families coincided with the findings of other researchers who had examined healthy families.[18,19,20,21] What is needed to develop these qualities?

Developing healthy families

Individuals need to be prepared for marriage and parenthood. Both marriage and parenting are complex and challenging responsibilities that affect not only individuals and family members but also society as a whole. Bradshaw8 proposed that families should be viewed as systems, with the marital partnership the chief component. If that is functioning well, the children will have an opportunity of growing up as happy, healthy people. He summarized the needs of families within that system: a sense of worth, a sense of physical security or productivity, a sense of intimacy and relatedness, a sense of unified structure, a sense of responsibility, a sense of being challenged and stimulated, a sense of joy and an opportunity for affirmation and spiritual grounding. A child needs a mother and father who are committed to each other in a basically healthy relationship. Thus, family enrichment programmes consider the couple, the children and the family as an interrelated unit.

Although a healthy family has many components, a significant one is the positive role models provided by parents. Positive parental role models help children work towards their own maturity. Child development specialists generally agree that the ideal setting for the healthy development of a child is two loving parents, mutually fulfilled in their marriage, who can provide their children with warm, non-possessive love. In such a family, a child identifies positively with the parent of his or her own sex, and learns by observation how to relate positively to the parent of the opposite sex.[22]

Many researchers believe the evidence for the emphasis upon strong marriages is compelling. Popenoe states:

"Social science research is almost never conclusive. There are always methodological difficulties and stones left unturned. Yet in the decades of work as a social scientist, I know of few other bodies of data in which the weight of evidence is so decisively on one side of the issue: for children, two parent-families are preferable to single-parent and step-families!"*

Popenoe's research strongly suggests the need for developing well-balanced programmes designed to strengthen existing and future family relationships.

Children who grow up in happy, intact, functional families unconsciously learn the roles they will later need in marriage and parenthood. They also gain a deep, satisfying sense of self-worth and a respect for others who share their lives. Such experiences help them to mature as self-confident adults capable of relating positively and creatively to other people, not only in the small world of the home but also in the community.

Family wellness is characterized by maturity in which parental roles model the following:

How to be a man or woman;
How to be a husband or wife;
How to be a father or mother;
How to achieve intimate relationships with others;
How to be a functional human being.

Parents can best model healthy roles when they are part of a functional, strong family.[8]

Realities: today's families at risk

Never have families and individuals had to live in such a complex, problematic world with so many choices to make, choices that often lead to feelings of guilt, fear, despair and helplessness. Families are at risk. Families are more transient and mobile and can no longer count on the extended family for support. The fragmentation and dissolution of extended families and the increase of families headed by single parents are all issues in today's world. Family life in the 1990s is unlike that of any other period in

---

* As quoted in Barbara Dafoe Whitehead, "Dan Quayle was right", The Atlantic Monthly (April 1993), p. 82.

history and is changing more rapidly than ever before. These changes are accelerated by the influences of recently developed technological advances including transportation, telecommunications and computers.

Environmental issues, overpopulation, and economic recession along with war, crime and violence, political upheaval, famine and the resettlement of refugees are some of the serious global problems concerning caregivers.

Acknowledging that these problems exist and have a direct and indirect impact on families is important. Poor relationships within the family are known to be closely related to many problems in society such as juvenile delinquency and domestic abuse. This interrelationship of what happens within the families, communities and the world needs to be considered in the development and implementation of family enrichment programmes.

Armand Nicholi expressed the relationship between families and societal realities in this way:

"The breakdown of the family contributes significantly to the major problems confronting our society today. Research data make unmistakably clear a strong relationship between broken families and the drug epidemic, the increase in out-of-wedlock pregnancies, the rise in violent crime, and the unprecedented epidemic of suicide among children and adolescents ... . We need a radical change in our thinking about family. We need a society where people have the freedom to be whatever they choose - but if they choose to have children, then those children must be given the highest priority."*

In the midst of a complicated, rapidly changing world, it must be remembered that every human being is a person of value. Every person has a basic need to belong. Every person wants to be a part of the smallest democracy at the heart of society. Over the years, the family has been the predominant means of nurturing and transmitting values to the next generation. Nothing could be more important. Children are culture's greatest natural resource. The future of the world depends on its children and its children's children. In a real sense, therefore, as go families, so goes the world.

While children are the greatest natural resource, they also require a greater economic investment than in the past. For example, in the agrarian societies of the past, children were seen as an economic asset. Large families were desired for work on the farm and, thus, increased productivity. Children were rarely sent to college and so did not drain the family budget with the sort of expenses more common in industrialized societies. In a sense, children provided the only security people could count

---

* Remarks taken from the text of a presentation delivered by Armand Nicholi in 1991 and compiled in a monograph entitled "What do we know about successful families", which is obtainable from Grad Resources, 13612 Midway Road, Suite 500, Dallas, Texas 75244, United States.

on in their old age. Increasingly, however, children require income instead of producing it. Still, they are the best investment that can be made with long-term benefits for humankind. Children need to be viewed as crucial members of the family unit whose needs must be met if families are to be healthy.

Family enrichment

Family enrichment programmes have existed for many years. Those who have developed and implemented programmes in the area of family enrichment, and written on the subject, agree that certain basic skills are derived from family functions and strengths. These skills are described below.

Learning to communicate

Positive communication means expressing oneself clearly as well as listening well. Communication can enhance close relationships because thoughts and feelings are expressed and clarified. Communication includes the expression of caring and affection. The expression of thoughts and feelings in positive ways consistent with actions can be learned.[22,23]

Accentuating the positive

Observing and sharing positive actions, making thoughtful gestures and acknowledging accomplishments makes others feel validated. Parents need to be encouraged to accentuate the positive. Simple actions can be used to emphasize positive qualities and actions. For example, a brief note to a child acknowledging something he or she did well could be put into the child's lunch box for school.

Expressing feelings

Human beings have a range of feelings that are normal and need to be expressed and validated. Expressing feelings in constructive ways is crucial in healthy relationships. Sadness, joy, anger and happiness all exist and are neither good nor bad; they exist. The way feelings are expressed can lead to close positive relationships where growth occurs or to non-constructive, often destructive, relationships.

Members of a family usually live so close together that unless they can share their feelings with each other, misunderstandings and tensions tend to develop and they become angry. What should families do with anger? Some people bottle it up and allow it to simmer. Others explode and get relief, often at the expense of someone else. Such an expression of anger is healthier than suppressing it. But there is an even better way: acknowledge anger; regard it as your emotional state; and ask the person with whom you're angry to help you handle it. This approach can lead to constructive results.[22]

Finding ways of expressing feelings that work well for each family member and the family unit is important. For example, some individuals prefer to express feelings in writing or drawing, others orally; some want time to reflect while others do not.

The following recommendations foster positive communication:

A   Avoid "you" statements;
B   Avoid "why" questions;
C   Express feelings. Begin sentences with "I feel ..." or "I believe ...". Share your own feelings and let the statement reflect back on you. In this way, you will avoid attacking the other person;
D   Allow time for resolving issues. To have meaningful family relationships, it is necessary to bring the issues and the feelings about the issues out into the open, and to work at resolving them. This needs to be done again and again. Acknowledging and dealing with differences is necessary in order for each member to live together in a modern democratic family.

Learning to cooperate

Parents with appropriate expectations and limits provide a foundation for cooperation. Children need limits with an external structure that will help them develop inner control. Their unbridled impulses can lead them into trouble and scary situations for children if they are not supported by adults. Children can best learn self-discipline with the cooperation of wise parents.[22]

In previous generations, many parents exercised discipline in an authoritarian manner. Most modern parents reject autocratic rule but have never been taught the more difficult cooperative method of discipline. As a result, many give up in despair and become "permissive", which often means indulgent, allowing children to do whatever they wish. These young people develop little inner control, intensifying their alienation from their parents and their parents' way of life. Parents who value autonomy and self-discipline set appropriate limits.

The cooperative method of parenting includes good communication and interaction between parent and child. This no longer means demanding unquestioning obedience as it once did when the job of parenthood was seen as just an effort to subdue the child's will.

Working cooperatively within the family develops the potential for cooperation and collaboration beyond the home.

Learning to negotiate

Healthy families have learned to deal with conflict in positive ways. This is certainly not to suggest that conflict is absent in their homes. The issue is not whether conflict occurs but how conflicts are resolved within families. How can parents teach their children to deal with conflict in constructive ways? In their behaviour, parents need to provide model ways of resolving conflict. Helping their children to resolve their differences is difficult for parents if they are not willing or able to work out their own. Parents must be encouraged to apply these skills as an educative responsibility to their children.

Many parents are plagued with doubts about whether they are doing the right thing. Healthy families talk things over with their children, especially when in disagreement. When parents feel that they must say no to their children's requests or set limits the children disagree with, careful explanations should be provided so their children understand the reasons for the decisions. Children must feel they deserve an explanation for parental decisions that affect them.

Parents must learn to negotiate if they want to influence their children positively. As children grow older, outside influences loom larger. For instance, because families are smaller than in the past, children often seek close companions outside the home, especially when siblings are far apart in age. In increasingly pluralistic societies, values children have learned at home are more likely to be contradicted by different values their companions have acquired in their own families. At quite an early age, children sense this conflict of loyalties.

The conflict grows acute for adolescents who in gaining independence may find themselves more and more alienated from their parents. At this time of family life, support groups are especially helpful for parents and adolescents as well as for the family.

Learning to release children into adulthood

Adolescence is, by definition, the state or process of growing up. Parents need to prepare their teenagers to make their own decisions, which means gradually releasing decision-making power into their hands.[24]

Parents of older children may support the increasing autonomy of their teenage children by expressing the process in a manner such as the following:

"My job is not to give you orders, but to help you make your own decisions and stand on your own feet. I'm also responsible for you and want to protect you from the dangerous situations you may get into because of your lack of experience. I'll give you freedom and responsibility a little at a time, as we both feel you're ready for it. If you can handle it, then you've earned the right to a little more freedom. If you can't, then we'll wait until you've gained enough new experience to try again."

Once this kind of agreement has been established between parent and child, the way is open for cooperation.

Passing the torch to the next generation is not easy, but parents can do some things to facilitate the transition from adolescence to responsible adulthood. Parents can do a better job of letting go if they understand the goals of adolescence.

In an adolescent-parent study that involved 8,165 young adolescents and 10,467 parents, Merton and Irene Stromm[25] identified seven goals that most adolescents intuitively seek to achieve during their teenage years:

A   Achievement: the satisfaction of achieving a standard of excellence in some area of endeavour;
B   Friendships: the broadening of one's social base by having learned to make friendships and maintain them;
C   Feelings: the self-understanding gained through having learned to share one's feelings with another person;
D   Identity: the sense of knowing "who I am", of being recognized as a significant person;
E   Responsibility: the confidence of knowing "I can stand alone and make responsible decisions";
F   Maturity: the transformation from a child into an adult;
G   Sexuality: the acceptance of responsibility for one's new role as a sexual being.

Parents can help achieving these goals through helping their adolescents understand themselves and the world around them. Parents need to encourage responsible citizenship and the equality of all, stressing the worth of the individual.

Basically the goal of parenting can be summarized in one phrase: "To prepare your child to function independently as an adult."[24]

State of the contemporary family

"The task of modern parents is much more complicated than it used-to-be."[26]
"Many parents just stand on the sidelines in a state of exasperated help-

lessness while their children are raised by the mass media![26]

The current situation in the United States illustrates how families are at risk and how family enrichment can be used in intervention as well as prevention programmes for families.

The high rate of marital breakdown and the growing trend of serial monogamy means that fewer and fewer children have the opportunity of growing up in stable and predictable family settings. Large numbers of children spend at least some years of their lives in one-parent families. For example, before they reach the age of 18, two out of three children born in the United States in 1993 could expect to live in a single-parent household.[27]

The following statistics are illustrative:

One out of four households in the United States is headed by a single parent with one or more children;

Nine out of ten (90 per cent) single-parent families are headed by the mother;

The United States has more than 14 million single parents;

The Census Bureau of the United States estimates that more than six out of every 10 children born in the mid-1990s will live in a single-parent home before they reach their eighteenth birthday.*

In a controversial collection of articles, *The Atlantic Monthly* took to task those who propose that single-parent families are as adequate for children as two-parent families. Boldly stated on the cover of the April 1993 issue was the statement: "After decades of public dispute about so-called family diversity, the evidence from social-science research is coming in: The dissolution of two-parent families, though it may benefit the adults involved, is harmful to many children, and dramatically undermines our society."[28] Moreover, the author, Barbara Dafoe Whitehead, argues that, "Family diversity in the form of an increasing number of single-parent and step-parent families does not strengthen the social fabric but, rather, dramatically weakens and undermines society".

The current situation is not encouraging. Children in single-parent families are two to three times as likely to have emotional or behavioural problems. They are two and a half times as likely to give birth out of wedlock. According to an article in The Atlantic Monthly, the out-of-wedlock birth rate jumped from 5 per cent in 1960 to 27 per cent in 1990.[28]

Often the parent who is parenting alone is experiencing considerable emotional stress. The trauma of divorce often means that a child has to

---

* Marriage and divorce statistics are from the Barna Research Group and taken from research studies the Group has conducted over the past decade and from data accumulated and reported by the National Center for Health Statistics in Washington, D.C. in a statistical abstract of the United States for 1991.

deal with parting company with one parent and sometimes adjusting to a step-parent, as well as to any other children brought into the new family circle created by a new marriage. Such changes can be traumatic experiences and result in the loss of security. While children suffer if their parents' marriages break up, they also suffer in homes where their parents are together but in conflict.

Judith Wallerstein, one of the pioneer researchers on the long-term psychological impact of family disruption on children, states that parent-child relationships are permanently altered by divorce in ways that society has not anticipated. She writes, "Divorce is deceptive. Legally it is a single event, but psychologically it is a chain ... sometimes a never-ending chain ... of events, relocations, and radically shifting relationships strung through time; a process that forever changes the lives of the people involved".

Five years after their parents had divorced, more than a third of the children experienced moderate or severe depression and performance problems in school, had trouble in establishing meaningful friendships, exhibited chronic responses to the resulting loneliness and feelings of rejection, and had unrealistic hopes of parental reconciliation.[29]

Wallerstein's research which was published in 1989 and summarized in The Atlantic Monthly, gives a sobering picture of divorce: "The child of divorce faces many additional psychological burdens in addition to the normative tasks of growing up."

By any measure, the disruptive and damaging effects of familial breakdown underscores the need to give families both intervention and preventive support. In an initial crisis as a result of divorce, death or an unwanted pregnancy, remedial supports are needed. Help is also needed with ongoing issues faced by families at risk as well as in developing strong marriages, educating for parenthood, and implementing early intervention when families are at risk.

Intervention

Intervention-based programmes are needed to deal with family crises such as a divorce, domestic violence or the death of one's partner. This is comparable to the hospital emergency room or intensive-care treatment. Offering this kind of support can help the affected parties stabilize their lives and ensure that basic protection and material needs are met.

Intervention programmes such as divorce-recovery workshops, emergency financial aid, and, where abuse is an issue, the provision and protection of safe houses or shelters of safety are necessary and required.

In any intervention programme, the goal is to sustain and move the individual or family towards self-sufficiency. If this goal is achieved, the economic cost to the State of such interventions is more than returned. Empowered healthy families have a potential to contribute to society that is not present in families with problems.

Enrichment

Examples of the community services that fall under enrichment programmes are providing parenting support groups and providing family-life education and short-term shelter services that help families in need with tasks and everyday necessities. Community services may include financial planning and food and baby-sitting cooperatives offered in a variety of ways.

Supportive networks, strategies on how to stay in touch with grandparents and other relatives, child care, tips for economical shopping, and even short-term financial support are all areas that may need to be provided for families at risk. Questionnaire research and other methods are indispensable in identifying current family needs.

While intervention and family enrichment programmes are vital, ultimately preventative measures must be emphasized so that families are able to avoid some of those problems requiring intervention.

Models for family and parent enrichment programmes exist that can be used in both prevention and intervention. One such programme, MOM's & DAD's Support Group,* has been used in schools, churches, businesses and organizations in Europe, Hong Kong and the United States.

Challenge to action

In this period of profound technological advances and unprecedented change, the family supports of the past are insufficient for meeting the

---

[1] MOM's & DAD's Support Group is a video-based curriculum designed for small groups of parents to help them prepare for the adolescent years of their children. At this high-stress time of family life, it is easy for parents to feel inadequate, frustrated and lonely. Such a parenting support group can help to counteract these feelings by teaching skills for building positive parent-child relationships and providing a support network. MOM's & DAD's includes a video series with practical tips for building positive family relationships. Small group discussions follow the video presentations that are geared to the specific needs of parents of adolescents in Western cultures. The small group provides an opportunity for parents to network with other parents and to support and encourage one another. These programmes have been successful in part because they are easily transferable and are parent-led. Characteristically, family enrichment involves active participation in carefully designed interactions and learning skills such as decision-making, problem-solving and conflict resolution as well as general open discussions about topics of concern to the participants. Family enrichment programmes provide parents with a network of supportive friendships and basic help in building strong relationship with their children. They give hope, help and encouragement.

familial needs of the present. Humankind is able to send people to the moon, to travel faster than the speed of sound, to fax information halfway across the world in seconds and to access think-tanks with computers, but lacks the interpersonal competencies needed to build loving relationships. Action on both the personal, local, national and international levels to make family wellness a priority needs to be encouraged.

Community-based, family-life education and enrichment programmes supported by policies, human and economic resources can contribute in major ways to the development of healthy families, and to building the smallest unit in democracy at the heart of society. Action for programmes and services to foster the healthy development of families must be a priority supported by individuals, families, Governments and non-governmental organizations. The future depends upon humankind taking responsibility immediately for this change in priorities from an emphasis on therapy to promoting healthy development.

Epilogue

The family and world peace*

"World peace". How easily those words fall from one's lips, and how eagerly and hopefully they come from one's heart, but in one's mind one must wrestle with the almost superhuman challenge of dealing with the persistent and ever-widening question: "How can this be?"

First, one must recognize that the question of world peace has become more urgent than ever before. Ten years ago, the author of the present epilogue and her late husband wrote in their Marriage Enrichment Newsletter:

"For the first time in human history, we possess instruments of war that could destroy the human race. In the past it was fists, then clubs, then spears, then bows and arrows, then rifles, then shells - and now nuclear bombs.

"But the human factor remains the same - from a quarrel in the kitchen to an argument at the work place, from a confrontation in the street to a feud between opposing families, from clans and tribes raiding each other to nations at war."

In the 10 years since these words were written, how have humans dealt with these increasing threats in their lives? Are they living in complacent

---

* Prepared by Vera Mace, who with her late husband, David Mace, worked for marriage enrichment during their 57 years of marriage. They became joint executive directors of the American Association for Marriage and Family Therapy and founded the Association of Couples in Marriage Enrichment in 1973. Having written numerous books and conducted workshops and seminars throughout the world, the Maces are known and respected throughout the world for their pioneering work in marriage and family enrichment. In her retirement, Vera Mace continues to write and influence families around the world.

acceptance? In a mood of doomed inevitability? In increasing helplessness? In fearful and overwhelming despair? There are no short answers to these questions, because the causes and effects of war are too numerous and too varied to list in a short paper. However, when reduced to their lowest common denominator, the questions focus on the fact that a breakdown in human relationships is basic to them all. So it is imperative to consider human relationships.

Patterns of human relationships have changed widely and deeply throughout the world, particularly in the last hundred years. But one factor has remained unchanged and universal, the complete dependence of all human life on relationships. A child is conceived as a result of a human relationship (even in the exceptional case of artificially contrived conception), and before birth is dependent for survival on a relationship with the mother. After birth, the child must learn to live with others, its own family of origin one hopes.

The potential for learning how "to live peace" starts from day one of a person's life. So many factors determine what form emerging family relationships will take - nurture, culture, experience, individual endowments and disposition - but through all of them the child is learning how to live. Confucius, the Chinese philosopher of the fifth century B.C. is reputed to have said:

"When there is love in the marriage, there is harmony in the home; when there is harmony in the home there is contentment in the community; when there is contentment in the community there is prosperity in the nation; when there is prosperity in the nation there is peace in the world."

The message of the present chapter is that in that kind of family, multiplied astronomically, the hope may lie of human beings ever achieving world peace.

Does this mean, therefore, that those persons who are no longer in families with children must wait until other generations can produce new families wholly dedicated to learning and promoting peace from the beginning of life? Happily, no. In his Foreword to Thich Nhat Hanh's book, the Dalai Lama says:

"Peace must first be developed within an individual. And I believe that love, compassion, and altruism are the fundamental bases for peace. Once these qualities are developed within an individual, he or she is then able to create an atmosphere of peace and harmony. This atmosphere can be expanded and extended from the individual to his family, from the family to the community and eventually to the whole world."[30]

This brings world peace right into the orbit of every person. In Thich Nhat Hanh's words: "The roots of war are in the way we live our daily lives - the way we develop our industries, build up our society, and consume goods."[31]

Thich Nhat Hanh then urges his readers "to look deeply" into their living in these areas so they may transcend their tendency to blame and take sides in situations of conflict and learn understanding, particularly of the suffering of "all sides" in any conflict.

Though no individual, however talented, can ever bring peace to the world, each person can create a tiny corner of the world where peace truly reigns. To this end, many people today are seeking, humbly but sincerely, to make their contribution. Over a hundred years ago, Alfred Lord Tennyson wrote:

"For I dipt into the future, far as human eye could see,
Saw the Vision of the world, and all the wonder that would be ...
"Till the war-drum throbbed no longer,
and the battle flags were furl'd.
In the Parliament of man, the Federation of the world."[32]

How far has humankind come since then? Is it travelling in the right direction? A. J. Muste of the Fellowship of Reconciliation put it best when he said, "There is no way to peace; peace is the way".

References

1. Nicholas Stinnett, "Strong families", in *Marriage and Family in a Changing Society*, J. Hemslin and others, eds. (New York, The Free Press, 1992), pp. 496-506.
2. David and Vera Mace, *Close Companions* (New York, Continuum, 1982).
3. Vera Mace, *365 Meditations for Women* (Nashville, Tennessee, Abingdon Press, 1989), pp. 126-127.
4. R. Catalano and P. Dooley, "Economic change in primary prevention", in *Prevention in Mental Health: Research, Policy and Practice*, D. Mace and others, eds. (Beverly Hills, California, Sage, 1983), pp. 21-40.
5. Luciano L'Abate, "Prevention as a profession" in *Prevention in Family Services*, D. Mace and others, eds. (Beverly Hills, California, Sage, 1983), pp. 49-61.
6. Carnegie Corporation of New York, "Foundation President urges action agenda for families and children", press release, 30 July 1992.
7. Ted W. Bowman, "Promoting family wellness : implications and issues", in *Prevention in Family Services*, D. Mace and others, eds. (Beverly Hills, California, Sage, 1983), p. 40.
8. John Bradshaw, *Bradshaw on: The Family* (Deerfield Beach, Florida, Health Communica-tions, 1988).
9. David and Vera Mace, *In the Presence of God* (Philadelphia, The Westminster Press, 1985), p. 9.
10. University of Nebraska-Lincoln, Department of Human Development and Family and Conferences and Institutes, *Building Family Strengths: A Manual for Families* (March, 1986).
11. Nicolas Stinnett, "Strong families: a portrait" in *Prevention in Family Services*, D. Mace and others, eds. (Beverly Hills, California, Sage, 1983), pp. 27-38.
12. Nicholas Stinnett and John DeFrain, *Secrets of Strong Families* (Boston, Little, Brown and Company, 1986).
13. D. Yankelovich, New Rules: *Searching for Fulfillment in a World Turned Upside Down* (New York, Random House, 1981).
14. David Mace, *Prevention in Family Services* (Beverly Hills, California, Sage, 1983).
15. Claudia Arp, *Beating the Winter Blues* (Nashville, Tennessee, Thomas Nelson, 1991).
16. James M. Hemslin, *Marriage and Family in a Changing Society* (New York, The Free Press, 1992).
17. Dave and Claudia Arp, *60 One-Minute Family Builder Series* (Nashville, Tennessee, Thomas Nelson, 1993).
18. H. A. Otto, "The personal and family strength research projects: some implications for the therapist", *Mental Hygiene* No. 48 (1964), pp. 349-450.
19. J. M. Lewis and others, *No Single Thread: Psychological Health in Family Systems* (New York, Brunner/Mazel, 1976).
20. J. M. Lewis, How's Your Family? (New York, Brunner/Mazel, 1979).
21. P. T. Nelson and B. Banonis, "Family concerns and strengths identified at Delaware's White House Conference on Families" in *Family Strengths* 3: Roots of Well-Being (Lincoln, Nebraska, University of Nebraska Press, 1981).
22. David and Vera Mace, Men, *Women and God* (Atlanta, Georgia, John Knox Press, 1976).
23. David Mace, *Love and Anger in Marriage* (Grand Rapids, Michigan, Zondervan, 1982).
24. Claudia Arp, *Almost 13* (Nashville, Tennessee, Thomas Nelson, 1986).
25. Merton and Irene Strommen, *Five Cries of Parents* (New York, Harper & Row, 1985), p. 6.
26. *Men, women and God* ..., p. 23.
27. George Barna, *The Future of the American Family* (Chicago, Illinois, Moody Press, 1993).
28. Barbara Dafoe Whitehead, "Dan Quayle was right", *The Atlantic Monthly* (April 1993), pp. 47-84.
29. Judith Wallerstein and Sandra Blakeslee, *Second Chances* (New York, Ticknor & Fiends, 1989), p. xvii.
30. Thich Nhat Hanh, *Peace is Every Step* (New York, Bantam Books, 1991), p. vii.
31. Ibid., p. 115.
32. Alfred Lord Tennyson, *The Works of Alfred Lord Tennyson* (London, Macmillan and Co. Ltd., 1897).

Partnership FAMILIES

Introduction*

In a recent speech, the Coordinator for the International Year of the Family referred to Virginia Satir's remark that if it were possible to heal the family, it would be possible to heal the world. He added, "This vision of family as the heart of the world's problems and at the Rubicon of its salvation is at once provocative, puzzling, frightening and hopeful".[1] This vision is provocative because of its simplicity, puzzling because it may be difficult to understand, frightening because it brings the problems of the world into an intimate domain and hopeful because the task of healing a family seems easier than that of trying to heal the whole world. Consequently, it seems important to examine the role of the family as a possible cause of the world's problems. Only then is it possible to see the family at the Rubicon of the world's salvation.

Building the smallest democracy at the heart of society

The family is the social microcosm that both creates and reflects the strengths and weaknesses of the larger social structures. The family, as the basic building block of society, is also the primary agent of socialization and acculturation. The family experience may be so powerful in shaping a person's behaviour that it creates an internal construct of reality that is then used to create the external world. From their experiences while growing up in their families, people use what they learn in social institutions, such as schools, businesses and Governments. Individuals who experienced democratic practices in their families are more likely to support, and expect, democratic social institutions, while those who experienced totalitarian practices in their families are likely to tolerate and create totalitarian social structures.

A child must be treated with respect and dignity within the family and be given proper nurturance and support for developing its talents and resources in order to become an adult who helps create and participate in a democratic society. If democratic social structures are to be created, they must be built upon democratic family structures and experiences. Consonant with this principle, the United Nations proclaimed 1994 as the International Year of the Family (IYF).

The motto for IYF, "Building the smallest democracy at the heart of society", recognizes that society sits on a foundation of common values, beliefs and behaviour learned in the family. The values, ideas and forms of

---

* Paper prepared for the IYF secretariat by Janae B. Weinhold and Barry K. Weinhold, Colorado Springs, United States of America.

behaviour of democracy must be taught and modelled in families to create sustainable democratic societies. Several ancient cultures that have been able to build sustainable democratic societies did so by first building democratic families.

One of the best examples of a sustainable democratic society is the Minoan civilization centred on Crete. It flourished for over 1,500 years (3000-1500 B.C.) using peaceful democratic practices such as equal gender relationships and democratic families. No modern civilization has been able to sustain peaceful democratic practices for that length of time. Even earlier than the Minoan civilization (from 7000 to 3500 B.C.) were smaller settlements in parts of south-eastern Europe and in what is now known as Turkey. There archaeological evidence indicates the presence of equal gender relations and peaceful relations with neighbouring settlements. This suggests that those societies used peaceful democratic practices and that their prevailing values emphasized the interrelatedness between humans and between humans and the Earth. More "feminine" in nature, these values stressed peaceful relations, life-giving (peace), nurturance, cooperation and horizontal linking. Social historian, Riane Eisler, who called these ancient cultures "partnership societies", says that people alive today could learn a lot by studying their ways of living.[2]

In Eisler's view, the archaeological findings from settlements flourishing in the Middle East during the period 3500 B.C. to the birth of Jesus Christ indicate that the domination of women by men began to appear during that time. Violent war-like conflicts erupted between neighbouring settlements. She suggests that men began to consider women as chattels: part of the booty of war victories. The value base of societies became more "masculine", emphasizing life-taking (war), intimidation, competition and hierarchical systems. Wandering and gathering societies were gradually replaced first by settlements organized around agriculture, then by city-States and finally by nation-States. This period of history Eisler identifies as the beginning of a "dominator" society, which she says prevails in most of the world today.[2] In her ground-breaking book, *The Chalice and the Blade*, Eisler indicates that the dominator society is currently showing signs of collapse, heralding a possible return to values and relationships based more on partnership.

In the present chapter, the term "partnership families" is used synonymously with the term "democratic families". The partnership-family model is contrasted with the dominator-family model, an expression of which can be seen in the widespread domestic violence in the world. The dominator model is a hierarchical system in which those who are more powerful use violence and threats of violence to exploit, victimize and control those who are weaker. Dominator-family structures are so common in many parts of the world that they are regarded as the only acceptable parenting model and are often accepted as the healthy and appropriate way of organizing a family. Recent research has focused on the dysfunctional aspects of the prevailing dominator model of family life and on how this model is self-perpetuating.[3,4,5,6,7,8] Some estimates suggest that almost all Western families (97 per cent) contain some elements of the dominator model.[6,7]

Domination and violence in families

Although violence has been visibly present throughout recorded history in the form of wars and violent conflicts between and within tribes, religious groups, racial and ethnic groups and nation-States, only recently has the amount of violence that exists within families become apparent. For example, a recent survey conducted in the United States estimates that 6.9 million children per year are gravely assaulted by their parents and that between 1.9 and 2.1 million women are the victims of severe violence at the hands of their partners.[9] Abuse of elderly persons in the United States by a member of their family is estimated to be as high as 2.5 million per year.[10] Another study from the United States concludes that "children may be the most violent family members", finding that over 29 million children a year commit one or more acts of violence towards a sibling in the family, with 19 million of these attacks being severe enough to be considered assaults if they had occurred outside the family.[11]

In both developed and developing countries, over half of all murders occur in the family. Most of the victims are women and female children. Since family violence is still not a category used in the official statistics of most countries, the true extent of family violence is not known. Added to this are traditional practices, such as female infanticide (often camouflaged by underreported birthrates), dowry deaths (often listed as suicides), the burning of women (classified as accidental deaths) and genital mutilation (categorized as a religious ceremony), producing a more complete picture of family violence. As many as 90 million girls may have had a clitorectomy performed on them by their mothers and grandmothers, according to researchers in Africa and the Middle East.[12] While there been no large-scale surveys in the developing countries to determine the level of family violence, some research has been begun in these areas. Preliminary results of limited surveys in Bangladesh, Chile, Colombia, India, Nigeria, New Guinea and

Zimbabwe reveal high levels of family violence against women.[13]

In some parts of the world, the family still operates as a sanctuary outside the laws of society. This often permits violent practices to exist within the family without offering much protection for its members, who are often subjected to cruel and inhumane physical, emotional and sexual abuse. Children and women are usually the targets of an abusive, dominating male, but in some families the mother may act out the dominating role on her children, passing on the cruelty that she has experienced in a society that does not give her equal rights with men. In either case, children are often threatened with severe punishment or physical abandonment if they tell anyone else about what is happening inside their family. Children usually will not do anything that might jeopardize the security of their family, no matter how bad their existence in it is. Even where laws protect women and children from abuse in families, evidence suggests that only about one in 10 cases is ever reported and few of these result in the punishment of the offender.[13]

Drawing on their long experience of clinical research and practice, the authors believe that violence in families and in the world is the result of the mismanagement of a natural human impulse known as the "talionic response".[14] The talionic response occurs naturally in the development of a child. If a child is not trained to manage this primitive response effectively by understanding and sensitive adults, it will probably develop violent or aggressive means for handling frustration and conflict.

Two Forms of Families: dominator and partnership

The list below summarizes the main characteristics of these two contrasting models of family life.[8]

Dominator families	*Partnership families*
COMPETITIVE STRUCTURES	COOPERATIVE STRUCTURES
MISUSE OF POWER	EQUITABLE USE OF POWER
NO EQUAL RIGHTS	EQUAL RIGHTS
FAMILY SECRETS	OPEN COMMUNICATION, NO SECRETS
RIGID AND COMPULSIVE RULES	FLEXIBLE RULES
RIGID GENDER ROLES	FLEXIBLE GENDER ROLES
NO SHARING OF HOUSEWORK	HOUSEWORK SHARED EQUITABLY
NO JOINT FAMILY ACTIVITIES	PLANNED FAMILY ACTIVITIES
ECONOMIC "BURDENS" UNSHARED	ECONOMIC RESPONSIBILITY SHARED

NO RESPECT FOR PERSONAL PRIVACY	RESPECT FOR PERSONAL PRIVACY
WIN-LOSE CONFLICT RESOLUTION	WIN-WIN CONFLICT RESOLUTION
NO SHARED DECISION-MAKING	SHARED DECISION-MAKING
NO SHARED PARENTING	PARENTING SHARED EQUITABLY
NO SUPPORT FOR FEELINGS	ALL FEELINGS ARE ACCEPTED
DISCIPLINE BY VIOLENCE AND SHAME	DISCIPLINE BASED ON RESPECT AND TRUST
MISTAKES NOT ADMITTED	MISTAKES ADMITTED
NO APOLOGIES GIVEN	APOLOGIES MADE WHEN NEEDED
PROBLEMS BLAMED ON OTHERS	PERSONAL RESPONSIBILITY FOR PROBLEMS
RESISTANCE TO "OUTSIDERS"	OPENNESS TO OUTSIDERS
LOYALTY TO FAMILY BASED ON "DUTY"	LOYALTY TO FAMILY BASED ON TRUST
RESISTANCE TO CHANGE	OPENNESS TO CHANGE
NO FAMILY UNITY	COHESIVE FAMILY UNIT
NO PROTECTION FROM ABUSIVE ACTS	MEMBERS FEEL SAFE, PROTECTED
CONFLICTS ARE IGNORED	CONFLICTS ARE RESOLVED IMMEDIATELY
LITTLE OR NO LAUGHTER OR JOY	FAMILY IS SEEN AS A SOURCE OF JOY
CHILDREN UNPLANNED AND UNWANTED	CHILDREN PLANNED AND WANTED

No family has all of the characteristics of either model; however, the characteristics of the dominator model are far more common in families in most countries of the world than those of the partnership model. As long as this is true, creating and sustaining democratic societies will be difficult or perhaps even impossible.

Seeking the Causes of Violence: a review of theoretical models

A number of theories have emerged to try to explain the causes of the violence men exhibit towards the women and children in their families. Both theorists and researchers have been searching for common threads that can be tied together in a meta-theory to predict which personal characteristics and social conditions are most likely to produce individuals with violent behaviour. To date no such unifying theory has been found. Most of the current theories and research can be grouped into two main theoretical frameworks.

The first set of theories, the most popular, seeks to find the origins of violent behaviour in the personal inadequacies of men and in the external stresses that cause them to act in dominating ways. For example, these theorists and researchers have focused their attention on such factors as alcoholism, a violent upbringing, mental illness or an addiction to another person (known as co-dependency). Added to this, the factors that have been studied include life stresses, impulse control and blocked goals that result from unemployment or poverty. Finally ethnicity, social class or lack of education have been identified as possible causes of forms of dominator behaviour. In study after study, the results show clearly that all these factors contribute in some important ways to the problem, but that they are not necessarily causal factors in themselves. These factors have to be taken seriously and must be examined more closely to identify the root causes of violent behaviour and understand the complex interaction of these contributing factors.

The second set of theories grows out of the realization that violence towards women is increasing and the awareness that earlier theories have failed to explain or account for the variability of these forms of violent behaviour. The common thread in this set of theories is a belief that the root cause of violent behaviour lies in the structure of the society itself. According to this set of theories, domestic violence is a reflection of broad social structures containing gender and economic inequalities. In this analysis, forms of dominator behaviour are not an aberration, but rather "... an affirmation of a particular social order"[15] that regards women as less important and less valuable than men and therefore does not offer them the same rights and privileges as men. For example, society may indirectly condone domestic violence because it protects the rights of privacy and the autonomy of the family more than it protects the rights of women and children. In many parts of the world, the right of the man to rule over the women and children in his own home is accepted. In this context, domestic violence is seen clearly as an acceptable way of maintaining social control.

Looking at domestic violence from this viewpoint has produced equally promising results. While the analysis of domestic violence as a structural problem began in the industrialized countries, recent studies from developing countries have confirmed the presence of cultural beliefs about women that support domination. Studies from India suggest that domestic violence is a by-product of a societal structure where authority lies with the male and the female is conditioned to accept a secondary role.[16] A Chinese study similarly identified a prevailing male-centred ideology where the husband has the right to abuse his wife if something is not done to his satisfaction. This includes his wife giving birth to a girl instead of a boy.[17] African surveys reveal a prevailing belief that a husband who beats his wife loves her. She expects to be beaten and will feel rejected if she is not beaten.[18] Other studies from developing countries show that violence occurs if the man wishes to take another wife, if he suspects his wife of infidelity and if he sees her as rebellious or if he considers that she nags him.[13]

This analysis is helpful by providing a broader context for understanding the causes of domestic violence, but again it does not sufficiently account for the variability of it. Violence against women and children is common but not universal. For example, a recent survey of societies in different regions of the world found that domestic violence was rare or absent in 15 of the 90 societies surveyed.[19] The study failed to identify any common structural elements clearly separating violent from non-violent societies, suggesting that a variable such as structural inequality may not be the basic cause of domestic violence that some theorists and researchers have thought it was. Certainly, inequality is an important context for understanding much about domestic violence, but it may still not explain how sociological and cultural factors, such as structural inequality, interact with individual personal behaviour.

What is needed is a perspective that brings together the theories that focus on the personal characteristics of people who commit domestic violence with the theories that propose the structural elements of a society as the primary cause of domestic violence. The present chapter presents an integrative perspective.

Integrating clinical research and social policy

Developing a psycho-social perspective to the problem is necessary to bring the two diverse theories together. This perspective permits the researcher to identify similar psychological processes that begin with the individual and reappear in more complex social systems such as couples and families.

First it is necessary to identify the psychological processes that characterize the development of the individual so they can be recognized in the development of couples, families and social or political organizations. Then re-examine all social policies and legislation to determine whether they support or inhibit the development of partnership families. Without an integrated approach that examines both the psychological and the social structures, the processes needed to create partnership families are unlikely to be understood or promoted effectively.

One such psycho-social attempt to analyse the consciousness of humans from both a personal and historical perspective is known as "psychohistory".[20,21] The basic premise of psychohistory is that every form of consciousness that emerges in the evolution of a person is also apparent in the history of the human species. This interactive process between the individual and the collective means that the limits of collective consciousness rest at the point reached by a critical mass of individuals. It also means that for an individual to extend his or her consciousness beyond the limits of the collective consciousness is difficult.

Other psycho-social approaches, including family systems theories,[22] information theories,[23] general systems theories,[24] psychodynamic developmental theories[25] and mind-body meta-theories,[26,27,28] propose a new understanding of how human systems grow and change. Most psycho-social theories support the notion that the early development greatly influences each individual, both socially and psychologically. If the early experiences are positive and support the fullest expression of the self, then the child will probably become an adult capable of altruistic values and behaviour. If the early experiences are negative or traumatic, then the child will probably become an adult who, out of necessity, focuses both on avoiding further traumas and on finding ways of inflicting trauma on others. This process is most likely at the heart of the psychological need to dominate.

Early childhood trauma is passed on to others primarily through intimate family and social relationships in identifiable and predictable patterns of adaptive behaviour involving abuse, neglect and abandonment. These individual adaptive patterns are carried into the social structure that people create: families, schools, churches, Governments and nation-States. From this perspective, it is possible to evaluate the evolution of any social structure using this individual baseline. It is also possible to see how these social structures contribute to the creation of intergenerational patterns of adaptive and abusive forms of behaviour.

Unintentional child abuse, which may begin during gestation and birth, is repeated in early childhood by parents and others seeking to act out their talionic response. The unconscious need of a person to take revenge by inflicting on others the hurt that he or she has experienced is recognized as the deepest and most ancient of responses and is behind the statement in the Bible, "An eye for an eye and a tooth for a tooth."[29] This impulse is probably responsible for most of the violence and cruelty in the history of humans.

The drive to victimize others sets up a pattern of victimization and perpetration that is called the "vicious cycle of cruelty".[7] Until very recently, the talionic response existed inside a vicious cycle of cruelty that was woven right into the social and legal fabric of society. In the Middle Ages, wrote Nietzsche,

"... to behold suffering gave pleasure ... a royal wedding or great public celebration would have been incomplete without executions, tortures or *autos-*

da-fé ... there was scarcely a noble household without some person whose office it was to serve as a butt for everyone's malice and cruel teasing."[30]

As these public expressions of the talionic response fell out of popular use, the impulse was internalized within the family by advocating socially sanctioned cruelty in child-rearing practices. Many books and authorities in the eighteenth and nineteenth centuries told parents that if they broke the will of children as early as possible "... by means of scolding and the rod, they will have obedient, docile and good children."[31] Elements of this expression of the talionic response is still found in many families, often supported externally by religious dogma or by so-called assertive discipline methods used in some schools.

Because humans are equipped with an innate drive for wholeness, they are unconsciously driven to find ways of healing these early psychological traumas. Since the original traumas occurred in intimate relationships, people seek to heal them in subsequent intimate relationships. People marry, have children, form groups and organizations and build nation-States as unconscious attempts to heal their early individual and collective traumas. Thus, a primary purpose of all relationships is to heal the effects of these traumas and achieve wholeness.[8]

Unfortunately, most people are unaware of their victimization as children. As a result, they are unable to stop the cycle of perpetration. When people are aware of their own victimization as a child, however, they often are able to stop the cycle. By understanding the healing purpose of intimate relationships, they are able to work together consciously and cooperatively heal their traumas and create new patterns of intimate relationships. Once people understand how to organize all their relationships to accomplish this, it will lead to a collective leap in human consciousness and in the evolution of the human species.

Stages of Human Development

Each individual must successfully pass through four psycho-social stages to achieve full self-development: co-dependence, counter-dependence, independence and interdependence. These stages have emerged from extensive research in developmental psychology[25] and recent research findings from prenatal and perinatal psychology.[32,33] The research has helped to identify the crucial developmental tasks that must be completed during each of these stages. Each stage requires the individual to complete successfully certain key developmental tasks before moving on to the next stage. If a key task is not completed successfully, it is carried along as excess baggage into the next stage where it can impede further development. These incomplete tasks continue to be recycled in people's lives until they have been completed.

Co-dependent stage

The co-dependent stage of development begins at conception. Because a foetus is totally dependent on the physical, emotional and nutritional condition of its mother, human trauma often begins in the womb. If the causes of foetal trauma were understood, however, it would be possible to reduce and maybe even eliminate prenatal trauma by having pregnant women avoid activities such as smoking, drinking alcohol, taking drugs or powerful medicines and by avoiding eating unhealthful foods.

The key developmental task of the co-dependent stage is bonding and attachment. Mothers who feel bonded to their unborn children and understand that their prenatal activities affect them do everything they can to prevent harm to the foetus. Many things can interfere with the completion of bonding and attachment prior to the child's birth. Economic difficulties, relationship problems between the parents, illness or a death in the family and other problems that remove the parents' attention from the unborn child will interfere with the bonding process. A mistaken belief that a developing foetus is unaware of environmental influences in the family also contributes to poor parent-child bonding. The biochemical systems of the mother and child are much more interconnected than once thought. Changes in the levels of adrenalin and noradrenalin because of maternal stress or intakes of caffeine or alcohol by the mother are felt almost immediately by the unborn child.[34]

The birth process itself can be traumatic. Leboyer's pioneering work showed that the birth trauma could be lessened and perhaps healed in children who were born in a dark, quiet room, given skin-to-skin contact immediately after birth and then laid in warm water to be massaged by the father. Leboyer's follow-up research indicated that these children grew up to display more peaceful personalities. Perinatal research has shown clearly that the optimal bonding period between mother and child and between father and child is the first 12 to 36 hours after birth.[35] The child requires extensive skin-to-skin contact during that time in order to activate the neurotransmitters in the brain and the nervous system. Infants must also be touched and talked to in loving ways, be held and sung to and mirrored effectively by their parents for solid bonding and attachment to occur. Early weaning or the absence of breast-feeding can also negatively affect bonding.

Premature or Caesarean births or other kinds of complications that produce a prolonged separation between mother and child shortly after birth also interfere with the bonding process. The serious illness of a child at birth can cause its parents to withdraw from bonding to protect themselves emotionally in case the child might die. A newborn child can safely endure a separation from its mother of only a day or two without suffering a lasting trauma.[36]

Experiences of neglect, abandonment or abuse during this period not only interfere with the trust-building process but also activate feelings of "abandonment rage."[14] The child's experiences during the co-dependent stage create a foundation for meeting the challenging experiences of the next stage of development. If the task of bonding is not completed successfully, it is difficult for the individual to complete the key tasks of exploration and emotional separation during the counter-dependent stage.

Counter-dependent stage

In the counter-dependency stage, the child has to complete two important developmental tasks. The first task is to pull away successfully from the constraints of the symbiotic relationship with the mother and form a separate, autonomous identity. The second is to learn to manage the feelings of frustration and pain encountered when the parents, and then the world, set limits. Both of these tasks typically activate responses of frustration and rage from the child. Because the rage is a natural response to these limits, it is important for adults to respond gently but firmly to the child's feelings. Temper tantrums and other forms of emotional outbursts must be accepted as normal and inevitable for a child on the way to emotional separation.

If the parents punish the child for these emotional outbursts by using corporal punishment, shame or humiliation, the child may suffer further wounds and experience a fear of annihilation. Rage then becomes a protective mechanism against this fear. This protective mechanism combines with any earlier feelings of rage from abandonment or from experiences of limitation, so by the age of three some children already have a reservoir full of unexpressed rage from these three sources.

Unexpressed rage from these three sources may cause the child to decide to avoid at all costs anything that activates the fear of annihilation. In this decision-making process, the child also usually resolves to take revenge on those responsible for inflicting the pain when he or she becomes big enough. This decision-making point is where the child instinctively reacts with the talionic response to defend itself against threats of annihilation. At this early age the response becomes woven into the character of the child as a survival mechanism. Because it is so deeply ingrained into the personality structure, to remove or change it later in life is difficult without some sort of external help through therapy or other interventions that penetrate deep into the individual's psyche.

Ideally, the needs of the child during the first two years of life should be met as completely as possible, for it is during this period that the child develops the ability to trust. Constancy and consistency from care-givers during this time provides the child with a solid foundation for beginning the next stage of development.

Unfortunately, most parents have not dealt with their own traumas before becoming parents, so they unconsciously try to use their relationship with their newborn infant to heal their own wounds. This makes it difficult for them to function effectively as parents and makes it more likely they will say and do things that traumatize the child. By becoming aware of the sources of their own traumas and by consciously forming adult relationships in which they can help each other heal their traumas, parents more likely will be able to help their children heal the foetal and birth traumas. This is how parents can provide their children with the foundation they need to develop their fullest capacities, teach them that this is the true purpose of relationships and support them in consciously forming their own relationships with this purpose.

A child who receives this kind of parenting will learn how to manage the talionic impulse in healthy ways and to release and direct whatever aggression remains in self-assertive efforts to develop mastery and autonomy. A child capable of managing this impulse will be able to trust and use effectively its own internal resources, rather than having to suppress or control the desire for revenge. When parents understand how to help their children do this, children will grow up without needing to take revenge or defend themselves against a fear of annihilation.

Instead, throughout history parents have created religious and civil laws or practices to legitimize the expression of their talionic impulses towards their children. Expressions such as "spare the rod and spoil the child" were probably used to hide this cruelty. Laws protecting the sanctity of the family were also used to keep society from interfering with abusive practices in the home unless they disturbed the public tranquillity.

The history of childhood reads like a horror story. Until recently no laws existed to protect the rights or the welfare of children. A recent review of the research findings on incest and the sexual exploitation of children showed clearly that these are universal phenomena widely practised in most cultures and in some cases tacitly sanctioned by religious and governmental institutions.[37] The dominator culture that supports the dominator family clearly pays only lip service to the basic rights of children.

Independent stage

During the independent stage of development (from the ages of three to six), the child seeks to become more and more emotionally autonomous and learns to master day-to-day skills of self-care. If the foundation of bonding is weak, the child will be consumed by fears and limit its mastery to a few essential things. If, in addition, little support is provided for exploration and separation, or if its efforts are punished, the child will not trust its own ability to be autonomous and constantly look to others for help and validation.

Interdependent stage

Only with the successful completion of bonding, separation and self-mastery in the three previous stages, will the child move fully to the interdependent stage (from the ages of six to 18). The major developmental task of this stage is learning the cooperation and negotiation skills needed to resolve conflicts and meet important needs.

Without a self that has been constructed during the previous three stages, true cooperation and negotiation are not possible. In distorted form, cooperation becomes taking care of the needs of others with the expectation of reciprocal caretaking. Negotiation becomes distorted into forms of manipulative behaviour for getting one's own way. The successful completion of all four stages is necessary for the creation of partnership families.

Major cultural differences in the parenting practices appear to nurture and support the completion of these developmental tasks. In more "child-centred" cultures, bonding with the children appears to be solid, but these cultures often lack similar practices that nurture and support exploration and separateness for the children.

For example, in a study of bonding practices in Kenya and Uganda,[38] Geber found that children were born at home and were never separated from the mother, who carried them unswaddled in a sling next to her breasts. Mothers massaged, caressed, sung to and fondled their children continually. They slept with the child and allowed it to breast-feed on demand. The mother knew instinctively when the child had to urinate and defecate and would take the child to the bushes when necessary. Geber found that these children were the most precocious, brilliant and advanced infants ever observed anywhere. They smiled contentedly from the fourth day after birth. When compared with European or American children, they were months ahead on all scales of development. These gains held steady as the children crawled, walked and talked, and advanced continuously far beyond Western children until the age of four.

Then, according to tribal custom, they were sent away to live in another village, never to see their family again. As a result, their psycho-social development was arrested. Severe depression developed and the children were totally overwhelmed by this trauma, unable to continue the developmental gains they had made earlier.

By contrast, many of the developed countries are less "child centred". They attempt to move the child out of the bonding stage as quickly as possible, often before the child is ready. This causes the child "to act separate" or independently when really it is filled with fear and uncertainty. This attempt to end the bonding stage prematurely can give rise to forms of addictive behaviour in adults as they seek substitutes to fill the psychological hole left by incomplete bonding. Addictions to substances such as food, alcohol or drugs are seen in this context as adaptive attempts to meet bonding deficits.

Because the knowledge of how to help children complete these important developmental tasks in childhood is so new, few adults alive today have successfully completed all the tasks of all four stages. The largest group still have unmet bonding needs from the first stage; most of the others are still learning to become emotionally separate and functionally autonomous. The few people who have completed these tasks are working on mastering emotional independence or working on developing forms of interdependent behaviour.

Since all incomplete developmental tasks are carried forward and continue to recirculate in peoples' lives, individuals can identify gaps in their developmental history at any age and then complete successfully these key psychological tasks.[8,39] Based on their clinical research, the authors of the present chapter have created clinical procedures and educational programmes to assist people in completing these tasks. The miracle of the developmental approach is that it is never too late for anyone to learn more effective ways of managing the talionic response as a defence and to develop other non-violent responses.

Moving from Dominator to Partnership Families

Few parents welcome a child into their lives expecting to become violent or abusive towards that child. Most parents see the newborn child as innocent and lovable and are able to create positive fantasies about its future. What happens within a family that instead makes this child a target of abuse and violence? What is it in the experience of family that activates the talionic impulse and then weaves it into the fabric of intimate family relationships?

Again, the answer seems to be systemic. Early in the evolution of humankind, the talionic impulse emerged and became accepted as part of human nature. It was then woven into the fabric of the culture by being institutionalized as various forms of socially sanctioned violence and cruelty. The vicious cycle of cruelty has provided a needed outlet for countless generations of people unable to manage their talionic impulses without resorting to abuse or violence. How can we stop this destructive cycle? This vicious cycle of cruelty can be stopped if parents are willing:

- A To learn as much as they can about the world of childhood, the nature of the child within each of them and the nature of the needs and feelings of children;
- B To learn where they have narcissistic wounds that interfere with their parenting and take the necessary steps to heal these wounds, rather than pass them on to their children;
- C To listen to and accept the needs and feelings their children express;
- D To set limits without using corporal punishment, shame or humiliation.

This destructive cycle can be stopped in two ways. The first involves helping adults learn how to heal the psychological wounds and how to manage their talionic response in non-violent ways. The second involves preventing the problem by teaching adults how to parent their children effectively so they will learn how to manage their violent impulses.

The step-by-step psycho-social process developed by the authors and summarized below describes how people can heal their psychological wounds from childhood and learn how to manage their talionic response effectively.[6,7]

1. **Become aware of conflicts, negative forms of behaviour and destructive relationship patterns**
    - A Identify early betrayals, abandonments, abuse and other traumatic events from childhood;
    - B Identify reoccurring themes related to these events;
    - C Identify addictive or compulsive forms of behaviour learned from the family of origin.
2. **Identify the unfinished relationship issues from childhood**
    - A Identify psychological wounds;
    - B Identify any unmet developmental needs from childhood that are causing problems in current relationships.
3. **Express the unexpressed core feelings related to these psychological wounds**
    - A Find safe, supportive relationships where feelings can be expressed in non-violent ways;

B Receive validation for childhood experiences from these friends;
   C Develop effective self-protective and self-nurturing skills.
4. **Contract with friends to receive help in completing these unfinished relationship issues**
   A Create cooperative healing contracts that complete these old issues;
   B Establish a therapeutic relationship, if necessary, to complete these issues;
   C Create regular self-nurturing activities;
   D Develop assertive communication skills to satisfy needs met and to resolve conflicts cooperatively.
5. **Develop autonomous forms of behaviour**
   A Set limits and healthy boundaries without using violence or shame;
   B Confront and change self-limiting beliefs;
   C Develop mastery in self-care and self-nurturing;
   D Reclaim personal responsibility for reaching life goals.
6. **Develop a programme of physical care**
   A Eat consciously to provide good nutritional support;
   B Exercise regularly;
   C Get structural body work to help break through the patterns stored in the body.
7. **Develop a spiritual life**
   A Use prayer, meditation and other spiritual practices to develop self-mastery;
   B Find a life purpose to help define a personal place in the events of the world;
   C Use forms of high service to others to help fulfil this purpose.
8. **Learn to live in partnership relationships**
   A Create relationships based on the principles of cooperation, negotiation, co-creation, mutual respect and intimacy;
   B Use vocations and hobbies to develop the highest personal potential;
   C Create support systems to develop a more conscious life living consciously with others and with the Earth.

Intimate relationships are one of the best places where people can heal their psychological wounds. Here people can begin to deactivate the talionic impulse by releasing the feelings stored in their emotional reservoirs. Because early conflicts in family relationships are the primary source of wounding, family relationships are the ideal place to begin healing these wounds. The authors have developed a Partnership Model[6] for resolving conflicts. It teaches people how to use conflicts that emerge in their intimate relationships as an opportunity for working cooperatively to heal the wounds they received while growing up in their families of origin. For example, when people involved in a conflict use the Partnership Model, they learn how to disengage from the current discord and to ask themselves the following questions: "Whom does this person remind me of from my past? What unfinished business from my family of origin is trying to get completed here?" Once people are able to articulate possible answers to such questions, they can ask for help from their partner or friend.

The transformation in this process occurs, for example, when the first person says to the second, "When you get angry and yell like that, you remind me of my mother. Then I feel about three years old and get scared. I was never able to yell back at my mother and tell her to shut up. I'd like you to help me complete this old problem with my mother. Would you be willing to play my mother for a few minutes and let me say the things to her that I could never say?" During such cooperative experiences, people find themselves able to help each other heal the past and also deepen the intimacy of the current relationship.

Sometimes a person's reservoir is so full of feelings from childhood experiences of repeated abuse, neglect or abandonment that the individual requires professional help to release the feelings. The authors have developed a system of psycho-therapeutic methods that help people first identify the experiences where their wounds occurred and then release their feelings in healthy and non-destructive ways.

Teaching children how to manage the talionic impulse in healthy ways and to release and direct whatever aggression remains in self-assertive efforts to develop mastery and autonomy must include the development of new parenting practices. This requires the parents to empty their own reservoirs of ill will first so they can serve as role models. Dealing with feelings of rage, violence and hatred within the family requires a new kind of family structure, one in which these important awarenesses are a primary part of the relationship structures between the adults and between the adults and the children.

When intimate family relationships between men and women and between parents and children become a resource for helping each other learn to manage the talionic impulses, the fabric of humanity will begin to change. Practical psycho-social processes, educational programmes for parents and children and effective social and family policies can open the way for healing the developmental traumas that currently block both cultural and personal evolution, providing a basis for an evolutionary leap in consciousness.

Practical Steps for Creating Partnership Families

Family functions can be defined in a variety of ways. The major family functions can be defined around the multiple relationships that exist between and among family members. For example, spouses can be husband and wife, mother and father, lovers, friends, parents, grandparents, business partners in handling the family's finances and have additional relationships with the extended family. This relationship-oriented method of defining family functions was developed in another chapter in this book.[40]

Some major functions of a family are:
A Establishing emotional, social and economic bonds between spouses;
B Providing a framework for procreation and sexual relationships between spouses;
C Exchanging goods and services;
D Protecting family members;
E Giving a name and status to family members, especially to children;
F Providing for the basic care of children, and, in many cultures, of the elderly and of disabled family members;
G Socializing and educating children;
H Providing emotional care, affection and recreation for family members

Establishing emotional, social and economic bonds between spouses

The first step in forming a family is usually some form of commitment between the two adults to live together. They can formalize their commitment by a legal marriage contract or by a less formal agreement to cohabitate. In addition to creating emotional bonds, the relationship establishes social bonds to relatives and in-laws and economic bonds related to common property. In Western cultures, this decision is usually preceded by a period of courtship; however, in some cultures arranged marriages are still common. In the latter situation, the couple need time after the marriage to establish a relationship. Even if there has been a period of courtship before marriage, a couple may still have a period of adjustment after getting married. The bonding stage of a relationship is much like the bonding stage of infancy. The couple needs to devote extensive time to talking in tender, loving ways to each other, touching each other, gazing into each other's eyes and learning to trust each other. In this process any unfinished business from the early bonding stage of each person will emerge as their relationship becomes close enough and safe enough.

For most people, this process is not conscious and, even if it were, they would probably be too embarrassed to admit to their partner what is really going on. They begin to "dream" they have finally found the perfect partner who will provide them with the unconditional love, attention and devotion they missed early in their infancy. This hoped-for "healing" has to be part of what the authors have called love. Each person in a new relationship has the same dilemma: "How can I get my partner to help me heal my wounds from my childhood without my having to admit that I actually still have them?" The approach that a couple uses to resolve this dilemma determines whether they will have a dominator relationship or a partnership relationship.

Dominator relationships

In dominator relationships people deal with this dilemma by trying to manipulate, trick or control their partner into helping them fulfil their unmet needs without ever revealing they have them. This is a difficult if not impossible task. Added to the problem is the fact that while people are using their partner in an attempt to get their needs met, their partner is doing the same thing. What typically happens is that a competitive struggle develops to see whose needs will be more important in the relationship. Suddenly, this kind, loving relationship becomes a competitive struggle that seems to have life-threatening consequences.

This struggle can quickly erase the goodwill and loving feelings that the partners developed early in the relationship. The dream of finally fulfilling their unmet bonding needs is shattered and replaced by a deep sense of betrayal, which touches the latent revenge-oriented talionic impulse. Most couples who have been together for a number of years have created a virtual reservoir of ill will in their relationship. Usually these couples do not have the understanding or the skills to drain the reservoir without some external help. This destructive process is responsible for almost all of the power plays, domestic violence and divorces in relationships as well as much of the hatred and violence that gets played out in the society at large.

Partnership relationships

In partnership relationships, this dilemma is resolved when each person admits that he or she has brought unfinished business into the relationship and then asks each other for help. This sets up a context for developing cooperative structures in the relationship that serve to preserve and enhance the bonds of love and goodwill that are usually present at the beginning of the relationship. If a couple understands that one of the purposes of their relationship is to help each other grow and mature and cooperate with each other so both get their needs met, the love and intimacy between them deepens.

The understanding about this purpose of relationships may have been known for centuries, but it has appeared only recently in the popular literature. However, the popular culture still presents an entirely different picture of relationships through its music, romantic novels and films and television shows. The popular culture inadvertently contributes to the continuance of destructive, dominator relationships in that it portrays relationships in romanticized and idealized ways, hiding this important purpose of relationships.

Practical steps for the creation of a partnership relationship

The steps[8] listed below have been used successfully by hundreds of couples with whom the authors have worked in therapy, classes and workshops. They have also been used by therapists they have trained, who have then used them with couples they have worked with. Other couples have used these steps to transform their relationship after taking a class. Couples who have been married or who have been together for over 10 years often need therapy or a relationship class to help them unravel their interlocking patterns and begin to drain the reservoir of ill will that may have been created in their relationship.

A couple must be willing to make the following series of agreements to begin creating a partnership relationship:

- A To recognize and reveal to each other any unmet developmental needs from childhood they are aware of and have brought to the relationship;
- B To help each other uncover any additional unmet needs that may emerge in a conflict;
- C To cooperate with each other to heal these childhood issues;
- D To stay together during any conflicts that emerge during the healing process;
- E To engage in self-discovery activities such as reading, workshops or therapy;
- F To learn and utilize win-win conflict resolution skills;
- G To ask for what they want directly from their partner;
- H To support equality of power, opportunity and responsibility in the relationship;
- I To tell the truth about their behaviour, feelings and needs;
- J To respect each other's psychological boundaries;
- K To keep all agreements to the best of their ability;
- L To use spiritual tools to support the development of partnership principles in the relationship whenever possible.

Providing a framework for procreation and sexual relationships between spouses

Laws related to marriage and, in some parts of the world, cohabitation are used as a way of regulating and controlling sexual behaviour. In many countries laws regulate the sexual behaviour of unmarried individuals and, in some cases, of married individuals as well. Contraceptives have allowed many people to separate sexuality from procreation, but many people (especially men) still have trouble separating the sexual touch from the non-sexual nurturing touch. This confusion is also one of the defining characteristics of dominator sexual relationships.

Dominator sexual relationships

Sexual relationships are one of the main arenas where people try to dominate others in order to get their needs met. Many people have unmet needs for a non-sexual nurturing touch, but they do not want other people to know about their needs. Instead, they attempt to get their needs met through sexual contact where they hope no one will know their secret. Since they usually do get some touch as part of sex, they decide to settle for that. This usually does not satisfy the need, requiring even more sexual contact, often leading to the creation of a sexual addiction. Using a substitute to meet a need serves only to increase the need and cause the person to become addicted to the activity. An addiction to sex can be difficult to break, particularly when the person does not know the real cause of the addiction.

Addiction to sex can also cause people to become more and more concerned about their sexual performance, hoping to "get it right this time" in order to get satisfaction. Sex is also a common way many men use to dominate women and children physically. Women can also dominate men by using seduction as a weapon. In many dominator families, the sexual abuse of children and spousal rape is common, a distorted and desperate attempt to satisfy unmet needs for touch and intimacy. According to recent estimates, in the United States, 5 out of 10 women and 4 out of 10 men were sexually abused in childhood.[37] Incest is a well-kept secret in many families in both the developed and the developing countries of the world. A recent comprehensive review of the research clearly indicates that incest is a world-wide problem of enormous proportions.[37]

Societal attitudes and behaviour related to sex make it even more difficult to separate the nurturing touch from the sexual touch. In many countries sex is hyped as the way to meet developmental needs. Sex is used in the developed countries in television commercials, advertisements, magazines, books, videos and films to convince people that sex is the only way of getting these needs met. The public responds by spending billions of dollars each year trying to look sexy, smell sexy, taste sexy, feel sexy and act sexy. People will try almost anything to look beautiful, thin and sexy from crash diets to radical surgery to having their bodies reshaped. Sexy female models in provocative poses are used to sell everything from soap to garage-door openers. Even male models are used to sell after-shave lotion, cologne and clothing that will drive women mad with passion. What people are actually buying is not a product but a fantasy. The fantasy, still based on the confusion between the sexual and the nurturing touch, is that if they have enough sex appeal they will attract the right person who will magically meet all their needs and transform their life.

Partnership sexual relationships

Sex is an important part of a partnership relationship, but it is not used to satisfy needs for non-sexual nurturing. When nurturing needs are met in appropriate ways through massage and non-sexual touch, this frees the sexual relationship to become much more meaningful and important as a celebration of the love and caring already present in the relationship.

In this way, partnership sex is more pleasurable and satisfying. Each person is in charge of his or her own sexual pleasure, so there is no need to use manipulation to get needs met. Sex becomes more spontaneous and creative, making it not only more physically satisfying but also more emotionally and spiritually satisfying.

Sex in a partnership relationship also can be a way of uncovering and healing old sexual wounds related to sexual abuse from childhood. The intimacy created in a partnership relationship can make it safe enough for deeply repressed sexual abuse patterns to come to the surface. Much can be done by a loving, cooperative and patient partner to help the person work through the old feelings that surface. Using the following set of partnership agreements as a foundation for working through these problems, many couples can help each other heal deep emotional and spiritual wounds from childhood abuse.

Practical steps needed to create a partnership sexual relationship

The key to creating a partnership sexual relationship is to have a common understanding of the difference between the sexual touch and the nurturing touch. This can be difficult for a man and may require the loving help of a partner who can gently confront him to make him more aware of these differences. Women have a better sense of the differences, probably because of their experiences in breast-feeding and nurturing their children. Until men are encouraged to develop their nurturing side and have more experience of providing a nurturing touch for their children, they will probably have difficulty in separating these two kinds of needs.

A set of basic agreements can help a couple move to more partnership sex.[8] A couple needs to agree:

A To be in charge of their own sexual pleasure and to be willing to ask for what they want sexually;
B To help each other distinguish between the needs for sexual touch and non-sexual touch;
C To respect each other's sexual boundaries;
D To help each other deal with any old hurts and wounds related to sexual abuse that are uncovered as part of sexual intimacy;
E Not to play seductive games with each other;
F To explore the spiritual aspects of sex;
G To refrain from using sex to resolve or escape from problems;
H To use sex as a form of celebration.

Exchanging goods and services

In industrialized countries, families by and large are considered as units of consumption rather than as units of production. In developing countries, the family is more typically involved in production tasks, with all family members contributing their labour to the production of goods and services.

The view of the family as a unit of consumption has contributed to devaluing the unpaid production of goods and services in the family, primarily those produced by women for their family. This category has no place in calculating economic figures such as the gross national product or family income. Yet without this contribution of labour, the family unit could not survive or it would require massive government spending to keep the family together. An Australian study has shown that people (mostly women) spend about the same amount of hours on unpaid work as they do in paid work.[41] In another study, it has been estimated that "... Australian households produce about three times the output of the manufacturing sector ... or ten times the gross domestic product of the mining industry".[41]

Government policies can also influence the role of the family as a provider of services for its members. The fewer the social benefits and public resources available to support the family, the more the welfare of each family member is dependent on the resources the family can provide for each member. Also, in times of social and economic transition, the family serves as the basic social safety net for its members. If the Government does not adequately support the family during these transition periods, the strain on the family and its members can be severe. High unemployment, housing shortages and low wages can all lead to increased alcoholism, poor health, domestic violence and divorce.

For most people, the family is the main provider of basic services such as shelter and housing, meal preparation, cleaning and care of clothing as well as money for education and recreation. As women have been able to work outside the home, their contribution to the family's income has greatly increased. However, this usually means that the division of labour within the home has to change or women end up with a double burden of work.

An Australian study has concluded that no matter how many hours of paid work a wife does, her husband's contribution remains relatively the same.[41] A British survey has shown more encouraging results. While women who are working part-time still have to do almost all the household chores, when women work full-time, men share equally with household shopping and meal preparation.[42] However, women who work outside the home face another inequity; they still earn considerably less than men for equal work.[41] This economic inequity more than any other economic factor supports the continuance of dominator relationships.

Dominator families

One of the primary forms of dominating women in families is economic in nature. According to an Australian study, women spend an average of 36 hours per week (70 per cent) in unpaid work providing for their family while men spend about 14.5 hours (30 per cent) in work at home. These percentages do not change, even if the woman works full-time outside the home.[41] Women are also discriminated against in most legal structures as well. Only 22 countries give equal rights to women in respect to marriage, divorce and family property.[43]

Usually the male controls the finances in dominator families. In many cases, men keep their income secret from their spouse and their children. All economic decisions are made by the male without consultation with his spouse or other family members. When a wife and children do not have accurate information about the amount of money available to the family, or access to that money, they are kept financially dependent and powerless.

Until women receive equal pay for equal work outside the home, they will not be in a strong enough "power" position to negotiate with men for more shared participation in household chores or in parenting. Without this equal pay, the economic argument can be used to justify the man's lack of shared participation in family activities.

Partnership families

A partnership family has clear agreements about creating an equitable economic relationship between the couple and in the family. This usually means recognizing the value of unpaid work done by women who stay home and care for young children, as well more equitably sharing household duties if both parents work outside the home.

The key to creating a partnership family is no secrets about money. The amount of money available to the family after taxes and the cost of benefits should be known to all family members. Economic equity has to be established if a true partnership relationship and a partnership family is to be created. This means shared decision-making about family finances regardless of who contributes how much to the family coffers. This is essential if children are to learn effective democratic principles related to money and how it is spent.

Regular family meetings need to be held to discuss how to divide up household chores equitably and how family resources might be allocated. These meetings can be used to discuss possibly buying a television set or a video recorder, to be shared by all family members. They can also be used to discuss family holidays and family recreation, with each person having a vote on how much money would be spent on these kinds of family activities.

Protecting family members

Society expects families to provide its members protection from all forms of abuse and violence, especially its women and children. Unfortunately, many families fail to perform this function well and considerable psychological, physical or sexual abuse occurs in families.

Rooted in ancient traditions, the concept of paterfamilias gave the father absolute authority over his wife, children and slaves. This concept is still behind much of the violence that occurs in families. For the most part, family violence has been accepted, ignored or hidden. Only recently have some Governments begun to intervene. One encouraging sign is that five countries have outlawed the corporal punishment of children by parents: Austria, Denmark, Finland, Norway and Sweden. In Sweden, where the law has been in effect for over 10 years, only one case has been tried in the courts.[44] Although information about domestic violence is limited in developing countries, evidence shows high levels of abuse of wives by husbands in parts of Africa, Asia and Latin America.[45]

Dominator families

The use of violence by men to control women and terrorize children is at the heart of dominator families. Until this is stopped by passing laws and enforcing them, the dominator family will not change. In addition, parents must be educated on how to help their children, especially male children, learn to manage their violent impulses. Adults must also be helped to find healthy non-violent ways of discharging their feelings and healing the wounds that are causing the violence. The processes described earlier in this chapter that help adults deal with these problems must be taught in schools and elsewhere so no adult is forced to use violence against others in order to deal with their old wounds.

Partnership families

A partnership family must be a safe family. Parents must learn and then teach their children effective ways of resolving conflicts non-violently where everyone wins. This has to be at the core of the democratic practices used in the family. All conflicts must be resolved peacefully and in such a way that everyone's needs are considered and met.

Parents must follow a few simple rules to teach their children how to live peacefully using democratic principles:

- A React calmly to their aggressive impulses and set limits without shaming them;
- B Support their attempts to become separate and autonomous people;
- C Teach them how to express their ordinary feelings of frustration, jealousy or defiance in healthy ways;
- D Encourage them to ask directly for what they want;
- E Offer to help them mediate the disputes they have with others;
- F Help them to identify their needs and learn to ask directly for help in meeting them when necessary.

Giving a name and status to family members, especially to children

Having a name and status within the family is the place where equity begins. Children who are given a family name and the right to inherit family property are accepted as part of the social and legal system. In the early partnership societies, women formed the social and legal core of the community. Temples were organized and operated by women, who owned much of the land, domesticated the animals and functioned as the controlling officers of the society. The lineage of children in these early societies was through the mother.[46] Because each child knew its mother, there were no problems regarding inheritance or naming.

When dominator practices overtook these early partnership societies, lineage was determined through the father. At that point, paternity rather than maternity began to determine name and legal status. A child with questionable paternity was denied a patriarchal name and the right to inherit patriarchal property. To assure certain knowledge of paternity, men began to control the expression of sexuality by women. The control of women's sexuality and the contempt for children born out of wedlock have been part of the accepted components of the dominator culture for the past 3,000 to 5,000 years. Paternity has been a way of enforcing male dominator practices directed at promiscuous women and the children of unwed parents as scapegoats for socially sanctioned violence.

Dominator families

In dominator families, the issue of providing a name and status for family members, particularly children, is used as a mechanism for controlling the sexual behaviour of women and for intimidating children. The need to control a woman's sexual behaviour frequently becomes an avenue for controlling other aspects of her life such as her ability to have male friends, the kind of clothing she wears and whether she works outside the home. Women who have children out of wedlock and the children who are born out of wedlock are frequent targets for physical, emotional and sexual abuse both within the family and outside it.

The practice of a woman assuming the name of her husband when she marries is also a form of patriarchal domination. It is a practice similar to the branding of cattle and horses to identify ownership and gives women the status of chattels or of property to be traded, sold, loaned, pillaged and plundered. Chattel status for women has been used as a reason for not permitting women to own or inherit property in their own right.

Partnership families

What is needed to address these dominator-based social regulations is first the adoption at both a national and individual level of the Convention on the Elimination of All Forms of Discrimination against Women.[47] Families with gender-equal practices in giving a name and status to women create a foundation for equity in other parts of the family structure such as shared legal power, common title to property and joint decision-making. On this concrete level, a man and a woman can then build gender-equal relationship practices into their parenting, sexual relationship and the daily operation of a household.

The second task is to emphasize the rights of the child. In 1989, the General Assembly adopted the Convention on the Rights of the Child,[48] which states that every child, including adopted children and those born out of wedlock, has the right from birth to a name and to acquire a nationality. This Convention must be ratified by all countries and woven into the fabric of social policies and structures. The rights of children must be a primary concern of parents and countries should pass laws guaranteeing these rights.

The selection of a name is an opportunity for individual expression. Both men and women should be free to decide on their own surnames. In some cases, a husband may assume the surname of his wife. When a child is born, the parents can consciously decide which surname will best serve the child's interests. In some cases, when the parents have different surnames, the children may be given surnames that are a combination of the parents' surnames or an entirely different surname. Changing the giving of surnames from a culturally determined condition to one based on individual needs supports the development of the healthy self-esteem of the individual and promotes the appreciation of diversity within the culture.

Providing for the basic care of children, the elderly and disabled family members

The basic care of family members is a crucial function of the family, and the care of children remains the most generally recognized primary responsibility of families. Basic care of family members includes the provision of adequate nutritious food, shelter, clothing and supportive social interactions. Because of the bonding involved, humans are best cared for by those who know and love them. People with special needs, especially the elderly and the disabled, often bring an added dimension of human experience to families. They often, because of their special needs, also add extra burdens to families. Social policies that support families in caring for their own members, such as paid family leave or family-leave subsidies, not only strengthen families but also keep social welfare programmes functioning at their most effective and efficient levels.

Extended family systems, whether biological or intentional, provide a solid foundation to support both the parents and the children during this period of long-term financial and emotional commitment. Nuclear families separated geographically from the support of their extended family system often experience a great deal of stress in trying to meet the needs of all their members, particularly those of the children.

Dominator families

The care of family members, particularly children, in dominator families becomes an opportunity for the most dominant member to have his or her needs served by the weaker members. Children are often used to serve the sexual, social, economic and physical needs of their parents. The care of children, the elderly and the disabled is often gender-based, typically assigned to women. Because of the low ranking of women and children in the dominator hierarchy, the care of children is given a low cultural or economic value. The devaluing of women and children, the carriers of evolutionary progress, has inhibited the growth of consciousness in the human species.

In dominator families, the tasks of basic human care are usually organized along rigid, culturally determined gender lines. The father is assigned the role of "provider" and works outside the home in a position that provides him with social status, social security benefits and economic resources. The mother assumes the role of "caretaker" and usually works inside the home to perform the tasks of cooking, cleaning, laundering and raising children, none providing her with social status, social security benefits or economic resources. Even if she does work outside the home, she will be paid less than a man and usually will be expected to continue to assume primary responsibility for the caretaking function. This imbalance in social and economic power keeps women dependent on men and helps to maintain the male-dominated social and economic system.

Partnership families

Partnership families are more person-centred and child-centred and make the psychological, emotional and spiritual welfare of each individual family member a priority. To accomplish this, the adults must create a home based on mutual respect that supports each person in achieving optimal development. Partnership families recognize the importance of the bonding between members, even those who are old or disabled. Children are viewed as the link to the future of the human species and should be provided with as much support for achieving their potential as possible. Partnership families use consensus decision-making to determine how the needs of all members will be met and negotiate differences when these needs conflict. Harmonious relationships and the continuity of the family as a social unit are of primary importance.

Care is taken to assure that members are not confined by gender-based role restrictions or expectations. Each person chooses responsibilities based on his or her age, ability, interests and need to learn or grow without regard to gender. Parents must model this kind of flexibility in their own relationship with regard to matters such as sharing household duties, parenting, home maintenance and money management. Conflicts regarding sharing responsibilities again must be used as opportunities for moving each individual forward in development by resolving them in win-win ways.

Socializing and educating children

The education and socialization of children is the primary way a society creates its future. The degree of responsibility of the family as the educator of children varies from one culture to another. In some societies, the education of children takes place primarily in the home, extended family or tribe. In more developed countries, the education of children has been taken on by the society in schools supported by public funds.

In either case, families provide a child's first educational experience, which is where values, beliefs, skills and family traditions are passed on from generation to generation. The first five to six years of a child's life are the formative years when the child strives to develop a sense of self, to explore the world, to master self-care, to develop autonomy and to learn social skills. By the time a child moves to a formal educational setting, the foundation for accurately processing information and appropriately assimilating life experiences should be in place.

This makes the role of the family, particularly the parents, critical. The more effectively parents carry out their roles as the child's "first teachers", the more children will be able to attain high levels of intellectual, social, emotional and psychological growth. Parents must understand that their children come into the world with certain cultural and genetic codings, making each of them unique. The task of parents is to identify the qualities of uniqueness in their children and then provide enlightened support for these qualities.

Children are also socialized in their family settings through their relationships with siblings. Here the child learns either dominating or partnering forms of social behaviour and often becomes involved in the vicious cycle of cruelty. As the talionic impulse appears in sibling relationships, the parents must help the children find ways of releasing their angry feelings and resolving their conflicts using non-violent win-win methods.

Dominator families

Children who grow up in dominator families often experience early the attempts of their parents to break their will. As the natural assertive qualities of becoming an individual emerge, the parents may experience this as a challenge to their authority. It is also this emergent self-expression that may activate the parents' own latent talionic impulses and the vicious cycle of cruelty. As a result, children find themselves struggling to survive the abuse of adults and older siblings rather than developing their own uniqueness. Children are often taught unquestioning obedience and threatened with violence if they do not comply. They learn they must be passive and deceptive or highly rebellious in order to maintain their sense of self.

Children in dominator families often find themselves the target of their parents' unresolved talionic impulses in the form of attacks of rage that lead to physical, emotional, sexual or spiritual abuse. In dominator families, children are often treated like dumb animals and shamed as a way of disciplining them. While this may not involve physical violence, the effects of it are just as damaging. This attitude of the family regarding the education and socialization of children can extend into the schools in developed countries where education has become a responsibility of the Government. This also permits the institutionalization of violence, shame and domination in schools to assure that the will of the child continues to be broken or suppressed.

Partnership families

In partnership families, the will of the child is tempered in ways that support both individual initiative and collective cooperation. To achieve this delicate balance, parents set firm limits and provide appropriate consequences for all forms of behaviour without using shame. Limit-setting emphasizes both physical safety and the rights of other people. This provides the child with concrete cause-and-effect experiences and teaching regarding his or her behaviour. Through this trial-and-error process, the child learns to interweave personal needs with the needs of the larger group.

When the talionic impulse appears at the age-appropriate time, the parents permit the children to express feelings in ways that do not physically harm themselves or others. The limits the parents set are defined in non-shaming ways, and they recognize the appropriateness of the children's behaviour. Parents need to provide love and limits during temper tantrums or episodes of aggressive behaviour. Appropriate outlets for this energy permit the child to release emotions in the moment; then the residual energy is gently guided into self-supportive activities for the child. Rage and violence are tempered and feelings of anger are channelled in functional ways that develop personal boundaries and help the child meet its needs. This is how children achieve the mastery and autonomy essential for their full development as individuals existing inside a family and society.

Providing emotional care, affection and recreation for family members

Home is the primary place where family members receive emotional care, experience intimacy and acquire understanding and support. It is the place of constancy in an often unpredictable, hurtful and insensitive world. Home is an experience often grounded in primal olfactory and sensory experiences related to food, touch and emotions. It is a place people return to regularly for nurturing, comfort and the reduction of tension.

Children as social beings require emotional involvement and interaction with their parents as well as physical care. Both the father and mother must be involved in parenting if a child is to complete successfully the tasks required during each stage of development, particularly the task of emotional separation. Parents also need a common long-term vision for the growth of the child so they can operate from a unified framework.

Adults need to complete most of their own developmental tasks before they have children, so they are emotionally available to meet the needs of a child. Parents must ensure that non-home environments, such as day care, also provide emotional support for the children. At the core of emotional care for family members must be a person-centred philosophy that fosters the development of peaceful, altruistic forms of behaviour.

Recreational experiences as a family unit are a way of supporting the exploratory forms of behaviour of its members in a safe environment. As children, in particular, leave the safety of the home, it is important they have the safety the family provides when encountering the larger world. New experiences can be put into a value framework that teaches tolerance of diversity, excitement about variety and support for the child's natural urges to explore and discover.

Dominator families

The emotional care of family members in a dominator family is almost always assigned to the mother. Her role is to serve as the manager of tension levels within the family, to provide soothing reassurance to both her husband and the children and to maintain the emotional equilibrium of the family system. She is expected to meet her own needs for nurturing and reassurance as she fulfils this role for others, even if she works outside the home and encounters situations that elevate her own tension levels. If the tension level of the home is too high, she is held responsible and expected to do something to relieve it.

The emotional climate of a dominator home often fluctuates between periods of repression and periods of violence. Conflict is avoided during the periods of repression until the tension levels reach a crisis point, when violence often erupts. The violence, usually directed at someone perceived to be less powerful, is abusive. Indeed, children often have a limited vocabulary and an even more limited understanding of their feelings. In dominator families, weaker members are expected to serve as the scapegoats of those who are stronger. The talionic impulse is usually unacknowledged and unmanaged by all members, who compete with each other for targets for their feelings of hatred and urges to be violent. In extreme cases, aggressive behaviour from the talionic impulse can cause the death of a family member.

Homicide statistics in Canada show that over two thirds of the child victims who died during the 1980s were killed by parents. In addition, parents or other family members were accused of committing 40 per cent of all violent crimes against children in Canada.[49]

Partnership families

Members of partnership families are each responsible for managing and expressing their own feelings, for finding effective ways of reducing their inner tensions and for managing their talionic impulses. Adults can find outlets for their sexual expression and for their needs for adult and cross-gender companionship with other adults. Self-care is stressed for each family member and children are supported in gradually assuming more personal responsibility when they appear developmentally ready.

A partnership home permits conflicts to surface the moment they occur and teaches effective skills for resolving them. Conflict is framed as an opportunity for intimacy and regarded as a self-regulating mechanism within the family structure. Feelings such as anger, sadness, fear, joy and love are acknowledged as vital aspects of humanness functioning as signals of people's inner experiences.

Vulnerabilities surface as doorways to emotional intimacy and honesty between family members. Parents who are able to speak their fears, admit their mistakes and share their regrets create an atmosphere of integrity for themselves and their children. Developing the ability to speak small truths of this nature in the family creates a pattern for speaking larger truths in the society.

Conclusion

In the course of human events it has become necessary to denounce the existing practices of the domination of weak or vulnerable family members by those with more strength or power. It is also necessary to call for these practices to be rapidly replaced by democratic practices that foster interdependence and partnership in families. This declaration of interdependence is not meant to supersede any previous declarations or statements of human rights, but instead to extend clearly these fundamental rights to the realm of family where all human rights initially must be preserved, protected and promoted.

This process could be accelerated if it were generally accepted that:

A All family members should be born into a family where they are planned for and wanted;

B All family members should be loved and cared for by parents who strive to understand the needs and behaviour of their children;

C All family members should have their basic needs for food, clothing and shelter provided for them by their family until they are able to provide for themselves;

D All family members should be seen and respected by their parents and other family members as unique individuals with talents, aspirations and dreams of their own;

E All family members should have their feelings and needs taken seriously and responded to with empathy by their parents and other family members;

F All family members should be raised in a family where they are disciplined and given appropriate limits without using violence, threats or shame;

G All family members should grow up in a family free from emotional, physical, sexual and spiritual abuse and violence;

H All family members should be taught effective non-violent ways of resolving family conflicts;

I All family members should share equally in family decision-making, particularly in decisions affecting them;

J All family members should have an equitable share of the resources available to the family.

FAMILY challenges for the future

References

[1] Henryk Sokalski, "Building the smallest democracy at the heart of society", statement given at the National Family Forum, Canberra, Australia, November 1992.
[2] Riane Eisler, *The Chalice and the Blade* (San Francisco, Harper and Row, 1987).
[3] John Bradshaw, *Bradshaw: On the Family* (Deerfield Beach, Florida, Health Communications, 1988).
[4] John Bradshaw, *Healing the Shame That Binds You* (Deerfield Beach, Florida, Health Communications, 1988).
[5] John Bradshaw, *Homecoming: Reclaiming and Championing Your Inner Child* (New York, Bantam Books, 1990).
[6] Barry K. Weinhold and Janae B. Weinhold, *Breaking Free of the Co-dependency Trap* (New Hampshire, Stillpoint, 1989).
[7] Barry K. Weinhold, *Breaking Free of Addictive Family Relationships* (New Hampshire, Stillpoint, 1991).
[8] Janae B. Weinhold and Barry K. Weinhold, *Counter-dependency: The Flight from Intimacy* (Colorado Springs, CICRCL Press, 1992).
[9] Leal J. Dickstein and Carol. C. Nadelson, eds., *Family Violence: Emerging Issues of a National Crisis*, Clinical Practice Series No. 3 (Washington, D.C., American Psychiatric Press, 1989).
[10] Rosalie S. Wolf and Karl A. Pillemer, Helping Elderly Victims: *The Reality of Elder Abuse* (New York, Columbia University Book Press, 1989), p. 20.
[11] Murry A. Strauss and Richard J. Gelles, "How violent are American families? Estimates from the National Family Violence Resurvey and Other Studies", in *Family Abuse and its Consequences: New Directions in Research*, Gerald T. Hotaling and others, eds. (Newbury Park, California, Sage Publications, 1988), p. 31.
[12] F. Ameen and others, *Linking Women's Global Struggles to End Violence* (Ottawa, Match International Centre, 1990).
[13] *Violence against Women in the Family* (United Nations publication, Sales No. E.89.IV.5), 1989.
[14] James Masterson, *The Narcissistic and Borderline Disorders: An Integrated Developmental Approach* (New York, Brunner/Mazel, 1981), pp. 182-193.
[15] M.D.A. Freeman, "Legal ideologies, patriarchal precedents and domestic violence", *State Law and Family* (London, Tavistock, 1984), p. 52.
[16] H. Singh, "Case study from India", cited in *Violence against Women* ..., p. 31.
[17] Wu Han, "A case study from China", cited in *Violence against Women* ..., p. 31.
[18] B. N. Wamalwa, "A case study", cited in *Violence against Women* ..., p. 20.
[19] David Levinson, *Family Violence in a Cross Cultural Perspective* (Newbury Park, California, Sage Publications, 1989).
[20] Lloyd DeMause, *Foundations of Psychohistory* (New York, Creative Roots, 1982).
[21] Gerald Heard, *The Five Ages of Man* (New York, Julian Press, 1963).
[22] David Fenell and Barry K. Weinhold, *Counseling Families* (Denver, Love Publishing, 1989).
[23] Richard Bandler and John Grindler, *Frogs into Princes: Neuro-Linguistic Programming* (Moab, Utah, Real People Press, 1979).
[24] J. G. Miller, *Living Systems* (New York, McGraw-Hill, 1978).
[25] Margaret Mahler and others, *The Psychological Birth of the Human Infant* (New York, Basic Books, 1967).
[26] Arnold Mindell, River's Way: *The Process Science of the Dreambody* (Boston, Routledge and Kegan Paul, 1985).
[27] Arnold Mindell, *Working With the Dreaming Body* (Boston, Routledge and Kegan Paul, 1985).
[28] Arnold Mindell, *The Dreambody in Relationships* (Boston, Routledge and Kegan Paul,1987).
[29] The Holy Bible, *Confraternity Version* (New York, Benzinger, 1961).
[30] Friedrich Nietzsche, *The Birth of Tragedy and the Genealogy of Morals*, Francis Golffing, trans. (New York, Doubleday, 1955).
[31] Morton Schatzman, Soul Murder: *Persecution in the Family* (New York, New American Library, 1973).
[32] Marshall Klaus and John Kennel, *Maternal-Infant Bonding* (St. Louis, C. V. Mosby,1976).
[33] Thomas Verney, *The Secret Life of the Unborn Child* (New York, Delta Books, 1981).

[34] Dennis Stott, Follow-up study from birth on the effects of prenatal stresses, *Developmental Medicine and Child Neurology*, vol. 15, 1973, pp. 770-787.

[35] Frederick Leboyer, *Birth Without Violence* (New York, Alfred A. Knopf, 1975).

[36] Ken Magid and Carol McKelvey, High Risk: *Children Without a Conscience* (New York, Bantam Books, 1987).

[37] Lloyd DeMause, "The universality of incest", *Journal of Psychohistory*, vol. 19, No. 2 (Fall 1991), pp. 2123-2164.

[38] Marcelle Geber, "The psycho-motor development of African children in the first year and the influence of maternal behavior", *Journal of Social Psychology*, No. 47, 1958, pp. 185-195.

[39] Janae Weinhold and Barry Weinhold, "Developmental systems theory", unpublished manuscript.

[40] United Nations, *Families: Forms and Functions*, Occasional Papers Series, No. 2, 1992.

[41] Selected findings from *Juggling Time: How Australian Families Use Time* (Barton, ACT, Office of the Status of Women, Department of the Prime Minister and Cabinet, 1991), p. 5.

[42] Peter Laslett, "Child, family and society", in *Report of the Conference*, Child and Society (Brussels, Commission of the European Communities, 1992), p. 37.

[43] L. Otero, "Conceptualization, typologies, structures and functions related to the familiar family", Paper presented to the Second Ad Hoc Inter-agency Meeting on the International Year of the Family, Vienna, Austria, 5-6 March 1992.

[44] Alice Miller, *Breaking Down the Walls of Silence* (New York, Dutton, 1991).

[45] Merlin Stone, *When God Was a Woman* (New York, Dial Press, 1976).

[46] *Violence against Women ...*, p. 17.

[47] *Official Records of the General Assembly, Thirty-fourth Session, Supplement* No. 46 (A/34/46), section VI.

[48] Ibid., *Forty-fourth Session, Supplement* No. 49 (A/44/49), section VI.

[49] "Children as victims of violent crime", *Juristat* (Statistics; Canada Service Bulletin), vol. 11, No. 8 (1991), p. 1.

FAMILY and Crime

Introduction[*]

In many countries, families are undergoing tremendous stress and change as a result of political strife, increasing urbanization, industrialization, economic hardship and changing social values. The role of the family as a primary institution of social control has diminished; the "traditional" family is vanishing in some parts of the world. These conditions have contributed to the instability of the family and to its diminishing role as a source of social support and control, phenomena that research has identified as causal factors in youthful crime and delinquency.

The need is to address the needs of families in the face of the serious challenges and obstacles of contemporary times and to strengthen their capability in the fulfilment of basic functions. By strengthening the valuable role and functions of a "holistic" family, individuals within the family will acquire the necessary skills to cope with the demands and pressures of the world without engaging in criminal activity.

In the delinquency prevention field, the socialization function can play a central role, as the primary responsibility for socializing the young rests with the family. Differences in types of families call for diverse strategies to strengthen the family as a whole.

When societal norms and expectations are in a state of flux, primary social control mechanisms, such as the family, have to be flexible. Nevertheless, the beneficial socialization processes which the family offers have certain common characteristics all over the world.

The role of the family is specified in the following three international instruments in the juvenile justice field: the United Nations Standard Minimum Rules for the Administration of Juvenile Justice (The Beijing Rules),[1] the United Nations Guidelines for the Prevention of Juvenile Delinquency (The Riyadh Guidelines),[2] and the United Nations Rules for the Protection of Juveniles Deprived of their Liberty.[3]

The Riyadh Guidelines, dealing with prevention of juvenile delinquency, highlight the important contribution that a healthy, stable family, as a primary socialization and social control agent and role model, can make in rearing children to be productive, integral members of society, free from crime, victimization and conflict with the law.

In the Riyadh Guidelines, paragraphs 11 to 19, the following statements are made concerning the family:

---

[*] The contents of this paper are drawn from the work of a consultant, Emilio Viano, of American University, Washington, D.C., as well as the work of the Crime Prevention and Criminal Justice Branch, United Nations Office at Vienna, and of United Nations congresses on the prevention of crime and the treatment of offenders in the field of crime and delinquency prevention.

A Every society should place a high priority on the needs and well-being of the family and of all its members;

B Since the family is the central unit responsible for the primary socialization of children, governmental and social efforts to preserve the integrity of the family, including the extended family, should be pursued. The society has a responsibility to assist the family in providing care and protection and in ensuring the physical and mental well-being of children. Adequate arrangements, including day-care, should be provided;

C Governments should establish policies conducive to bringing up children in stable and settled family environments. Families in need of assistance in resolving conditions of instability or conflict should be provided with requisite services;

D Where a stable and settled family environment is lacking and when community efforts to assist parents in this regard have failed and the extended family cannot fulfil this role, alternative placements, including foster care and adoption, should be considered. Such placements should replicate, to the extent possible, a stable and settled family environment, while, at the same time, establishing a sense of permanency for children, thus avoiding problems associated with "foster drift";

E Special attention should be given to children of families affected by problems brought about by rapid and uneven economic, social and cultural change, in particular the children of indigenous, migrant and refugee families. As such changes may disrupt the social capacity of the family to secure the traditional rearing and nurturing of children, often as a result of role and culture conflict, innovative and socially constructive modalities for the socialization of children have to be designed;

F Measures should be taken and programmes developed to provide families with the opportunity to learn about parental roles and obligations as regards child development and child care, promoting positive parent-child relationships, sensitizing parents to the problems of children and young persons and encouraging their involvement in family and community-based activities;

G Governments should take measures to promote family cohesion and harmony and to discourage the separation of children from their parents, unless circumstances affecting the welfare and future of the child leave no viable alternative;

H It is important to emphasize the socialization function of the and extended family; it is equally important to recognize the future role, responsibilities, participation and partnership of young persons in society;

1   In ensuring the right of the child to proper socialization, Governments and other agencies should rely on existing social and legal agencies, but whenever traditional institutions and customs are no longer effective, they should also provide and allow for innovative measures."

The Beijing Rules and the Rules for the Protection of Juveniles Deprived of their Liberty, dealing with the treatment and handling of young persons who have already come into conflict with the law, highlight the important role of the family in relation to young persons in custodial detention.

General Assembly resolutions 40/35 of 29 November 1985, on development of standards for the prevention of juvenile delinquency, 40/36 of 29 November 1985 and 45/114 of 14 December 1990, on domestic violence, and 45/115 of 14 December 1990, on the instrumental use of children in criminal activities are also relevant to the role of the family in juvenile justice issues. Relevant documentation includes: reports of the sixth,[4] seventh[5] and eighth[6] United Nations congresses on the prevention of crime and the treatment of offenders and the working papers presented by the Secretariat to those congresses entitled "Juvenile justice: before and after the onset of delinquency",[7] "Youth, crime and justice",[8] "Women as victims",[9] "The fair treatment of women by the criminal justice system",[10] and "Juvenile justice, delinquency prevention and the protection of the young: policy approaches and directions";[11] the International Review of Criminal Policy, numbers 39 and 40, special double volume on juvenile justice in international perspective;[12] and the Crime Prevention and Criminal Justice Newsletter, number 9, of December 1983, special issue on domestic violence.

The General Assembly, in its resolutions 40/35 and 40/36, recognized the highly detrimental effects of domestic violence on children in relation to delinquency prevention. Both male and female children are battered and abused, but the primary victim is the female.

An unfortunately large number of children witness to their detriment degrading battery and abuse between familial adults or by adults against siblings, mostly committed by the male against the female. Such practices traumatize and demoralize the young, as it is not easy to be victimized by or to observe the victimization of a loved one. This relates to both the direct experience of intrusive violence, as victim, and the indirect experience, as observer. Both experiences inculcate in the young a social attitude that violent conduct is an acceptable, normative form of interpersonal relations and promote the adoption of destructive behaviour. Moreover, such practices denigrate the status of women, placing serious obstacles in the path of achieving equality of the sexes.

Community: the essential human habitat

The strongest support for the family unit comes from the community where it exists. Community identity, competence and self-direction rest on human relatedness, on the sense of belonging and being "in place". Relatedness is the essence of community, the foundation of communities, and involves the reciprocity of caring and being cared for. A well-functioning community, rich in natural support systems, offers its members a firm sense of identity, stability and self-direction.

In the world today, the stability of many communities and their anchoring and support functions are challenged by vast population migrations, political upheavals and transitions, shifts in economic productivity and power, as well as by dramatic improvements in the availability and ease of travel. With few exceptions, most areas of the world are experiencing vast and unsettling population movements from rural to urban areas and from one country or even continent to another. Consequently, many different groups may share the same geographical area within a city, leading to the establishment of different communities that coexist and at times compete for resources and services.

Individuals frequently move in and out of local communities. What was once a homogeneous rural village becomes a boom town, attracting people of different lifestyles and placing stresses on existing values, norms, institutions and services. Demographic changes affect many rural areas. Many young persons depart for the cities, leaving their elders behind. In cities, young adults may move out of one neighbourhood into another one while their ageing parents cannot follow them. These young persons, and the parents left behind, face the challenge of having to accept, respect and interact with newcomers who are frequently of a different ethnic and other background.

In both rural and urban situations, conflicts may arise as old folkways and mores confront a multiplicity of lifestyles and norms. Time is required for newcomers and permanent or established residents to develop a new community identity. Without this identity, a community will find it difficult to identify its needs and goals, to develop a commitment to them and to deal effectively with wide-ranging problems and demands. Identity and community pride are interdependent with community competence, self-direction and relatedness - essential elements for a well-functioning community.

Participation in community affairs helps otherwise powerless individuals develop some measure of community and personal self-direction and experience a greater sense of relatedness or solidarity with others. This in turn increases their personal competence and self-esteem both as family and community members. Without these positive elements, a community is in danger of internal disorganization and progressive degeneration, on the one hand, and of external control and social neglect, on the other. The more powerless a community is because of denial of basic infrastructure, in terms of resources, facilities and services, the more its residents are blocked in their attempt to acquire needed skills and strengthen their communal ties, the greater the potential for disorder, conflict and crime. All impinge on the basic constituent unit of the community, namely the family. Weak connections to the larger environment or a failure to provide the needed resources to a community may entrap the members and begin a negative process fuelled by the disempowerment of the community.

The family and the socialization process

The family, as the primary, most intimate and influential environment in which human development takes place, is universally regarded as an essential building block of the community and, ultimately, of society. Traditionally, the family has been considered as a group of persons related by blood or marriage, living together and cooperating economically and socially, including in child-rearing. In various cultures around the world many forms of family can be identified, each with its own characteristics, dynamics and problems - the nuclear, extended and reorganized families with several variations. The nuclear family, until recently assumed to be the dominant structure at least in the Western world, has been steadily declining in number and as a percentage of total families. In contrast to the centrality of the marital couple as the governing relationship in the nuclear family, the significant or governing coalition in some other families may be that of father and son, as in traditional families in China and Western Asia, mother and son, as in traditional Hindu families, or between brothers, as in families in some African cultures. Extended families, as well as ethnic families in transition, value intergenerational continuity the most.

Family functions are in a state of flux, as are its definition and structure.

Over time, the family has surrendered some of its functions to other societal institutions, has reclaimed some of them and has assumed new ones. An especially interesting example of a function considered lost but rediscovered is education. During the first decades of the twentieth century, the family appeared to surrender its role of educating the young to compulsory education. However, the family is now steadily recognized as continuing to function as an important educator of all its members. The family certainly influences, positively or negatively, the results of formal schooling. More importantly, all family members teach and learn from each other. Children learn from their parents in countless ways; parents learn from their children as well. Immigrant and refugee parents often learn the language and customs of their new country from their children. Siblings learn values, attitudes, skills and information from one another. All the members of the family may learn from the grandparents or great-grandparents who often fulfil the role of custodians of the family's history, cultural values, traditions and rituals.

The family's "world within"

The family can be aptly described as a system interacting and transacting with its environment and within itself. Families are influenced and shaped by a variety of biological, psychological and social forces, such as the following:

A   The interactions of the family with its social, economic, political and physical environments, *inter alia*: the societal context of oppression and disempowerment; the community and its institutions, including formal and informal support networks; and the mass media and its portrayals of family life;

B   The cultural values and norms of the family, as affected by race, ethnicity, religion, occupation, socio-economic status and urban, suburban or rural residence;

C   The personalities of the family members, including that part based on the earlier experience of the parents in their own families of origin;

D   The health conditions and biological maturity of the family members;

E   The internal organization or structure that results from the unique experiences of the family over time, including roles and tasks, boundary processes, levels of authority and decision-making and its world-view.

The interactions of all these forces shape the behaviours, interpersonal relations and communication patterns constantly created and recreated by the family among its members and between its members and the larger society over its lifetime. They also serve to balance common tensions in family life, like those between closeness and distance, constancy and change and authority and self-direction.

Much analysis, policy and practical work with families has failed to take into account their historic, social, economic and political context, including the patriarchal social order where women's status, power and resources are curtailed. This in turn leads many to accept and reinforce oppressive gender-typed family roles and to use a reciprocal view of causation that, for example, blames the victim for precipitation of battery and abuse rather than the perpetrator of the offence.

One must realize that families, like all other human systems, are firmly anchored in the historical, cultural, economic and political environments in which they exist and function. Theory construction and research are similarly affected. Consequently, all those who study or work with families must confront and resolve their own attitudes, beliefs and values, including those influenced by gender. If this is not done, scholars, practitioners and legislators will not advance gender equality, will continue supporting gender-powered relations and "ignore women's and children's issues, reframe them as something else or recast them as (their) fault",[13] and families may remain unaware about the connections between their own turmoil and suffering and the social order in which they live. The principal of a family environment free of gender bias is certainly an ideal well worth striving for.

To understand crime and violence, a perspective is needed that examines the intricate way numerous factors interact to negatively impact certain individuals, families and their social interconnections or groups. This standpoint must incorporate an examination of historical, present and future interactions among families, their primary social network and the society at large. It must also encompass the singular capacity of individuals to be or not to be influenced in a foreseeable manner by family and other social systems. No single prevailing social and behaviourial science discipline can furnish such a perspective.

An important analytical tool advanced by epidemiology is the web of causation, that is, the concept of multiple interacting factors, rather than a unique root cause. Epidemiological studies indicate it is often more advantageous to search for a causal web at a remote but critical juncture than to look for a large and, on the surface, more direct cause. At the same time, one of the main tenets of human ecology is that families and the social structure in which they are intertwined can generate both pro-social and antisocial individual and group behaviours. These ideas and tenets and what is known about child development suggest that the family is the one institution in society that a country should target to attack crime and violence and related social problems.

However, the importance of the family cannot be credibly discussed without giving adequate consideration to the complex but specific way in which the central structural elements in society, political, economic, educational and religious, affect the one family task intricately connected with crime and violence: child-rearing.

Child development

The interactional process between parents and their children is considered one of the major components of the socialization process, although, as the family is not a closed system, other influences impinge on the child besides those of the parents. The ability and motivation of parents or caretakers to raise children properly is in great measure affected by past, present and future conditions in society and by the child-raiser's own capabilities.

To sustain a decent civilization, society must ensure that children are raised to become adults competent in constructive self-expression and in finding purpose and value in life without violating the rights and denying the needs of others, and able to recognize, accept and fulfil civic responsibilities. Parents are the primary members and representatives of society responsible for producing such results. Humans cannot exist independently of the influence of other persons. Any consideration of human development must take into account the context or setting in which the development takes place. This interaction between individual and environment constitutes the foundation of an ecological approach to human development. From this point of view, the process of development unfolds as the child's perception of the world and his or her ability to act upon it expands. The individual and the environment mutually interact, each influencing the other in a constantly changing give-and-take of biology and society mediated by intelligence and emotion.*

For most individuals, this environment includes, most immediately, family, friends, then neighbourhood and school, and then, although less evidently so, laws, social attitudes and institutions that directly or indirectly have an impact on the child. The total outcome of these forces affecting the individual is called environmental press. Environmental press stems from the situations and events confronting and enveloping an

---

* This view of human development was initially and most prominently developed by Urie Bronfenbrenner. See Urie Bronfenbrenner, The Ecology of Human Development: Experiments by Nature and Design (Cambridge, Massachusetts, Harvard University Press, 1979).

individual that give rise to a psychosocial momentum and lead that person in a specific direction. Multiple factors, multiple levels and a complicated combination of forces are at work here, requiring an interdisciplinary approach to understand them and their consequences.

Many and different developmental routes exist. Appropriate psychological, cognitive, social and ethical development is required to prevent crime and violence in society. These developmental routes are the primary points where a society can and should undertake major crime prevention efforts.

The quality of child-raising is influenced by the existing social situation through a varied and changeable individual, family and societal interactional dynamic. Parents and families live within different social networks, depending on the complexity of the particular society. They are members, by birth or choice, of religious groups, social organizations and groups of friends and relatives. This represents their primary and normally most important social web. It is from here that the family and its members derive their sense of belonging, meaning and security. The attitudes, values and cultural ways of this social structure greatly influence its members, who strongly identify with them. Influenced by this social structure are attitudes and behaviour concerning raising children, learning, opportunities, work, norms, relations with other persons and with organizations within and outside the primary social network and more. This primary social web is often influenced and organized along ethnic, racial and religious lines.

In less tiered and usually pre-industrial societies, the primary social network of a family encompasses elements distinct from the family in more stratified and industrial societies, such as work, education, governance and other features of social organization. These elements constitute a significant basis for identity for the entire membership. Through this process of association, even persons of moderate competence and success can perceive themselves as capable, prospering and safe. Social pressure to satisfy the expectations of society can thus be considerable and effective, and the returns for conforming, like belonging, inclusion and safety, are also considerable.

Clearly the family, as the basic building block of society and the primary agent of socialization, plays a significant role in crime and delinquency prevention. Unfortunately, the family is not always the perfect, safe, and loving institution it is expected to be. There can be just as much criminal activity within the family, by the family and against the family as in society at large or in any other group. Yet, among scholars, no group of researchers has focused solely on the study of "crime and the family".

Role of parents

Parents model behaviour that children identify with and emulate. They exercise considerable influence in encouraging or discouraging certain conduct, approving or rewarding them or, conversely, disapproving of and sanctioning it. In this way, they push, pull, entice and cajole their children to follow a certain socialization. While doing this parents reflect and respond to their environment, a complex web of activities, beliefs, values and practices. Decent behaviour must be proactively, painstakingly and lovingly taught, nurtured and rewarded. The presence of values and support systems inculcate and favour lawful conduct.

Often parents are so overwhelmed by their own problems, which may include money, work, marital difficulties, drug dependency or illness, that they have no energy left to pay much attention to their children. They may also face the burden of negative influences of the environment and little support in child-rearing. Interaction in the family is not only one-way. The children have considerable effect on the life of their parents and siblings. Furthermore, feedback of the children's conduct from teachers, relatives, neighbours and others, reinforces some of the beliefs and feelings which parents have towards their children.

Parents who have acquired a criminal record do not necessarily seek to promote crime in their children. They may disapprove of the delinquent acts of their children as much as other parents. However, they may use inadequate child-rearing methods, usually based on the lack of a model of good parenting.

Crimes within the family

It should not be overlooked that crimes are committed within family units and these have a deleterious effect on the socialization process. Crime within the family, as a category, applies to criminal conduct where both the perpetrator and the victim are members of the same family. The expression "within the family" encompasses acts between parents, between siblings, between parent and child and between generations, for example, when a grandchild and grandparent are involved. A full range of criminal acts can take place within the family.

Ambiguities and variations

What acts can be considered criminal within the particular context of the family? Certain actions are criminal specifically because they take place in the family context. On the other hand, some acts may not be deemed criminal for precisely the same reason. Then, there are many grey areas, subject to debate and differences of opinion. Stealing money is generally considered a crime, but if the money is taken from a close relative, there is probably a reluctance to call it a crime. Other problematic situations include assault, non-consensual sex between spouses, the destruction of property and the unauthorized selling of goods belonging to the family or to one of its members.

These problematic situations exemplify the inclination of society to use one set of definitions and standards for conduct that takes place within the family and another for some of the same actions involving strangers. Considerable normative uncertainty is based on substantial differences in perceiving and approaching a similar situation. In some families or cultures, everything that happens within the family is considered private, a "family matter". In other families or cultures, people may instead take a dim view of what others would consider relatively minor. For example, the first incident of domestic violence may cause a spouse to terminate the marriage, or at least cause individuals to advise the spouse to do so. Certainly, the view from the inside and the outside can be quite different. Parents may tolerate certain conduct of their children that a schoolteacher, neighbour or social worker may consider unacceptable and as requiring vigorous intervention.

Even within a family different opinions exist on what is acceptable and what is unacceptable. In other words, a family, like society, uses numerous yardsticks to judge the appropriateness of the behaviour of its members. Gender, age, status, roles and functions have an impact on the family's, and particularly the parents', assessment of the actions and behaviours of different family members over a continuum ranging from praiseworthy conformance to the rules of society and the family to misconduct and to crime.

Thus, taking money without permission from a parent's wallet is judged differently if the perpetrator is five years old or 17 years old. Freedom to come and go without regard for the family mealtimes or curfews may be extended to an adolescent who is working and contributing to the family budget, but this may not be the case for a sibling of similar age who is still wholly dependent on the parents. The power and authority of the parents allows them to do with impunity what is not permitted of their children: "borrowing" money from them without permission; disregarding claims for privacy; excepting themselves from agreed-on family rules when convenient or expedient.

Because of the ambiguities involved, police are often reluctant to intervene in family cases, notwithstanding that, had the same behaviour been engaged in by strangers, it would have been regarded as criminal. This legal tolerance is especially evident in the case of sexual assault. The same behaviour defined as rape when it occurs between strangers is often ignored and overlooked if it happens within a marriage. Thus, the so-called "marital exemption" specifically shields husbands from being charged with the rape of their wives, although this has changed, or is in the process of changing, in a number of countries. As a consequence, many situations of exploitation and victimization have traditionally been ignored by society. Only now, after much effort, issues like marital rape, domestic violence, child abuse, bride burning and abuse of the elderly are beginning to be addressed and corrected.

To counteract this vagueness, it has been proposed that society should simply consider any act that takes place within the family to be a crime if it would be defined as such when the persons involved are not related.[14] While superficially this seems like a simple and plausible solution, it is far from perfect. For example, there are crimes within the family (for example, sex between unmarrieds who are closely related) that are not necessarily crimes if the participants are not so related. Also, many would consider it wholly inappropriate to apply and enforce within the family all the rules defining and sanctioning criminal conduct in the outside world.

Violence in the family

Prevention of domestic violence is of utmost importance. Recourse to physical force by parents on children and by spouses when dealing with each other promotes the use of violence outside the family.

Verbal and emotional maltreatment and abuse can be as intimidating, demoralizing, damaging, troubling and terrorizing as physical abuse. Verbal insults and humiliations, repeated constantly in a young lifetime, are what socializes children into violence and sets them apart from the other youngsters who learn quite different lessons in their family and social interactions.

Violence causes feelings of entrapment, degradation and humiliation. Self-blame is common to all victims of family violence. The deleterious effect of violence in the family underscores the need for effective preventive and treatment strategies. Once family interactions become dominated by violent processes, the situation is difficult to alter.

However, numerous programmes around the world prove that families can be helped even in these situations. Activities of immediate protection and assistance include shelters, emergency telephones, self-help and governmental groups for battered women and children, and therapy programmes. For offenders, only limited therapeutic treatment is available.

In some countries, self-help efforts have been the response to perceived police inactivity or insensitivity to the occurrence of domestic violence. Numerous countries have voluntary mutual defence groups. In one community, "habitant groups" take measures to prevent domestic violence from escalating by placing the victim with another family for a short period and disciplining the offender. "Neighbourhood watch" programmes and other community self-help programmes can effectively expose and intervene in maltreatment, diminishing the level of tolerance for it. The importance of providing immediate protection has been borne out by cross-cultural studies highlighting the readiness of kin and neighbours to intervene in violent or potentially violent situations in societies with non-violent child-rearing practices and relatively low incidences of wife battery.[*]

Special measures have been introduced to protect children from both domestic abuse and violence outside the home. Examples include neighbourhood car pools organized to drive children to and from school and extracurricular activities and the designation of certain homes in the neighbourhood with special decals as safe houses where a child in danger or fear may seek refuge and assistance.

What complicates the prevention of violence is the fact that violence in the family is frequently influenced by broader cultural patterns. Research suggests that battery in the family is related to the general level of violence that exists in a particular society.

Violence constitutes an abuse of power. It often emerges from the desire to dominate, degrade, subjugate, possess and control others. In the long run, the promotion of human rights, better education and the improvement of the status of women are needed, as well as a change of attitude towards domination, be it sexual or any other kind. Training individuals in the dynamics of successful family relationships includes the promotion of gender equality, equality in partnership between spouses and teaching coping skills. The starting-point is to strengthen the strong and well-functioning aspects of families.

Society and the family: policy dilemmas

The relationship between society and family privacy is not easy to solve. On the one hand, creating and maintaining a civilized society

---

[*] See reports of the Secretary-General to the Seventh Congress on the situation of women as victims of crime (A/CONF.121/16) and on the fair treatment of women by criminal justice systems (A/CONF.121/17 and Corr.1 and Add.1). See also the report of the Secretary-General to the Eighth Congress on domestic violence (A/CONF.144/17).

requires that it consistently and vigorously combat crime. On the other hand, society has a strong stake in assisting and safeguarding the family as a key social institution requiring certain protections and exemptions. What has not been adequately recognized is that the latter contributes to the former.

The family is regulated through a series of stipulations, immunities and privileges that do not impact other groups. For example, clear regulations control the formation and even more so the dissolution of the family, for instance, by divorce or legal separation. In other words, people need the permission of society to start and particularly to dissolve a family. Alarmed by the dramatic increase in the rate of divorces, some people in the United States of America have called for legislation that would forbid married adults with minor children to divorce until their children have reached majority. In other words, parents cannot or should not, they argue, be able to simply walk out on their children. Needless to say, counter-arguments exist.

In most cases, maintaining the unity of the family is a strong interest. This explains and justifies the reluctance of society to intervene in private family matters and to break up the family by applying the same criminal law it uses in cases involving unrelated people. This explains why those who argue forcefully for invoking criminal penalties and strong State intervention in cases of domestic violence, child abuse, incest, physical punishment of children, marital rape and other crimes within the family are, at times, perceived and criticized as being anti-family. There is no question that the family is different from other arrangements and institutions in society. This is true not just in the legal sense but in myriad other ways.

Life in the family is all-encompassing and thus very different from, for example, life at school, at the office or in the factory. This difference must be acknowledged and taken into account. Crime is only one among many different areas of behaviour and social relations where there are special rules and expectations for the family as contrasted to other groups. This complex of differences and protections constitutes, expresses and symbolizes the uniqueness and importance of the family as a social institution that addresses and, ideally, serves the needs of the whole person.

In a number of countries certain behaviour within the family previously overlooked has now been clearly labelled as criminal. The criminalization of previously tolerated conduct under reformed notions of child abuse, spouse abuse and marital rape is a clear indication that the status of women and children in many societies is changing from that of a possession to being an equal and having autonomous rights. The children's rights movement has made tremendous progress in obtaining the recognition of many children's rights and in significantly challenging the belief that children are the unquestioned property or wards of adults.[15, 16, 17] The Convention on the Rights of the Child[18] is a milestone in this quest for children's rights. The Convention on the Elimination of All Forms of Discrimination against Women[19] is another major instrument which aims, inter alia, at overcoming obstacles to achieving full gender equality.

The juncture between the family and the criminal justice system is delicate and fragile. On the one hand, some call for an increased involvement in family life by various State agencies, particularly the justice system, to protect those perceived as vulnerable in it: children, women and the elderly. On the other hand, others point out that the justice system and the State in general are poorly equipped to understand the unique requirements of the family and to deal with them in a manner that is positive, constructive and in the best interest of the offender, the victim and the family as a whole.

The dilemmas concerning intervention can be agonizingly difficult. For example, if the authorities intervene in a punitive way to remove an offending parent to protect one of the children, this may result in emotional loss experienced by the other children and the spouse. When that parent is the main provider it will result in economic hardships and possible loss of the family home. It can also result in shame, loss of reputation and social ostracism, often referred to as secondary victimization. These difficulties cannot be used to justify failing to intervene to stop violence, abuse and exploitation. However, relying principally on the criminal law to solve these painful situations is not always the best answer.

Considerable effort and resources must be invested to reconsider the manner of intervention in family affairs. To assume that the same action should be taken as in the case of a similar crime between strangers is simplistic. Such an assumption does not take into account the legitimate and real differences between the family and what it means to its members and other social institutions and relationships; at times they are as fleeting as a casual encounter. Solving the problem of crime within the family in an equitable and sensitive way challenges society's creativity, compassion, concern and willingness to allocate the needed funds and resources. It also requires that the parties involved, who may have different perceptions and assessments of the situation, be willing to set aside their differences and craft a solution that is in the true interest of the entire family and, because of the socialization role of the family, ultimately of society.

Families and the treatment of offenders

Families also have a pivotal role in the "treatment" and "rehabilitation" of a family member who has been convicted of a crime. Additionally, a consequence of crimes often overlooked in research and policy making is the negative impact the arrest, conviction and prison sentence of members of the family have on the remaining ones who may be deeply dependent on those members emotionally and financially.

Non-custodial sanctions

To find effective measures of dealing with offenders without the disruptive effect of imprisonment, an increasing variety of non-custodial sanctions are being introduced around the world. Besides being a more humane way of dealing with crime and of facilitating rehabilitative efforts, non-custodial measures also reduce the workload of frequently overburdened penal systems.

Alternatives to imprisonment include provisional probation (in Austria), home arrest (in Indonesia), home detention (in Australia), fines, suspension of sentence or of enforcement, and work release. Community service, known for over a century as a substitute for detention for fine default, or even as a substitute for imprisonment in traditional societies, is a promising alternative to imprisonment. The advantage of community service lies in the fact it gives offenders an opportunity to make amends by working for the well-being of others, and makes it possible for the community to contribute actively to their reintegration into society.*

Instead of legal interventions, or in addition to them, mediation may be used. In such cases, the offender and the victim, with the assistance of a neutral person, try to reach an understanding and find ways to compensate for the harm suffered.

Within a framework of a given non-custodial measure, supervision may be provided to assist the reintegration of the offender into society. In appropriate cases, various schemes, such as casework, group therapy, residential programmes and specialized treatment can be developed to meet the needs of offenders more effectively.

Non-custodial sanctions rely greatly on the informal and formal social support the offender is able to find. Thus the support of the family is one of the factors that should determine the sanction to apply if alternatives exist. For instance, a significant proportion of juveniles who commit minor offences may not warrant any legal intervention, especially where the family, school or other informal social control institution reacts in an appropriately constructive manner.**

---

* See the report of the Secretary-General to the Eighth Congress on alternatives to imprisonment and the reduction of the prison population (A/CONF.144/12).

** See the working paper prepared by the Secretariat, and submitted to the Eighth Congress, on prevention of delinquency, juvenile justice and the protection of the young: policy approaches and directions (A/CONF.144/16).

The acceptance of non-custodial sanctions by the general public and the family concerned is vitally important. Generally, the reactions of the society have been positive. On the other hand, the selection of offences and offenders for non-custodial sanctions must be carefully made. They should not be applied, for instance, if the offender continues his or her misbehaviour or uses threats and violence. Many families also need some kind of support in order to cope with their own feelings and to have control over the situation at home.

Non-custodial measures are most effective where efforts are coordinated, with adequate support, by the family of the offender, the correctional system and social welfare agencies. The use of alternatives to imprisonment must be coordinated with competent social services in facilitating, if needed, the social resettlement of the offender and his or her family.

Incarceration of adults

Countries vary considerably in their use of imprisonment and the length of custodial sentences. Concern has been growing about the effectiveness of different forms of such sanctions. Studies have shown that custodial sentences do not have significant effect on the deterrence of crime; on the contrary, the increasing incarceration population and prison overcrowding create additional social difficulties. Imprisonment may also have unintended harmful effects on the psychological and social state of the offender and his or her family. Reduction of the incarcerated population is also an economic question.

The sixth, seventh and eighth United Nations congresses on the prevention of crime and the treatment of offenders recommended that imprisonment should be a disposition of last resort. According to the Standard Minimum Rules for the Treatment of Prisoners,[20] incarcerated persons should be allowed, under the necessary supervision, to communicate with their family and reputable friends at regular intervals, both by correspondence and by receiving visits. These contacts often serve to establish the offender's hope for a better future which may also affect his or her subsequent career.

Incarcerated persons themselves may also be able to make a contribution to their families, even during imprisonment. The Basic Principles for the Treatment of Prisoners[21] state that conditions should be created enabling them to undertake meaningful remunerated employment to facilitate their reintegration into the workforce of the country and permit them to contribute to their own financial support and that of their families.

For the families of incarcerated persons to be an important and effective component in the rehabilitative process, a number of policies would be useful. For example, resources may need to be allocated for the transportation of relatives who cannot afford to visit detainees. Visiting schedules may need to be kept flexible to deal with the varied circumstances of the families of incarcerated persons. In a number of countries, prisoners depend on family members to provide food, clothing and other things that the institution does not provide. To facilitate this kind of material support, the prisoners should be kept close to their families.

Conjugal visits are important to preserve a marriage. Especially during long sentences, it still may happen that the non-sentenced spouse does not want to maintain the relationship and wants to divorce. In such cases, special help is needed for all parties, as these situations can create strong feelings of guilt, animosity and desertion.

Nowadays, planning interventions to reduce further criminal activity of an offender and lead to reintegration into society is considered important.[22] Rehabilitation of an offender should be a leading principle in all "treatment", sanctions and after-care. Since the family is most often the environment to which an offender returns, it should be taken into consideration from the very beginning of rehabilitation. A reality is that a number of families will not be willing to continue contact with the offender. With some support, however, they might reconsider their position. Having the offenders reintegrated into their natural environment is in the best interest of society. Family ties form a considerable part of a person's relatedness and commitment to society.

In ideal conditions, the penal institutions and community-based corrections include educational and therapeutical elements that help the offender and his or her family reconstruct their lives on more solid ground. Trained teachers and volunteers, educational and library facilities, and the access to religious representatives or other supporting personnel would serve this aim. A number of rehabilitative programmes have been developed. All offenders should benefit from arrangements designed to assist them in returning to family life, society, education or employment after release. Special courses might be devised to this end. After return to the community, services are needed to assist in finding accommodation, employment, as well as to assist in the reintegration process.

In many countries, volunteer or professional associations contribute to rehabilitation and augment the work of state authorities. Their work may include the provision of housing, the development of employment opportunities, group interaction, the counselling of offenders and their families as well as behaviour modification or supportive therapies.

Custodial detention of young persons

The imprisonment of young persons represents a special situation governed by United Nations standards, in particular, the United Nations Standard Minimum Rules for the Administration of Juvenile Justice (The Beijing Rules) and the United Nations Rules for the Protection of Juveniles Deprived of their Liberty. They require, inter alia, a distinctly separate and specialized "child-centred" juvenile justice "system", procedures and operations. Familial contacts are usually vital. Such contacts not only provide emotional and psychological support, but they also are an integral part of the right to fair and humane treatment. Maintaining contact with the young is as important to the parent as to the young offender. It helps both parties keep a realistic image of each other and helps to sustain interpersonal relationships.

Conclusion

In practically every society in human history the family has been the pivotal institution, the building block of society. The fact that the family is found everywhere across the millennia is because it performs certain vital functions that ensure the survival of the members of society. The most important of these functions is the reproduction, nurturing and socializing of the next generation.

One of the central themes of the present study is that the structure of social relationships shapes the style, form and effectiveness of social control systems, and that the family plays a key role.

In recent decades, especially in North America and Western Europe, social relationships have undergone rapid change. Weakening ties between individuals and families and between families and communities have led to a deterioration of the ability of families and communities to exercise the most effective form of social control, the informal one. This weakening of informal social controls has been accompanied by an increase in formal types of controls, some demonstrably ineffective. The numbers of police, judges, correctional officers, lawyers, psychotherapists, social workers and other official agents of social control are constantly growing with the crime rate.

Probably the most effective way to prevent crime and delinquency is to support, strengthen and nurture the family and the community as creators of those social bonds indispensable for successfully combating deviance. In particular, partnerships need to be formed between families and the institutions sharing family responsibilities.

Because of its role in socializing the young, the most effective primary crime prevention measures are clearly those that emphasize providing support to and strengthening the family unit, whatever the form of that unit. This could be accomplished, inter alia, through measures aimed at the elimination of impoverished living conditions, specific education in family life and parenting skills, and, particularly in urban society, through the development of community-liaison schemes and programmes.

For the family and subsequently the school to function successfully as crime prevention agents, the community must identify, develop and support a variety of essential services for the young, including counselling for both offenders and victims, community-based corrections and addiction-awareness campaigns. In particular, community services can provide mechanisms for rendering assistance to young persons of school age who have special problems the school and the family cannot deal with effectively.

Stable relationships between the family, the school and the community are especially useful in assisting young persons in developing skills in interpersonal relations and in finding their place in society. Priority should be given to community solutions for minor offences; whenever voluntary solutions to a conflict situation are possible, these should be encouraged, preferably with the participation of the local community. However, caution has to be exercised as regards the impact not only of formal but also of informal control networks, since both can and do exert positive and negative influences. Programmes should involve policy measures aimed at enhancing positive behaviour, improving learning and academic achievement, strengthening aspects of school life and promoting better relations between the school, the family and other segments of the community.

In support of families, assistance is needed. Health services, social welfare, housing, education and post-compulsory-education training can all contribute to a well-functioning family producing contributing members of society. Social support services should also be given to "troubled" families. This support should be as integrated, informal and non-interventionist as possible, always bearing in mind the long-term interests of the children.

For Governments the message should be clear: to maintain a well-ordered, contented society, an investment in the family is an investment in the future. The major challenge facing society is to balance the competing, deeply felt human needs for autonomy and belonging and the consequent need to develop fine-tuned solutions to the inherent contradictions between the desire for freedom, liberty and privacy and the need for law and order.

References

[1] General Assembly resolution 40/33, annex, of 29 November 1985.
[2] General Assembly resolution 45/112, annex, of 14 December 1990.
[3] General Assembly resolution 45/113, annex, of 14 December 1990.
[4] *Sixth United Nations Congress on the Prevention of Crime and the Treatment of Offenders, Caracas, 25 August-5 September 1980: Report prepared by the Secretariat* (United Nations publication, Sales No. E.81.IV.4).
[5] *Seventh United Nations Congress on the Prevention of Crime and the Treatment of Offenders, Milan, 26 August-6 September 1985: Report prepared by the Secretariat* (United Nations publication, Sales No. E.86.IV.1).
[6] *Eighth United Nations Congress on the Prevention of Crime and the Treatment of Offenders, Havana, 27 August-7 September 1990: Report prepared by the Secretariat* (United Nations publication, Sales No. E.91.IV.2).
[7] A/CONF.87/5.
[8] A/CONF.121/7.
[9] A/CONF.121/16.
[10] A/CONF.121/17 and Corr. 1 and Add. 1.
[11] A/CONF.144/16.
[12] United Nations publication, Sales No. E.90.IV.3.
[13] Morris Taggart, "The feminist critique in epistemological perspective: questions of context in family therapy", *Journal of Marital and Family Therapy*, vol. 11, No. 2 (1985), p. 104.
[14] Alan Jay Lincoln and Murray A. Straus, *Crime and the Family* (Springfield, Illinois, C. C. Thomas, 1985).
[15] Beatrice Gross and Ronald Gross, *The Children's Rights Movement: Overcoming the Oppression of Young People* (Garden City, New York, Anchor Press/Doubleday, 1977).
[16] Robert H. Mnookin and others, *In the Interest of Children: Advocacy, Law Reform and Public Policy* (New York, Freeman, 1985).
[17] Samuel M. Davis and Mortimer D. Schwartz, *Children's Rights and the Law* (Lexington, Massachusetts, Lexington Books, 1987).
[18] General Assembly resolution 44/25, annex, of 20 November 1989.
[19] General Assembly resolution 34/180 of 18 December 1979.
[20] *Human Rights: A Compilation of International Instruments* (United Nations publication, Sales No. E.88.XIV.1), sect. G.
[21] General Assembly resolution 45/111, annex, of 14 December 1990.
[22] Susan E. Martin, Lee B. Sechrest and Robin Redner, eds., *New Directions in the Rehabilitation of Criminal Offenders* (Washington, D.C., National Academy Press, 1981).

FAMILY and Youth: Issues, Problems and opportunities

9

Introduction

Historically, the family has performed a fundamental role in the process of socialization. The socialization of youth, however, is no longer seen as merely a simple transmission of types of behaviour, values and attitudes. First, there is a common perception that the family is in a state of crisis owing to changing moral values, rejection of family ties and bonds in favour of individualism, economic stress and the breakdown of the family, a phrase often associated with explanations of social maladies. Second, most countries have experienced shifts in women's roles, declining fertility rates, delayed marriages, unmarried cohabitation, ageing populations and an increase in single-parent households as well as out-of-wedlock births. In addition, rapidly increasing changes in society combined with cultural, economic and other factors have contributed to a perceived distance between youth and other family members. Yet, the family remains at the core of the socialization process and has, in modern societies, a critical supportive role in education. What families invest in their young members, it is generally agreed, determines in large measure their future opportunities and development.

Similarly, young people play a significant role in the democratization of both the society and the family. In families, youth are often the catalyst for positive change and serve as carriers of emerging trends and information from the greater society. They introduce new ideas to redistribute family responsibilities among male and female members, and they promote intergenerational cooperation between the young and the elderly members of the family. Through their exposure to schools, peers and the media, young people are often the most informed members of families. Their aspirations and opinions are frequently a major source of strength in families, and their sensitivity to the changing environment adds immeasurably to the adaptability of families. Youth also contribute financially or materially to families, or by their own labour. In many cases, these contributions are vital to the survival of family members.

The global conviction that intensified action and international cooperation on behalf of families were needed as an integral part of the worldwide effort to advance social progress and development led to the unanimous proclamation by the General Assembly of 1994 as the International Year of the Family (IYF).[1] Increased awareness of family issues and improved institutional capability of countries to tackle family-related problems with comprehensive policies were among the major objectives of the IYF. By the same token, the tenth anniversary of the International Youth Year: Participation, Development, Peace (1995) provides an opportunity for a reassessment of the effectiveness of existing youth policies and programmes and the philosophy upon which they are based. Changes in the context in which young people live, while not occurring uniformly, have nevertheless penetrated almost all aspects of life everywhere.

To better understand and appreciate the role of the family in the socialization of youth, the Secretariat for IYF and the Youth Policies and Programmes Unit of the Department for Policy Coordination and Sustainable Development of the United Nations Secretariat, in cooperation with the Government of China and the All-China Youth Federation, organized an Interregional Meeting on the Role of the Family in the Socialization of Youth. It was held in Beijing from 31 May to 4 June 1993. The present chapter is based on a working paper[2] commissioned for that Meeting by the United Nations and contains some major recommendations that were discussed and subsequently adopted by the participants.

Definition of adolescence and youth

Adolescence has generally been defined as being the time in a person's life between the ages of 10 and 19 years, and youth as being the time between 15 and 24 years. The present chapter considers youth as beginning with mid-adolescence and deals with the whole group of young people from the ages of 15 to 24. While chronological definitions are statistically convenient, in fact great variation exists in the timing and duration, though not the sequence, of the biological, social and psychological changes that characterize this period of transition. In most cultures the period is considered to begin with puberty.

In general, the terms adolescent(s), youth and young people tend to be used interchangeably. Adolescence is broadly regarded as the period of transition from childhood to adulthood in a developmental perspective, where biological, psychological and social maturation takes place. The characteristics of such development are interrelated, dynamic and interactive, but each culture has its own ways of acknowledging the social and psychological aspects of maturation.

Social status as an adult is granted in many countries when a young person reaches physical maturity or a particular age, or gains a certain level of ability. Where menstruation has been recognized as the entry to womanhood for girls, early marriage and parenthood are often the norm. There may be traditional procedures, such as initiation ceremonies to mark the transition of young people into adulthood, although many of these are breaking down. In such societies, there is often a rapid passage from childhood to adult life and the young person is usually given guidance about the rights and responsibilities that accompany it. Adolescence, as perceived in industrialized societies, scarcely exists in these situations.

In other societies, particularly those with high levels of urbanization and industrialization, there tends to be a period of time when a young person is considered to be no longer a child, but not yet an adult. He or she may be biologically mature and physically capable of parenthood, but may still be seen as being socially, psychologically and legally immature for a period of several more years. Longer education and later marriage and parenthood are the common pattern in this case.

Even with the differences found between (and even within) cultures in the ways young people are recognized to have become adult, it is still possible to identify common elements in their experience. They begin to look and feel different and must learn to cope with fundamental changes in their social roles and relationships and their rights and responsibilities. They find others responding differently to them and holding different expectations of them. As young people become more aware of themselves, there is a growing consanguine awareness of the wider world where they must take their place as adults. They increasingly face problems with long-range consequences and must prepare themselves for decisions about work, relationships, marriage and parenthood.

In many respects, both the generic problems of transition and the long-term aspirations of young people today are similar to those of their parents. What is different for so many is the world in which they are growing up. So often, parents and others who would traditionally have provided guidance have little experience of much of what today's young people have to face. This factor provides a most pressing challenge for both youth and families in a supportive, socialization role.

Youth is receiving increased attention today, partly because the experience of young people differs in so many ways from that of earlier generations, and partly because the number of young people is growing. Clearly, young people represent a major demographic, economic and political force whose needs cannot be ignored. Furthermore, there has been a trend over the last 150 years for both boys and girls to mature earlier physically. The average age for the onset of menstruation, for example, has dropped from 17 years in 1830 to 12.6 years in 1960, and there are indications that this downward trend is continuing. Improved nutrition appears to be the major factor. But while physical maturation is occurring earlier, the assumption of adult roles is being delayed in most urbanized and industrialized societies.

The socialization process

The family is clearly a powerful socializing institution. Because of its primacy, it has a significant long-term influence on a child's personality and future life. Families touch the lives of adolescents on a daily and personal basis, exercising some degree of power on their actions and behaviour. The family remains a constant, influential element despite fluctuations in its relative importance when, from time to time, peers, the community and media may seem strong external influences.

Parental involvement in the socialization of youth varies widely. In simple communities, the association is often close. As children accompany parents as they go about their daily business, young people are able to make a complete identification with their own future roles. Traditional societies contrast with modern cultures in the degree of emphasis given to the significance of parents. In most industrialized societies, children are taught to relate to contemporaries and peers from quite an early age. Similarly, much attention is given to these peer relationships by parents in assessing behavioural problems of children or in advising children on modes of conduct. In traditional cultures, however, children seem to be brought up to be more highly receptive to parental sway, the father particularly serving as a model for, and as a symbol of, traditional authority. Such a family structure, while based largely on an inappropriate gender-based distribution of power within families, provides social stability and continuity of behaviour between the generations; looks backward as much as forward and is highly resistant to social change. Yet, everywhere, the state of societal change exceeds all precedents, and the process of transition to adulthood is now often more complex, difficult and painful for young people than it ever was for earlier generations.

Some argue that the socialization role played by the family is becoming less and less meaningful as society grows more complex, as people become more alienated from one another, and as formal agencies outside the family increasingly begin to take over the responsibilities traditionally entrusted to the family. An example of this trend may be in the realm of sex education, as schools in some countries begin to assume a greater responsibility for imparting knowledge and values concerning sexual behaviour. Furthermore, the enormous effect of the mass media in conveying values to both children and adults may erode the traditional responsibility of parents to be the prime transmitters of values.

In general, emancipation from parental authority and emotional dependence is greatly accelerated during adolescence. In order to function effectively as adults, adolescents tend to detach themselves from their families and develop some independence in their behaviour, values and beliefs. The ease of transition to fuller independence in later adolescence depends to a great extent, however, upon the attitudes and behaviour of parents during the preceding years.

As they mature, adolescents are more likely to demand a nearly equal and active role in family discussions and decision-making. Families that allow latitude for the participation of young people in family decisions have, on the whole, fewer problems during the youth years than is the case in more rigid and authoritarian families. Young people need to learn to assume increasing responsibility for behaviour and decision-making within the context of their close relationships, if they are to be able to assume such responsibilities in their extra-familial relationships. Relationships with parents need to be renegotiated so that youth can assume greater autonomy while remaining connected with parents in a relationship of mutuality and friendship, rather than one predicated on parental control.

Two types of parent that seem to have the most positive outcomes for young people are the authoritative and democratic type of parents, both characterized as being highly responsive, moderately demanding and not restrictive. Democratic parents are less conventional, directive and assertive in their control than authoritative parents but, like them, they are supportive, caring, committed and manifest no problem behaviour or family disorganization. Young people from such families are better adjusted in terms of mental health, self-image, social integration and the ability to make independent decisions than their peers from authoritarian homes where parents exert rigid control or permissive homes where parents are either uninvolved or are lax in controlling behaviour. Adolescents from rejecting, neglecting or indifferent families are the least socially competent, and suffer most from psychological dysfunction and from problem behaviour during their youth years.

Positive family influences on youth have received scant attention from researchers, compared with negative parental influences that are more widely documented. The conflict with parents so often described as the generation gap is perhaps not as real as it seems. It is much more common to find young people and their parents sharing the same fundamental values. The differences are likely to occur in relation to less important subjects such as style of dress and taste in music, restrictions in the use of money or dating, choosing friends and driving. Parents, however, are often disturbed by their adolescent's adherence to peer standards.

Most family conflicts during youth years centre on the desire of adolescents for more freedom than parents think they are ready for. However, the unwillingness of youth to assume some of the responsibilities that parents feel should accompany increased maturity and independence is another common source of contention.

The adolescent subculture

If adolescents can find secure relationships with others of their own age, they are freer and abler to emancipate themselves from home ties. The support and values of contemporaries help in making the transition from parental control to individual autonomy. Perhaps because of the value of this supportive network in meeting the difficult challenges of transition, adolescents place such great importance upon acceptance by their peer group.

The need for group security may also lead to the formation of in-groups, such as gangs and cliques. Members of an in-group feel especially close to others within the group and are very much aware of the distinction between being "in" and "out", between those who belong and those who do not.

In either case, relations with peers help adolescents to prepare for adult love and friendship and to reduce dependence on parental standards. To some extent, the peer group takes over the controlling function exercised by parents. This, in turn, expands and changes the repertoire of acceptable and non-acceptable behaviour. Impulsiveness or self-centredness, for example, might be overlooked by parents yet may not be tolerated by one's peers.

Delinquency and gangs

Contrary to the popular view, peer group activity alone rarely produces delinquency. The roots of delinquency lie across a much broader platform drawn from the social context within which it operates. Social delinquency is a symptom of broader problems in society, such as the alienation of many adolescents from culture and institutions, particularly young people in minority and low-income groups and their inability to find jobs. Children from poverty-stricken homes are often ill-prepared to meet the demands of schools, which tend to value middle-class standards. Those who encounter a great deal of frustration and humiliation in their attempts to meet school standards may gather together in groups to express their defiance. They may drop out of school and, failing to find employment, turn to theft and acts of violence in their boredom, resentment and desire for the material things so temptingly advertised by the mass media. Delinquent gangs give them the status that they cannot get elsewhere. That desire for status is a crucial factor. Poverty, broken homes and rejection by parents: all contribute to the other, complex forces that induce high delinquency rates in slum areas.

The peer group, however, does play a heavy role in enabling delinquent activity. The non-peer-oriented adolescent is less likely to engage in delinquent behaviour. Similarly, females, who have been traditionally socialized to adopt a passive role in respect to authority, have tended to be less frequently involved in delinquent behaviour. However, these same traditional roles make young women vulnerable to victimization by criminal activity and exploitation. Recent changes in patterns of female delinquency are attributable, at least in part, to positive changes in sex roles in contemporary society.

Delinquency has long been thought to be a problem of poorer urban youth and of school drop-outs. Evidence is growing, however, of a substantial amount of delinquent activity among middle-class adolescents, especially suburban youth. Individual delinquency, not associated with gangs, bad neighbourhoods, poverty or cultural conflict, is more puzzling. The subtle influence exerted by child-rearing practices is suggested by data pertaining to the influence of childhood discipline on later aggression and crime. Additionally, many severe family problems, such as domestic violence, are found in all types of families at all socio-economic strata. The fact that the tendency towards delinquent careers starts early has been pointed out in several studies in which delinquent or criminal careers have begun between the ages of 6 and 10.

Juvenile delinquency is correlated with a number of microsocial and macrosocial factors, including large family size, lack of participation in groups, lack of religious beliefs, lower socio-economic levels, working mothers, divorced parents, parental alcoholism, low aptitude, poor school achievement, and with processes bringing about social disorganization such as rapid industrialization. To establish simple casual relationships between the above-mentioned factors and the occurrence of delinquency is not possible, especially as many of the factors are interrelated. Furthermore, while such factors can be coincident with delinquency, they may signal other issues, such as inadequate supportive infrastructure for working mothers or benefit systems for the poor.

The changing social environment

The family serves as the primary agent of socialization, plays an important role in the transmission of human values and cultural identity and is a major focus for material and emotional support essential to the growth, development and well-being of its members, especially children and youth. In the broader sense, the family educates, trains, socializes, motivates and supports its children and young people, thereby investing in their growth and acting as a vital resource for development.

There is no universal pattern of families. Families may be nuclear or extended; they may consist of one generation or several; they may contain children and one or two parents or a number of adults who take on parental roles. They may be bound together by birth, by marriage, by adoption, by love and affection, or by economic or social advantage. Culture, religion and the political, social and economic organization of societies influence the ways families function, how they have evolved, and the ways they try to meet the physical, social and emotional needs of their members.

In traditional societies, the extended family, which may include several generations plus cousins, uncles and aunts, usually assists in the socialization of young people. This structure provides great social material and moral support to the young as well as a variety of role models preparing the way for adulthood. In this model, adults exert a relatively high degree of influence on youth, and yet young people have a broader base for consultation, advice and opinion than in nuclear families. In the nuclear family, consisting solely of parents and their children, there may be less adult control, and the young usually have greater freedom in choosing friends, education, career, work and spouse. Both types can provide a basis for the healthy development of youth. In modern times, however, the traditional symbols of stability in the family have been threatened. The divorce rate has risen, the number of single-parent families has increased, and large numbers of young people have left their families prematurely and migrated to towns. Even where young people remain within their families, because of the radical changes in social and economic conditions, many parents feel ill-equipped to help their children prepare for experiences they themselves have never had.

Furthermore, single-parent families living in poverty are often forced to leave children unattended or compelled to take their older children out of school prematurely to enter the workforce. Poor parents often have neither the energy nor the time to invest in interpersonal relationships, resulting in neglect of their children's emotional needs. In extreme circumstances, they are compelled to abandon their children, thereby relinquishing their parental functions. Public concerns about the effects of such problems on children and the young and society, in general, has demanded the introduction of interventions, external to the family, for its protection and the fulfilment of its obligations, especially those of child care. This includes provisions for the material support of poor families, often based on the number of children present.

In some places, the ability of families to fulfil essential functions has been eroded to the extent that there is a complete functional breakdown, putting the health and well-being of their young at risk. Family-support functions and structure, and opportunities for the development of new relationships, roles, behaviour and skills appear to be weakened in relation to other societal factors as societies become more modern.

This changing social environment has important implications for adolescent and youth development. In so far as the changes include the breakdown of family functioning and premature separation from family relationships, youth are deprived of a factor that builds resilience and might otherwise protect them from adversity later on. Such problems also often radically alter the nature of the new relationships with other young people and adults, at a time when patterns for future relationships are being set, having a profound long-term impact on their development and lives.

The levels of intra- and international migration have increased. Young migrants often encounter a hostile environment and are vulnerable to a range of emotional and behavioural problems. Migrant youths include those who are homeless, refugees and victims of war. A disproportionate number of urban migrants are young; about one fourth are between the ages of 15 and 24, with a somewhat larger number of males than females. Children and young people together account for over 70 per cent of the total rural-urban migration in less developed countries. This is not surprising, as the primary motive for migration is to seek education or employment. The switch from what is a traditional and often relatively stable rural society to an urban conglomeration that often lacks the infrastructure for family support is one of the major barriers to the healthy development of young people today.

As technology grows more complex, more education and training are needed to achieve economic independence. While reproductive maturity is essentially biological in origin, economic independence is more often a result of national and international factors. With high levels of youth unemployment, young people are often trapped between a growing sense of individual maturity and a lengthening of economic dependence. In traditional rural societies, the transition from childhood to adulthood is fairly short, with predetermined roles waiting to be assumed. In such situations, young people can be reasonably certain that their lives will be substantially similar to those of their parents. In modern affluent societies, however, more support is available for young people during the longer periods of training and education required for them to fit into technologically sophisticated economic systems. Young people can be fairly sure that their lives will be substantially different from those of their parents, and that their children's lives will be substantially different from their own.

The FAMILY and Youth: Issues, Problems and Opportunities

In transitional societies, young people may simultaneously be involved in two cultures: the traditional one in which their parents grew up and which they may still value, and the modern one that may be taught in schools and portrayed in the mass media. A similar clash of cultures may occur in the lives of young people whose families have migrated to another country or from a rural to an urban area. For a young person experiencing the natural stresses of the transition from childhood to adulthood, the tension is heightened, the frustration aggravated and the likelihood of problems increased.

Families and societies perpetuate gender inequalities in child-rearing in many countries. The profile of the girl child shows numerous deprivations. They are more frequently sick, less well-fed, more likely to be illiterate than boys, and they lack the opportunities to better themselves. Like their mothers, they often work long hours to meet family needs, such as caring for their younger siblings, fetching fuel and water, cooking meals, shopping, washing clothes and cleaning homes, as well as looking after the old and the ill. Such responsibilities are often so demanding they can be met only at the expense of their own development. While the burden of poverty has serious implications on the life of the girl child, other factors such as seclusion, traditional practices and customs and social sanctions for early marriage (in some cases at less than 10 years of age), further inhibit development opportunities for girls. These inequalities are evidenced in the lower life expectancy, literacy, school enrolment, participation in the labour force and in the social and political activities of girls.

Many children and youth of the working poor, whether in a rural or urban society, have hardly known a childhood. Parental expectations of their children's contribution often exceed helping with household chores and can include work outside the home in unskilled, low-paid occupations. The implications of the missed opportunities for education, recreation and normal family life on the development of these children and youth are tremendous, with repercussions on their interactions with family and society. More significantly, childhood is not used as a time of preparation for adulthood by these families, which binds them further into the cycle of poverty, illiteracy and inadequate environments for the child care of successive generations. The roles, commitments and expectations of the individual members in such families overlap as children and youth take on familial responsibilities and obligations that their parents are unable to meet.

Children and youth separated from or abandoned by their families because of armed conflict, poverty, breakdown of family ties (sometimes described as social orphans or street children and youth), learn to fend for themselves, sometimes at very young ages. These young people are extremely vulnerable to exploitation, drugs, crime, prostitution and other social problems, leaving them few choices and options for the future. In the case of the girl child, these conditions are accentuated through her additional vulnerability to exploitation.

The contemporary nuclear family is more often geographically isolated from its relatives than previously. More children survive than die, older family members are much older and the proportion of the old and very old is rising. Isolation and ageing can strain affective ties and are calling into question traditional roles and patterns of family functioning.

Another factor altering family functions, but with positive effect, are the changes in the roles and status of women: a new dynamic linked to longer education, literacy, the means to control fertility, changing economic values and the ability to earn. Another important development is the rise of the one-parent household. Nearly 30 per cent of all families in some countries, often concentrated among the most disadvantaged groups, belong to this type. Elsewhere, single-parent families arise as a result of war, migration and hunger. Finally, the acquired immunodeficiency syndrome (AIDS) is already devastating a growing number of families, leaving many infants, children and youth orphaned, often in the absence of any viable support system.

Large numbers of families are at risk in a variety of circumstances, such as war, drought, famine, racial and ethnic violence, and economic deprivation. Poverty-induced labour migrants, single-parent families, refugee and displaced families, and those whose livelihoods have been destroyed by environmental degradation are a few examples of families at risk.

Some groups of families, for intra-familial reasons, lack the capacity to meet the basic needs of their members. These families may manifest a variety of problems, including domestic violence, drug and alcohol dependency, sexual and child abuse and neglect. Damage to childrens' and adolescents' mental health and psychosocial behaviour, and to their ability to form lasting relationships, is most commonly observed as a result of such serious family problems.

Despite all these negative forces, many families respond to challenge with surprising resilience, and the essential functions of the family continue to be served under extreme hardships. Thus, groups of abandoned street youth sometimes care for their younger members as if in families. Local communities may look after their elderly and sick, supporting them emotionally as well as physically. Responsibilities usually recognized as being those of the family are often readily assumed by other groups. In some cases, these responsibilities become incorporated into the culture before evolving into national social policies and sometimes becoming laws.

The role of youth in socialization

Young family members often play a considerable role in socialization within the family. They can have a positive impact on their parents' personalities. Parents can receive from their children information on many issues with which they normally do not deal. Young people bring into the family fresh ideas and information, and they propagate social, cultural and political changes germinating in schools and colleges. They motivate parents with new ideas, social and political thinking. Young people, with their idealism and receptivity to change, have significantly contributed to programmes and campaigns of social development. Immigrant and refugee parents often learn from their children the language and customs of the new country.

Young people have also contributed to bringing about a change of behaviour in family settings Parents have been forced to adopt certain ideas because of their teenage children, and also because of their fear of being left out of the new and emerging culture.

Many examples of youth-to-youth programmes and also youth solidarity efforts serve to channel their idealism, energy and vitality for the good of others, particularly other youth. As members of organized groups, youth not only bring family values to the groups but also bring new values to the family. They participate in the betterment of the community. They mobilize peers, family members and others in the community for a cause or on other social issues.

Young people also make significant contributions to sharing household tasks. In African families, where the number of young people is disproportionately high, youth in the family are often called upon to assume adult productive responsibilities, even at an early age. In Western culture, for young people to share many household tasks is becoming common practice, even though young female members do more than the males. In many developing countries, mainly young girls share the household tasks while boys look for extra family income. As a consequence, a large number of the young are part of the labour force. In industrialized countries, teenagers often work after school to earn money for their own consumption and occasionally to assist the family. Access to extended families is the only stable form of social support in many societies; children take care of their parents and grandparents and support them for the rest of their lives. Youth in families make major contributions to caring for other family members.

Major issues and problems affecting youth

Because of the rapid communications in modern society, the environmental stresses associated with psychosocial problems are more or less common to the whole industrialized and urbanized world. The way children or adolescents react to such stresses, however, is influenced by local conditions and varies considerably between and within countries. In general, nevertheless, three categories of reaction are frequently encountered. The first is a passive form of coping, which includes varying degrees of withdrawal ranging from school-leaving to dropping out of society in general, and to its most extreme form, suicide. The second is an aggressive form of coping, including juvenile delinquency, gang violence and terrorism. The third category includes some compromise reaction, such as instability at school or work and substance abuse.

Socio-economically deprived children and adolescents are at higher risk of falling victim to psychosocial problems. Children and adolescents living in sub-optimal social and economic conditions are prepared less well for school, more likely never to attend and more likely to leave early. Furthermore, the socio-economically deprived are always among the most vulnerable to the effects of demographic, economic and political upheavals.

Growing evidence suggests that manifestations of problem behaviour are not isolated from and independent of one another. They include alcohol and drug abuse, cigarette smoking and early sexual activity. For example, heavy drinking and the use of some other drugs is often associated with antisocial behaviour and implicated in traffic accidents, a major cause of death and disability in young people. The use of tobacco, alcohol and other substances is associated with poorer performance at school, at work and in sport. Peer pressure plays a significant role in problem behaviour and may be particularly significant for the young person from a divided family, one that lives in an unrewarding environment, or who is less successful at school, in sport or in making friends.

The use of alcohol and drugs

Drinking alcohol is often seen as a way of appearing to be adult, which may be encouraged by the example of older family members or the media. If the family is either excessively tolerant or full of discord, the risk is greater. Peer pressure plays a major role in sustaining drinking behaviour. It is seen as a way of gaining social approval, although it may lead to the opposite if associated with drunkenness. Drinking also often has a positive image among the young, being associated with toughness, rebelliousness, attractiveness and sociability. Some young people, unable to cope with the pressure to achieve some of the developmental tasks of growing up, whether in the family, in their social relationships, at school, or in seeking or doing work, turn to alcohol for emotional relief.

The average age of drug users has declined in recent years, and multiple drug use has become more common. The use of one drug is likely to lead to the use of many, often in the search for ever stronger effects and with more dangerous consequences. As with alcohol abuse, the drug user is likely to fail in many ways, at school, in relationships and at work. Many young people have turned to crime and prostitution to maintain their supply of drugs. Among the factors commonly associated with drug use are family and peer tolerance or active approval of drug use, weak parental control and discipline, ready access to drugs and alienation.

Suicide

Suicide rates among young people are rising in both developed and developing countries more than in all other age groups. In many countries, suicide ranks second after accidents as the leading cause of death among the young. Young men commit suicide much more commonly than young women who, however, attempt suicide with much greater frequency, sometimes causing permanent damage to themselves.

The disruption of family relations is one of the most frequent causes of suicidal behaviour. The pressures arising from urban migration, isolation, intense competition at school and unemployment are other important stress factors. For some young people, the pressures become overwhelming, resulting in low self-esteem and depression. The causes of suicide may be multiple, however, including lack of any emotional support. Recent evidence shows that increased suicide rates are strongly related to the concurrent presence of all these social factors. It may also be associated with drug and alcohol dependence and mental instability.

Violence and accidental and intentional injury

Social violence in which young people are both victims and instigators of aggression is dramatically on the rise. In the industrialized world and in many less developed countries, violent death, including suicide, murder and accidental death, heads the list of causes of mortality among those between 15 and 24 years of age, especially young men.

This violence is likely to have multiple causes. Some factors commonly identified as related to violence include poverty, unemployment, crowding and reduction in the control exercised in the socialization of young people. But individual factors are also likely to contribute. They include experimentation, risk-taking, defiance of adult authority, drug and alcohol abuse, a sense of failure, frustration and hopelessness, and heavy exposure to violence in the streets. Other reasons for youth violence are the absence of recognized social status for the young, loosening traditional links within the family, community and society and uncertainty about the future.

Accidents are one of the major causes of mortality and morbidity among young people aged between 10 and 24 years throughout the world. As much as half of all deaths in many countries are caused by accidents and injuries. Road accidents are often accompanied by intoxication with alcohol or other drugs. Other behavioural factors that contribute to accidental injury in young people are exuberance, lack of experience, a feeling of invulnerability and risk-taking. But environmental conditions can contribute greatly to risks, and often a combination of risk-taking with an unsafe environment leads to injury.

Sexual harassment or abuse of young people is another problem receiving increasing attention. Intercourse with a minor (other than a spouse), whether forced as in rape, or enticed as is sometimes the case in incest or paedophile relationships, is universally condemned. Incest is particularly difficult to deal with since the adolescent who experiences it, most commonly a girl with a father or stepfather, is likely to face extreme hazards if she reports it. Typically, the abuser employs threats as a form of coercion and to enforce silence. Other family members may be implicated or are in a state of denial concerning the incestuous abuse. The victim may be condemned, punished, or the family broken up, and is likely to retain feelings of guilt.

Problems related to school

Formal education is becoming accessible to a greatly increasing number of children and adolescents each year. But school attendance does not necessarily mean that effective learning is taking place or that the education the schools are providing is relevant to their students' needs. In families where the values, languages, attitudes and milieu are more distant from the school, such as among poor families in non-poor areas, rural families in urban areas, migrant and immigrant families, the stress of adjustment to the school setting will be greater than usual.

The pressure to perform in school is often a major source of problematic stress for young people. This pressure comes from all sides (parents, teachers, older peers) as a by-product of the emphasis placed on education in industrialized society. Schools often adopt policies such as streaming (dividing students by performance levels), which greatly increase the stress resulting from the pressure to perform. Psychosocial problems may result if the stress of schooling is too great. The reactions to schooling stress are varied: phobia is common; antipathy, truancy and school-leaving are more widespread; and psychosomatic symptoms occur at all ages. In extreme cases, a quite small but significant number of suicides are associated with the stress of schooling.

Youth and work

Work is one of the important elements in developing the self-image of the adolescent. The employee role links individuals closely to other people of the same age group and, at the same time, anchors them firmly in the economic life of the community. It provides deeper social roots and enhances self-dignity and a sense of usefulness. With employment, the young person achieves a measure of financial independence and, in some cultures, it also brings standing in the family and a voice in family affairs. Financial independence also creates opportunities for marriage and family formation.

Failure at the economic level brings feelings of inadequacy and insecurity and may result in peer rejection. Such problems create disharmony in the family and lead to several family and social problems, such as vandalism, stealing and other criminal activity.

Leaving school and entering work

Three aspects of modern industrial society seem to generate problems related to school leaving and work entry: the trend towards prolonged, mass, general education; the fact that education is the key to social mobility; and the fact that the economic crises of recent times make it less and less likely that adolescents will be able to realize their chosen vocational aspirations. These factors provoke parental and school pressure on children and adolescents and result in stress.

When young people leave school and enter the labour market, they soon encounter the disproportion between high job qualification requirements and the low potential associated with unskilled employment. Widespread unemployment, which is highest among the young, or inappropriate employment (young people obtaining jobs below their qualifications and education) are key problems affecting young people.

In addition, the stresses resulting from prolonged schooling and a lack of suitable employment upon completion of studies undermines the incentive for education and may contribute to social problems. One common reaction is to withdraw from school before the completion of studies. When the educational and employment systems fail to deliver on expectations, youth are much more receptive to various forms of antisocial behaviour.

For many young migrants and those who have grown up in an urban environment, the town and city are unable to fulfil their aspirations; not enough employment is available in the modern sector to absorb them, and huge numbers become part of the unorganized or informal sector, living in the squatter and slum areas that are growing more rapidly than the modern cities they surround. Alcoholism, drug abuse and crime among adolescents and youth can often be attributed to the stresses of school leaving and work entry. Adolescent prostitution is another problem that sometimes arises out of economic hardship.

Sexual behaviour and reproductive health

Of all the changes that occur during adolescence, none arouses more interest and anxiety than those related to sexuality. For adolescents and youth, the way sexuality is dealt with in their families, the degree and soundness of the information they are given, and the nature of the relationships they have with other people, including their sexual partners, will determine whether their sexual behaviour contributes positively or negatively to their overall socialization.

Many cultures are witnessing changes in established values about sexual behaviour, at a time when many of the traditional systems of preparation for adult sexual life have begun to break down. An important factor is that young people are reaching physical maturity at an earlier age as a result of improved nutrition, environmental conditions and health care.

Cohabitation among young people has become a common phenomenon and has resulted in many other significant changes, such as fertility patterns and inheritance rights. The distinction between children born in wedlock and those of unwed partners has become irrelevant in some countries. The number of children born out of wedlock has increased dramatically in many countries, presenting novel and pressing social policy issues.

Adolescent pregnancy is a serious worldwide issue associated with many health and other related emotional, social and economic problems. In developing countries, it frequently arises from early marriage, sometimes just after menarche, but in most countries an increasing proportion of young people are becoming sexually active at earlier ages and pregnant prior to marriage. The pregnant adolescent is often reluctant to seek medical attention early enough, because of fears of negative reaction to her sexual activity. Similarly, contraception to prevent pregnancy is often absent or ineffective in this population group, whether because of the pressure to conceive among married girls in traditional societies, or because of anxiety about the anticipated negative reaction of others to their sexual activity. Shortcomings in sexual education also contribute to adolescent pregnancy.

The damaging consequences of childbearing too young are not only bio-medical, however. Adolescent pregnancy or marriage is likely to bring an abrupt end to education, and arrest social and economic development. In extended family systems, the adolescent mother may have the support of kin in raising her child. With the nuclearization of family units and increasing numbers of women employed away from home, however, the traditional support systems of adolescent mothers are not available to the extent they might once have been. The unwed adolescent mother and her child are likely to suffer great social and economic hardship. She may have to bring up the child single-handed in poor economic conditions while she herself is not sufficiently mature to provide the necessary psychological and material support for her child. Fathers of children born to adolescent mothers are generally uninvolved in the responsibilities of child care and only rarely provide material support to the mother and child.

A second hazard of unprotected sexuality in adolescence is the possibility of contracting one of the many sexually transmitted diseases (STD), including the human immunodeficiency virus (HIV)/AIDS. The incidence of STD among adolescents has increased markedly during the last 20 years. Young people are often reluctant to ask for medical help because, as with the pregnancy of an unmarried adolescent, they fear the reaction of the health provider and the possibility of disclosure to others.

The new scourge of AIDS poses special problems for a number of reasons. It is not only, at present, incurable but, unlike other STD, it is also fatal. Transmission may come through sexual contact, through sharing a contaminated needle among drug users, or through the mother to the baby. Problem behaviour is often clustered, and this makes drug users among adolescents particularly vulnerable. For an adolescent to seek help for a suspected infection may well mean facing the suspicion that he or she has been sexually active, possibly homosexual and/or using drugs: suspicions that might be particularly difficult to tolerate. Furthermore, learning about the presence of an HIV or AIDS infection can have devastating personal consequences. Disclosure to others may lead to varying degrees of social ostracism and economic hardship. Despite vast publicity, many myths remain, perhaps particularly among the adolescent population who have limited access in most societies to sound information about sexuality and sexual behaviour.

Where the traditional systems for providing information and guidance on sexuality, reproduction and parenthood and for supervising courtship and marriage are breaking down, they must be rebuilt or replaced. The problems faced by so many sexually active young people demonstrate that this has become a matter of urgency. If parents or other elders lack confidence or are embarrassed about discussing such matters, then their children will be forced to rely on their peers for their sexual knowledge, possibly with disastrous results. Most school curricula have little place for education about sexuality, and it is often excluded on the grounds that it may lead to sexual activity. However, many young people are already adopting new patterns of sexual behaviour and the consequences of ignorance are invariably more harmful than those of knowledge.

Opportunities for action

A sound knowledge of what constitutes proper development in diverse cultures is essential when planning and implementing appropriate interventions in support of youth and families with young members. Research is also needed to assess the impact of policies and legislation, to determine ways of promoting effective intersectoral and interdisciplinary action, and of identifying the best approaches to the involvement of young people themselves in planning and implementing programmes for their wellbeing. Knowledge alone is insufficient; skills in communicating and applying knowledge is also essential. For this purpose, training all those who can effectively interact with the young is needed. Advocacy, too, is important to achieve appropriate policies, legislation and public attitudes that support such needs. Whatever programmes are developed require systematic evaluation, taking into account both objective and subjective measures of effectiveness and impact.

Policies and legislation

Providing services to prevent or correct problems arising among youth can be supported by policies and legislation in many sectors, including health, education, social services, criminal justice, youth sports and culture, employment and others. But policies are rarely effectively coordinated and often push in conflicting directions. Legislation is often inconsistent as is the case, for example, in the widely divergent minimum legal ages for contracting marriage, performing military service, driving motor vehicles, drinking alcohol, voting, leaving school and taking up employment. These difficulties are complicated by a lack of information about the laws that exist, as well as the failure to implement them.

Legislation can be effective in addressing issues affecting youth. Examples include laws that reduce or eliminate advertising and the availability of, and accessibility to, harmful substances such as tobacco, alcohol or drugs; that strengthen the requirements for obtaining a driving licence; that introduce safety measures in the workplace; that raise the minimum age of marriage; and that permit and encourage the provision of appropriate sexual education and services to prevent teenage pregnancy. Policies and legislation, however, need to be implemented not only formally, but also by all those who influence the lives of young people. Similarly, legislation should not be seen as merely an instrument for control, but also as a source of protection for young people.

The need to reconsider the present philosophy of social policies is urgent in many countries so as to determine joint objectives and integrated mechanisms to be oriented towards the family and youth within one framework. National family legislation, policies and programmes should be related to those concerned with youth to integrate better the formulation, implementation and evaluation processes. Both governmental and non-governmental organizations and agencies concerned with family and youth issues should coordinate their work more closely.

National youth policies should keep in perspective family issues, consider youth as important members of the family and include programmes in areas such as youth rights, age at marriage, adolescent health, housing, employment and poverty. Youth and family issues should be considered in the context of tradition, culture, values and the family background. The principal concern of programmes should be the overall development of youth as responsible members of the family, society and country.

The family should be assisted and encouraged to fulfil its responsibility of nurturing and work as a conduit for the transmission of values, culture and information to young members of the family. Since family functions are diminishing as a result of modernization, the State needs to protect and provide services to families, especially those at risk, by the formulation of appropriate family legislation, policies and programmes. These measures should result in the effective functioning of the family for the socialization of youth and youth participation in the socialization of the family.

All Governments should adopt a comprehensive national youth policy to be continuously reviewed in the light of emerging social changes, including the family perspective, the spirit of volunteerism, the principles of integration, responsible leadership, involvement and participation in decision-making and training opportunities.

The provision of services to prevent or correct problems confronting youth should be supported by policies and legislation encompassing various sectors such as health, education, social services, criminal justice, youth sports and culture and employment. These policies and legislation should be conducted on an intersectoral basis.

All countries should establish or strengthen national bodies or similar mechanisms dealing with youth, with the active participation of youth leaders, and representatives of business communities, national unions of family organizations and national family planning associations as well as other family-related non-governmental organizations.

The family-welfare sector

Families should be assisted and encouraged to fulfil their responsibility of nurturing, as well as to work as a conduit for the transmission of values, culture and information to young members of the family. Special efforts need to be made to educate and encourage young adults to practise appropriate parenting techniques, including shared responsibility for child-rearing. Families should be encouraged to understand the importance of education for all members of the family, especially women and girls, and to enhance their involvement in providing formal and informal educational opportunities. At the same time, young people should be encouraged to share their feelings and aspirations with their parents, while parents should create opportunities to involve youth in decisions affecting them.

Established and effective lines of communication are essential to supporting families for youth welfare and maintaining intergenerational understanding. The ability of families to provide basic health care, including proper nutrition, improved food storage and clean water needs to be properly acknowledged and assistance provided. Young members of the family require appropriate information and other forms of support to prevent delinquency, crime, drug and alcohol abuse, irresponsible sexuality and the spread of diseases, such as HIV/AIDS.

Governments, as well as appropriate intergovernmental agencies and international relief organizations, should take urgent action against violence and atrocities committed against families, in particular against children and young women, in order to bring to an end such injustices, including all forms of discrimination, aggression, repression, violence, racism and segregation. Immediate treatment for the victims and their families should be provided.

Governments should set priorities and maintain a balance of care vis-à-vis the various sectors of concern to the family and youth, and provide services aimed at target categories of the population, such as those living in rural and urban areas, families at risk, and the educated and illiterate.

The social-welfare sector

Social welfare services differ from country to country. In some countries, financial assistance is an integral part of the family welfare service and families are provided with supportive assistance to bring up children and adolescents. In such situations, youth are often also provided with assistance to seek vocational or other training. The lack of resources in developing countries make these services generally unavailable, although providing guidance, case-work help and other assistance to deal with psychosocial problems is often possible.

Many young families, especially single-parent and female-headed families, find the constant need to balance work and family responsibilities to be among the most demanding aspects of daily life. Greater attention should be given to the reduction of stress caused by such demands and to the provision of adequate support systems.

Governments, as well as the private sector, should provide day-care facilities for children and the aged, nursing care for the elderly or infirm, and flexible work schedules. Young parents, both male and female, should not be penalized at work in terms of job security and promotion for meeting familial obligations.

The income-generating function of family units, especially in developing countries, is often crucial for their survival, particularly for poor and young families. Governments, non-governmental organizations and the private sector should give increased attention to encouraging such self-reliance through productive family projects by means such as credit facilities, technical assistance, training, the use of cooperatives and market assistance.

Governments, non-governmental organizations and the private sector should pay urgent attention to the situation of young families living in poverty, resulting in such problems as street children and homeless youth. Young people from such families should be the target of youth programmes for income-generation and skills-training.

Social welfare services should be designed to enable families to meet their needs, cope with stress, develop harmonious interpersonal relationships and improve family functioning. Such services should also include assistance to youth in vocational and other training.

"Drop-in" centres where young people may turn in the absence of their family or peer support systems should be provided. Phone-in or hot-line services have also proved useful to meet the needs of young people in stress.

Through a series of activities, guidance should be provided on the purpose, contents, methods and ways of the socialization of youth in the family in accordance with the situation confronting youth and the cultural heritage of the country.

Agencies that provide social welfare services need to be strengthened to accommodate growing needs. In view of the paucity of qualified professionals in the public social welfare sector, it is necessary to promote legislation that would provide incentives for qualified volunteers in the areas relating to the family and youth to ensure adequate and qualified support, irrespective of budgetary constraints.

The health sector

Several models for adolescent health services exist, including special services for young people embedded in a general service; specialized services for adolescents only, which deal with all aspects of adolescent health; single-issue services, such as those provided for alcohol or drug problems; and health services for young people which exist in other contexts, such as the school system or youth organizations. Young people can be helped best with an integrated approach, rather than by approaches that focus primarily on single issues. Many of the problems are interrelated and share common roots. Promoting the healthy development of youth will likely preclude the need for a curative response later. For the health sector to be effective, however, well-articulated policies are required that give priority to promoting health and preventing problems. These efforts must be coordinated across sectors, and require trained staff who are knowledgeable and skilled in working with adolescents or in training others who influence their health.

Family members, school staff, community and youth workers should be trained in the early detection of warning signals of high-risk youth, such as young persons with poor self-esteem and a low self-image, who are unsuccessful in the eyes of peer groups.

The education sector

After the family, perhaps the most important influence on the socialization of young people are their teachers. The school, as a formal institution of learning, imposes a particular set of conditions on the educational process quite different from the type of learning taking place in the family, in peer groups or in the community. The school system offers an ideal opportunity to reach many young people, and elements of family-life education are, in fact, sometimes found in subjects such as social sciences, biology and home economics. Unfortunately, where they do exist, they tend to be provided more for girls than for boys, often reinforce gender stereotypes and focus too heavily on traditional, home-making skills. School curricula are also sometimes dominated by a system of formal, written examinations; however, many aspects of family-life education, particularly those concerned with values and personal development skills, do not easily lend themselves to such examination. Consequently, family-life education is too often neglected because of the demands of a crowded timetable or else is seen by teachers, students or parents as having little value because it will not be directly assist in the search for a job.

Although in some countries family-life education or its equivalent is being more formally and prominently included in the school syllabus, in most countries formal family-life education is still in the early stages of development. Therefore, many of the children and adolescents currently in school do not have systematic access to family-life education.

The need is to recognize that after the family teachers are perhaps the most important influence on the socialization of young people. Thus, the socialization function of education needs to be strengthened. Schools should be agents of cultural transmission and continuity and help transmit accumulated knowledge, skills and values.

Formal and non-formal education in families, schools and communities should be emphasized for responsible citizenship and leadership for, by and with youth, and the promotion of peace, mutual respect and understanding among youth across different ethnic and socio-economic backgrounds.

Adolescent peer groups and peer-group relations, both in schools and universities and in out-of-school activities, need to be promoted as they serve basic functions in society. Information and materials with regard to these activities must be disseminated so the target sector will be aware of the programmes available. Student councils and other youth groups should provide young students with their own avenues to participate in society both at the level of educational institutions and public service activities. Programmes for youth who are disadvantaged and/or victimized on account of poverty are sorely lacking. Specific programmes addressing street children, drug addicts, the physically and mentally abused, drop-outs, under-achievers and other vulnerable groups need to be developed; furthermore, national programmes and plans of action for specific areas should include such programmes. The adoption of policy and legislation to support such measures should be encouraged.

Literacy and educational activities should be promoted to help young school drop-outs develop further the knowledge and skills acquired in school or through literacy courses, and to enable young people to find employment through appropriate information and skills development.

Where family education exists in schools (such subjects such as social services, biology and home economics), these courses are likely to be provided more for girls than boys and to focus largely on traditional, female home-making skills. The need is to re-focus this emphasis on the equitable sharing of household roles between male and female family members and to teach such courses on a more systematic basis, including courses on family planning, education, appropriate sex education and the rights of the child, youth and women.

Concerted efforts are needed to educate and encourage young adults to practise appropriate parenting techniques where the responsibility of child-rearing is shared by both parents, resulting in vastly improved health, education and socialization of children.

The youth sector

Although school enrolment rates and the school-leaving age have generally been increasing throughout the world, a significant number of adolescents are not in school and must be reached in other ways. Here the role of non-governmental youth organizations at international, regional, national and local levels becomes particularly important. They can reach young people at all levels, especially out-of-school youth. Given appropriate technical and financial support, much more could be done by these organizations. Youth centres can also cater effectively to a variety of young people's needs, and can provide the advantage of enabling them to seek help without publicly acknowledging problems in more threatening circumstances. These centres can also provide a good conduit for information and serve to identity problems on an individual or community basis.

Many youth organizations have accepted the importance of playing an even greater part in helping young people to prepare for adult life. The greatest challenge, however, lies in reaching those who are the most disadvantaged and have little access to sources of information and guidance. Youth organizations, particularly those with a large membership, have direct access to young people, including many who are outside the school system. With well-organized structures, roots in communities, established systems of training, communication and programme development and networks of committed and experienced youth leaders, many youth organizations are able to reach those who are the most difficult to contact.

The participation of young people in planning and providing services is a key consideration. Given the opportunity, they can best articulate their needs and comment on the acceptability of approaches intended to promote their development. Peers have a powerful influence on the behaviour of adolescents. With appropriate skills and support by knowledgeable adults, youth are in an ideal position to provide effective counselling, information and social support for other young people.

Policy makers, as well as researchers on family and youth issues, should direct increasing attention to the problems and challenges posed by the rural-urban migration of youth, as well as by the emergency situations of refugee families, including children and youth in especially difficult circumstances.

Youth services should be provided to young migrants who often encounter new cultural problems and, frequently, a difficult and unfavourable environment. They may have to face these situations without parental/family support, contributing to an increase in a number of problems. Among the most vulnerable are homeless youth, young refugees and young victims of war and civil conflict.

The socialization roles of non-governmental youth organizations at all levels should be strengthened and involve both in-school and out-of-school youth. Such organizations should promote among youth the ideals of mutual respect and reciprocal rights and obligations within the family. Voluntary youth organizations should be encouraged to undertake projects concerned with the delivery of family support services, especially targeted at families at risk.

The mass media, culture and recreation

Young people are strongly influenced by the images of popular culture reaching them through the various mass media. These images have crossed cultural boundaries with unprecedented speed and intensity. Popular figures in entertainment and sports are influential and provide both positive and negative examples to the young. Much more could be done to promote the healthy development of youth through these channels.

The mass media should be utilized to highlight the importance and significance of family education and the participation of youth in the design, implementation and evaluation of such activities. Public knowledge of family education should also be increased to improve parents' understanding and sense of responsibility for family education.

Both governmental and non-governmental organizations and agencies concerned with family and youth matters should closely monitor the ways and means the media portrays the family and youth in society. Particular attention should be paid to the problems of how the girl child and female youth are presented in the media.

International bodies, especially the United Nations, should be encouraged to contribute to instilling desired values (via examples and/or role models) through the positive endorsement of value-oriented television and radio programmes that address issues related to the family, specifically youth.

Just as many countries have adopted logotypes to endorse appropriate environmentally friendly products, a similar endorsement could be made for value-oriented programming in various countries.

Appropriate policies and measures should be adopted to enable and encourage youth to participate in cultural, artistic, sports and leisure activities, paying special attention to disadvantaged youth.

Families, schools and communities should not underestimate the importance of providing young people with opportunities and facilities (such as youth centres and recreational parks) to channel their ideals and energies in constructive ways.

The judicial system

Governments should pay particular attention to the imprisonment of young persons within the framework of international standards, in particular the United Nations Standard Minimum Rules for the Administration of Juvenile Justice (The Beijing Rules)[3] and the United Nations Rules for the Protection of Juveniles Deprived of their Liberty,[4] which require, inter alia, distinctly separate procedures and operations and a specialized juvenile justice system.

Family contacts are usually vital because they provide emotional and psychological support, and they are an integral part of the right to fair and humane treatment. Governments should provide special training for professionals, such as police officers, judges, prosecutors and youth and social workers on the treatment of juvenile delinquents.

The research sector

Member States and the non-governmental organizations concerned should develop more action-oriented and applied research, particularly in specific areas such as refining the concept of youth in the national context; identifying subcategories of youth and their needs and aspirations; studying the role of the family in the socialization of youth as well as the positive role of youth in the socialization of the family, which has received scant attention; and reviewing existing policies and legislation affecting the status of youth in a given society.

Comprehensive data collection and interdisciplinary research is needed on the interactive roles, problems and challenges of the family and youth in the 1990s and beyond. Both intersectoral and sectoral issues should be reviewed and evaluated, obstacles identified and forward-looking strategies formulated from the perspective both of the family and youth.

References

[1] *Official Records of the General Assembly, Forty-fourth Session, Supplement No. 49* (A/44/49), vol. I, sect. VI.

[2] "A working paper on issues and problems related to the interactive roles of the family and youth in society" by Shiv Khare, World Assembly of Youth.

[3] *Official Records of the General Assembly, Fortieth Session, Supplement No. 53* (A/40/53), sect. V.

[4] Ibid., *Forty-fifth Session, Supplement No. 49A* (A/45/49), sect. VI.

The Elderly and the FAMILY in Developing Countries

10

Introduction*

Responding to the General Assembly resolution 44/82 proclaiming the IYF, and as a contribution to IYF, the International Institute on Ageing (INIA), in Malta, supported by the IYF secretariat, conducted the present study in developing countries on the role and obligations of the family in providing support to the elderly and in preserving their dignity, status and security.

The dramatic increase in the number and proportion of older persons has been one of the most significant developments of the twentieth century. The developing countries may experience the most intense ageing trends during the period 1980-2025. Projections suggest that despite their currently young populations, those countries will contain the vast majority of the world's older persons after the turn of the century. Within the elderly population itself, the older age groups are expected to show even faster growth, namely, a sevenfold increase from 1950 to 2025.

Socio-economic trends and the decline in fertility and mortality accompanying the ageing of populations are affecting the family both positively and negatively. In addition, urbanization, modernization, industrialization, migration and the increasing participation of women in the labour force are also greatly modifying the traditional role of the family.

The present study provides information on the changing role of the family, the extent and causes of such change and its implications on the aged at the individual as well as the societal levels and in terms of the socio-cultural, economic, functional and environmental consequences.

One of the major policy questions examined in this study is whether the goal of providing services for the ageing should be to support the older person in the context of the family, as well as through informal social networks. Another policy question is whether policy makers should aim at keeping older individuals in their familiar environment as opposed to focusing on their care requirements in isolation. The question of older persons and their roles in the family is also examined in this study, as those roles are increasingly being redefined.

Demographic considerations

Demographic factors have been important determinants in the sweeping changes experienced by the family in developing countries. Declining

---

* This study was commissioned by the International Institute on Ageing (INIA), which acted as the coordinating agency, and was prepared by Tarek Shuman (United States of America). It is based on existing literature, surveys, data and information as well as on four regional studies carried out by the following consultants: Mustafa Benyaklef (Morocco) for Africa, Vladislav Bezrukov and Natalia Lakiza-Sachuk (Ukraine) for eastern and central Europe, Lita J. Domingo (Philippines) for the Asian and Pacific region and Luiz R. Ramos (Brazil) for Latin America. Additional input was provided by a number of national and international gerontological societies and non-governmental organizations as well as the collaborative network of INIA.

The Elderly and the FAMILY in Developing Countries

fertility, coupled with the increased rate of survival has resulted in an increase in the relative burden placed on family members in supporting the elderly. Even in regions where cultural norms of caring for the ageing remain strong, the physical capacity of the family to provide such care has been weakened. The fall in the birth rate has begun to accelerate in many developing countries and, by the twenty-first century, it will be common for many elderly persons to have few or even no children to care for them in old age. The role of the elderly within the family will be modified, and the traditional role of the family itself in providing services and security to the elderly will be severely affected. Shifts from extended to nuclear families imply the loss of older persons' roles as heads of families, and thus of their decision-making functions and financial responsibilities. Changes such as these will have a net effect of marginalizing the ageing and removing them from the mainstream of development, weakening their traditional sources of material support and eliminating purposeful social and economic roles.

Number, proportion and distribution of older persons

The dramatic increase in the number and proportion of aged persons has been a significant development of the twentieth century. According to United Nations projections, the total number of persons aged 60 or over in the world population will increase fivefold, from 214 million to 1.2 billion, between 1950 and 2025. Concurrently, their proportion of the global population is expected to increase from 8 to 14 per cent. It is also projected that the developing countries will experience the most intense ageing trends during the period 1975-2025. Despite their current youthful populations, those countries will contain the vast majority of the world's older persons after the turn of the century. Within the elderly population itself, the older age groups are expected to show even faster growth, from 15 million in 1950 to 111 million in 2025, a sevenfold increase.

Although the developing countries accounted for 52 per cent of the world's 347 million persons aged 60 or over in 1975, they are expected to contain 72 per cent of all older persons by 2025, with their older population increasing from 180 to 806 million persons. Similarly, in 2025, the developing regions will account for 75 per cent of all persons aged 60 to 69, 69 per cent of all persons aged 70 to 79 and 60 per cent of persons aged 80 or over.[1]

The Asian and the Pacific region is the world's most populous one. According to United Nations estimates, over 2.5 billion persons, 55 per cent of the global population, lived in that region in 1980. Of that figure 170 million persons were aged 60 or over, or 45 per cent of the world's elderly. Projections indicate that by 2025 the region will account for 4.3 billion persons, or 52 per cent of the world's population, of which 623 million persons will be aged 60 or over, or 56 per cent of the world's elderly. China and India, the region's most populous countries, are projected to account together for over 33 per cent of the global population and 38 per cent of all elderly persons by 2025.[1]

While marked trends towards ageing population structures characterize a significant portion of the Asian and Pacific region, some countries will remain youthful throughout the 1980-2025 projection period. According to the categorization of countries used by the United Nations, which is based on the timing of significant fertility decline, the Asian countries fall into the category of "late initiation", that is, countries where fertility decline began between 1950 and 1990.[2] This indicates that in 1970 the population of all Asian countries under consideration in this report could have been characterized as fairly young, with less than 4 per cent of population aged 65 or over. Transition to lower rates of fertility and mortality underlying population ageing has occurred, or is projected to occur. There are and will be considerable variations in the timing and rate of change in the countries and territories in Asia. China, Singapore, Sri Lanka and Thailand, for example, moved to the "youthful" category in 1990 when the ageing population accounted for 4-6 per cent of their populations. Further reclassification of Asian countries is expected, owing to a continuing decline in fertility and improvement in life expectancy by 2010. Three countries (China, Sri Lanka and Thailand) will "mature" and register as aged more than 7 per cent of their populations. Singapore will join the "aged" societies, as 10 per cent of its population will be 65 years of age or older. A relatively modest decline in fertility has been projected for India, Indonesia, Malaysia and the Philippines; consequently, their populations will remain youthful through 2010.

Projections for Asia indicate that the dominant trend over the next 35 years will be the ageing of the population. Asian countries' populations will mature considerably by 2025, with the percentage of the aged ranging from 7.7 to 20.6 per cent in Singapore and 12.6 per cent in Thailand. The countries of the region have experienced a rapid increase in the absolute number of the elderly population and in their elderly support ratios. Those findings have either been overlooked or given low priority by most of the Governments in that region because of the daunting task of providing for the needs of young populations. The continued growth in numbers of the elderly will be increasingly difficult to ignore, however, as it will create demand for new services and affect the allocation of resources by Governments.[3]

The United Nations projections for the period 1980-2025 indicate that Africa will experience one of the largest increases in numbers of persons aged 60 or over of any region. It is estimated that its older population will increase by a factor of 4.4, from 22.9 million in 1980 to 101.9 million in 2025 - a larger increase than that projected for its total population. Another distinguishing feature of the ageing situation in Africa is that the older segment of the population will remain primarily rural in coming decades. Recent projections indicate that approximately 64 per cent of the elderly in Africa will live in areas defined as rural in the year 2000, compared with 58 per cent of the total population. It is necessary to note here that the chronological age of 60 used in the present report to demarcate the beginning of old age does not necessarily correspond to cultural conceptions of old age in Africa. The lack of vital statistics in many areas accords with the frequent finding that persons do not know their chronological age exactly; they refer instead to a "social age", according to which a person may be considered old if he or she has become a grandparent or has amassed a level of knowledge or leadership associated with old age. Also, in regions where life expectancy is low and where malnutrition, disease, high rates of childbirth and adverse working conditions contribute to premature ageing, the cultural definition of old age may refer to a relatively young age group, compared with perceptions in developed countries.

The distinctive demographic features of Latin America are its high level of urbanization, the highest among all developing regions, and the current youthfulness of its population. In 1980, the United Nations estimated that 65.4 per cent of its inhabitants lived in areas classified as urban, and nearly 40 per cent of its population was aged 14 years or younger. Projections for coming decades indicate increasing urbanization, with 75.7 per cent of the total population and 78.6 per cent of the population aged 60 or over living in urban areas by the year 2000. At the same time, the region's age structure is expected to become less youthful. According to United Nations projections, persons aged 60 or over will increase from 6.4 to 10.8 per cent of the total population between 1980 and 2025. Rapid shifts towards ageing population structures are expected in a number of countries, particularly in the Caribbean and temperate South American subregions. The regional projections thus mask great heterogeneity in ageing trends at the national level.

As to the number of persons aged 60 or over, significant increases are projected for Latin America during the period 1980-2025. While an estimated 8.2 per cent of the total world population and 6.2 per cent of the total elderly population lived in the region in 1980, those proportions are expected to increase to 10.6 per cent and 8.3 per cent respectively by 2025. The region's two largest countries, Brazil and Mexico, ranked sixteenth and twenty-fifth worldwide in the number of elderly in 1950. By 2025, it is predicted that Brazil will rank sixth, with its elderly population increasing by 24.4 million persons, and Mexico will rank ninth, with an increase of 13.9 million elderly. A survey of Latin America confirms that in Brazil, those aged 60 or over represent the fastest growing age group in the population. An increase of 105 per cent is projected in this age group in the last two decades of this century, and of more than 130 per cent in the first quarter of the twenty-first century. By 2025, the projection is that Brazil will have the sixth largest elderly population in the world, representing 14 per cent of the total population of the country.[4]

For the region as a whole, a fourfold jump is forecast in the group of persons aged 60 or over. That age group is expected to increase from 23.3 million persons in 1980 to 93.3 million persons in 2025. At the subregional level, an increase of 5.7 million older persons is forecast for the Caribbean during the same period, an increase of 18.7 million for Central America, an increase of 5.8 million for temperate South America, and an increase of 39.7 million for tropical South America.[*] The largest factors of increase in the population aged 60 or over are thus expected in Central America.

The growth of age groups within the elderly population in Latin America is also projected to increase. Brazil and Mexico, for example, will experience the largest increases in numbers of persons in the age group 70 or over; 10.2 million for Brazil and 5.4 million for Mexico, between 1980 and 2025. In the region as a whole, an increase of 28.5 million persons aged 70 and over is foreseen for the 1980-2025 period.

One of the most typical demographic features of the east and central European countries is the increasing number and percentage of the elderly in the general population structure. At the end of the 1980s, for example, the elderly of Bulgaria, 60 years of age or over, constituted 19.2 per cent of the total population; in Poland and in Russia that figure was 15.3 per cent; and in Ukraine, 17.9 per cent. The percentage of older persons in this region will increase a projected 1.6 times between 1990 and 2025.

In brief, looking at the changes projected for the distribution of the elderly population by regions of the world, a marked shift towards less developed areas can be seen. In 1950, about 40 per cent of all persons aged 60 or over were living in Europe, North America and the former Union of Soviet

---

[*] Temperate South America includes Argentina, Chile and Uruguay; tropical South America includes Bolivia, Brazil, Colombia, Ecuador, Guyana, Paraguay, Peru, Suriname and Venezuela.

Socialist Republics, with an additional 25 per cent in South Asia and 23.6 per cent in East Asia. With the exception of a transitory dip in the percentage in South Asia, this regional breakdown remained constant until 1975.

By 2025, however, this configuration is expected to have changed significantly, as the rates in more developed countries decrease and those in developing countries greatly increase. Between 1975 and 2025, the proportion of the elderly living in Europe, North America and the former Soviet Union is expected to decline to approximately 25 per cent, while the proportion living in East and South Asia may jump from 48 per cent to over 57 per cent. Concurrently, the proportion in Africa and Latin America together is expected to increase from 11 per cent to over 17 per cent. Throughout the period 1950-2025, the elderly population of Asia will be increasing; nearly 50 per cent of the world's elderly population lived in this region in 1950, and it is projected that almost 60 per cent will be living there by 2025. This shift in the distribution of older persons from developed to developing countries is emphasized by differential rates of increase in their 60 or over populations. For example, while the number of elderly persons in Bangladesh, Brazil, Mexico and Nigeria are expected to increase by factors of 6.5, 15, 13 and 12, respectively, between 1950 and 2025, the 60 or over population of Germany is expected to increase by a factor of only 2, and that of Italy by a factor of only 2.8 during this same period of time.

Age structure and gender balance

Although the increasing number of the elderly is often associated in the public mind with improvements in life expectancy, demographic analysis shows that declining fertility is the most influential factor in the ageing of populations, with decreases in mortality playing a secondary role.

At the regional level, Africa is still characterized by high rates of fertility and mortality and a low life expectancy at birth, although improvements have been registered over the past several decades. Crude death rates are at the level of 16 per 1,000 population or higher in the majority of countries during the 1980-1985 period. Crude birth rates are registered at the high level of more than 40 per 1,000 population during the same period, producing an age structure in which over 40 per cent of the region's population is under 15. Life expectancy in many countries of the region remains under 50 years.

For the developing countries of the Asian and the Pacific region, the transition to the lower levels of mortality and fertility, which underlie the ageing of populations, has occurred or is projected to occur during the period 1950-2025. Considerable variation occurs, however, in the timing and rates of decrease in various countries of this region.

Latin America's currently youthful age structure is a product of the improvement in mortality recorded since the Second World War, in association with continued high levels of fertility in most countries of the region. Life expectancy at birth, in the majority of countries, is at the level of 70 years or more, and this trend is expected to improve in all but two of the region's countries (Haiti and Bolivia) by the year 2025.

The average life expectancy in the eastern and central European countries is much lower than in most developed countries of the world. In 1990, the life expectancy at birth was 69 years for Russia, 70 years for Hungary, 71 years for Bulgaria, Belarus and Ukraine, 72 years for Czechoslovakia and Poland, as compared to 76-77 years for Italy, Netherlands, Norway, Spain and Sweden.

As to the sex composition of the elderly population, the preponderance of women over men is characteristic of the elderly population now having particular significance for the more developed regions. Also, evidence indicates that, in these regions, sex imbalance increases with age. In the case of developing regions, United Nations estimates show that the numbers of men and women are more balanced.[1] The markedly higher life expectancies for women in the more developed regions, and the relative parity between the sexes in developing areas, may be explained by such factors as high maternal death rates and high levels of infant mortality.

Urban/Rural distribution

Another important phenomenon of the twentieth century is the dramatic increase in the number and proportion of persons living in urban areas. In 1900 an estimated 218 million persons lived in urban areas, 13.6 per cent of the world's total population. In 1980, this number had increased to 1.8 billion with an increase of proportion to 41.3 per cent. A recent United Nations report projected that the urban population of the world may reach 2.85 billion by the year 2000 and 4.93 billion by 2025.[5] This growth of urbanization is expected to continue, particularly in the developing countries, but at a slower pace owing primarily to projected decline in total population growth.

Within the developing countries, Latin America, by far, was the most urbanized region in 1980, at 65 per cent, which is projected to reach 75 per cent by the year 2000. Southern Asia was the least urbanized region in 1980 at 22 per cent, and it will remain the least urbanized by the end of the century, at 35 per cent. Africa was 29 per cent urban in 1980 and will increase to 45 per cent by the year 2000. Asia as a whole will increase from 27 per cent urban in 1980 to 39 per cent by the end of the century.[5] For the period 1960-1990 urbanization progressed in all eastern and central European countries, although unevenly. For example, the percentage of urban population increased by 30 to 40 per cent in Poland, Russia and the Ukraine, and by 60 to 65 per cent in Romania and Hungary and by 75 to 85 per cent in Bulgaria and Yugoslavia and its former republics.

The intensification of efforts of the developing countries to achieve accelerated development through industrialization has resulted in pushing agricultural labour cityward, curtailing rural growth and the capacity of the urban centres to absorb labour. This rural to urban migration has accelerated in developing countries during the past decade, even when job opportunities in the cities were limited. Rapid urbanization, accompanied by rapid population growth and scarce resources, has contributed to a state of diminished returns and to chronic and acute urban problems. Squatter settlements and shanty towns are mushrooming in the developing countries. In many cities, 40-50 per cent of the people live in slums or squatter settlements, some of them growing at rates of up to 20 per cent per year. Newcomers to the city, predominantly poor, tend to settle in shanty towns as squatters in home-made, makeshift living quarters in areas usually devoid of even minimum urban amenities such as electricity, water, sewerage and transport (Shuman, 1991). Many studies on the subject concluded that the inhabitants of such blighted residential areas are the poorest elements of their respective populations, characterized by limited literacy, low occupational skills and inadequate preparation for urban life. Such problems, in both developed and developing countries, remain chronic and, in some cases, become acute and unmanageable.

Looking at global trends of urban-rural distribution of older persons, a small majority in 1980 (53 per cent) of the world's elderly population lived in rural areas, according to United Nations estimates. However, these estimates indicate that by the year 2000 a preponderance of older persons will be in urban areas (55 per cent), with corresponding decreases in the size of the population of rural elderly. Throughout the 1980-2000 period, elderly women appear more likely to reside in urban areas than their male counterparts, with 49 per cent of all women aged 60 or over living in urban areas in 1980 as opposed to 44 per cent of elderly males, and 57 per cent of all elderly females in the urban category in the year 2000, as opposed to 52 per cent of elderly males.[5]

As to regional trends in urban-rural distribution, the elderly of Africa tend more to live in rural areas than their counterparts in any other world region, and this segment of the population will remain primarily rural in coming decades. Recent United Nations projections indicate that approximately 64 per cent of Africa's elderly will live in areas defined as rural in the year 2000, compared with 58 per cent of the total population.

The elderly population of the Asian and Pacific region was estimated to be predominantly rural in 1980. However, comparison of projections for the year 2000 with the 1980 estimates suggests a trend towards urbanization of the elderly, although a substantial majority will continue to be rural in most subregions. In absolute terms, the projections indicate that the elderly population of the region will grow by 124 million persons between 1980 and 2000 and, of these, 69 million will be living in urban areas and 55 million in rural areas. The enormous numerical increases of the elderly, their projected distribution and the change in family structure suggest that the traditional support networks for the elderly have been weakened by age-selective migration and that service networks in both urban and rural areas will have to be greatly expanded during the coming few decades. Much more effort will have to be made in building up new infrastructures in rural areas as in strengthening urban-based resources.

The distribution of the older population in Latin America is reflected in the trend of its high level of urbanization, as noted above. Of persons in the age group 60 or over, 69.4 per cent were estimated to have lived in areas classified as urban in 1980. United Nations projections for the year 2000 show a continuation of trends towards urbanization. It is expected that 78.6 per cent of older persons will be living in urban areas in the region as a whole at that time.

Socio-economic implications of ageing populations

Recent worldwide economic trends have severely affected the well-being of peoples and the family, and profound and disruptive social changes have transformed the way people acquire their livelihood. Recent years for the majority of developing countries have been characterized by falling per capita incomes and standard of living. Rapid inflation and a severe slow-down in economic activities in the industrialized countries were transmitted to many developing countries. Such stress has been particularly acute in recent years where Governments have taken steps to reduce social costs as part of their efforts to bring their revenues and expenditures into balance and implement structural adjustment programmes. In highly indebted developing countries, falling prices for export commodities, rising real interest rates and a rapidly growing debt service have led to a need for austerity programmes to restore conditions for sustainable growth. In Africa and Latin America, where the setback to economic growth has been most pronounced, unemployment and underemployment became more severe. Real wages fell as devaluations, wage restraints and inflation in many countries reduced purchasing power and resulted in shortfalls in national income. Many Governments were forced to reduce expenditures for essential social services, and real per capita spending for health, education and housing has declined.

In addition to this severe worldwide economic recession, in many developing countries the need for services is increasing with the spread of urbanization, migration, changing family and kinship support systems and greater participation of women in the modern economy. But as economic decline in some countries is placing greater demands on the limited capacity of current public systems, Governments are seeking to maintain existing family support systems. Social welfare programmes in many developing countries emphasize the creation of income-generating opportunities for the poor, vulnerable, dependent and disabled. The family as a basic social unit has undergone profound changes. The most important are those related to family formation and fertility, and to the family as a system of support. As part of the process of rapid demographic and socio-economic change around the world, patterns of family formation and family life are continuing to undergo considerable change, altering the composition and structure of the family in many societies. The coming decades will be increasingly concerned with population ageing issues. Public and private sectors will be pressured to assume responsibility for some of the functions traditionally provided by the family. Within these economic realities, the socio-economic implications of ageing populations are worthy of further consideration.

As to the eastern and central European countries, the social and economic implications of the ageing of populations are compounded by the drastic political and economic changes in these societies. These countries following the path of market-oriented economies are going through a transitional period characterized by diverse features for each country affecting all segments in the population including the elderly. Political instability and economic recession or even crisis in the post-communist eastern and central European countries have led to changes in priorities particularly with regard to social programmes and to an impaired functioning of existing institutions responsible for the welfare of the family and the vulnerable groups within society.

Economic implications

Evidence is increasing that the ageing of populations can profoundly affect the socio-economic development of society as a whole. In this context, development denotes steady improvement in the quality of life of all population groups, in addition to being construed in terms of technological progress, capital formation and increases in per capita income. This concept accords with the International Development Strategy for the Third United Nations Development Decade, adopted by the General Assembly in its resolution 35/36, which defines the ultimate aim of development as "the constant improvement of the well-being of the entire population on the basis of its full participation in the process of development and a fair distribution of the benefits therefrom". As mentioned earlier, evidence is accumulating that the ageing of populations can have a strong influence on the course of development, both in economic and social terms. When older persons retire and become economically inactive, their increasing weight in the population implies deteriorating ratios between the labour force and ageing dependants. Underlying the economic impact of the ageing process are changes in the ratio of the economically active dependent population. In this respect, for developing countries, special attention should be given to the significance of demographic change for agricultural productivity and rural economic conditions, since the impact of ageing processes in agrarian societies is in some cases intensified by extensive rural-urban migration of young people. Also, careful attention should focus on the effect of demographic change on family structure and accompanying shifts in the physical and financial capacity of family members to support older relatives.

In developing regions, to a growing extent, the trends in ageing dependency ratios are associated with increasing national expenditures for social security and social services, as well as higher financial burdens on the working population. The economic impact of the ageing populations in some rural areas is heightened by the extensive out-migration of young people. In some cases, however, such as Africa, available evidence indicates that the magnitude of economic dependency is not greatly affected by the costs of supporting the ageing, because even in 2025 the weight of the ageing will be small within the overall dependency. Also, in East Asia, the evidence is that the fertility decline will compensate both for the increase in the numbers of the elderly and for the assumed greater costs of supporting them.

In brief, demographic ageing trends are currently associated with decreasing economic potential, in terms of variables such as growing age-dependency rates, government expenditures for social security, tax rates for the economically active, reduced labour productivity and increased need for government support of families caring for the ageing. Many of these impacts are shaped by socio-economic policies as well as by quantitative changes in population structure.

Social implications

As to the social implications of population ageing, it should be recognized, from the outset, that the social component of development encompasses the equitable distribution of the benefits of economic growth to all sectors of the population and, even more broadly, the improvement of the intangible social, cultural, psychological and political factors shaping the quality of life. Elements of social development thus include the promotion of human dignity, of social equity in access to goods and services and of participation in the process of development.

In this respect, there is evidence that the older sector of the population is not sharing equitably in the process of development and may be negatively affected by the modernizing, industrializing and urbanizing trends accompanying development. As the older population grows, in both relative and absolute terms, social development issues impinging on this population group are becoming more acute.

Furthermore, demographic factors, specifically the decline in fertility and mortality accompanying the ageing populations, are affecting major social institutions such as the family. Because the availability of children will decline and the survival of older members will increase, the burden placed on family members in supporting the elderly will increase. Thus, even in developing regions where the cultural norm of caring for the ageing remains strong, the physical capacity of the family to provide such care will be weakened. In turn, this situation has significant economic implications, for a reduction in family resources will be accompanied by an increased need for public services, both to strengthen the economic capacity of the family to perform its caretaking role and, where necessary, to substitute for the traditional family support.

Available data on the social implications of the ageing populations indicate that the changes in value structures and upheaval which accompany the development process in many cases work to undermine the status and material security of older persons. Increasing marginalization is resulting from loss of traditional roles, authority, opportunities for productive work and family support. As the proportions and numbers of the ageing in the total population grow, the danger is an overall lag in social development, in the sense of inclusion of all population groups as participants and beneficiaries of economic, social, political and cultural progress. Analysis of these issues leads to the suggestion that promoting the active participation of ageing persons in all areas of community life is as important for equitable social development as for enhancing the productive potential of society.

The role of the family in the care of the elderly

No doubt family ties are particularly salient for the aged. Indeed, older people rely on the family bonds of affection and obligation to make up for the shortcomings in society's provisions for their well-being. Kin can function as important resources for the elderly, meeting health or financial needs with services, gifts and monetary contributions. They can provide affection and companionship at a time when the older person's social network may be circumscribed by infirmities and budget restrictions.[6]

In most developing countries, the predominant form of the family is the extended family where reciprocal obligations felt by family members for one another arise from strong kinship bonds. This extended kin regulates the relationships of older persons to their children, grandchildren, aged parents, siblings, cousins, in-laws, and other peripheral kin by blood or marriage. Extended kin usually display cohesiveness transcending generational, geographical and socio-economic differences.

The ageing in the traditional extended family enjoy high prestige as custodians of morality. As family heads, they enjoy honour and exercise some degree of authority over younger family members. As long as they are physically able, they also contribute to productive work. Within this type of family, the elderly thus enjoy a sense of belonging, as well as emotional and physical security.

Changing family structure and roles

The extension of the family over time from two and three to four and five generations, all living at the same time, is one of the fundamental correlates to individual ageing in present day societies. Increasingly, the generation survives beyond the sixth or seventh decade of life. Persons in their fifties may have living parents and grandparents, carrying the role of child and grandchild, while at the same time being parents and grandparents themselves.

An added complexity to this extension of the family over time is its increased extension over space through increased migrations and mobility of populations on intra- and international levels. This is particularly true of the younger age group in search of occupational, educational and economic opportunities.

From a regional perspective, countries of the Asian and Pacific region have begun to experience significant changes in their age structure as they move from conditions of high to lower levels of fertility and mortality. As a result, the number of children being added to the base of the age pyramid has been decreasing while the improved life expectancy has resulted in more people surviving to the older ages. The extent to which this transformation of age structure has proceeded varies across countries in this region.

While emotional ties and mutual support among family members remain strong in developing regions, clearly demographic change will affect more and more the capacity of the family to continue its care-giving role. Most salient is the reduction in the birth rate and the resulting decrease in the number of children available in a family to care for ageing parents. The fall in the birth rate is now beginning to accelerate in many developing countries. By the twenty-first century, it will become common for many older persons to have few or even no children to care for them in old age.

Evidence is also increasing that trends towards urbanization and industrialization are transforming the structure of the extended family, although it continues to function in traditional ways in rural areas. Socio-economic factors tending to weaken this family framework include out-migration from rural areas (reported from the African region), the small size of urban housing units (reported from the Latin American region), as well as international migration and the increasing tendency of women to join the labour force (reported from the Asian and the Pacific region). For the eastern and central European region, the collapse of communism and the struggle to adjust to a market-oriented economy are adversely affecting the structure as well as the traditional role of the family.

Today's potential care-givers are faced with options and opportunities that were not available to previous generations. Educational attainment in particular has opened more opportunities to improve their status, mainly through increased involvement in income-generating activities. Participation in these extra-familial activities directly benefited women and fundamentally altered the structure of care-giving support to the older members of families.

Migration

Closely associated with the increase in work participation is the migration from rural to urban areas. This widely observed shift of population from rural to urban settings has placed greater responsibilities on nuclear families and has denied many older persons the assistance they once received from extended family support networks. The opportunities in the countryside and the availability of services in the city lead to mass migration, the most severe being witnessed in Latin America. To a lesser degree, this has been the case in other developing regions. For Asia, not only have population movements increased in scale and complexity, the gender selectivity of migrants has likewise been gradually changing - more and more women in the region are reported to be migrating independently not only within the country but also internationally.

The adverse effects of the oil crisis, for example, led to a large pipeline of Asian workers to the Western Asian region. In 1981, there were 2.5 million Asians working in the region.[7] The industrialized countries of Asia also emerged as the new magnets in the 1980s. The demand for domestic helpers in Hong Kong and Singapore, and for other occupational groups dominated by women, further enhanced the participation of women in overseas employment.[8]

Despite their disadvantaged position, migrant women have become significant economic actors at the national and international levels. In 1988, women accounted for 78 per cent of registered migrants in Indonesia. In Sri Lanka, by the mid 1980s, women represented some 60-70 per cent of all Sri Lankan labour migrants.[9] A continuing study of Filipino immigrants to the United States of America has shown that migrant women have higher levels of labour force participation (68 per cent) than native-born white women.[8]

The debate continues over whether the benefits of labour migration outweigh the costs. Possibly the greatest benefit to migrants' countries of origin has been the massive flow of remittances, which have become the top foreign exchange earner in several Asian countries. In Sri Lanka, foreign remittances, largely from women working in the Arab States in the Persian Gulf area, were second only to tea as a source of foreign exchange.[9] Rising incomes through migrant remittances can provide more material support for the elderly. A village-based study in West Java found remittances to be essential to the welfare of many elderly villagers.[2] About 16 per cent of Filipino families receive income from abroad which accounts for 30 per cent of their total income.[10]

Non-economic consequences of labour migration have received relatively little attention although analysts surmise that the social and psychological effects on both the migrants and their family must be profound. Migration may have mixed consequences on the living arrangements and care for the elderly. In as much as migration involves the young, fewer care-givers will be left for the elderly. This is particularly true for many of the Asian countries where women, who are likely to be the preferred caregivers, are mobile in both intra- and international migration. Evidence of neglect of the elderly on account of migration has not been established, but it remains to be seen whether or not the continuation of this trend, coupled with changes in lifestyle, will eventually lead to the loss of an important source of care for the elderly and other members of the family. This important area remains largely unexplored by researchers.

A number of studies carried out in rural areas of Africa,[11] Asia[12] and Latin America[13] repeatedly show that the villagers who migrate are, for the most part, young, male, single and better educated. The reduction of the agricultural labour force would normally be welcomed as a prerequisite to national economic growth. However, when migration from rural areas takes a steady toll of the young, able and more educated males over a period of years, the accelerating population decrease will have serious economic and social consequences for the remaining ageing rural population.

For the eastern and central European region the predominant trend of population migration from rural to urban areas, observed in the countries of this region prior to the transitional period, has been drastically reduced and has given way to intensive emigration flows, both from rural and urban areas, to destinations beyond the boundaries of these countries. This is destabilizing the family, particularly for those migratory families who traditionally would have maintained their role in caring for their ageing members.

The family in urban areas

The above examples from different regions clearly indicate that, in the urban areas of developing countries, the extended family structure has often given way to the nuclear or conjugal family, consisting of a couple and their unmarried children sharing a dwelling. The ability of families to care for older relatives in the urban context is seriously impaired, with crowded housing, limited financial resources and the increasing employment of women. Although the proportion of one-person households remains low in developing countries, the average size of households in the majority of Asian and Latin American countries has been decreasing because of declining fertility levels and a reduction in the proportion of composite and extended households.

In Morocco, for example, a reported 49 per cent of households have more than five persons, 32.5 per cent of these families live with an average of two persons in a room, and only 4 per cent of households consist of one person and 8 per cent of two persons. This is also true of Brazil, where the majority of the elderly live with their children or grandchildren; 56 per cent live in multigenerational households, and only 12 per cent live alone, and those are mostly women.

As to the Asian and the Pacific region, a number of studies emphasize that a small proportion of the Asian elderly live alone. Available data indicate that 2 per cent in Singapore to 8 per cent in Indonesia of those aged 60 or over live alone. In 1987, 3.4 per cent of those 60 years or over in China lived alone, while Sri Lanka registered a relatively high 7.6 per cent. For rural India, only 2 per cent of those 60-69 years old were living alone.[14]

Surveys in the 1980s reveal that more than half of the elderly in the Association of South-East Asian Nations are in intergenerational living arrangements; 68 per cent of those aged 60 or over in the Philippines; 77 per cent in Thailand; and 85 per cent in Singapore.[15] Such high levels of co-residence indicate that, in Asia, the elderly continue to live with and be cared for by the family. Although Asian societies are going through a number of changes - fertility decline, economic transformations, increasing women's participation in the labour force, rising levels of education - these changes do not seem to have greatly affected co-residence levels. Even where fundamental changes have taken place, such as in Singapore, co-residence remains the norm. Data from the Philippines, Singapore and Thailand indicate a strong sense of moral obligation for children to care for their elderly parents instilled in them from an early age. Evidence also reveals that, for many families, affection and not simply obligation is the main driving force behind co-residential arrangements underscoring the importance of the quality of interpersonal relationships between generations.[16]

Available evidence suggests that in many developing countries the urban elderly are concentrated in slums and squatter settlements characterized by substandard housing, inadequate services and lack of sanitation. The living conditions in most urban areas of developing countries are not conducive for younger persons to care for their elderly. These trends are multiplying the cases where urban people, preoccupied by absorbing daily problems of modern life or suffering from material constraints, fail to fulfil their duties and obligations towards the old.

The family in rural areas

In rural developing countries, where the majority of the population lives, the predominant form of the family is still the extended family, consisting of a couple, married and unmarried children, grandchildren, collateral and other relatives, often living together in the same shelter or compound. In this traditional extended family, the ageing enjoy high prestige as custodians of village lore and morality, and exercise some degree of authority over younger family members, as headsmen, landowners and bearers of vital information on agriculture, artisanal skills, medicine, child-care and warfare. They enjoy a sense of belonging, as well as emotional and physical security. As long as they are physically able, they contribute to productive work in farming and in the household.

In most developing countries, rural-urban migration has significantly affected the age structure, producing disproportionately high aged dependency rates in rural areas. The emigration of the young and the concomitant ageing of the rural population relate not only to family structure and provision of services by family members, but also to the serious economic and social consequences for the remaining family members. Draining the rural areas of the most dynamic and educated individuals, who have been raised, educated and trained at the expense of their families and the rural community, will inevitably depress the rural areas including the family and consequently decrease the ability of family members to provide for their elderly.

At the regional level, available evidence indicates that the extended family and community are ingrained in the social system of Africa's traditional agrarian societies, and they still constitute primary sources of care for the elderly. Examples from many African countries confirm that protection and care are not given to the elderly in a spirit of charity, but rather they stem from the roles, rights and obligations traditionally assigned to each age category within the social structure. In the case of North African countries, for example, bonds of family solidarity and values and respect for older persons are embedded in the Arab-Muslim culture, tradition and religion. Similarly, in almost all rural Africa, the male elders traditionally function as the heads of extended families, counselling in marital conflicts or family disputes, and socializing children and youth in the cultural norms and values of their society. At the same time older women have important domestic roles, teaching young girls a variety of skills and explaining social norms and taboos.

African observers can see that, although the relative weight of the elderly in the population will remain quite low, the rapid growth in the number of older persons and widespread social changes will weaken the traditional family and community support systems for the elderly, with age-selective increase in migration from rural areas and reduced opportunities for older persons to remain economically active.

Although the percentage of the ageing living in rural areas will most likely decline, more than 60 per cent will still be rural by the turn of the century. In numerical terms, the number of rural elderly in Africa is projected to increase from 7.5 million in 1980 to 27.7 million in

2000. The number of urban elderly, though growing at a faster rate, is estimated to reach only 15 million by the turn of the century.[1]

For Asia, the respect and care accorded to older persons by their families in traditional societies have been emphasized. Available evidence suggests that at the present time these traditional forms of support remain largely intact in rural areas, where the majority of the elderly and of the population as a whole lives. Still, literature from some Asian countries notes that the effects of industrialization and modernization are beginning to be felt even at the village level; mass media such as television, radio and the press are becoming increasingly available, with the effect that the simple village society is changing into one of complex needs and wants. Increasingly, in many Asian countries, the gradual shift from an agrarian society to an industrial economy has affected traditional power structures. Throughout the region, migration among the young and urbanization are associated with shifts from extended family structure to nuclear families, with concomitant declines in the accessibility of care from the younger family members.

For Latin America, the most urbanized of the world's major regions, about 70 per cent of the elderly live in urban areas. As in other developing regions, the impact of rural migration and increased urbanization on the traditional extended family and its role as a care-provider for the elderly is a major concern; this trend could lead to increased demand for costly State-based assistance. However, regional source materials consistently stress the patterns of reciprocal intergenerational support characterizing the traditional extended family in Latin America.

Effects of demographic change on the capacity of the family to support older persons

The influence of demographic change on the family will more and more affect the capacity of the family to continue its care-giving role. The reduction in the birth rate and the resulting decrease in the number of children available in a family to care for ageing parents have serious implications on the capacity of the family to support older persons.

The increase in numbers of the extreme aged is another factor taxing the resources of the families as care providers. Linked to this is the increasing probability of families encompassing four or five generations. For a middle-aged person to care for two generations of elderly relatives, in addition to carrying out the roles of parent and grandparent, is becoming increasingly difficult.

Widowhood in later life

The last stage of the family life cycle, the marital dissolution and the new role of widowhood of the surviving partner, usually the wife, warrant special consideration in this study. Widowhood touches most ageing families and demands dramatic adaptations in the lives of survivors. Widowhood means the loss, reorganization and acquisition of social roles and disruption of many social relationships.

The preponderance of widowed women among the elderly is a major factor affecting the availability of family support. The tendency of men to marry women several years younger than themselves and the longer life expectancy of women in many areas means that older women have a high probability of experiencing a long period of widowhood in later life. The loss of a spouse means loss of socio-economic support and companionship and makes older women vulnerable to poverty and social isolation.

Although loneliness is reportedly the greatest difficulty faced by widows, remarriage, in many societies, is not a commonly employed recourse. In most developing countries, marriage rates for older people are low, despite variations by sex and previous marital status. Remarriage for older people is considered improper in many traditional societies. Available data, indicate, however, that men are more likely to marry after the age of 60 than women, since they are not restricted by social norms to marrying older women.

Although older men have an easier time finding partners, they also may have more to gain from marriage than do older women. According to a number of studies on the subject, widowhood seems to be a more devastating experience for men because so few husbands can expect to survive their partners. Widowers may suffer from greater social isolation than do widows,[17] since they do not only lose a companion, but they also experience a greater decline in kin interaction,[18] presumably because the wife typically maintains contact with family members and relatives.

Support systems: institutional vs. traditional

In major developing regions of the world, decreasing family size and increasing numbers of older persons, as well as other demographic and social factors affecting family structure, have given rise to formal institutions to share or take over some of the families' traditional responsibilities. This trend is expected to continue. While these institutions are necessary and respond to a real need, particularly for physical care, many studies indicate that none of these institutions has proven to be an acceptable substitute for the family in providing emotional, psychological and social support. The debate continues, however, as to the proper balance between the family and government assistance, and the appropriate means and ways of helping the family to continue to be responsive to the effective needs of its elderly members.

While the family provides the most important source of support for the elderly, Governments more and more recognize the special needs of this rapidly growing sector of the population. The commitment of Governments to address the rights and needs of this target group is reflected in their development plans, as in the case of India,[19] and even in their constitution, as in the Philippines.[20] However, even with the rapid growth of the number of elderly population, from the perspective of the planners who have to consider competing demands and limited resources, the elderly still represent a minority and continue to be relegated to low government priorities.

In most developing countries, ageing is often viewed as a welfare rather than a developmental issue. As such, in the design of welfare policies and programmes, the elderly are categorized together with groups of poor, disabled and victims of disasters.[19]

Institutional and non-institutional services for the elderly have been developed in many developing countries. The degree of development, however, is determined by available financial resources. For example, in the Philippines, geriatric clinics/hospitals are mainly urban-based. A programme of free medical care for those aged 60 or over is gradually being introduced in Thailand. In countries such as Singapore, however, medical services for the ageing are considered adequate.[19]

In many Asian countries, Governments have adopted a strategy to encourage the participation of the private sector in providing social services for the needy elderly. In India, for example, assistance for the needy elderly, who have no means of livelihood or support, is left to voluntary organizations and local bodies. Starting in 1983, the Government of India decided to give grants to voluntary organizations for services to the aged as well as grants-in-aid to voluntary agencies for a variety of services including health care, training and homes for the elderly.

To deal with its problems of ageing, China is currently considering five programme areas, namely, income security, medical care, educational services, leisure and opportunities for the elderly to make socially useful contributions.[21]

Senior citizens' clubs and committees have become favourite media for the elderly to interact with peers, articulate their needs, participate in volunteer work and to derive recreational and other services in Indonesia, the

Philippines, Singapore and Thailand.[22]

For Africa, according to available evidence, the extended family and the community still constitute primary sources of care for the elderly, maintaining traditional responsibilities for providing them with necessary shelter, clothing, food and health care. However, from available statistics, it has become clear that health and social services should be targeted, in the next few decades, towards a primarily rural population of persons aged 60 or over. The service infrastructure will have to be strengthened in both urban and rural contexts to complement the family support and to meet the needs of growing numbers of the ageing. But as in other developing regions, the historically weaker service networks in rural areas should be a particular focus for policy makers. Furthermore, unless family and community traditions of mutual aid can be preserved and strengthened, a vast service infrastructure will be required in coming decades to replace and expand previous informal care-giving. With the current scarcity of economic resources, the lead times needed to develop social security systems, for example, providing universal coverage to the population and competing demands from a large population of youth, the socio-economic feasibility of creating such systems may well be questioned. Thus, maintaining and strengthening the resources of traditional care-givers, rather than creating new and costly institutions, are a central recommendation to African policy makers.

For the Asian and the Pacific region, evidence is strong that respect, honour and care are accorded to older persons by their families in these traditional societies. In many cases, these attitudes are instilled through religious teaching, as in Sri Lanka, where the extended family system is strengthened and nurtured by the Buddhist and Hindu cultures and religions. As indicated in the African and Asian contexts, care given to the elderly is reciprocated in many ways. In the extended family, grandparents play important roles in the socialization of children, teaching social values and moral codes, providing instruction in agriculture and artisanal skills as well as giving care and affection. The support accorded to the elderly in return includes providing shelter, financial help, clothes, food and nursing care.

For Asia, even with the variability in experience and action, one feature of ageing has remained largely similar across countries, that is, the reliance upon the family rather than governmental and institutional sources in the provision of care and support for the elderly. Similar conditions were reported in our survey for the African and Latin American regions.

Evidence shows the continued performance of the traditional role by the family, particularly in the Asian and Pacific region where urbanization was less intense than that of Latin America. But as with all other aspects of society, the family has not been immune from social and demographic changes. Family relationships have been put under great pressure by such changes. Owing to these developments and given resource constraints faced by their Governments, concern has been expressed about whether or not this system of care and support will be sustained in these developing regions.

Available information suggests that at the present time, in the Asian and the Pacific region, these traditional forms of support for older persons remain largely intact in rural areas. There, as in other developing regions, the majority of the elderly and of the population as a whole live. In urban areas, the impact of socio-economic change on social institutions, and thus on the availability of family care for the elderly, is strongly felt. Urbanization is associated throughout the region with shifts from an extended family structure to nuclear families, with concomitant declines in the accessibility of care from younger family members, and the emergence of formal governmental substitute services.

In Latin America, regional source materials stress the patterns of reciprocal intergenerational support, characterizing the traditional extended family in this region. As in other developing countries, the elderly commonly share a household with their adult children, particularly in rural areas. In Costa Rica, almost 90 per cent of the elderly live with relatives and in Argentina three or more generations of rural families live in one household. However, as in other developing regions, trends towards urbanization and industrialization are reported to be weakening the family as a source of support for the elderly, particularly in urban areas.

In a number of the eastern and central European countries such as Belarus, Bulgaria, Poland, Russia and Ukraine, the elderly traditionally take an active role in the life of their children. In contrast, the patterns of West Europe are followed more often in the Baltic States, Czechoslovakia and Hungary. In a 1987 investigation conducted in Poland, slightly over 25 per cent of elderly families provided material and financial support to their children. This especially applied to families in rural areas. The data of a Ukrainian study showed that elderly people in large towns provided more assistance and support to their children and their families than they received from them.

Despite the clear evidence that, in developing countries of the world, the family is still the major provider of support to the elderly, an important aspect of assistance where government is most visible is in the provision of social security. The degree and coverage of assistance and benefits, however, are determined by the level of development of each country.

Examining the Association of South-East Asian Nations countries, Chen and Jones observe a wide range in the coverage and benefits of pensions, superannuation or central provident fund schemes.[23] The level of coverage ranges from about 80 per cent of the labour force in Malaysia and Singapore to only 3 per cent in Thailand.

Gender in care-giving

As to the gender dimension of care-giving, in the Asian and Pacific region[3] in patrilineal societies, norms on care-givers are defined - parents live with their sons, and daughters-in-law are the care-givers. This custom persists in many countries of the region, even in highly urbanized Singapore. Changes in lifestyle, however, strained the family's ability to care for the frail elderly. Governments, therefore, are stepping in to provide amenities and services for the elderly. And possibly alternative care-givers will assume more important roles in the future. For example, already many families in Singapore hire domestic helpers to free women to work outside the home.[24]

Although custom and tradition mainly determine the care-giving pattern among the Chinese and Indians in Singapore, for the Thai and Filipinos relational considerations were more important. The care-giver designate was an open-ended matter, that is, anyone among the children could fill the role. This was also found among the Singaporean Malay elderly.[16]

Another gender-related aspect of care-giving stems from the increasing longevity of individuals. Spouses are increasingly surviving together. The combined effect of younger age at marriage of women and their longer life expectancy has resulted in wives ending up as care-givers for their older husbands.[25] This is illustrated in a recent study of the elderly in Singapore showing that the spouse is the main care-provider when the elderly are ill or in need of care. Close to half of the males reported their spouses as the care-giver compared to only 9 per cent for the female. As to the elderly female, close to 40 per cent are cared for by the son- or daughter-in-law.[26] A related finding in Malaysia shows that the main support for the elderly during their illness is their children, especially the "old-old". Most of the "young-old" either look after themselves or are looked after by their spouse.[27]

In brief, family care in developing regions generally means female care, as women are traditionally the main providers of services within the family. However, women's participation in the labour force, combined with demographic changes in family structure, is beginning to change the traditional support system for the elderly. In addition, because of sex differences in life expectancy, women are expected to outlive men by several years and thus create a situation whereby those at the oldest ages and with the greatest need for care are far more likely to be female.

Spouses and children in developing countries are most often the primary, and in many cases the only, care-givers to the older members of the family. Due to the role of women as family care-givers, they are much more likely to be the major care-providers to older persons. A recent study has shown that, although male relatives may be equally likely to help with certain tasks, they are more likely to help when needs are intermittent, whereas women are more likely to help when consistent aid is required.[28]

Clearly, the ability of the family to care for older relatives is very much influenced by reproductive behaviour in conjunction with increased longevity. At the family level, five children easily provide a relatively reasonable environment in old age for one grandparent; it is less likely when three children still have two grandparents out of four. This effect of the demographic transition on ratios of surviving children to surviving parents implies an increasing need for public support to families caring for older relatives, even in areas where cultural values strongly uphold the responsibility of children to care for their parents.

The literature on care-giving is reported to be limited in its ability to describe fully the assistance given by family members to elderly relatives.[29] These limitations are due to the non-representative samples used and the reliance on cross-sectional studies. Without longitudinal data it is hard to put together a complete picture of family system changes, starting from before the onset of any care-giving crisis. Finally the viewpoint of the elderly must be incorporated in any intervention programmes.[30]

Conclusions and recommendations

CONCLUSIONS

The examination of the demographic trends and their implications on the ageing and their families in the present study is intended as input to policy makers responsible for drawing up development plans at the regional and national levels in developing countries. Knowledge of projected increases in numbers of older persons, and of their distribution by age, sex and place of residence, is vital for determining the necessary dimensions and structure of future health and social welfare services, family support, housing, employment opportunities and income security schemes for the ageing, particularly the most vulnerable among them, such as isolated widows, inhabitants of remote rural areas and frail very old persons.

At the same time, information about the changing weight of the elderly and other age groups in the population is crucial in considering issues, such as the allocation of societal resources among different age groups, deployment of the labour force and financing of services including income security schemes. This study reveals that, while ties and mutual support among family members remain strong in most areas of the developing regions, clearly demographic change will increasingly affect the capacity of the family to continue its care-giving role. Within this context, the present study considered the socio-economic implications of ageing trends, particularly as they affect the family as a support system to the elderly.

Decreasing family size and increasing number of older people, as well as other demographic and social factors affecting family structure, were discussed. The rising number of formal institutions established to share or take over some of the families' traditional responsibilities were examined. It was concluded that, while these institutions respond to a real need, none has proven to be an acceptable total substitute for the family in providing psycho-social support.

The study gives particular attention to the increasing number of widowed women among the elderly and its effect on the availability of family support. The cultural and traditional tendencies of women marrying men several years older than themselves, and their longer life expectancy of women in many developing countries, mean that older women have a high probability of experiencing a long period of widowhood in later life, with loss of socio-economic support and increasing vulnerability to poverty and social isolation.

A common theme in the source materials of this study is a commitment to meet the individual needs of the elderly, to the greatest degree possible, within the context of their family and community. This principle is adhered to equally strongly among major developing regions of the world. In all the humanitarian spheres, health, housing, social welfare, income security, employment, emotional and psychological support, provision of services to the elderly through their families are a priority objective. Development of State-based schemes is considered appropriate only for those sectors of the elderly population that have lost their family support through widowhood, childlessness, extreme poverty or the destruction of war and natural disaster. In the regions of both Asian and the Pacific and Africa, in traditional agrarian societies the family group secured the financial, educational, social, psychological, emotional and cultural needs of all its members, through bonds of mutual aid and interdependence. In Latin America, although the family remains a primary source of support to the elderly, and the extended family continues to maintain its traditional role in rural areas, its structure is being transformed and weakened by the high degree of urbanization and rapid industrialization.

Because of the instrumental role of the family in meeting the needs of the elderly in developing countries, a central objective which emerges from the present study is to strengthen the resources of the family to permit it to remain a primary care-giver for the elderly, and to fulfil the needs of the elderly in the contexts of their families and communities. The ultimate goal, in this respect, is to enable the elderly to remain with their families and in their familiar environment for as long as possible, to promote their independence and to give them the right to choose their own lifestyles.

At present, the eastern and central European countries are in an exceptional political, economic and social position. They cannot be defined as either "developing" or "developed" countries. They are a group of countries whose economies are in transition and who have common characteristics and tendencies as well as certain common socio-economic political and demographic structures. Any of the following recommendations should take into consideration the unique situation of this region and should be adjusted accordingly to respond to the specific needs of the family and their elderly.

Recommendations

The following recommendations should be considered within the framework of other international, regional and national strategies and plans. They are only a further elaboration of the recommendations and guidelines contained, inter alia, in the resolutions and decisions of the United Nations concerning the International Year of the Family, the International Plan of Action on Ageing[31] and its follow-up reviews and strategies, the World Population Plan of Action,[32] and the Nairobi Forward-looking Strategies for the Advancement of Women.[33] Furthermore, the study and its recommendations reaffirm the principles and objectives of the Charter of the United Nations, the Universal Declaration of Human Rights (General Assembly resolution 217 A (III), annex) and the Declaration on Social Progress and Development (General Assembly resolution 2542 (XXIV)). This study recognizes that, in suggesting recommendations, each country will deal responsibly with the question of individual needs of the elderly within the context of the family, on the basis of its specific national needs, objectives and capabilities. The family is widely recognized as a fundamental unit of society, and should be maintained, strengthened and protected, in accordance with the traditions and customs of each country. Its instrumental role in meeting the needs of the elderly should be supported to permit it to remain a primary care-giver. The International Institute on Ageing, in contributing this study to the Year of the Family, calls upon the United Nations to invite Governments of developing countries to take the recommendations into consideration in the formulation of their national plans and programmes.

Recommendations for international action

1. Recognizing the diversity in developing countries, with different political, economic, cultural and social systems, and at different stages of development, international meetings to exchange information and experience should be held on a regular basis to explore effective means of fulfilling the needs of the elderly in the context of their families and communities.
2. The United Nations should recognize the family as an important issue that deserves an identifiable unit within its system. The Secretariat of the Year of the Family has accumulated a wealth of experience, knowledge and information and should serve as the core of the above proposed entity.
3. The International Labour Organization should encourage Governments to provide work opportunities to elderly workers, and to allow them to continue to participate in the process of development. Governments should also be encouraged to strengthen the coverage of their old age social security systems and the benefits of their pension schemes.
4. The United Nations, through technical cooperation, should promote social policies that strengthen and maintain family solidarity among generations.

Recommendations for policy

5. In order to respond effectively to the challenges of various factors changing the structure and form of the family, national Governments, as appropriate, are encouraged to adopt specific policies and programmes to support and strengthen the resources of the family to permit it to remain a primary care-giver for the elderly.
6. In developing policies, Governments should be advised to develop programmes that can effectively supplement and support families in their traditional roles without supplanting them. The ultimate goal of these policies and programmes should be to enable the elderly to remain with their families and in their familiar environment for as long as possible.
7. Policy makers are encouraged to ensure that all social and economic development policies are sensitive to the diverse and changing needs

of families, and provide necessary support particularly to the most vulnerable of them. Promoting the independence of the elderly and their right to choose their own lifestyle should be the objective.
8. Governments are advised, in developing their national plans, to establish concrete policy measures and to provide a flexible range of options, taking into consideration the heterogeneity of the older population, the wide differences in their family status, their physical capabilities and income as well as their own perceptions of need.
9. Governments should be encouraged to give support to the families caring for elderly members in the form of financial incentives, such as income tax deductions, special monetary assistance or subsidized housing.
10. Also, Governments should be encouraged to provide temporary relief to care-givers, and counselling services to help the family better understand the problems and needs of the ageing.

Recommendations for research

11. While emotional ties and mutual support among family members remain strong in developing countries, it is clear that demographic changes will increasingly affect the capacity of the family to continue its care-giving role. Governments and international organizations should monitor these demographic changes and, in particular, the United Nations should study, on a regular basis, the various factors affecting the family and its care-giving capacity, and disseminate this information to policy makers and planners.
12. Many social policies relating to the elderly have proven dysfunctional, tending to isolate older persons from their families. Serious research should be undertaken in this area to ensure a proper balance between the family and the government assistance.
13. Studies should be undertaken to understand the changes in intergenerational relationships and their effect upon the role of the family as care-giver.
14. Studies should be undertaken focusing upon support systems for childless elderly, and widowhood in later life.
15. To assess the extent to which progress is being made in achieving the goals and objectives of family-related policies and programmes, a set of indicators should be developed.

References

1. *World Population Prospects* (United Nations publication, Sales No. E.91.XIII.4).
2. G. Hugo, *Population Mobility in West Java* (Yogyakarta, Gadjah Mada University Press, 1978).
3. L. Domingo and M. Asis, "Living arrangements and the flow of support between generations", *Journal of Cross-Cultural Gerontology*, 1994.
4. L. R. Ramos, R. P. Veras and A. Kalache, "Population ageing: a Brazilian reality", *Revista de Saude Publication*, vol. 21, No. 3 (1987), pp. 211-224.
5. *World Urbanization Prospects 1990: Estimates and Projections of Urban and Rural Populations and of Urban Agglomerations* (United Nations publication, Sales No. E.91.XIII.11).
6. J. Treas, "Aging and the family", *Scientific Perspectives and Social Issues*, J. E. Birren and R. B. Sloane, eds. (Englewood Cliffs, New Jersey, Prentice-Hall, 1975).
7. Fred Arnold, *Asia's Labor Pipeline: An Overview* (Boulder, Colorado, Westview Press, 1986).
8. Maruja Milagros Asis, "International migration and the changing labor force experience of women", paper presented at the United Nations Expert Group Meeting on International Migration Policies and the Status of Female Migrants, held at San Miniato, Italy, March 1990.
9. F. Ealans, "Sri Lankan Women in the Middle East", paper presented at the United Nations Expert Group Meeting on International Migration Policies and the Status of Female Migrants, held at San Miniato, Italy, March 1990.
10. Maruja Milagros Asis, "Between choice and circumstance: the dilemas of international labor migration", Quezon City, University of the Philippines, 1994.
11. J. Gaude, *Phénomène migratoire et politique associée dans le contexte africain : Études de cas en Algérie, Burundi, Cameroun, Haute-Volta* (Geneva, International Labour Organisation, 1983).
12. R. D. Singh, *Labour Migration and its Impact on Employment and Income in a Small Farm Economy* (Geneva, International Labour Organisation, 1983).
13. P. Peek and P. Antolines, *Labour Migration in the Sierra of Ecuador : Causes and Incidence* (Geneva, International Labour Organisation, 1980).
14. Kevin Kinsella, "Living arrangements of the elderly: a cross national data comparison", paper given at the International Conference on Population Aging, held at San Diego, California in 1993.
15. L. Domingo and J. Casterline, "Living arrangement of the Filipino elderly", *Asia-Pacific Population Journal*, vol. 7, No. 3 (1992), pp. 63-88; and J. Knodel, Chayovan Napaporn and Siriboon Siriwan, "The familial support system of Thai elderly; an overview", Asia-Pacific Population Journal, vol. 7, No. 3 (1992).
16. Domingo and Asis, op. cit.; Knodel, Napaporn and Siriwan, op. cit.; and K. Mehta and others, "Living arrangements of the elderly in Singapore; cultural norms in transition", *Journal of Cross-Cultural Gerontology*, 1994.
17. W. Bock, "Aging and suicide; the significance of marital, kinship and alternative relations", *The Family Coordinator*, vol. 21, No. 1 (1972).
18. F. Bernardo, "Social adaptation to widowhood among a rural-urban aged population", Washington Agricultural Experimental Station Bulletin, No. 689, reprinted in *Ageing, the Individual and Society: Readings in Social Gerontology* (New York, St. Martin's Press, 1967).
19. United Nations, Economic and Social Commission for Asia and the Pacific, Population Ageing; Review of National Policies and Programmes in Asia and the Pacific, Asian Population Studies Series, No. 109 (New York, 1992).
20. L. Domingo, "Government and non-government response to the issue of aging in the Philippines", paper presented at the Round Table on the Ageing of Asian Population sponsored by the Economic and Social Commission for Asia and the Pacific in collaboration with San Diego State University, held at Bangkok, 1992.
21. C. Wu, "Ageing process and income security of elderly under reform in China", paper prepared for the Round Table on the Ageing of Asian Population, 1992.
22. Ai Ju Chen and Paul P. L. Cheung, "The elderly in Singapore", country report of Singapore on the socio-economic consequences of the age-

ing of the population, prepared for the Phase III ASEAN Population Project, 1988.

[23] Ai Ju Chen and Gavin Jones, *Aging in ASEAN. Its Socio-economic Consequences* (Singapore, Institute of South-East Asian Studies, 1989).

[24] Mehta and others, "Living arrangements ...; and K. Mehta, "Women's role in family support system", paper given at the Workshop on Population Aging held at the National University of Singapore, sponsored by the Japanese Organization for International Cooperation on Family Planning, March 1994.

[25] M. Garrett, "International conference on population and development", paper given at the United Nations Expert Group Meeting on Population Growth and Demographic Structure, held in Paris, November 1992.

[26] Mehta, "Women's role ...".

[27] M. Yatim, "Population Aging in Malaysia", paper given at the Workshop on Population Aging held at the National University of Singapore, sponsored by the Japanese Organization for International Cooperation on Family Planning, March 1994.

[28] E. P. Stoller, "Males as helpers; the roles of sons, relatives and friends", *Gerontologist* (Washington, D.C.), vol. 30, No. 2, 1990, pp. 228-235.

[29] Gatz, Bengston and Blum, "Caregiving families", in J. Birrin and W. Schile, eds., *Handbook of the Psychology of the Ageing, 3rd ed.* (New York, Academic Press, 1990).

[30] *The Situation of Elderly Women* (United Nations publication, Sales No. E.91.XIII.12).

[31] *Report of the World Assembly on Aging, Vienna, 26 July-6 August 1982* (United Nations publication, Sales No. E.82.I.16), chap. VI, sect. A.

[32] *Report of the United Nations World Population Conference, 1974*, Bucharest, 19-30 August 1974 (United Nations publication, Sales No. E.75.XIII.3), chap. I.

[33] *Report of the World Conference to Review and Appraise the Achievements of the United Nations Decade for Women: Equality, Development and Peace, Nairobi, 15-26 July 1985* (United Nations publication, Sales No. E.85.IV.10), chap. I, sect. A.

FAMILY and Disabilities

Each family is unique*

"WE ALL COME FROM FAMILIES. FAMILIES ARE BIG, SMALL, EXTENDED, MULTIGENERATIONAL, WITH ONE PARENT, TWO PARENTS AND GRANDPARENTS. WE LIVE UNDER ONE ROOF OR MANY. A FAMILY CAN BE AS TEMPORARY AS A FEW WEEKS, AS PERMANENT AS FOREVER. WE BECOME PART OF A FAMILY BY BIRTH, ADOPTION, MARRIAGE OR FROM A DESIRE FOR MUTUAL SUPPORT. AS FAMILY MEMBERS, WE NURTURE, PROTECT AND INFLUENCE EACH OTHER. A FAMILY IS A CULTURE UNTO ITSELF, WITH DIFFERENT VALUES AND UNIQUE WAYS OF REALISING ITS DREAM; TOGETHER, OUR FAMILIES BECOME THE SOURCE OF OUR RICH CULTURAL HERITAGE AND SPIRITUAL DIVERSITY. EACH FAMILY HAS ITS STRENGTHS AND QUALITIES THAT FLOW FROM INDIVIDUAL MEMBERS AND FROM THE FAMILY AS A UNIT. OUR FAMILIES CREATE NEIGHBOURHOODS, COMMUNITIES, STATES AND NATIONS."

New Mexico Governor's Task Force on Children, Youth and Families, 1991[23]

One family in four worldwide has a relative with a disability. These families are as different from one another as any other family. But many such families daily experience discrimination and marginalization in their own immediate neighbourhoods and communities. They are also vulnerable to generalizations about families made by people without personal experience of the actual situation of families. A typical example is the assumption that "a handicapped child means a handicapped family".

The reality is more complex. All families have different strengths and needs. Furthermore, every member of the family also has individual needs, which differ from person to person, depending on their basic personality, their coping styles and their response to stress in general.

Generalizations about disabled people are as suspect and as dangerous as generalizations about families, and for much the same reason. The experience of disabled people is affected by the social and family environment they live in as well as by the nature of the disability. Attitudes to disability vary not only from country to country but also within relatively small areas within a single country. People with visual impairments may be treated very differently from those with speech and hearing impairments. Learning or psychiatric impairments or chronic epilepsy are still relatively the most feared or shunned in both developed and developing countries.

Much depends also on the extent to which disabled people receive the

---

* The present paper has been prepared for the IYF secretariat by Peter Mittler, Professor at the University of Manchester and Helle Mittler of Stockport Social Services Division, United Kingdom of Great Britain and Northern Ireland, in their capacity as co-chairpersons of the IYF Task Force of the International League of Societies for Persons with Mental Handicap (ILSMH).

necessary supports, aids and interventions. These range from spectacles and hearing aids, mobility aids, chemotherapy for epilepsy or psychiatric disorders, to schooling and vocational training.

A good deal of the literature about disability concerns children whose disability was obvious at birth or became apparent at an early age and who are living with their families. In developing countries, a larger proportion of children become disabled after a period of normal development as a direct result of illness or injury (e.g. meningitis, encephalitis or poliomyelitis) or as a consequence of malnutrition. Many more become disabled as a result of road traffic and other accidents, violence, war and its aftermath and as a direct result of abuse. The age of onset and the nature of the impairment will affect different individuals and families to a different extent.

People who become disabled as adults may no longer be living with their own parents but may receive a great deal of support from them or from the extended family. Other adults with an acquired disability may be living a long way away from their families or may no longer be accepted by their families. As a result, many such adults are dependent on the support of the communities where they are living. Local attitudes as well as local services determine whether they continue to be accepted, whether rehabilitation services are available and whether they will be able to resume their work and their place in the community. This applies particularly to soldiers and civilians disabled by wars or armed conflicts, many of whom experience major problems in finding jobs and a valued place in society.

Definitions and concepts

Because attitudes to disability are deeply rooted in the social and cultural values of a society, definitions of disability are problematic. Scientists and research workers striving for precision and clarity in the use of terminology have developed complex systems of classification, with the aim of facilitating research and scientific communication. The clearest expression of this trend is the classification published by the World Health Organization (WHO) that is being revised. But the assumptions underlying it have been questioned by disabled people as well as by professionals adhering to a more social model of disability.

The distinction made by WHO[32] in its definitions of impairment, disability and handicap has been widely used and quoted. Briefly, the definitions are as follows:

- An *impairment* is any loss or abnormality of psychological, physiolog-

ical or anatomical structure or function
- A *disability* is any restriction or lack (resulting from an impairment) of ability to perform an activity in the manner or within the range considered normal for a human being
- A *handicap* is a disadvantage for a given individual, resulting from an impairment or a disability, that limits or prevents the fulfilment of a role that is normal (depending on age, sex and social and cultural factors) for that individual.

These definitions have been increasingly criticized, particularly by organizations of disabled people on the grounds that they focus too much on the individual with the disability and fail to reflect how extensively the lives of disabled people are disadvantaged by the social structure of the society in which they live. Although the WHO definition of handicap includes the concept of disadvantage, its origins are located in the individual and not in society and its institutions. These definitions also make no direct reference to environmental or family factors.

Social model of disability

The social model of disability insists that social structures and the barriers they give rise to need to be modified. For example, there are still countries where a child whose intelligence quotient (IQ) falls below a certain point is denied access to education in schools, either ordinary or special. Similarly, many disabled adults are denied the opportunity of obtaining vocational training or of securing paid employment, not because they have been shown to be incapable of work but as a direct result of negative attitudes by decision makers or because the workplace is inaccessible. For disabled people who are denied access to opportunities and facilities, discrimination is a daily experience.

The social model does not seek to minimize or deny the presence of impairments and the restrictions that these may impose on the independence and autonomy of the disabled person. But it does place more emphasis on the importance of society and its institutions being modified to meet the needs of disabled persons. This contrasts with the traditional assumption that it is disabled people who should be trained to adapt or adjust to society. The models can be seen as complementary rather than as mutually exclusive in meeting the needs of individuals within their own social and family settings.

Terms such as disability and handicap are therefore socially and culturally relative. In an example[13] from Mali:

"The most disabling condition for a woman is to be ugly. This condition is defined in very clear terms. These women do not get married and consequently do not fulfil the normal parental role.

In other countries, dwarfs, people missing an eye, toe or finger or having an extra toe or finger or with a facial disfigurement or albinism may have no functional limitations but still be labelled as disabled."

Helander suggests that disability might simply be defined as follows:

"A disabled person is one who in his/her society is regarded or officially recognised as such because of a difference in appearance and/or behaviour, in combination with a functional limitation or activity restriction."

Disabled Peoples' International (DPI), a world federation of organizations of disabled persons, have proposed alternative definitions:
- Impairment is the functional limitation within the individual caused by physical, mental or sensory impairment
- Disability is the loss or limitation of opportunities to take part in the normal life of the community on an equal level with others due to physical and social barriers

The DPI definition therefore dispenses with the concept of handicap altogether, regarding it as misleading and discriminatory.

Equalization of opportunities

The concept of equalization of opportunities is fundamental not only to definitions, but also to the total process of planning and provision and ensuring the full participation of disabled people in society and in determining their own needs and priorities. It is derived from the Universal Declaration of Human Rights.

The most recent United Nations definition of equalization of opportunities is incorporated in the Standard Rules on the Equalization of Opportunities for Persons with Disabilities, which were adopted by the General Assembly[30] in 1993:

"Equalization of opportunities means the process through which the various systems of society and the environment, such as services, activities, information and documentation are made available to all, particularly to persons with disabilities."

What we know and do not know

The quality and quantity of information about disability on a global scale is not impressive, and there is some disagreement about the accuracy of such data as are available. The best summary source is the Statistical Office of the United Nations Secretariat in New York, which collects and tabulates information supplied by most Member States of the United Nations. A number of countries have also undertaken detailed surveys and censuses.

A major problem in the interpretation of disability statistics arises from the lack of an agreed definition of disability, which would differentiate people with a "marked or significant" disability from people with one that does not seriously impede the day-to-day functioning of the affected individual or that can be easily compensated for (e.g. by spectacles, a hearing aid or a walking stick).

Clearly, such distinctions depend on local customs and attitudes as well as on the availability of aids, appliances and services. For example, people with a mild degree of intellectual disability often participate fully in community activities in most developing countries. In a developed country, however, they are more likely to stand out in schools and may experience difficulty in finding work or taking their place in their local community.

It also goes without saying that in any community much depends on the support provided by the family for their disabled relative in going to school, getting and keeping a job and living with as much independence as possible. In turn, families themselves need support in this task from neighbours and from local services.

Estimates of prevalence

Most of the published information relates to the number of disabled persons in a country and may also provide information about the nature of their disability. However, little or no statistical information about families as such appears to be available on an international scale.

United Nations sources originally estimated the total number of disabled people in the world to be around 500 million in 1990. These numbers were expected to increase to 600 million by the year 2000, which amounts to approximately one person in ten. The figure of 500 million includes 140 million children, of whom 127 million live in developing countries - including 88 million in Asia, 18 million in Africa and 13 million in Latin America. Another 11 million are in North America and a further 6 million in Europe.

These figures are now thought to be an overestimate by the United Nations Development Programme (UNDP). Considering only people with "moderate or severe" disability, Helander[13] puts the current total figure at around 276 million, of whom 183 million are in developing countries and 93 million in developed countries. Helander also estimates that an average of 8.5 million severely or moderately disabled people are added to this total every year, or around 23,000 a day. By 2025, the number of disabled people will rise from 183 million to 435 million in developing countries and from 93 million to 138 million in developed countries. Based on these projections, the total number will be 573 million in 2025, or 8.2 per cent of the world's total population.

Each year, 35 million children die and another 35 million become disabled. At least half of all of these occurrences could be prevented by the use of knowledge and skills already in humankind's possession.

Ninety per cent of infant disability is related to environmental causes related to poverty, which include malnutrition, poor sanitation and persistent abuse.

The global prevalence of specific moderate and severe disabilities is estimated as follows:

TYPE OF DISABILITY	PERCENTAGE
Movement	2.5-3.0
Seeing	0.5-1.0
Hearing/speech	0.5-1.0
Learning	0.2-0.4
Fits	0.3-0.6
Psychiatric	0.1-0.2
Feeling (hands and feet)	0.1-0.2
Combinations of the above	0.2-0.3

Eighty-five per cent of adult disability is caused after the age of 13. Major causes include domestic and industrial accidents, wars and armed conflict and its consequences (particularly undetected plastic land mines), malnutrition and environmental pollution.

The relative increase in the number of disabled people, particularly in developing countries, can be attributed to a variety of factors. These include not only the rise in the number of births, but also the survival of many children who would previously have died at birth or in the first year of life. This applies particularly to very low birth weight babies and to those with profound and multiple impairments, as well as to children with Down's syndrome or spina bifida who, while not necessarily severely intellectually impaired, are physically vulnerable to respiratory and other infections, unless appropriate medical and nursing treatment is available.

In addition, advances in the quality of health care are associated with increasing life expectancy for both children and adults. Greater longevity in the whole population leads to an increase in the number of older disabled people and in the survival of disabled people who would previously have died at an earlier age. This has clear implications for the need to develop appropriate services to match these demographic trends.

These figures relate to people with marked or significant disabilities. But growing urbanization and an increase in the complexity of educational and occupational demands will increasingly affect people with relatively mild degrees of impairment. For example, European experience in the early twentieth century and current experience in many developing countries indicates that as more children go to school, those who experience difficulties in learning are more readily noticed. Many are still forced to repeat one or more years, thus singling them out as educational failures and isolating them from their friends. Others are simply excluded from school and left to fend for themselves.

Experiencing discrimination

FOR EVERY DISABLED PERSON IN THE WORLD, AN ESTIMATED MINIMUM OF FOUR MEMBERS OF THE IMMEDIATE FAMILY WILL BE DIRECTLY AFFECTED THROUGH HAVING TO ADAPT TO AND MEET THE NEEDS OF THEIR RELATIVE.

All families will be profoundly affected by the nature of the society they live in and by the value that that society places on the contribution disabled people can make. These values are reflected in social structures and institutions that may provide pathways or barriers to disabled people taking their place in the community and making a valued contribution to its growth and development. Just as some families are victims of oppression and discrimination, others have been enriched and strengthened by their experiences both within the family and as a consequence of contacts and supports outside the family.

Families will be affected to an extent and in a manner that will vary in relation to age, gender, degree of dependence and the amount and nature of the support available from the rest of the family, the local community and service agencies. It will depend as well on social attitudes and structures.

Most societies and cultures discriminate against disabled people and their families to some degree: in the school, the workplace, on the street and in community settings. Many families have encountered stereotyped assumptions about disability. Indeed, as members of their local and national communities, their initial reaction to the experience of disability may well be identical to that of their neighbours.

Although there are few detailed studies on this subject, the many anecdotal accounts from disabled people and their families, as well as the accounts by a range of observers suggest that many people still regard disability as a direct result of magic or of some transgression earlier in life or in a previous life. In many countries, attitudes towards disabled people and their families are still affected by myths and superstitions. These are widespread in the society and are by no means confined to rural areas or to people without education[16 and 27].

At one extreme, typified in mid-twentieth century Europe, disabled people have been systematically exterminated or permanently incarcerated in institutions. In many developed countries, people with psychiatric or intellectual impairments have been kept in appalling conditions, often without treatment or rehabilitation and with little or no prospect of a return to the community. Some have been (and still are) subjected to compulsory sterilization or been forced to take part in noxious and illness-inducing drug trials. Many are victims of emotional, physical and sexual abuse.

Just as the Incas banished disabled persons from their cities on festival days, reports exist of similar practices in some modern States on special occasions such as an international sports event or the visit of a foreign dignitary. In certain areas of the world pregnant women are warned against encountering a disabled person because of the risk to their unborn child.

In many countries, disabled people are still isolated from the community and denied access to its resources and facilities. Many have been excluded from work not because their condition precluded work but simply on account of the presence of a disability or because the workplace is not accessible or unsuitable for a disabled person.

Disabled people and their families are also subject to all other forms of discrimination, as are non-disabled members of their communities and countries. Discrimination and disadvantage relating to a family member with a disability may be increased if he or she belongs to a minority ethnic group; if they are female; if they are a member of a low socio-economic group; if they have a minority religion; if they are homosexual or lesbian. Some family members with a disability may therefore be subject to multiple severe discriminations and disadvantages.

Poverty is one of the most common forms of disadvantage experienced by disabled people and their families. Disabled people in all countries are economically disadvantaged. Many are living in severe poverty at or beyond the margins of society. This applies also to disabled people in countries with advanced systems of income support, because the allowances available to disabled people are judged to be inadequate to meet basic living costs. An official study in the United Kingdom showed that families of children with disabilities have incomes on average 22 per cent lower than those of equivalent families in the population as a whole[26].

The costs of meeting the needs of a disabled person will vary considerably, but many studies have demonstrated the need for additional expenditure of clothing (particularly footwear), laundry, transport and additional furniture as well as replacement costs where children may be destructive of household furniture and fittings.

These are examples of direct costs but there are even greater indirect psychological as well as financial costs that arise from the inability of one or more family members to be free to obtain paid employment. It is almost invariably the mother who is prevented from working outside the home, reflecting the stereotype of the community and of the family that it is the mother who must, by definition, be the main carer. In the study of the United Kingdom mentioned above, 32 per cent of parents had no earners within the family unit, compared with 18 per cent of the general population of parents[26].

Yet in few societies are disabled people and their families regarded as full and equal members of their local community, where the birth of a disabled child may be seen as a special gift of God. There are reports of disabled people in Samoa being included in ceremonial dancing and blind people being regarded as being under special divine protection in rural areas of Mexico[9].

A detailed study of proverbs, poems, riddles and folk-songs from Kenya and the United Republic of Tanzania involving references to disability, and interviews with tribal elders and with primary and special school teachers noted that most of the elders attributed disability to God's will or witchcraft and did not believe that education had anything to offer, whereas most of the teachers referred to illness and felt that education would enable children to be accepted and to make a contribution to society[16].

Kisanji concludes that:

"Difficulties notwithstanding, the communities accepted the presence of disabled persons in their midst as part of a continuum of individual differences which must be tolerated, respected and its members assisted to develop within the cultural boundaries."

"The Masai do not stigmatise people who have a disability, however serious the condition may be, by excluding them from the community. Disabled people marry, become parents and perform many other tasks[29]."

Another well-documented example of community acceptance and inclusion is the island of Martha's Vineyard in Massachusetts where a large number of the population have a hereditary form of hearing impairment but where the whole population are easily able to communicate through American Sign Language[10]. In fact, normally hearing families are reported to use sign language when they do not want their children to understand a conversation.

Combating discrimination

Fortunately, individual families as well as individuals within families and groups of families working together have themselves, in a variety of ways, worked to modify negative attitudes and striven to secure the acceptance of disabled people into the community. The extent of their success varies greatly not only from country to country but also within countries.

Growth of voluntary organizations

The 1940s and 1950s witnessed the spontaneous development of groupings of parents and family members. At first, these groups provided a foundation for mutual support and learning and a sharing of ideas and experiences. But many developed into effective forces for change, first at the local, then the national and finally at the international level. Their members were not only determined to gain access to basic supports and services for their relatives, but also to create better conditions for families with similar needs in the future. Over the years, they have campaigned vigorously for changes in legislation and provision and often became powerful advocates for changes in social structures[7].

Public attitudes

Voluntary organizations and family members have been at the forefront of the movement to bring about changes in public attitudes to disabled people. They have done so partly by their own example and partly by attempting to influence the way disabled people are portrayed in the media: in local and national newspapers and on radio and television.

In general, disabled people are now less often depicted as helpless victims, needing the charity of the public or as fighting bravely to overcome their disability. More and more the emphasis is on their similarity to other people, rather than on differences. Similarly, families are less often depicted as overburdened and handicapped by having to look after a disabled relative. The emphasis is more on the supports that families need to help the family as a whole to lead an ordinary life. However, all countries still have a long way to go before disabled people and their families are depicted in ways that they themselves can accept. International organizations such as ILSMH have produced some helpful guidelines to this end [28].

Development of self-advocacy organizations

During the 1980s, groups of disabled people themselves began to form their own organizations and to distance themselves from bodies that claimed to represent their interests but that were in fact controlled by a majority of non-disabled people.

Some of these organizations are now highly influential bodies that operate at national and international levels. The best known of these is DPI. It was founded in Singapore in 1981, with some support from the United Nations, as a direct consequence of the International Year of Disabled Persons: "Full participation and equality" (1981). It draws its membership from organizations of disabled people at the national level and also has strong regional networks.

DPI has been highly influential in the United Nations and played a major part in the development of the World Programme of Action concerning Disabled Persons (1983) and in the launch of the United Nations Decade of Disabled Persons (1983-1992).

The self-advocacy movement tends to be led by articulate or well-educated people with physical, sensory or invisible impairments. More recently, people with intellectual disabilities have also started to develop self-advocacy organizations (e.g. People First), although for families to advocate on their behalf is still common.

A potential source of tension exists between advocacy and self-advocacy organizations. Organizations of disabled persons wish to speak for themselves and tend to resent and reject statements made on their behalf by organizations for disabled persons. "Nothing about us without us" is the slogan of DPI. However, there is no reason why organizations of disabled people cannot make common cause with other organizations, provided they perceive common goals, and they will be seen to be more effective in securing their aims if they work together rather than separately.

Within families, too, the natural tendency is for non-disabled members of the family to represent the interests of their disabled relatives, especially if they are children or have significant difficulties in speaking for themselves (e.g. as a result of severe intellectual or language impairments). Many examples of such a tendency can be seen in ordinary social encounters; disabled people have frequently complained that people "talk over the top of their heads", literally if they are in a wheelchair or figuratively in other situations. Many people address the carer or family member in situations where it would be more appropriate to ask the disabled person directly. This is sometimes described as the "Does he take sugar in his tea?" phenomenon, the title of a weekly radio programme in the United Kingdom.

Experience of families

Although most disabled people live in families, little published information or research is available on the situation of such families worldwide. Several symposia have been held where reports from different countries have been presented under specific headings (e.g., legislation, family support systems, basic social welfare provisions and respite care) and then analysed for common themes[9]. Despite major cultural and social differences, a number of common themes do emerge from such comparative studies.

Despite the shortage of international and comparative studies, many examples from individual countries have been published in which family members including disabled people have spoken and written eloquently about their needs and aspirations and about the improvements they would like to see in the ways their needs are met and not met.

The stories they tell are not all about isolation, prejudice and discrimination, numerous and moving though these are. They are also about shared learning and growth, about the enrichment of experience of all family members and about the joys of achievement and success. The experience of disability can be positive and often adds a new dimension to the lives of individuals and families.

Family stories collected by a Task Force

ILSMII set up a Task Force to ensure that families who have a relative with a mental handicap were included in activities for the International Year of the Family (IYF) at the local, national and international level. The Task Force consisted of one mother and one father from each of the main regions of the world. To raise public and professional awareness of the situation of such families, the Task Force collected a wide range of family stories from the main regions of the world. In addition, members of the Task Force devised a series of Learning Messages specifically for IYF. These are reproduced in the annex. Although the experience of most members of the Task Force concerned mental handicap, both the family stories and the Learning Messages are equally relevant to all disabled persons and their families.

Nearly all Learning Messages demonstrate families' strengths in combating difficulties and discrimination and their ability to learn and develop positively, gaining from their experiences, however difficult and painful they may be. Most of their experiences will be similar to those of families with members who have other kinds of disability.

Information given to families

The situation of the families and the condition of their disabled member varied a great deal. Some disabilities had been diagnosed at birth; others were a result of illness, an accident or war. However, learning about the disability presented the first common difficulties. It often took months or even years to obtain an accurate diagnosis, even for families with money, a high level of education and some medical knowledge. Local doctors, including paediatricians, were often too ready to offer reassurance that a child who was demonstrably delayed in development would "be all right" or "catch up later". Parents themselves, understandably, wanted to believe this statement and felt unable to challenge it, even when they felt sure that something was wrong. Only the top national hospitals and facilities seemed to have the necessary expertise to assess and diagnose correctly.

The experience of being told that their child is disabled is usually unforgettable for most parents. Parents valued the rare occasions when the specialist told them with sensitivity and enabled them to retain some hope that their child could learn and develop. Too often this was not the case and doctors gave a globally negative picture, telling parents and grandparents only what the child would not be able to do. To these families' credit and the credit of the member with the disability, these gloomy predictions were often disproved.

In Muslim and many Asian cultures, only the father as head of the household was given the information about the disability. Many fathers carry this knowledge alone for weeks, months, even years before they are able to share it with any other member of their family, often another male member and before telling their wife. One Korean father waited for 10 years before informing his wife about the diagnosis he had been given shortly after his son was born.

Advice and support given to families

Often parents are not given advice about how they can help their child to develop when the disability is diagnosed, nor are they offered adequate support. In developed countries, the understanding now is that the effects of impairment can be minimized by the provision of learning programmes and appropriate technical aids from the earliest stage. Because of this, support and advice are often offered and educational programmes are available from the age of two years or even earlier. In some developed countries, such as Italy and the United States of America, all children, including the most severely disabled, attend mainstream schools, resulting in greater understanding and acceptance from others [24].

Access to such support in developing countries is often rare and problematic. Many families receive no advice or support until their child is of school age, if then. When they seek school or pre-school facilities, they often encounter rejection or teachers who are untrained or unequipped to enable their child to learn. In the local schools, their children are often taunted and even bullied.

In many countries, facilities to teach disabled children with learning, sensory and/or behaviourial difficulties were set up initially by parents and parent groups themselves. Many mothers of these pioneering families trained as teachers of children with special educational needs and began to help other children and other families as well as their own. Once appropriate educational and, later on, vocational provision was made available, families almost universally reported progress in learning and development. However, sometimes there is a mismatch between the diagnoses given and the intelligence test results and the level of progress achieved. Some children assessed at a low IQ level progress well and achieve considerable independence in self-care skills while other children with a higher tested IQ make little progress[1 and 20].

Roles of family members

The day-to-day care that disabled children need varies greatly and depends both on their level of impairment and on the social environment, circumstances and attitudes among which they live. Some young children need much more intensive care because of sleeping, feeding and health difficulties.

Almost universally, responsibility is most likely to fall upon women, usually mothers. Working mothers often give up their jobs to care for their disabled child. In China, after the mother's statutory maternity leave, grandmothers often take over the caring task. Older sisters too have an important role to play and some research suggests that they are the most likely to be adversely affected among brothers and sisters.

Although in some cultures the father's main role as a parent is that of breadwinner, there is now greater variety in the way fathers parent. In many families the roles are more shared. When both parents shared their fears and feelings and also the care of their disabled child and other children, this also contributed to a more positive view and outcome. In a minority of families, fathers or grandfathers were the main carers of their disabled child, particularly where this was a son who needed intimate personal care.

A common situation is that of women as single parents, either as unmarried mothers, separated or divorced or widowed parents. Unless they are well supported by their families or communities or are wealthy enough to buy support, they are likely to be among the most financially disadvantaged families.

The reaction of extended family members and of friends and local communities to a disabled child or adult and their family will vary greatly, depending on the values and beliefs of the society in which they live. Where families are shunned or rejected, an intolerable strain can be put on family members and lead to extreme experiences of isolation and depression. It can also exacerbate marital difficulties and result in separation and marital breakdown.

Where families are supported by at least some members of the extended family and community, this makes a significant difference to their lives and to the opportunities for the disabled child or adult to interact and have access to ordinary everyday experiences. Supervision and even some practical tasks can be shared, enabling the mother and brothers and sisters also to have some time to participate in the life of the community and to pursue their own interests. Parents and family members greatly appreciate and value such support and count themselves fortunate to receive it.

Families with a disabled member are often themselves educators in disability issues within their own families and communities. Through their interaction with others and by giving explanations to neighbours and friends, even by involving neighbours and friends in local associations and training events, they raise awareness about disability and help the community increase its knowledge. Contact with disabled children or adults often enable others to enjoy the relationship when they get to know them and appreciate their personal strengths and qualities.

As their child grows older, families begin to think about the future. Often it is at the stage of adolescence that parents' hopes and expectations for their disabled son or daughter begin to contrast most sharply with those for their other children. Sometimes this in itself leads to pressure on mothers to produce more "normal" children and (especially in some cultures) sons to carry on the family name and tradition. In one such case, a mother was persuaded to have eight children; seven were handicapped.

Parents would like their sons and daughters to live as normal a life as possible; to earn their livelihood through employment; to marry and have friends; and to live in their own accommodation with the support they need to lead safe and full lives. In many parts of the world where sufficient local or State services do not exist, families with means band together to set up vocational schemes and, increasingly to set up trust or insurance schemes to provide for their children when they are no longer able to care for them. Often they are again discriminated against in these areas. Few insurance schemes will offer plans for people with disabilities. The majority of families do not have the means to contemplate any such schemes. Indeed, some have to resort to exploiting their disabled child or family member as beggars, where they are often prey to unscrupulous entrepreneurs.

Many parents look to their non-disabled sons and daughters to provide for their disabled brother or sister. However, both parents' and brothers' and sisters' attitudes to this varies considerably. While some families take this approach for granted, others are reluctant to place such a major responsibility on their children, who may already have difficulties of their own. Some children who may be the only sibling are also apprehensive and resent the fact that they themselves will receive no support in this task.

Many parents feel the need for facilities when they will no longer be able to provide the necessary care and support to their older family members with a disability. The few institutions that exist are often isolated from family life and do not allow for regular easy contact. Stories of older disabled family members included that of a mentally handicapped man in his sixties who had only recently re-established contact with one brother and whose sister attended his funeral after not having seen him for over 50 years.

Effects on family members

Often there are no major differences in family life. If the disability is not severe, multiple or progressive, it need not interfere with the normal daily routines or with the way families live their lives. Some disabled children, young and older people are well integrated members of their communities, with rewarding relationships and lives that they enjoy and that enrich others. Often they make a valued contribution to the economic and social life of the community. Some disabled people are key members and leaders in their fields, whether it be political, scientific or in the arts. They too are often influential in changing attitudes and social structures for the benefit of disabled people and their families.

Sometimes, however, the interplay of the social environment and severe and/or multiple impairment leads to some restrictions on family life. In addition to the isolation and the increased intensity of caring already mentioned, family members also report an inability to go out or undertake activities spontaneously, as would other families, unless there are supportive relatives, friends, neighbours living locally or local supportive services that they can access.

The time parents need to look after their disabled child or relative clearly also affects the time available to devote to their non-disabled children and to each other. Some families think their non-disabled children are neglected or held back as a result of this. Sometimes, when the needs of all the family members cannot be balanced adequately and the strain is too great, family breakdown results and either parents separate or disabled children are sent to live outside the family. This can also happen because there are no adequate educational or vocational facilities locally. Again, this affects the closeness of family relationships. But it may have some advantages. As a disabled African leading figure explained, he would not as a non-disabled person have had the advantages of an international education, which enabled him to reach a high post and later return to visit his farming family.

The role of grandparents is often influential. They can be supportive and share the care and take a lead in seeking expert opinion and advice, as in a Chinese family that was interviewed. Often they can provide support financially and emotionally. They can also be rejecting and oppressive: in blaming the mother; in hiding the truth about a history of disability in the family; in putting pressure on a mother to ignore medical or educational advice or to have more children. Aunts and uncles and other extended family members can also play similar roles.

Brothers and sisters can develop warm, loving relationships with their disabled sisters and brothers. They may be the best at understanding them when there are communication difficulties; they may become playfellows. They can be supportive when the disabled child starts school or is taunted or bullied at school. But if this happens then they too can suffer. Some children take on some of the attitudes around them and become ashamed to bring their school friends home to meet their disabled brother or sister and in turn became isolated and withdrawn. Some are disturbed in their activities or their studies by their disabled brother or sister, especially in crowded accommodations.

A key factor seems to be how or whether the disability is explained to them. Some parents are reluctant to give explanations for a variety of reasons, but when they are given from an early age children seem better able to cope, perhaps because the parents are sharing their own ability and positive attitude. Being involved in activities and programmes with their disabled brothers and sisters also seems mutually beneficial.

In countries where the standard of living is comparatively high and medical services are more advanced and better equipped, the number of older disabled people are increasing with the increase of life expectancy.

This has led to situations where ageing people whose own infirmity may be increasing are in a position to care for their own disabled parents or other older relatives. The marked increase in the number of older people, who may soon be more numerous than the number of employed people to support them, poses a new and as yet unfamiliar problem both socially and economically for the next millennium.

Living with a disabled child or relative brings important benefits. Nearly all parents or family members, no matter how painful or difficult their experiences are or have been, report important fundamental gains. Many of these relate to knowing and loving the person with disability for his or her unique and individual personality. Many recount with pride the achievements their child or relative has made in developing independence and in contributing to society. Many report how much such persons are loved and appreciated in their local community. However, there are important gains beyond these.

Some people express this in terms of gaining a different perspective in the way they see life and relate to other people: their experience has given them a new dimension of understanding and humanity. They have shed many of their previously held judgements and are better equipped to understand other disadvantaged people, whether they are disabled, poor or socially weak. Previously, they were critical and perhaps arrogant in their judgements; now they feel better able to understand. Some parents, indeed, offer support and advice to others.

Families' experience of professionals

Throughout the life of a disabled person, the family can come into contact with a variety of professionals. Parents and family members are appreciative of those professionals who:
- Treat them and their disabled child or adult relative with consideration and respect
- Communicate with them openly and honestly
- Share their information and skills
- Give clear and full explanations:
  A Of their role and their agencies' responsibilities
  B The legislative framework in which they operate
  C The disabled member's rights and entitlements
- Advocate on their behalf or alongside them for better service provision, more relevant and humane policies and social and economic conditions
- Explore needs and plan services in conjunction with families.

In many countries there are good examples of true partnership between professionals and family members working and training together and jointly combating discrimination and disadvantage. However, this is the experience of only a minority of families. Too many families still complain of inadequate information, both oral and written. Information is often given in a language full of professional jargon, which families have difficulty understanding. An overly negative view is taken of their disabled child or relative and of themselves. They are often excluded from assessments and from decision-making and planning when services are delivered. These may be offered on a take-it-or-leave-it basis, with little possibility of choice or negotiation. When consultation does take place, it is often felt to be on an unequal basis and only to a point before "the barriers come down".

Direct communication with the disabled child or adult is not always, or even in the majority of situations, the norm. Even where the law insists that the disabled child or adult's views must be sought, there are limits to how seriously they are considered, especially when intellectual impairments exist or when professionals find it difficult to understand the disabled person.

Low expectations remain a significant form of discrimination and result in reduced life-enhancing opportunities for many disabled children and adults. The arrogance, lack of understanding, insensitivity and judgemental attitudes of some professionals add considerably to the distress of many families.

Many disabled people, parents and other family members, especially those disadvantaged by poverty, low levels of education and low class or status, remain in awe of professionals. Dependence on professionals for those services that exist makes it difficult and risky to challenge their assessments, views and decisions. However, with the gradual growth of United Nations initiatives to promote the rights of disabled people including disabled children and the development of strong parent and self-advocacy groups, families are increasing in confidence in their own knowledge, experience and skills and, above all, in the knowledge of the rights of their disabled members to equal social justice. New assertive generations are emerging to claim and work towards these rights, preferably in partnership with professionals but, if this partnership is not forthcoming, without them.

Disabled people and their family members have always had an informal role in raising the awareness of professionals in relation to the experience of disability in society and to their needs. Many parents explain to teachers and other professionals how to communicate and respond to their children and also how to explain this to other children and parents. Relatives of older disabled people do the same. In many countries, family members now play an active role in the formal training of professionals.

Recent reviews of research on parental needs has suggested that professionals need to adopt a much wider and more comprehensive perspective in working with families [19]. For example, professionals should inform themselves about existing family and social networks, to what extent individual family members are able to support the child and the parent(s), particularly mothers. Families also differ greatly in their coping style and in their ability to obtain support both from the rest of the family and from their existing social networks. Professionals need to learn to take these factors into account in assessing the social and family context within which the child is living and developing. In the words of this author[19]:

"Families differ greatly not only in how they organise themselves and in the resources that they have but in how they perceive the challenges they face. The same event will have different meanings and different effects for different individuals. Ultimately, the implication is that families differ in the types of services which they will find most helpful in supporting their own coping strategies."

Implications for policy and practice

Access to information

One of the foremost needs of families is for accurate and honest information about the condition of their family member. This may be at the time of birth, if the disability is already apparent; or when it becomes clear that a child's development is delayed or at any time of life when disability is the result of illness or accident, malnutrition, abuse or war.

Because "knowledge is power", information enables family members to begin to understand their situation and to make choices about what they can do to minimize the effects of the disability on their member's and their own lives. However great a shock a diagnosis may be, it is often more helpful than uncertainty.

The information families need is much more than a diagnosis or an account of the impairment. Adequate information will include some explanation of biological processes in clear lay language and also some idea of the range of possible prognoses for the person with the disability. An exclusive focus on what the person will not be able to do is experienced as destructive and unhelpful by families. Even more important is to know what they will be able to do and what are the range of future possibilities, from the most pessimistic to the most optimistic.

Families also need information about what options for services and supports are available to them. These should include local, regional, national and international organizations; health, education and welfare services; employment and vocational opportunities, as well as informal networks.

The manner in which information is given is almost as important as the information itself. A number of guidelines are offered below, drawn from various sources.

The knowledge gained from assessment, whether it is medical or educational, should be shared with family members as early as possible.

Family members should not, in general, be told alone.

Because such information is likely to be upsetting, telling parents or partners together or enabling a parent to have a relative or friend present is supportive and will enable such support to continue.

The fact that such information is not easy to give or receive should be acknowledged.

There are cultural differences in how emotions are expressed, but giving family members opportunities to express their feelings privately and encouraging them to share their feelings with others whom they can trust is helpful.

It is important to give opportunities for the first "telling" or information-giving to be repeated or followed up.

If this information comes after birth or a trauma such as an accident or sudden illness, it is likely to be a shock. In these cases, the information is unlikely to be fully heard or understood. It is therefore important to give some information in writing and to arrange for a second appointment or for a professional such as a doctor or nurse or social worker to visit the family a little later to explain anything that was not understood or to give further information in response to questions the family want to ask after reflection.

Professionals should demonstrate a positive approach, which reflects respect and valuing of the child or person with the disability. Information should be given honestly but with an emphasis on positives.

Families of disabled persons consistently express the need for a single point of contact to ask for information or advice. Their needs cross traditional departmental boundaries between departments of health, education, housing, social welfare, vocational training and employment.

Practical advice

Although families value information, they also say that information alone is not enough. They need, from the earliest days, some guidance as to how to support their disabled family member and, wherever possible, how to minimize the disadvantaging effects of the impairment.

Parents of young children appreciate advice on how to stimulate and help their child to learn, explore and socialize. At each age and life stage, both common life needs such as the need for loving relationships and a sense of self-worth and security are essential. Particular needs that have to be met are likely to be educational needs, sexual and vocational needs and accommodation and care needs when family members may be no longer in a position to offer the necessary support and care themselves.

Professionals may be able to offer such advice themselves or be in a position to direct families to other agencies or organizations who can. Other parents of disabled children or families with a disabled member are often able to support those facing similar issues.

Family support

Many families with a disabled child or adult member live their lives and cope in much the same way as other families. However, the availability of support from family, friends, neighbours and communities is a crucial factor in how they do so.

The support families need and value takes many forms and includes support from informal social networks, local communities and governmental and non-governmental agencies.

Attitudes

The acceptance of and liking or love for the person with the disability is central. Positive attitudes among their family members or from neighbours are of great importance. Families are often instrumental in generating positive attitudes themselves by giving the people around them an opportunity of getting to know the disabled person.

Practical help

Caring for a disabled child and adult usually takes more time and effort than caring for those without an impairment. In these situations, any help with practical tasks may be supportive, whether it is help with other household duties, help with other children in the family or help in caring for the disabled person, which again may take many forms. It can include looking after the disabled person in the home while other family members are engaged in other activities, undertaking a particular programme with the disabled person to enable him or her to acquire a new skill, or taking the disabled person out of the home for activities and experiences to broaden his or her life.

Practical help in the home may also take the form of special aids such as wheelchairs and appliances, and adaptations to the home, such as hoists or wider toilets.

Respite or shared care

The term "respite care" is problematic, since it again reflects the model of disability being an inevitable burden that must be relieved. Terms such as "shared care" or "alternative or second families" are increasingly used. Similarly, the concept of care may be too limited and under-emphasize the positive aspects of stimulation, new experiences and enjoyment associated with family life.

A number of countries have schemes whereby a family with a disabled child or young person is linked with another family who gets to know the child and invites him or her to stay at regular intervals or from time to time. This gives children with a disability an opportunity to mix with different children and adults in a different environment and to broaden their experiences. It also enables them to gain greater independence from their own families. At the same time, it gives their families the opportunity of participating in activities the disabled member might not be able to do or of giving more time than they are usually able to give to other members of the family.

A major national study in the United States showed that although 46 out of the 50 States provided shared care in some form, many families experienced problems in being aware of what was available and in gaining access to the service of their choice[2]. Many of the arrangements were inflexible and failed to meet families' needs. Examples of accessible family support systems from the United Kingdom have recently been reported[25].

In addition to benefits for the family or for the individual, these schemes bring benefits to the community as a whole. Families who offer to share their home with a disabled child or adult demonstrate their commitment to sharing such roles and tasks by the community as a whole. They also provide valuable examples to neighbours and fellow citizens.

Financial support

When a family includes a disabled member, the family almost always experiences additional costs. In many countries, financial support is offered only by other members of the family or in some societies by the disabled child or adult begging for alms.

In many developed countries, providing social welfare acknowledges a responsibility for all citizens to support those who are vulnerable and disadvantaged. The State offers some financial support to those who care for disabled children or adults in their family and who may, by so doing, forego their own work or career opportunities. Care within the home is also often seen as a more desirable and certainly also as a cheaper form of care than alternative residential care if such support is not available.

When disabled persons reach adulthood, they are also entitled to financial support if they are unable to work or support themselves financially. This includes the cost of support they need to live in the community, including staff to support them in practical ways by helping them with personal care, shopping, cooking, cleaning and additional costs for travel.

Some families themselves are taking out insurance or setting up trust schemes for their disabled sons and daughters for the future when they will be no longer able to offer their children the care they need.

Counselling

In addition to practical support, families or individual family members sometimes need and can benefit from psychological support, particularly when negative reactions to disability persist and/or become overwhelming. Counselling is a broad term to describe several methods of offering support. The main principles include helping people express their feelings and thoughts, however negative these may be, in a supportive, non-judgemental environment and help them look at all the choices available to work out what they think is best for themselves and their family. This type of support service is accessible to only a limited number of people in developed countries and those in developing countries wealthy enough to find and pay for such a service.

Family-to-family support and self-help

Almost all services and policies for disabled people and their families have their origins in families and family members coming together and supporting each other; in initiating programmes to help their disabled children and relatives; and in pressing Governments for social policies to give them the support and services they need.

Families have a unique ability to support others in a similar position to their own. Although all families are different, they can understand better than others the experiences of caring for and living with a disabled family member in their social context and environment. They can empathize with each others' feelings, share ways they themselves have coped with any difficulties that arose and how they sought and found solutions. They can be a source of information and advice and offer mutual practical and emotional support. Some of the types of support described in previous sections may be offered by other parents and family members.

Different family members can gain support for their particular situation and role from others: mothers, fathers, grandparents, brothers and sisters. Disabled people gain from the friendship of other disabled children and adults who have had similar experiences of struggle and achievement and of facing prejudice and disadvantage.

Much can be gained from groups and associations of disabled people meeting together and from other family members and families meeting in groups and associations. Not only is there a pooling of knowledge and experience and a breaking down of feelings of isolation, but also these groups can gain strength from each other in initiating new methods of support; in modifying the attitudes of others; in advocating for the rights of people with disability and their families; and in pressing for more appropriate policies to address these rights.

Self-help groups can be appropriate and helpful at any age or stage in the life cycle of the disabled person and his or her family. Children gain from sharing activities; adolescents and young adults from discussing views and experiences as well as having fun together; older people gain from meeting and sharing memories of their past lives, as do all older people.

Groups of parents can meet in each others' homes, in community halls and, as happened in Côte d'Ivoire[11], in the local market-place.

Self-help groups can also invite professionals to give them information, advice or support. They can involve professionals in advocating on their behalf or jointly press for improvements. They can also demonstrate their own abilities to contribute to training professionals.

Conflict and advocacy

Conflict may arise from time to time in all families, particularly when children reach the adolescent or young adult stage and may make choices different from those favoured by their parents. Most young people will grow in independence and make their own way. To what degree they take account of their parents' views and wishes will vary from culture to culture and from individual to individual. This development is even more difficult for those young people who remain dependent on their families for their physical care throughout their lives.

Common areas for potential conflict include young people's wish to experiment and take risks and try new experiences, even if these are later discarded as mistakes. Young disabled persons may wish to go further afield than their families consider safe; they may wish to try new skills; they may, like other young people, want to form sexual relationships; they may want to marry and to have children of their own.

Their parents and relatives may well be sympathetic to these choices and wishes; they may, indeed, encourage them. However, in other families, young persons may meet with discouragement, disapproval and blocking of their wishes. This negative response may spring from the best of motives: other family members may fear for the disabled young person and wish to protect him or her from harm, upset or emotional pain. However, this may nevertheless constitute a denial of the right of disabled persons to self-determination and to make choices about their own lives.

Similar conflicts may occur when disabled persons are older. They may also want to do things that other family members feel may be a risk to themselves.

In these situations, disabled children, young people and adults should have access to an independent person who will act as their advocate and who will argue their case, try to ensure their rights and enable them to exercise control over their own lives. This may need to be done at the same time as offering some support, advice and/or counselling for the rest of the family.

Abuse and protection

Even more serious and difficult are those situations where disabled children or adults are abused. While the majority of families care adequately or well for their disabled members, in some family situations the disabled member may be scapegoated, neglected or ill-treated.

A growing body of research, at least in developed countries, is about the abuse experienced by disabled children and adults. People with disabilities, including older people, have also expressed their feelings and views about experiencing abuse, which in some cases may have occurred many years ago.

Sexual abuse has been reported in most cultures and all classes of society. The pre- conditions for the occurrence of sexual abuse include both the accessibility of a more vulnerable person and the ability to ensure their silence about the abuse. Clearly these conditions are present in relation to disabled people.

Studies in the United States estimate that abuse has occurred in up to 25 per cent of adolescents with learning difficulties; 50 per cent of young people in institutions with hearing impairments; and as many as 50 per cent to 75 per cent of children with severe learning difficulties and behaviour problems[15 and 31]. In the United Kingdom an estimated 5 per cent of adults with learning difficulties have been sexually abused at some time.

Among many reasons for this, some relate to the negative social attitudes of prejudice and discrimination that lead parents of disabled children to neglect or ill-treat such children or even leave them to die. Family members may adopt the social attitudes and behaviour of others and taunt such children, and criticize or reproach them for their difference and for what they cannot do.

Many different forms of abuse exist. Abuse is also cumulative and multiple. All sexually abused children and many physically abused children are emotionally abused. About a quarter of the children who are physically abused are also sexually abused. Once a child has been sexually abused, he or she is more vulnerable to further abuse.

Recognition is growing that the abuse of disabled children and adults occurs all too often and more frequently than in other populations. Such abuse occurs not only within families, but also in institutions and with alternative families and carers.

The very dependence of the disabled member may make him or her the target for all the frustrations caused by a variety of stresses in the family such as poverty, overwork, tensions in family relationships, unemployment, poverty and ill health.

Lack of knowledge may also lead to some forms of mistreatment, such as emotional neglect and lack of stimulation, that are likely to affect significantly the disabled person's degree of disability in coping with his or her environment.

Disabled children and adults are perhaps the most vulnerable to abuse of all kinds including severe physical and sexual abuse. Disabled children and adults often require more intimate physical care that enables others to have access to them in private. They may have less access to sexual education and to an understanding of what is normal and acceptable touching and what is sexual behaviour. They are often less free to move about and find independent people to whom they can talk about the abuse, and they may also find it harder to communicate and be understood, and, even more crucially, to be believed.

Behavioural signs indicating the possibility of sexual abuse of other children or adults may be too readily interpreted by professionals as due to the disabling condition. For too long professionals and society at large have failed to consider abuse as a possible origin of changed, perhaps challenging, behaviours in people with disability and have not considered that such behaviour may provide one means - sometimes the only means - for disabled people to communicate their anger and distress in response to abusive experiences.

Strategies for protection

Many countries have now developed or are developing ways of protecting children and vulnerable adults from abuse both within their families and by others outside the family, including other carers and professionals. These procedures were set up initially for non-disabled children but the frequency of abuse makes it necessary to extend them to disabled children and adults.

Understanding is now greater that professionals, communities and families must be more alert to the possibility of abuse occurring and ways of responding if abuse is suspected. Additional complexities in doing this may be present in investigating and dealing with the abuse of disabled children and adults, particularly in situations where there are difficulties in communication or where the child or adult has an intellectual impairment. Most legal systems discriminate against children and people with learning difficulties or communication impairments, although a few successful prosecutions have been brought in such situations. This remains an area where professionals in all disciplines require more training, knowledge and skills.

Again, training and raising awareness of the possibility of abuse and its damaging long-term consequences are essential, particularly for professionals and carers of disabled children and adults.

Sexual education for disabled children is at least as important as for other children. Support for families and for disabled people to increase their opportunities for communication where there are speech, hearing or comprehension difficulties should include signs or symbols that will enable disabled people to tell of abuse if it exists.

Because of the long-term damaging effects of abuse, all survivors of abuse must have the opportunity of working through their feelings and experiences, with the support of a trained worker.

Families cannot always be the best or safest places for disabled children or adults; alternative provision and care are sometimes needed. This may be only on a temporary basis if appropriate work is done with family members as well as with the survivor of the abuse.

Support in the life cycle

Some useful general principles can be derived from what families have reported.

General principles of support
- Support should always be mindful of the rights of the disabled person
- Support should always be offered on the basis of needs identified

either by families themselves or in collaboration with families
- Support should be offered in an appropriate way to the individual family
- Support should remain flexible. The mode, amount or timing of support should change as the needs of the disabled person and the family change
- Support should retain a focus on the similarity of needs of the person with the disability and the family to those of others
- Support should maximize the degree of control exercised by the disabled person and the family
- Support should facilitate the integration of the person with the disability and the family into the life of the local community.

While these principles apply throughout the life span, the support has specific aspects offered at key stages in the life cycle.

At birth

Many parents have written about their experiences and feelings on learning they had given birth to a child with a disability. The experience is never forgotten, and it affects their relationships with other professionals for many years. Many parents are still angry and bitter when they remember the pain caused by the way they were first informed that their new baby had a disability. Considerable improvements have taken place over the past 20 years, but many parents still complain of insensitivity, lack of information, understanding and support[5].

Some writers automatically assume that giving birth to a child with a disability will always be seen as a tragedy and that new parents inevitably pass through periods of mourning and chronic sorrow before they finally adjust to the reality of having a child with a disability. Professionals and well-meaning friends try to help the new parents accept the disability, somehow implying that parents deny their child has a disability or that they reject the child.

The reality is that parents' reactions vary greatly. Some will have been told before birth that their baby will have a particular impairment and will have made a conscious decision to continue with the pregnancy. Some will realize at once that there is an abnormality in the baby before anyone tells them. Others will suspect something is wrong from the behaviour of the staff of the maternity unit or because the hospital procedures are different.

Preschool years and early intervention

Since it is universally accepted that the first five years of a child's life are all important, parents of children with disabilities must be given every possible support in helping their children's development. The nature and amount of support will vary from family to family in relation to the needs of the child, the family as a whole and individual members of the family. Each family therefore needs to be aware of what is available and be able to discuss how their needs can best be met.

All families must be able to express concerns if they are worried about any aspect of their child's development. Their child should be thoroughly assessed by a multidisciplinary team including doctors, nurses and specialists in child development with a knowledge of assessment of young children. Ideally, the assessment should be carried out in an environment familiar to the child, preferably the child's own home, rather than in the strange environment of a hospital or clinic.

In some countries, specialist child development teams are available to carry out a detailed assessment of the level the child has reached in various areas of development (e.g., physical, self-care, social, language development). On this basis, the team suggests activities that can be carried out at home.

In Kenya, for example, about 30 such teams have been established at the local level to work with families and schools. The teams are supported by the Ministries of Health and Education[27].

The team has to have some knowledge of the family situation to ensure that the suggestions made are realistic and manageable. Suggestions for additional family activities, over and above what they would do naturally, should be the outcome of negotiation rather than prescription. If the parents agree, it may be helpful and informative for a member of the team to visit the family beforehand and keep in touch with the family to provide support and encouragement and to modify the suggestions if they prove unrealistic.

Many of the concerns of families at this point relate to ordinary routines such as feeding and sleeping and the extent to which the baby needs to be treated differently as a consequence of the impairment. At a later stage, they will need support in methods of stimulating the child, the right kind of activities and play materials and playing with other children.

Wherever possible, assessment and early intervention programmes should have a multidisciplinary input. To identify additional complications, including medical surveillance, is particularly important. Children with Down's syndrome, for example, frequently have additional impairments involving ocular, auditory, respiratory and cardiac functions. Similarly, children with epilepsy may not have access to the right medication. Preventing secondary impairments is important in children with intellectual deficits. Because these may not be apparent at birth, comprehensive medical monitoring must be provided so treatment will be timely and effective. Obtaining full medical check- ups is sometimes difficult, as parents' concerns tend to be dismissed as examples of fussiness or over-protectiveness.

Portage home intervention programme

The Portage home intervention programme is perhaps the best-known example of a home-based family support programme for young children with a developmental delay or disability. This programme was originally developed in rural areas in North America but has since been translated into 30 languages and adapted for use in many developing countries; for example, Guyana, India, Jamaica and Nepal[3].

The Portage programme is based on the parent and home visitor carrying out a joint assessment of the stages a child has reached in key areas of development; for example, physical, fine and gross motory skills, social, emotional and language development and in a range of spontaneous play activities. This joint assessment is based on the parents' detailed knowledge of the child, supplemented by the home visitor's own observations and experience of other children's development.

The next stage involves discussion and negotiations between the parent and the home visitor concerning priorities for the next steps in the child's learning and, above all, of ways the family can help the child reach these targets in a comparatively short time, within one or two weeks. To this end, the home visitor uses a set of activity cards suggesting ordinary games that can be used by members of the family to help the child achieve short-term targets, mainly using ordinary household routines and activities.

A range of other home-visiting and support programmes have been reported in a number of developing countries. One of the best known is the Zimcare project, developed by a voluntary organization in four rural areas in Zimbabwe[18]. These were run in association with existing locally active organizations (e.g. the Red Cross).

While independent evaluation suggested this was a successful programme, not all families and primary-care givers can commit time and motivation to meeting the demands of such programmes. This raises a general issue about the commitment needed to implement Portage-type programmes by families already overwhelmed by the day-to-day demands of work and never-ending domestic tasks. There is also the issue of the nature of the participation demanded by the programme. Even when adapted to suit local conditions, family members (nearly always mothers) have to find time to be alone with the child, to record progress (however simply) and to plan further activities with the home visitor.

Those developing these programmes should take account of the potential resources of the extended family and adapt them to whatever extent is practicable and desirable. Many grandparents, uncles and aunts and brothers and sisters have become involved in early intervention programmes and have played a major part in helping to give families a sense of common purpose in working together to help children with disabilities to learn and to develop and to be accepted in the neighbourhood and the local community.

Inclusion in mainstream preschool programmes

In addition to specialist initiatives such as Portage, opportunities should be created so preschool children can be integrated into whatever programmes are available to other preschool children. Many countries have developed a range of preschool facilities: nursery schools, nursery classes in primary classes and day-care centres, as well as many privately run kindergartens and playgroups, often run or controlled by the parents themselves.

Many children with developmental delays and disabilities have been successfully integrated into these programmes. No doubt they are a much-needed source of support for parents. Not only do they provide a break from the day-to-day care of the child, but they are also an opportunity to meet other parents and professional staff on a day-to-day basis, people with whom they can exchange ideas and experiences.

Yet preschool provision is not common in developing countries. A summary of provision in Asia indicates that only India, Sri Lanka and Thailand have extensive provision[17], though China seems to be rapidly extending nurseries and including children with developmental delays. There are reports of an experimental integration programme in Anhui Province, with some support from the United Kingdom charity, Save the Children Fund.

Towards partnership with parents

In all projects involving young and preschool children, utmost care is needed to ensure that professionals and volunteers work with and through full and equal partnership with families at every stage. Parents have frequently complained that professionals have a tendency to take over and to know best, forgetting it is the family who lives with the child for 24 hours a day and has the experience of understanding and trying to meet the child's needs. Professionals are there to support not supplant families.

In countries where comprehensive assessment and early intervention programmes are available, parents should not be overwhelmed and confused by conflicting advice from different professionals whom they encounter in clinics or on home visits. To avoid this, many teams have developed the concept of a key worker. After the initial assessment, this person provides a single point of contact between the family and the rest of the team. A close relationship develops between the family and the key worker who must be a good listener and mediator, whatever other qualifications they may have. Sometimes this function is carried out by another parent.

Services need to be planned and delivered to respond to these individual needs. Services must not be delivered in inflexible packages or be based on a stereotype of family needs and priorities. These have to be discussed and negotiated.

The same dynamic interaction between the needs of families and the nature of available services and supports applies at all stages in the lives of families who have a disabled relative.

School years

Disabled children do not go to school at all in many developing countries. Surveys conducted by the United Nations Educational, Scientific and Cultural Organization (UNESCO) indicate that less than 2 per cent of disabled children attend any form of school in many African and Asian countries and that few who do so will complete four years of primary education[12]. Yet studies in several countries have indicated that a certain amount of casual integration does take place. Children have been accepted by the local school, because their parents have taken them and because they and their families were already known to the school[21 and 22].

Integration dilemmas

Western countries widely agree that all disabled children should attend the same local schools as other children in the neighbourhood. This is probably the view of most parents of younger children and of many parents of older children as well.

But the issues are far from simple from the point of view of families and the children themselves. While the inclusion of children with physical impairments is widely accepted, teachers are less ready to accept children with significant learning or behavioural difficulties and are anxious about teaching children with sensory impairments without additional resources provided by equipment or trained support teachers.

Many industrialized countries have a well-resourced and highly developed special school system, with well-trained staff and staff ratios as low as one adult to three children in some classes. The classrooms are often well equipped and the schools are likely to be visited by speech therapists, physiotherapists, medical and nursing specialists and advisory teachers and psychologists.

Yet however well resourced a special school may be, it still separates its pupils from other children and therefore deprives them of the opportunity of a shared learning environment with other children and of helping them in turn to value and include disabled children. The challenge is one of integrating and combining the educational advantages of special schools with the social benefits of ordinary schools; some call this making ordinary schools special and special schools ordinary.

Many links have been developed between special and ordinary schools. Children from special schools may spend part of each week attending classes in a neighbouring ordinary school. Ordinary schools have in turn set up special classes or developed resource rooms and learning support teams to enable children with disabilities to spend all or most of their time in the ordinary class, with carefully planned support from other teachers.

It is tempting to advise parents in developing countries to avoid the mistakes of developed countries by adopting integrated education from the outset. This is indeed the preferred option for many parents. Others however feel that ordinary schools are simply not ready or properly resourced to meet the needs of children with severe disabilities, particularly those with severe intellectual impairments. Teachers may be hostile or negative, the classes are likely to be too large and the needs of such children may be overlooked. In this situation, some parents prefer to put their energies into lobbying for a special school to be set up, often with funds they have raised themselves or with limited support from public funds. Many parents have set up their own schools and indeed trained to teach in the schools themselves.

Home-school links

Whether or not children go to school, parents and the wider family are just as much in need of support then as they were during the first few years of the child's life. Some will need support in insisting on the rights of their child to attend school. Others may not be convinced of any benefit in their child attending school. They may feel that little or nothing can be done by schools to help the child and they may fear that the child will be teased, mocked or unhappy both in the classroom and in the playground.

Where children do attend school, developing an active partnership of equals between parents and professionals must be a top priority. Unfortunately, this is far from being a reality in many countries, developing or developed. Indeed, it may well be the exception rather than the rule.

In many countries, parents of all children and not just those with disabilities are still kept at arm's length by schools. Failure to mobilize the interest of parents and to work for their close involvement in the life of the school and the education of their child is a tragic waste of human resources and family commitment.

Where disabled children are concerned, everything is gained by developing close working relationships between teachers and parents and other family members. The rationale for such partnerships is overwhelmingly convincing but, with some notable exceptions, not many examples are found throughout the world.

Some years ago, UNESCO commissioned ILSMH to prepare guidelines for collaboration and partnership between parents and professionals working with disabled children and young people[23]. The guidelines reflected the best examples of good practice available from reports by some 70 member societies throughout the world.

The main recommendations concerning school-age children are summarized below. They appear to be relevant to different degrees to children with a wide range of disabilities and to schools and families in many countries.

Guidelines for collaboration between home and school

- Opportunities for parents and teachers to discuss their aims and priorities for the child should be available, both in the long term and the short term.
- To plan the most appropriate curriculum, teaching objectives and methods, teachers should try to learn about the child's home environment in general and as it relates to the child's learning opportunities in particular.
- Teachers and family members should jointly assess the child's skills, abilities and needs.
- Successful collaboration between parents and teachers depends on the extent to which information is shared.
- Educational goals and methods need to be shared with families.
- Parents and teachers should share and celebrate success.
- Teachers need to find the time to listen to parents' concerns and priorities ("Your choice is our choice", as expressed by teachers in Bangladesh).
- Parents and teachers will find it useful to list possible ways they can work together; for example, through teachers visiting parents at home, parents taking part in school activities, recording children's work through photographs and videos to illustrate progress or share ideas on joint work.
- Parents can be much more fully involved in training professionals.
- Opportunities need to be created to involve both the parents and the student in the formulation and monitoring of plans and policies in the school and the locality.

Needs of school-leavers and young adults

The age children leave school varies greatly across the world, both for disabled and non-disabled children. In many countries, the majority of children do not complete even four years of primary education and can expect to leave school between 10 and 12 years of age. Many drop out after one or two years and others attend sporadically. Only a minority proceed to secondary education or beyond.

If this is the norm for many children in developing countries, all the more important that a firm foundation of partnership is laid between parents and teachers during the years when children are at school. Many parents will be able to build on these foundations once their child leaves school and transfer what they have learned from this partnership to new challenges and situations the family will encounter as their son or daughter leaves school and becomes an adult.

Leaving school presents challenges both to the young person and the family. The routine of daily attendance at school and the structure this provides are suddenly disrupted. The young person often feels disorientated and confused by the change of routine and lifestyle and may be left with little or nothing to do during the day. Finding a useful role and adjusting to the changes brought about by leaving school may take time.

All this may coincide with the whole range of social, physical and sexual pressures associated with the normal process of adolescence, in this case complicated by disability and by doubts and uncertainties about the future.

The family will also be faced with a number of adjustments. Too often a member of the family, usually the mother, is forced to give up her work or some of her outside interests to look after a disabled son or daughter. This in itself can be a cause of stress, all the more so because in most countries the prospects of daytime occupation for young disabled people are small. The family situation is therefore potentially tense and explosive.

At this time worries about the long-term future can become prominent; concerns about what arrangements can be made for the young person when the parents are too old or themselves too disabled to look after their son or daughter and what will finally happen after their death. This is a particular concern when the young person is severely intellectually impaired and needs a level of support and care not available in the community.

Housing trusts have been set up in some countries to ensure that a home can be provided with appropriate levels of care when this becomes necessary. Parents who can afford to do so may make payments into a trust fund specifically set up for this purpose. Sometimes, all too rarely, plans are made by public authorities to prepare the young person to live in alternative accommodation in the community when the time comes. But schemes such as this are available only to the few. Many families cannot see any resolution to this problem and fear that their son or daughter may be sent to an institution for the rest of their lives.

Planning for the future

Few countries in the world provide for disabled school-leavers and young people so as to meet the whole range of needs identified at this time in the young person's life or where it is planned in partnership with the family. In most countries, even families who have been reasonably well supported while their child was at school are often neglected and left to fend for themselves. Because few services are available for the young people themselves, the situation at home can be highly charged and reach crisis point.

Families must be able to voice these concerns and to know they will not only be listened to with understanding, but also that plans will be made with their full participation as well as that of the young people concerned, which will result in an exploration of whatever alternatives are available, however limited these may be.

This process needs to begin while the young person is still at school. Some developed countries have legal requirements that a transition plan be developed for all disabled school-leavers. The school is not only responsible for preparing the young person to be as independent as possible, but also for involving parents and the student in discussion and decision-making on future provision, together with other professional staff such as social workers and health professionals who are well placed to advise on these options. Increasingly, schools are helping their students anticipate some of the problems they will face in finding a job and taking their place in society.

The first need of families is for information about facilities and resources that are or can be made available. In some countries, this information is summarized in leaflet form, listing the names of key organizations and individuals. These agencies may be scattered and uncoordinated, making it difficult for families to know where and how to begin to secure the support and services they and their son or daughter need.

Because families are at their most vulnerable at this transition point between school and community services, one person must be designated as a single point of contact and families should have a say in choosing him or her. Then this person should try to coordinate the information available from the various agencies and act as a friend or advocate of the family in securing the most appropriate provision for the family as a whole and for the disabled person in particular. Their needs are now, as before, inseparable.

Continuing education

In many developing countries, continuing education facilities are becoming available to disabled young people. They are usually in local community colleges attended by other young people and have a wide range of vocational and non-vocational courses. Colleges such as these offer a fresh start both educationally and socially. Many young people who have attended special schools or classes are more than ready for the more adult and challenging environment that a local college can present.

As most colleges are by definition for all members of the community, the initial assumption is that disabled students will be fully included in the classes of their choice. This means the college staff will need some preparation and support in ensuring that the curriculum and activities of the class and of the college as a whole are fully extended to all disabled students. Some students will need additional support; for example, access to and mobility within the building, taped or Brailled material, sign-language interpretation and learning support. Some of these supports are expensive; others call for a greater degree of awareness, knowledge and skills among all levels of college staff.

The role of parents whose son or daughter is attending college is ambiguous. Although they have a great deal of valuable information to share with the college, their sons or daughters are likely to be of an age when they should be able to speak for themselves and make their own needs known. Staff may be inclined, therefore, to keep parents at arms's length in the interests of consistency with other students whose parents may have little or no formal or social contact with the college.

Parents should be at least centrally involved at the time of admission to the college. At this stage, other professionals such as teachers, health professionals or social workers may also be involved with the young person and the family in developing a transition plan in collaboration with college staff. Parents should then have an opportunity to share their views and information on a basis of equality with other partners in the transition process.

Because choosing the right courses is one of the most difficult decisions facing any student entering college, all concerned must be made aware of what is available and that the choice really meets the needs of the student who should have the final say. The risk is underestimating the student's abilities and assuming that certain courses may be too difficult or that vocational courses may not lead to employment at the end of the course.

Family members, college staff and former teachers may all have different views. In this situation, the voice of the student is sometimes drowned in a chorus of well-intentioned advice.

Preparation for employment

Despite world recession and high levels of unemployment, disabled people insist on their rights to paid employment. This is in line with International Labour Organisation Convention 159 of 1983 concerning Vocational Rehabilitation and Employment (Disabled Persons)[14] and also with the Standard Rules on the Equalization of Opportunities for Persons with Disabilities[30]. A small number of countries have introduced legislation making it illegal to discriminate against disabled people in respect of employment, as well as housing, education, leisure and transport (e.g., the Americans with Disabilities Act, 1990). Others have introduced disability quotas and levies (Germany, for example).

In reality, the number of disabled people in full employment is low in most countries. Nevertheless, a growing number of disabled people have found and kept jobs, despite families or professionals underestimating the likelihood of their doing so.

Many disabled people in developing countries are working with their family, especially in rural areas. In other cases, they are working in family businesses or selling goods from a family stall in the market-place. This not only benefits the individual and the family, but also provides a good example to the general public that disabled people can make a positive contribution to society.

In other cases, parents and voluntary organizations have themselves set up sheltered workshops and vocational training centres to ensure that disabled people have access to some form of training and vocational preparation (e.g., Kenya). Some of these workshops specialize in making certain products and then marketing them directly to the general public. This aim may at times conflict with that of preparing people to work in the open market or at least of securing supported employment.

Many industrialized countries have long established day centres or sheltered workshops but their success in placing people in open employment is limited. Several countries, however, have reported successful schemes where a disabled person is given whatever support is needed to enable them to do a particular job in a given environment. The support may be in the form of grants for the employer to adapt the workplace or for individuals to acquire physical or electronic supports so they can operate machinery or carry out tasks that would otherwise be difficult or impossible for them.

In some countries, human support is given for a disabled person to learn and become proficient in the tasks required in the work setting. This support is sometimes provided by a staff member from the day centre or sheltered workshop or by a volunteer from the workplace who provides essential social support in helping particularly those with intellectual impairments to make friends and join informal social networks (e.g., the Pathway scheme in the United Kingdom, started by the voluntary agency, the Royal Society for Mentally Handicapped Children and Adults (MENCAP) but later developed from public funds).

Living in the community

The principle of living an ordinary life in developed countries implies that disabled people should be supported in leaving their families and living as independently as possible. Some progress has been made to this end. An increasing number of adults, including some with severe physical and intellectual impairments, are living in their own homes and apartments, with as much support as they need as individuals. This comes from publicly funded social-care assistants who help them with those tasks and activities they cannot carry out for themselves.

In most developing countries, however, young people traditionally remain with their families until they marry. In these situations, the concept of moving out of the family in late adolescence would not be considered appropriate, as the family expects to provide a home for some years and also to include new daughters-in-law as the sons marry, at least for a period. Furthermore, the extended family has a key role in supporting all members of the family, including those with a disability. This may include a job and a home being provided by a member of the extended family. Although a greater number of small nuclear families are now found in developing countries, the traditional supporting role of the extended family remains strong in most countries.

Marriage and parenthood

Disabled people often have restricted opportunities to meet people of their own age and background. Similarly, families of young disabled people may over-protect their son or daughter and discourage friendships and more intimate relationships, for fear of exploitation or disappointment.

In the past, there has been little open recognition of the sexual needs of disabled people and that these needs are no different from those of the rest of the population. Disabled people, particularly those with intellectual impairments, have been regarded as asexual both by their families and by professionals, despite clear evidence to the contrary. Consequently, sexuality, sex education and support in personal relationships generally have rarely been provided for young people or discussed by their families.

More recently, the social and sexual needs of disabled people of all ages have received increasing recognition, stimulated in part by growing evidence of their vulnerability to exploitation and sexual abuse as well as by the more positive motivation of supporting them in forming relationships, in marrying and in becoming parents.

Recognizing, respecting and supporting disabled people in forming relationships, marrying and becoming parents again calls for understanding and collaboration between disabled people themselves, their families and the various professionals with whom they may be in contact. Although many disabled people will need relatively little help, others, particularly those with intellectual or communication impairments, may well encounter greater obstacles and need sensitive support.

Many disabled people marry and become successful parents, and some marriage partners and some parents may become disabled when they already have a family. Again the variety of experience is great, just as among the non-disabled population and depending on the social environment.

Although many disabled people have married and become parents, they face many obstacles. In part these spring directly from cultural and social attitudes to disability. For example, some will fear that the disability may be inherited and passed to children, or there may be concerns about the ability of the disabled person to support a family.

Disabled people who have pioneered by pressing for their right to share these common human experiences have helped to shape society's thinking on these issues, and some disabled parents and some children of disabled parents have begun to document their experiences.

Challenge of ageing

The increasing life expectancy both of disabled people and their parents is bringing new challenges. Ageing disabled people themselves often become carers of their elderly and infirm parents. This may provide a valued and indeed indispensable role for them, but it also creates barriers to their own independence and autonomy in the community. Their situation parallels that of countless women who have sacrificed opportunities for a career, marriage and motherhood in order to devote themselves to the care of their or their spouses' elderly and dependent parents.

Some disabled people enter willingly into such a role but others will feel that new restrictions are being imposed on them against their will.

These issues should be considered by the whole family in advance of emergencies, therefore, and the disabled member of the family should express a clear view and take appropriate action. Families should expect to receive support from professionals and service agencies in the community.

The process of ageing can be particularly difficult for disabled people. Any physical or psychological difficulties they experience are all too often assumed to be an integral part of their disability. When this happens, they may find it hard to obtain investigation and treatment for conditions not directly related to their disability at all.

A further dilemma arises in individuals with Down's syndrome who show signs of rapid ageing consistent with Alzheimer's disease at a comparatively early age. Although many have lived successfully and with varying degrees of support in the community, the ageing process can affect them so severely that some form of residential care becomes necessary. Should they then be integrated into ordinary old people's homes and geriatric hospitals where they will be much younger than other residents and where they might have to live in poor conditions for many more years? A preferred solution is to provide them with an increasing amount of support to enable them to remain either in their own homes or in supported accommodation. Funds for this option are hard to come by.

Preparing for death and bereavement

Children and adults with disabilities are as, or perhaps even more, likely to experience the death of their relatives, carers and friends as anyone else. They themselves may have a progressive, terminal condition. For carers to explain and prepare disabled people for death and bereavement, as well as to support them through their grief and mourning, may be particularly painful. This is understandable when attachments are all the more crucial because of the additional dependency needs. However, it is all the more important to involve the disabled person in what is happening, to explain and to provide opportunities for them to express their feelings, fears and anxieties as well as the confusion, anger and powerlessness that are well-known features of bereavement. Giving information and explanation, and involvement in planning for their own future, are all ways for those supporting disabled people to help them retain as much control over their own lives as possible.

Conclusions

Disabled people themselves and their families have already made and are continuing to make a significant and powerful impact on the way the societies they live in think about and respond to disabled people. An increasing number of disabled people are making an outstanding and inspirational contribution to the life of their communities as teachers, politicians and artists. The various United Nations conventions and charters and guidance to Governments in relation to disability issues are a useful spur to further action. But profound changes are needed before disabled people are granted equal rights and can fully take their place in society and, most importantly, before society itself can fully benefit from the creativity, strengths and abilities of disabled people and their families. IYF can provide a starting-point for a major reappraisal of the extent to which families can be better supported in helping their relatives take their place in the community and make a significant contribution to society.

In preceding sections, the focus has been on individual families and services to support people with disabilities and their families in particular. But what disabled people and their families most want is to have the same access and rights to life-enhancing opportunities as their non-disabled friends and neighbours. For this to be possible, the needs of disabled people must be considered alongside those of all other groups.

To make this happen, the built environment will need to change so disabled people can become as mobile and as able to use buildings, transport and other facilities as everyone else.

Education, employment, housing, health, social welfare, income security and all other services must also become as accessible to disabled people and to members of their families as to all other members of society.

Above all, social attitudes in all cultures must become informed by true knowledge about disabled people and their families, their strengths, their needs, their difficulties and their gifts.

These changes can come about in a variety of ways through:
- National and local policies and social education
- A more informed portrayal of disabled people and their families by the media
- A greater degree of interaction between disabled people and their families
- The perseverance of disabled people, their families and supportive professionals in continuing to campaign for all these necessary changes.

More positive social attitudes, policies and structures will bring about a greater contribution from disabled people and their families. This in turn will provide a foundation for achieving the goal of a Society for All in the twenty-first century.

References

1. Baine, D. Handicapped children in developing countries. Edmonton, Canada, University of Edmonton Press, 1988.
2. Bradley, V., J. Knoll *and* J. Agosta, *eds.* Emerging issues in family support. Washington, D.C., American Association on Mental Retardation, 1992.
3. Brouillette, J., M. Thorburn *and* K. Yamaguchi. Early Intervention. In P. Mittler, R. Brouillette and D. Hornis, *eds.* World yearbook of education: special needs education. London, Kogan Page, 1993.
4. Byrne, E., C. Cunningham and P. Sloper. Families of children with Down's syndrome: One feature in common. London, Routledge, 1988.
5. Carr, J. The effects on the family of a severely handicapped child. In A. Clarke, A.D.B. Clarke *and* J. Berg, *eds.* Mental deficiency: The changing outlook, 4th ed. London, Methuen, 1985.
6. Dunn, W. Personal communication. 1993.
7. Dybwad, R. Voluntary organisations in the field of mental handicap. Boston, Brookline Publications, 1989.
8. Fryers, T. Epidemiological thinking in mental retardation: Issues in taxonomy and population frequency. *In* N. Bray, *ed. International review of research in mental retardation* (New York and London, Academic Press, 1993).
9. Gartner, A., D. Lipsky *and* A. Turnbull, *eds.* Supporting families with a child with a disability: An international outlook. Baltimore, Maryland., Paul H. Brookes, 1991.
10. Groce, N. Everybody here spoke sign language: Hereditary deafness on Martha's Vineyard. Cambridge, Massachusettes, Harvard University Press, 1985.
11. Haddad, H. Personal communication. 1993.
12. Hegarty, S. Education of children with disabilities. *In* P. Mittler, R. Brouillette and D. Harris, eds. World yearbook of education: special needs education. London, Kogan Page, 1993.
13. Helander, E. Beyond prejudice and dignity: An introduction to community based rehabilitation. Geneva, United Nations Development Programme, 1993.
14. International Labour Organisation. *International labour conventions and recommendations,* 1919 -. Geneva, International Labour Office.
15. Kelly, L. The connection between disability and child abuse: a review of the research evidence. *Child abuse review,* 1:157-167, 1992.
16. Kisanji, J. Interface between culture and disability in the Tanzanian context. *International journal of development, disability and education:* 41, 1994 (in press).
17. Kohli, T. Special education in Asia. *In* P. Mittler, R. Brouillette *and* D. Harris, *eds.* World yearbook of education: special needs education. London, Kogan Page, 1993.
18. Mariga, L. and R. McConkey. Home based learning programmes for mentally handicapped people in rural areas of Zimbabwe. *International review of rehabilitation research,* 10:175-183, 1987.
19. McConachie, H. Implications of a model of stress and coping for services to families of young disabled children. *Child: care, health and development,* 20, 1994 (in press).
20. Miles, C. Educating mentally handicapped children. 2. ed. Peshawar, Pakistan, Mission Hospital, 1991.
21. Miles, C. and M. Miles. Children with learning difficulties. In P. Mittler, R. Brouillette and D. Harris, eds. World yearbook of education: special needs education. London, Kogan Page, 1993.
22. Miles, M. Action study on integration of handicapped children in Pakistan. Peshawar, North-West Frontier Province, Mission Hospital, 1985.
23. Mittler, P., H. Mittler and H. McConachie. Working together: Guidelines for collaboration between professionals and families of children and young people with disabilities. UNESCO Guides to Special Education No. 2. Paris, United Nations Educational, Scientific and Cultural Organization, 1986.
24. P. Mittler, R. Brouillette and D. Harris, eds. World yearbook of education: special needs education. London, Kogan Page, 1993.
25. Mittler, P. and H. Mittler, eds. *Innovations in family support.* Chorley, Lancashire, Lisieux Hall Publications, 1994.
26. Office of Population Censuses and Surveys. Survey of disability in Great Britain; Part 5: Financial circumstances of families. London, Her Majesty's Stationery Office, 1988.

[27] Serpell, R., L. Mariga and K. Harvey. Mental retardation in African countries: Conceptualisation, services and research. In N. Bray, ed. *International review of research in mental retardation* (New York and London, Academic Press, 1993).

[28] Shearer, A. *Think positive: Presenting a positive image of people with mental handicap*. Brussels, International League of Societies for Persons with Mental Handicap, 1984.

[29] Talle, A. Notes on the concept of disability among the pastoral Masai in Kenya. In F. J. Brown and B. Ingstad, eds. Disability in a cross-cultural perspective: Working Paper No. 4. Oslo, Department of Social Anthropology, 1990. pp. 61-78.

[30] United Nations, *Official Records of the General Assembly*, Forty-eighth Session, Supplement No. 49 (A/48/49), resolution 48/96, annex.

[31] Westcott, H. The abuse of disabled children and adults. London, National Society for the Prevention of Cruelty to Children, 1993.

[32] World Health Organization. International classification of impairments, disabilities and handicaps; A manual of classification relating to the consequences of disease, Geneva, 1980.

Annex

LEARNING MESSAGES

The Learning Messages that the IYF Task Force of ILSMH wants to communicate to its member societies, and to Governments, international agencies and to all individuals and organizations concerned with IYF are as follows:

A All people are valued members of their communities;

B People with a disability and their families are equal participating members of their communities and have the same rights:

   i To participate in decisions that affect their lives;

   ii To diversity of choice of housing, education, work, recreation and leisure;

      a To equity and justice;

      b To be empowered to take their full place in the community;

      c To dignity and privacy in all aspects of their lives;

C Everyone is likely to experience disability at some time in their lives, either personally or through members of their family or community;

D Society can add to or lessen disability;

E People with disabilities have abilities;

F People with a disability have the right to be consulted, to make informed choices and to exercise control in planning their lives;

G People with a disability and their families and carers have an important contribution to make to policy development, planning and delivery of services and to training about disability issues;

H It is normal to be different;

I People with a disability have useful knowledge about their own needs, strengths and abilities;

J Families with a member who has a disability have knowledge about their own strengths, needs and abilities;

k Families need information;

l Support for families with a member who has a disability makes economic sense;

m Definitions of the family must reflect the wide range of family arrangements and forms found in society;

n Usually it is in the best interests of the family member with a disability to remain within the family environment, at least during childhood. Families require practical support in order to fulfil this role. Exploitation of families by the State needs to be avoided;

o The interests, safety and welfare of the person with a disability must always be safeguarded;

p In two-parent families, the task of caring for a family member with a disability should as far as possible be shared by both parents. Fathers and mothers both have a vital role in creating a beneficial family environment. Both can make a valuable contribution to the functioning of supportive organizations and where possible should be actively involved in such organizations.

Migration and the FAMILY

Introduction[*]

The unprecedented increase in levels of population mobility in both developing countries and developed countries has been one of the most significant and ubiquitous changes in the last decade. Movement away from the home place on a permanent or temporary basis has become an option to improve life chances for a much wider spectrum of the population than ever before, particularly in developing countries. Whereas in the past possible relocation was usually only part of the calculus of choice for narrowly defined socio-economic, gender, age, ethnic and cultural groups, it has now become available much more broadly across societies. Population mobility remains a selective process, but it is now not only increasing exponentially in scale but also in the diversity of the groups involved. Population movements have also become more complex with respect to the types of movement (especially the huge diversity of important non-permanent mobility) and the spatial patterns of that movement. This is important not only from the perspective of its influence in causing interregional differences in the level and nature of population growth but also because of its significance for economic development and social change. Population movements have profound effects upon economic and social changes in the areas of origin and destination and among the migrants themselves. Equally, social and economic processes are important in shaping the pattern of population movement. This complex two-way relationship between population movement on the one hand and economic development and social change on the other is little understood and remains the major focus of migration research. One dimension of this complex relationship that has been inexplicably neglected, however, is that involving the family.

In both developing countries and developed countries the last decade has seen parametric shifts in the structure and functioning of families with the most profound demographic, social and economic consequences. The extent to which this shapes, and is influenced by, changes in population movement has not been addressed to any substantial degree in the literature. The neglect of the family dimension in migration research, however, extends further. Much of this research adopts as a unit of study the individual migrant and ignores the significance of the family as an important and meaningful group in shaping migration decision-making. Moreover, a large amount of migration is of families or parts of families rather than of

[*] The present paper has been prepared for the IYF secretariat by Graeme Hugo, Professor of Geography, University of Adelaide, Australia.

individuals, and the adjustment at the destination is frequently undertaken by persons as a family group rather than as totally isolated individuals.

The present chapter explores some aspects of the role of the family in population movement as well as the influence of migration upon changing patterns of family structure and functioning. While families have undergone massive changes in both developing and developed countries, the major focus will be upon developing countries where, it could be argued, changes in both family and migration patterns have been more substantial and more profound in their impact than those in developed countries. This is not to say that the relationship is not important in developed countries; some dimensions of it will be reviewed in the latter part of this paper. Nevertheless, most attention is placed upon developing countries, especially in Asia where the present writer has had the most firsthand experience.

Changing patterns and types of population movement in developing countries

In traditional societies the family was not only the basic social unit but also the fundamental unit of economic organization. In their attempts to survive under especially difficult conditions, or in more normal circumstances to improve their life chances, families have long developed and employed particular mobility strategies. These strategies could either involve the entire family moving or could involve families (or more usually the patriarch) allocating some of their constituent members to work in other localities. Some of the earliest forms of human organization such as hunting and gathering and shifting cultivation involved population mobility as an integral part of the family's survival strategy. However, in such societies, family members tended to range over a very restricted "well-trodden social space" [88]. This situation has been totally transformed in recent years in a number of ways. Such allocations of family labour to locations other than the area of origin have been used by a broader spectrum of types of families in a wider variety of contexts and, most importantly, ranging over a much more extensive territorial space. These processes have been an important element in the enormous increase in the scale, complexity and significance for economic and social change of population mobility in developing countries over the last decade.

Permanent relocations of people within developing countries have become greater, in particular the displacement of people from rural to urban areas has gathered momentum over the last decade, especially in

Africa and Asia. It has been pointed out[82, p. 151] that the rate of urbanization is a sensitive index of intensity of the redistribution of population from rural to urban areas. This can be defined as the average annual rate of change of the percentage urban and is equal to the difference between the urban population growth rate and the total (urban and rural combined) population growth rate. Table 12.1 shows that the rate of growth of urbanization increased from 1.86 per cent per annum in the late 1970s to 2.42 per cent in the late 1980s. Hence population redistribution from rural to urban areas was intense in the 1980s and will continue into the 1990s as the table shows. The extent of rural-urban migration has been highest in Asia where the rate of urbanization in the 1985-1990 period was 3.1 per cent per annum.

TABLE 12.1.
RATE OF URBANIZATION,[a] LESS DEVELOPED REGIONS BY MAJOR AREAS, 1975-2025

Major area	1975-1980	1985-1990	1990-1995	1995-2000	2020-2025
Less developed regions	1.86	2.42	2.10	1.80	1.01
Africa	1.91	2.02	1.92	1.75	1.15
Latin America	1.20	0.87	0.72	0.59	0.31
Asia[b]	2.04	3.05	2.57	2.22	1.14
Oceania[c]	0.67	1.41	1.57	1.76	1.71

Source: *World Urbanization Prospects, 1990* (United Nations publication, Sales No. E.91.XIII.6).

[a] Rate of urbanization is defined as the average annual exponential rate of growth of the percentage urban. It equals the difference between the growth rate of the urban population and the growth rate of the total population.
[b] Excluding Japan.
[c] Excluding Australia-New Zealand.

While the increase in permanent migrations in many developing countries has been substantial in the last two decades, the increased volume of non-permanent movement has been especially marked in most contexts. This has involved a vast array of types of commuting, circular migration involving periods of absence from the home place ranging from a few days to several years and a range of seasonal movements. This mobility is extremely difficult to quantify since it is usually not detected in conventional migration questions routinely used in censuses and national surveys[28]. However, an impressive and growing array of field evidence (e.g.[32, 57, 58 and 75]) indicates that movements of this type are of greatly increased significance in most developing countries. For example, in Java an estimated one in four rural households at least have a worker employed in an urban area[32]. Much of the mobility occurs between rural and urban areas and is adding to blurring the distinction between urban and rural areas since many people who have their permanent place of residence in rural areas actually work for considerable periods of the year in urban areas.

Perhaps one of the most unexpected of the many changes in the migration situation in several developing countries over the last two decades has been the substantial increase in international migration in and out of these countries[40]. These movements have many dimensions that vary in significance from country to country but the following are particularly important:

A The growing flow of migrants (both permanent and temporary) from developing countries to developed countries. This South-North flow not only involves movements into the longstanding destination countries of Australia, Canada and the United States of America but also areas that for centuries have been regarded more as regions of emigration than of immigration: Europe and even Japan;

B Massive movements of labour from developing countries, on an intentionally temporary basis, into capital-rich, labour-deficit countries. In particular these include the oil-rich countries of the Middle East and the newly industrializing areas of Asia such as Hong Kong, Malaysia, Republic of Korea, Singapore and Taiwan Province, China[72];

C The increasing significance of refugee-humanitarian flows out of developing countries;

D Increased flows of transient highly skilled labour from one country to another[66]. Some developing countries, especially in Africa and Latin America[65], continue to be detrimentally affected by brain-drain-type net losses of their most highly skilled citizens. Nevertheless in some countries such as India, the Philippines and the Republic of Korea it is argued that such movement makes a greater contribution to the development of the home country by the backflow of remittances than would have been the case had the migrants remained at home[9].

E The totally unprecedented increase in the extent of illegal undocumented migration is particularly significant. The Mexico-United States flow is best known but only one of the myriads of these flows. These are sustained by well-developed family and institutional networks.

In such a limited space it is not possible to do justice to the transformation that has occurred in the population movement patterns in developing countries. A number of general observations should be made, however, about these burgeoning flows. The first important element is the tremendous increase in the significance of women in these flows[11 and 82], which is true of both internal and international movements, permanent and temporary flows and legal and illegal migrations. A second feature of the present pattern is the interrelatedness of different forms of mobility. Clearly various forms of temporary movement for business or tourism encourage and channel more permanent movements. In this context an important question is to what extent the rapidly increasing circular migration will eventually be transformed into permanent relocation. The evidence here is mixed, with some studies showing that temporary migration is a first stage when movers gradually establish themselves at a destination in preparation for eventual relocation while in other contexts circular migration is an entrenched and enduring mobility strategy in its own right. However, no matter how temporary a migration stream may seem to be, usually some settlement of migrants takes place at the destination. A third major trend has been the increased involvement of government intervention in attempting to influence the scale, direction and composition of population flows both within and between countries.

In summarizing these changes, however, one must observe that improvements in the methods and procedures to measure and analyse population mobility have not kept pace with the increasing scale and significance of the phenomenon itself. Indeed little progress has been made. Even with respect to permanent internal migration, many developing countries do not include a question on place of previous residence in their censuses[81], and even where such questions are incorporated they often use concepts that greatly compromise their effectiveness in obtaining a comprehensive picture of permanent relocations of population within boundaries[71]. Similarly, important national surveys such as annual labour force and socio-economic surveys rarely include a question on migration. Even demographic surveys have failed to recognize the significance of population mobility as an important explanatory variable. The situation with respect to non-permanent movements is worse. Despite almost two decades of field surveys producing incontrovertible empirical confirmation of the scale and significance of the phenomenon, no advances in methodology have allowed representative data to be collected in national censuses and surveys. More effort needs to be expended in developing appropriate questions on place of work to detect important non-permanent flows of people within developing countries.

A similar failure regarding methodology and data collection must unfortunately be reported for international population movements. A few developing countries have adequate systems of recording inflows and outflows of people across their national borders, although a great deal of expertise and knowledge has been accumulated in the experience of countries such as Australia, Canada and the United States. This information is becoming not only demographically significant in developing countries but also crucially important in social and economic planning. Bangladesh, Pakistan, the Philippines and Sri Lanka are just four countries where the outflow of people is the major foreign-exchange-earning "export". There may well be some advantage for those countries experiencing significant emigration outflows to include in their censuses and national surveys a question on whether a family member is absent overseas.

Hence the lack of quantification of the evolving trends in the patterns and types of population movement in developing countries is only partly due to limitations of available space and is largely due to a lack of adequate available data. Improvements in data collection procedures and a focused and thorough analysis of the relevant new data sources that will become available in the next few years (especially the 1990 round of censuses) must be an important priority for the 1990s. It should also be pointed out that a significant shortcoming of migration research based on surveys of various kinds is the failure to utilize the family as the unit of research. By focusing upon individuals, these surveys are structuring their results so important roles played by the family in shaping the migration process are not detected.

Macrostructural forces shaping population mobility in developing countries

The causes of the huge increase in population mobility in developing countries are many and complex and cannot be elaborated in detail here. However, in large part the increasing tempo of economic and social changes must be at the core of any comprehensive explanation. Massey[49] has made the important observation that it is economic development rather than stagnation that engenders population movement, at least in the short to medium term. Hence in developing countries with large rural populations, developments in agriculture have been tremendously significant in pushing large numbers of people out of rural areas. Land enclosure, increased commercialization of agricultural practices, mechanization and replacement of labour with capital inputs have continued apace in many developing countries. To take one example, at the 1980 census, Indonesia had 55.9 per cent of its 51 million workers employed in agriculture but by 1990, for the first time in its history, Indonesia had fewer people employed in agriculture than in other activities[36]. Moreover, during the 1990s a significant displacement of labour from this sector is anticipated. This is partly due to ongoing changes in wet rice cultivation, evident since the 1970s, involving the substitution of mechanical hulling for hand milling, the increased commercialization of labour use and the use of more efficient methods of harvesting. However, a new round of labour-displacing changes are taking place in the 1990s including the direct seeding of rice instead of transplanting, the use of pesticides instead of labour-intensive weeding and the increased use of hand tractors that could displace as much as a third of the agricultural workforce, many of them women[36]. Another important development has been the tremendous increase in education provision since 1970 in developing countries. Many developing countries in several years have achieved the goal of universal education, at least to the primary level. This has encouraged migration by making young people unhappy with a career in agriculture, thereby increasing their aspirations and opening up a wider world of opportunity to them.

Other important influences include the internationalization of capital, enabling many transnational corporations to establish manufacturing operations in low labour-cost developing countries. The enormous improvements in the speed, cost and ease of transport have made the most remote village accessible to the wider world. Similarly, the spread of mass communications is an underrated force in disseminating information about opportunities apparently available at distant locations. In Indonesia, television ownership has increased from less than one in ten households in the mid-1970s to one in three in 1990. Moreover satellite-based systems ensure the instant transmission of information to the most remote villages. Another underestimated (and understudied) element in the proliferation of population mobility has been the growth and expansion of a migration industry that seeks to facilitate (and profit from) various types of internal and international population movements. This involves an enormous variety of recruiters, agents, lawyers, transport operators, factory supervisors and travel facilitators of various kinds who have become key actors in many migration systems. Important political interventions encouraging population movement such as government involvement in immigration and labour recruitment programmes should also be noted, political insecurity creating refugee flows and government land-settlement schemes.

This rapidly changing economic, social and political context in developing countries has been favourable to the development of an increased scale of population mobility. However, it is the contention of the present writer that to understand fully the evolving level, pattern and implications of this population movement, supplementing such macro-level analysis with a consideration of processes operating at the micro-level is important and necessary. Pre-eminent among these elements in many developing countries is the role of the family in shaping who moves, what type of movement they engage in, where they go, what they do at the destination and what are the effects of the movement.

The family as a unit of analysis in population mobility in developing countries

Classical and neo-classical economics theories of migration explain migration as occurring as a result of differences in wage rates between one region and another[42 and 60]. Todaro[77] made the theory more realistic by explaining that migration occurs due to expected wage differentials between the country of origin and the potential destination. However, these theories were found to have limited explanatory power in developing countries. It has been argued (e.g.[76]) that one of the reasons for this was their assumption that movers were atomistic[49]; that is, they operated in a totally individual way. In fact, a great deal of migration in developing countries clearly occurs as a result of decisions taken by families rather than individuals. Moreover, even when migration is undertaken by individuals rather than a family unit, it is often as a result of family members being allocated to different labour markets by the family. Although models based on individuals may have considerable applicability in the context of developed countries, it is crucially important to understand that in developing countries the family has traditionally been the unit within which most decisions about production, investment and consumption are taken. Many decisions about the population movement of individuals in such contexts therefore are taken by the family or the senior member(s) of the family, usually older males. Hence decisions about movement may or may not coincide with the wishes and interests of the individual who moves. A great deal of the decision-making regarding population movement is carried out at the family rather than at the individual level, as is well established in the case-study literature[e.g. [15], [23], [68], 86 and 87]. Moreover, these writers maintain that a focus on the family rather than on the individual allows broader macro-structural forces as well as those forces operating on the individual to be better taken into account. They in effect argue that focusing on intermediate units such as families, household, village communities or kin groups can be viewed as bridging the gap between social and individual levels of analysis.

In some traditional situations where the family is the unit of production, the family, usually by its participation, distributes its labour resources over the range of tasks necessary to achieve a satisfactory level of production. Since the range of tasks have difficult requirements and individual family members have different capacities, characteristics and skills, there is a division of labour so as to make what is thought to be the best possible use of the human capital available to the family. In many traditional systems, this often involved allocating to individual family members off-farm as well as on-farm tasks, although in most cases the off-farm tasks would be located quite close to the land that the family was cultivating. In allocating its labour, the traditional family sought to achieve two objectives: the maximization of production and income on the one hand and the minimization of risk on the other. The latter is especially important since many such families led a knife-edge existence and had no surplus available to absorb the effects of failure. One of the important strategies of risk minimization was the diversification of sources of income and types of production so that failure in one area would not necessarily result in a total economic disaster for the family. Hence in such contexts families adopt survival strategies involving the allocation of their labour between a range of tasks in a range of locations, which represents a trade-off between maximizing total production or income and minimizing risk. Population mobility is an important part of this strategy because the family not only gains access to new and additional sources of income at locations other than in the vicinity of the family home place but also diversifies its portfolio of different types of sources of income. Hence the risk of the family not having any income at all is minimized since it would be unlikely that both on-farm and off-farm sources of income would be likely to fail at the same time.

Rahmato[59] has suggested that coping with risk is a central part of the peasant economy and that peasants develop particular anticipatory strategies to insure themselves against death and hardship. Hence survival strategies involving some form of population mobility can take the form of either a response to the onset of a crisis (e.g., crop failure, destruction of a major family source of income by fire or flood) or as an "insurance policy" against the possible future failure of an important source of family income.

In some cases, the family makes the decisions about population mobility only for certain members of the family group. For example, Torres[79, p. 31], found that in the Philippines a distinct gender differential exists in poor families. Whereas males generally were found to make relatively autonomous decisions, the dynamics of decision-making with young girls was different. Usually girls who have left school are expected to stay indoors or to work in the company of their parents and other elders. Young women even require permission from their elders and brothers to leave the house. More often than not, they move around with relatives. Hence, information on job opportunities in metropolitan Manila for girls is filtered through the social group who are vested with normative authority to decide for the girls. Filial piety, or respect for elders, is another strong Filipino value. Young women, therefore, would be expected to respect decisions from their kin group, including those pertaining to accepting work in Manila.

In fact the kinship system often determines who in the family will migrate[63]. This can be determined on the basis of age, order of birth within the family and gender as well as the particular skills and attributes of the different individuals making up the family group. In some situations, families adopt deliberate strategies whereby older children are kept away from school to work on the family farm while younger children are given schooling in preparation for migration[13, p. 46]. In the Philippines, Lauby and Stark[41, pp. 481-482] point out that, for farm work, sons are considered less dispensable so daughters tend to be sent to urban centres to remit money back to their village-based families to alleviate economic pressures at their origin. Table 12.2 below, for example, shows in a study of Filipino migration[19, p. 259] that when a woman makes her first rural to urban migration the decision maker is frequently not the woman herself.

TABLE 12.2.

PERSON WHO MADE DECISION IN FIRST RURAL-URBAN MIGRATION BY AGE AT TIME OF MOVE, PHILIPPINES

Decision maker	Age at the time of move			Total
	15-19	20-24	25+	
	(Percentage)			
Migrant herself	58	47	46	54
Husband	5	25	37	13
Parents	16	8	5	13
Other relative	16	15	3	15
Non-relative	5	4	9	5
Total[a]	100	100	100	100
Number of people in sample	704	214	117	1 035

Source: E. M. Go, "The relationship between female migration and economic activity in the Philippines", doctoral dissertation, Australian National University, Canberra, 1992.

[a] Owing to rounding, some totals may not add up to 100.

The simple adaptive or survival strategies outlined above, or some versions of them, have operated in many traditional societies. They rely on sets of intergenerational relationships where primary loyalties and the flows of wealth produced are directed to the parents[8]. The changed contexts in developing countries over the last decade or so have expanded enormously the geographical extent of the area over which the family can allocate its labour resources. Whereas the bulk of the mobility associated with the family's deployment of its labour resources has previously been in and around the locality the family is located in, the contextual shifts briefly summarized earlier have widened the area where family members can range in search of work.

A huge geographical expansion of labour markets over the last decade or so has taken place within countries so that whereas labour markets for most jobs were previously local or regional, many markets now cover a whole country, or most of it. This especially applies to those labour markets centred on major metropolitan areas, which typically draw labour from the total national space. Indeed, many labour markets overlap national boundaries. Labour markets are practically global for some highly specialized occupations, so managers, professionals, highly skilled individuals and academics move frequently between countries as they acquire experience and seniority within their particular labour market[66]. However, such international extension of labour markets is no longer confined to a highly skilled élite. For example, the agricultural industry in the United States draws its labour from well beyond the Rio Grande. Similarly Filipino women seem to have made the market for domestic workers an almost global one while the interflows of workers between Indonesia, Malaysia and Singapore is increasingly great in scale and diversity[34 and 35] so that some labour markets traverse all three countries.

The sum of individual migration decisions does not necessarily add up to a family migration strategy since the overall imperatives of the family may necessitate an individual family member being allocated a quite different task (and pattern of movement) from what they may wish or expect given their particular individual characteristics. Families tend to be careful in the way they allocate their labour. Massey[49] describes a situation where rural Mexican families send their better educated children to Mexico City where they can obtain white collar employment and the lesser educated members to the United States where they can gain work in agriculture or blue-collar occupations. Such a strategy is not only a realistic matching of family members' characteristics to available opportunities, but also spreads the families' income risk over three locations.

Indeed, such a spreading of risk may even reduce the pressure on the family's farm so it can experiment more with innovative crops and new and different agricultural techniques.[76].

The issue of risk minimization in family-migration decision-making is important. It means, for example, that wage differentials between areas are not necessary for migration to occur since the family member may be allocated to an area to work predominantly to expand the portfolio of the family's income-generating opportunities and not because wage rates are higher at the destination than at his or her place of origin.

The enormous expansion in non-permanent forms of population mobility in developing countries can not be explained in terms of conventional classical and neo-classical economics migration theory. It can only be understood when the family perspective outlined above is adopted. The deployment of individual family members for periods at distant locations allows the family to take advantage of periodic lulls in demand for labour in the home area or of temporary upswings in demand at the potential destination. The family's interest is to inject an element of circularity into the mobility of its members because it still allows the family to access the labour of the individual at the home place during periods of peak demand. The family is allowed to keep control of those individuals or, more significantly, the wealth they generate. The evidence is that remittances back to the village-based family tend to attenuate over time as the migrant becomes more settled at the destination. Moreover, patriarchal authority over the migrant is also likely to diminish the longer the family member is away from its direct influence. In addition, the costs of deploying a single family member rather than the entire family to a particular destination on a temporary basis can reduce the overall costs of movement and maximize the returns. This is because a single male may be able to live more cheaply at the destination than a family can by sharing crowded barrack-type accommodation or even sleeping at his workplace or in the open. Similarly, earning in the city but spending in the village ensures that earnings go much further because the cost of food and housing tends to be cheaper in the village. This especially applies if a family member is being deployed to an overseas or often distant location. In some cases particular types of family members are sent away because the family feels they are more likely to be reliable in remitting their incomes back to the village. For example, Ong[54, p. 30] reports that in Malaysia unmarried daughters are subject to greater pressure from their families than the sons are to share their urban-based income with other family members. This also has been found to be the case in the

Philippines[67, p. 96 and 80, p. 95] and Thailand[18]. Tongudai[78, p. 148] found in a study of female migrants in Bangkok that three in four sent back remittances to their village-based families. In some cases wages for up to one year were withdrawn in advance by parents as soon as the job had been arranged. This was especially the case for domestic and factory workers.

The fact that the family or household is the key unit in migration decision-making should not be necessarily interpreted as reflecting a democratic discussion among family members resulting in a consensus decision about a particular mobility strategy. Often it is a patriarchal decision as to what would be in the best interests of the family group. Recent research suggests, however, that the hitherto widespread belief that women played little role in family migration decision-making is being strongly challenged. In many contexts, women are in fact active and central in decision-making processes affecting family groups and characterizing them as passive associational followers of male migrants is incorrect[33].

At several points in the present chapter, it has been mentioned that family-based population mobility decision-making may take the form of a survival or an adaptive strategy. This is an important distinction although in many cases the strategies have elements of both. The allocation of family labour over a wider area can first take the form of a response to a specific crisis situation in which the deployment of family members is indeed a survival strategy; the survival of the family will depend on it. Hence Corbett[14] shows how households who live in a context with periodic problems in obtaining stable and adequate access to food develop strategic plans to minimize the impact of food shortages. From the African literature she was able to identify sequences of household responses to the onset of famine, and a simple model of famine-coping strategies is presented in table 12.3 below.

The table shows that family migration responses are involved in two of the three stages. In the first stage of the onset of declining entitlements to food, families will undertake a series of responses that do not lead to a disposal of their key productive assets. One such response is to deploy family labour as widely as possible to earn income for the family's subsistence from areas not effected by the famine. As Corbett[14, p. 1107] points out, the responses undertaken in this first stage of a coping strategy can be interpreted as forms of self or interhousehold insurance, and many of them may have been developed to cope with predictable and non-severe risks.

Families may be able to support themselves using these strategies for long periods, but if the famine persists there will come a time, a second stage, when their key productive assets will be disposed of.

Finally, in a third or terminal stage households are destitute or virtu-

TABLE 12.3. FAMINE-COPING STRATEGIES, AFRICA

Stage	Strategy
1. Declining entitlements to food	Increased petty commodity production and trading^a Dispersed grazing^a Change in cropping and planting practices Migration to towns^a Collection of wild foods^a Interhousehold transfers and loans Credit from merchants and moneylenders Migration to rural areas^a Rationing of food consumption
2. Sale or loss of productive assets	Sale of productive household assets Food distributed by relief programmes Sale of possessions
3. Full crisis response	Break up of household or family^a Distress migration of the entire family^a

Source: Jane Corbett, "Famine and household coping strategies". World Development, vol. 16, No. 9 (Oxford, 1988), pp. 1099-1112.
^a Strategy often involving mobility.

ally assetless. In these circumstances a household's ability to generate either current or future income is severely diminished. Even the sale of its own labour power may no longer be as possible if household members are weakened by hunger or hunger-related disease. Both African and Asian case-studies suggest that distress migration of the whole household in search of relief may be the only option that remains[14, p. 1107].

The mobility elements in the sequence shown in table 3 represent the survival strategies, but in certain situations families deploy their labour through some form of population mobility not because the very survival of the family is in question but as an adaptive strategy to shifts in the pattern of available opportunities. In such contexts the strategy is not so much one of survival as one of maintaining the family's level of living (or in some cases enhancement of it) and insuring against any possible future threat to that level.

An important element in the use of population mobility by families as a labour allocation mechanism is that the family (or, more commonly, the patriarch) can maintain sufficient control over the absent family members so the earnings they generate are repatriated back to the family of origin. The system is predicated on the movers continuing to observe the traditional system of intergenerational obligations, although they are not co-resident with the figures of authority in that system. In some contexts (e.g., in Malaysia and the Philippines), this control is more effectively exercised over young women than young men. Rodenburg[62] found that in north Sumatra, Indonesia, a strong mutual moral obligation was felt between family members living in the village and members who had moved elsewhere. Clearly a circular strategy is more likely to enable the family to access resources generated by family members working elsewhere than if the family members migrate permanently away from the home area.

In sum, a comprehensive explanation of the increased scale and complexity of contemporary population mobility in developing countries needs to go beyond an understanding of the macroeconomic, social and political changes occurring in those countries. It must encompass an appreciation of how family and household strategies of decision-making operate in that changing environment. One important element in such an appreciation is the operation of family-based social networks.

Social networks in the migration process in developing countries

An important element in understanding how population mobility operates within the framework of family-labour-allocation strategies are family-based social networks, which link origin and destination. Migrants in developing countries are stereotypically characterized as wide-eyed, naive individuals arriving at their international or large-city destination not knowing anyone and overwhelmed by the alien nature of that destination. The majority of movers, however, move along well-trodden paths. Even if they have not travelled them before themselves, these paths have been traversed earlier by family members and friends. The movers tend to travel with friends or family and have a range of family-based contacts at the destination. The networks established, linking origin and destination, become key elements in sustaining and enhancing the population flows between them. These networks inject a self-perpetuating dynamism into flows of population, allowing movement to continue long after the original, usually economic, reasons for the flow may have been superseded or rendered redundant. Whenever a person in a developing country migrates, every individual they know acquires some social capital in the form of a contact at the mover's destination and the quality of that social capital is greatly enhanced if the contact is a family member.

The networks established by earlier generations of movers from families and localities act as conduits to channel later generations of movers to those destinations in an atmosphere of certainty. Previous generations of movers have not only supplied valuable information and encouragement, but also often paid for or arranged and eased the subsequent migration of other family members. Moreover, when the migrant arrives at the destination, that end of the network lends valuable assistance in the adjustment process, especially by assisting in gaining access to housing and employment. The fundamental role of networks is to reduce significantly the risks associated with migration. Indeed, many movers in developing countries operate in an environment of almost total certainty owing to family-based conditions. Hence, again, the risk minimization factor is important.

The role of family-based networks in facilitating the bulk of population movement in developing countries can scarcely be exaggerated. While other factors undoubtedly are necessary to initiate the beginning of a new limb of the network, once the pioneer(s) is (are) established at a new destination the subsequent flow can be rapid. The pioneer migrants constitute anchors to chains along which much larger numbers of subsequent migrants are drawn. They are especially important in international migration. The pioneers can be people who gain access to a destination country through some form of recruitment or refugee migration but then can facilitate substantial subsequent movement through a legal family reunification movement. Indeed the family migration programmes of countries such as Australia, Canada and the United States institutionalize the role of social networks in facilitating international migration. Yet illegal migration is virtually impossible unless an informal network links origin and destination to facilitate the clandestine movement. The pioneer migration may have occurred for quite adventitious reasons but, once established, the flow may take on mass proportions.

The important point about the development of family-based networks is that, once created, they totally change the entire environment in which subsequent movement occurs. The networks established not only link individual family members with friends and other family members at a range of destinations, but also often with potential employers as well. Frequently a patron-client, mutual dependence relationship develops between an employer and a family or groups of families from a particular origin. This relationship not only guarantees work for the potential migrantspotential migrants but also assures the employer of a regular and trusted supply of labour. Hence employers are drawn into the family-based social networks. Indeed it is incorrect to characterize these networks purely as social, based entirely on the connections of family and longstanding friendship. Over time they became more complex, involving not only employers but also other elements whose role is to facilitate movement along the networks for profit. A myriad of agents, recruiters, travel agents, transport operators and supervisors position themselves at critical points along the networks to facilitate the flow of movers along it. One example[72] of such a pattern is presented in figure 12.1. It shows the number of these intermediaries involved in a network along which illegal migrants flow from a village in east Java to work on plantations in peninsular Malaysia. The growing complexity and institutionalization of networks over time is thus an important feature in many developing countries.

Another example of these complex networks of agents is in the substantial flow of Filipino (mostly female) entertainers into Japan. Torres[79, p. 57] reports that a complex network of underground travel agents, talent promoters and job brokers are known to expedite the illegal entry of entertainers into Japan.

While networks have an important function of informing potential new migrants of the availability, or lack of availability, of job opportunities, one of the most important features of the networks established by migrants is their role in sustaining population flows quite independently of objective economic conditions in the communities of origin and destination. Moreover, they can operate largely outside the area of influence of policy makers. Migration flows occurring along such networks are notoriously difficult to influence by policy interventions, let alone stop. Almost all attempts to prevent such movements in the past have failed. The networks are enormously resilient and tenacious even in the face of the most vigorous and draconian actions of Governments. Hence, once established, the networks became a strong force for perpetuating particular streams of movement. Knowledge of the persistence of these flows along networks in the long term, however, is extremely limited. Particular flows may follow a logistic curve with a few people moving initially, then a rapid increase in movement, followed by a tapering off when a particular threshold level is reached.

The linkages established between the communities of origin and destination not only become channels for the movement of people back and forth, but they also operate as important conduits of information, money and goods in both directions. The issue of remittances from the destination to the place of origin is of major significance. The conventional wisdom about remittances in the 1970s was that they usually had little impact on development since they generally were small in size and were spent on non-productive investments in the place of origin[45]. However, as more careful studies of remittances have been made over the last decade, this wisdom has undergone a substantial revision in the following respects:

A   Past measurement of remittances has at best been partial and has severely underestimated their scale because of severe deficiencies in the definitions and time scales used in surveys. Moreover, the most important remittances can often be those supplied in an emergency situation; indeed, the certainty that support will be available from family members based elsewhere when and if needed can have a significant effect on development activity in the home area[30];

B   The dismissal of using remittances as being non-productive has been too hasty because it has ignored the multiplier effects of investments in land and housing and the second and third round effects of such investments in the place of origin.

In the case of international migration flows, remittances not only have a significant impact in the communities of origin of migrants, but also important macroeconomic impacts upon national economies.

The crucial significance of networks in sustaining and developing particular migration flows has been overlooked in many attempts to explain migration in developing countries. Clearly, however, the development of networks is facilitated where the extended family is the rule. In these systems the patriarch (or in a few cases, the matriarch) is able to deploy family members to particular areas and retain control over them and the wealth flows they generate.

FIGURE 12.1. EXAMPLE OF A RECRUITMENT NETWORK OF PROSPECTIVE LABOUR MIGRANTS (ILLEGAL) FROM EAST JAVA TO MALAYSIA

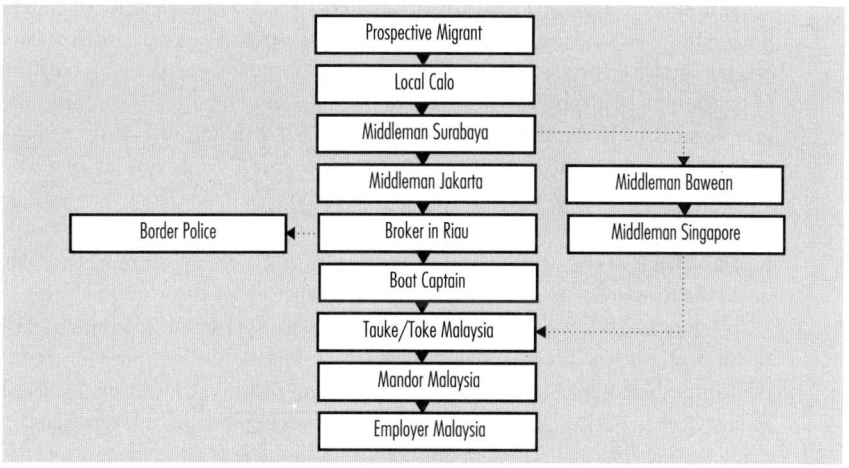

Source: Based on data supplied by E. Spaan, Taikongs and Calos, "The role of middlemen and brokers in Javanese international migration", International Migration Review (New York, forthcoming).

The development of networks explains (where the classical and neo-classical theories fail to) why neighbouring communities with apparently identical economic and social circumstances can have totally different levels and patterns of population movement. Communities that have established a network of external linkages will tend to have a substantial level of out-movement while those without such linkages will have low levels of mobility. Networks can not only function to facilitate and sustain the movement of family members, but they can also be used to exert and maintain the family's control of the member who has moved. Hence Rodenburg[62, p. 59] describes the movement of Toba Batak traders from their rural origins in north Sumatra, Indonesia, to cities in the following terms:

"Upon their first arrival in town, most of the traders stay with friends or relatives. Related affines usually provide shelter and funds during the initial period when the new migrant is still struggling to find his way to set up his enterprise. Living with co-villagers also gives the men the opportunity to send messages or money when one of them returns. For a wife, this network is also important in another way since, to a certain extent, it means social control of her husband's activities. In case her husband should have an affair she may soon find out."

Family-based social networks, once established, can also operate so as to facilitate the migration of groups who previously were not permitted to move by the family. Torres[79, p. 66], for example, maintains that the existence of these networks has been crucial in Filipino families overcoming traditional taboos and deploying their educated single young daughters to work in metropolitan Manila.

The increasing participation of women in migration is evident across both internal and international migration streams. These moves are encouraged by the demands of the labour market, as well as by cultural expectations from the social network. Young, single, educated women are encouraged to leave their towns or villages for Manila, not only because there are few (or no) jobs for them in the rural countryside, but also because the work in Manila will generate incomes. From their own admission, a sizeable portion of their salaries will be used for their families' sustenance back home. Given this expectation, it is not uncommon that the girls' families are the ones who make the decision for their migration.

Understanding the operation of social networks in facilitating and sustaining migration processes is hampered by the failure of many conventional methodologies for the collection of migration data to take account of networks. Although most migration surveys question migrants about prior contacts with their destination, few studies explore in detail exactly how these networks operate; who the actors in them are; who has access to them; how long they operate for and so on. While the literature on the role of networks in migration is substantial[6, 16, 22 and 47] many dimensions remain little understood. For example, little is known of the significance of the quality of ties between groups and their influence on migration. It may be possible to recognize a hierarchy of support networks according to how much support an individual can access from them. One such hierarchy could range from immediate family to broader family, then to friends and acquaintances in the locality through to ethnic group links and regional and nationality groupings.

The impact of migration on the family

Keep in mind that the interrelationship between migration and the family is a two-way one. However, the body of research relating to population mobility as an independent variable influencing change in family structure and functioning is limited.

Families of migrants at the place of origin must adjust not only to the permanent or temporary absence of family members, but also to the influences of the newly acquired money, goods, ideas, attitudes, behaviour and innovations transmitted back to them by the movers. The adjustments to these active impacts that families must make depend upon which family members move, the length of the absence and the sociocultural system at the place of origin, especially dominant types of family structure and the degree of flexibility within that structure. Gonzalez[21] shows how various types of migration, differentiated by degree of permanency, have different impacts on family structure. Other studies suggest that kinship linkages and family residence patterns influence the households' adaptation to migration. Patrilocal societies are generally more adaptable than matrilocal, as are those in which the joint family dominates over the nuclear family[13, p. 47].

Where temporary rather than permanent absence from the village is the norm, it is highly selective of economically active men, and separation of these men from their wives and children necessitates adjustments not only in the nuclear family but also within the community at large. Whereas temporary migration usually involves separation of nuclear family members, permanent migration is often associated with a separation of the nuclear family from other kin and is hence characterized by a greater reliance by the spouse and children on the nuclear family, a weakening of wider kinship relationships and a consequent widening of the roles of nuclear family members, especially women[21, p. 1274].

Female headship of incomplete nuclear families is common in areas where temporary mobility occurs. In such circumstances women and children must perform tasks traditionally done by men. Siegel[70], for example, found in Indonesia that the outmigration of Acehnese men, usually for periods of almost a year, has led women to handle additional agricultural tasks. The extent of this depends partly upon the periodicity of male mobility. Whereas on the Indonesian island of Bawean[83, p. 121] absences may last several years, in western Java[27] most movement is over relatively short distances so that movers can return to their villages at times of peak labour demand.

Another important factor in the family's adaptation to migration is whether an extended family and kinship structure exists to allow other male family members to fill roles normally assigned to the absent male. Lineton[44, p. 66] reports that in southern Sulawesi, Bugis women have little difficulty coping with their husbands' absence because members of the extended family move in and provide companionship and other support. Naim[53, p. 425] found that the extended absences of Minangkabau migrant men from their western Sumatran homes created strains within the family and may have been responsible for an unusually high incidence of Oedipus complex among children and of mental disorders among women in the Minangkabau heartland.

The effects of population mobility on women's traditional roles in rural areas need systematic study. Research should encompass changes affecting women who themselves migrate and those who remain in villages where men are absent for long periods. The field work undertaken by the present writer in outmigration villages in western Java and southern Sulawesi indicated many cases of expanded roles for women. In southern Sulawesi, for example, some women in heavy outmigration areas were appointed to head their villages, although traditionally that role is reserved for males. One of the few detailed studies of the impact of heavy male circular migration from rural areas in Indonesia[12] found that in eastern Kalimantan, women's involvement in rice and vegetable production increased as a direct result of male movement. More than half of the women interviewed reported that life was difficult during their husband's absence. Most of the difficulties they mentioned related to agricultural labour, especially tree felling and fence and field-hut construction. Colfer[12, p. 233] stresses, however, that such comments tell only part of the story. What impressed her most during her fieldwork was the women's competence in providing for their families during their husband's absence and their pride in their autonomy and competence. Their efforts to cope received strong support from other members of the community. Hetler's[26] study conducted in a village of central Java categorizes women whose husbands were absent for long periods as de facto household heads and shows how they frequently assumed the roles of de jure heads by paying taxes, providing labour and household representatives for village activities and attending meetings.

Less information is available about the impact of gender differentials in migration at urban destinations. Some studies suggest it may lead to reduced rates of marriage in the cities and a decline in fertility[e.g. 43, p. 74]. Certainly at the urban destination a greater incidence of non-traditional family structures and living situations exists than in the village of origin. Households tend to be considerably larger in urban than in rural areas because of urban housing shortages caused by rapid population growth. According to the 1980 Indonesian census, the proportion of households with nine or more members was almost twice as large in urban (11.8 per cent) as in rural areas (6.1 per cent).

Rural-to-urban migration does lead to the separation of family members, creating a greater dependence on the nuclear family, weakening wider kinship relationships and consequently expanding the roles of nuclear family members, especially women[21, p. 1274]. Caldwell[8] has identified such changes as being critical to the transition from high to low fertility, which requires a reversal of the net flow of wealth. (In traditional societies the net flow is from children to parents, but in modern societies the flow is from parents to children.)

Caldwell says that from a demographic viewpoint, the most important social exports from Europe have been the predominance of the nuclear family with its strong husband-wife ties and the concentration of concern and expenditure on one's children rather than on one's parents and other kin. Some evidence indicates that if such changes are not initiated by urbanization, they are certainly assisted by it. Although wider kinship linkages exhibit considerable tenacity in the face of the physical separation caused by mobility, the processes encouraging the physical and emotional nucleation of families are likely to impinge most strongly upon families living in urban areas. Even the strong linkages migrants maintain with their village-based families and friends and reinforce through return migration, encourage the diffusion of these ideas and attitudes to rural areas. Studies explicitly investigating the social effects of rural-to-urban migration on the family are lacking despite the fact that the family is often the unit of migration decision-making. Research into this important interface between migration and social change is sorely needed.

The influence of urbanward mobility on marriage has also attracted the attention of researchers. Gonzalez[21, p. 1268] suggests that the migration-induced imbalance in sex ratios has led to a decreased incidence of arranged marriages and to marriages being contracted at a later age. In Indonesia researchers have noted strains created by difficulties in finding a spouse, inflation of dowry size[53, p. 428], and migrants being able to marry women of much higher status or caste than would normally be the case[44, p. 106]. Evidence of the impact of temporary migration upon divorce is mixed. Hathaway[25, p. 3] suggests that the mobility induced separation of family members, even for short periods, leads to marital instability and the consequent permanent break-up of the family unit, whereas Gonzalez[21, p. 1266] cites several studies of societies where the temporary separation of husband and wife has been consistent with marital stability. A study of western Java[27, pp. 616-617] revealed a substantially greater incidence of divorce among mover households than among stayer households, especially in households experiencing prolonged separation. A high incidence of divorce among the Minangkabau of western Sumatra has been attributed to high rates of male outmigration[53, p. 426], whereas Lineton[44, p. 65] suggests that the low incidence of divorce among the Bugis of Wajo is partly because nuclear families migrate as a whole.

Although differences between the urban and rural way of life in developing countries can be exaggerated, no doubt some elements of social change are more evident among urban populations; for example, "the emergence of the nuclear family, the enrichment and multiplication of individual social relationships, the challenge to collective solidarity by individual freedom"[84, pp. 157-158]. Changes in intrafamily and intergenerational relationships in developing countries are usually of interest because of their effects on fertility. However, the strengthening of ties between economically active adults and their nuclear families and the weakening of ties with older parents have major implications for the welfare of older persons. In traditional societies the net intergenerational transfer, not only of wealth but also of care and attention to older persons, has meant that older people could count on their children for security in old age. The reversal of net intergenerational wealth flows associated with intrafamilial changes suggests that the older generation may no longer be able to count on as much support as in the past. Signs of this are already evident in some developing areas, especially cities[29]. According to Frons, Jeffries and Nelson[17, p. 10], "as the younger generation becomes more affluent, more materialistic - and more preoccupied with a youth-oriented Western culture - the traditional regard for the elderly is vanishing". In highly urbanized and industrialized centres of Asia such as Hong Kong and Singapore, the abandonment of old people has become a social problem. By 1982 it had become so widespread in Singapore that the Government passed a law making it compulsory for children to support their elderly parents.

Public social security programmes for the elderly in developing countries are generally inadequate[85]. Many countries have no formal programme, and in most that do, provision is extremely meagre and confined to limited eligibility groups.

Various case-studies document the contribution of rural-to-urban migration to the reduced status and increased neglect of the aged population. In Malaysia, for example, Chan[10, p. 10] found that in depressed states like Kelantan, age-selective outmigration leads to the neglect of elderly persons who, for various reasons, are much less mobile and consequently have been left behind. In urban areas the elderly are sometimes not much better off than their rural counterparts, where they themselves are physically and socially segregated from their families because of acute urban residential space pressures that do not facilitate the continuance of the extended family system.

A growing body of research indicates that the accelerating levels of migration of women in developing countries[36] is leading to an increased incidence of children living separately from their mothers. A recent analysis of data from an international series of demographic and health surveys conducted in many developing countries from 1980 onwards has indicated a relatively high incidence of mothers and children living separately, especially in Africa[55]. Several explanations can be put forward for this including divorce and a high incidence of fostering out of children. However, migration does play a significant role. Hence mothers may leave behind children in the village when they go elsewhere to work since conditions at the destination are not conducive to child care. Another common practice is for urban-based parents to send their children back to their home village to grow up under the care of grandparents, aunts or uncles in what is considered a more conducive, traditional environment. The separation of the nuclear family by migration in developing countries is therefore an increasingly important phenomenon and its effects need to be investigated.

Richter[61, pp. 44-45] has investigated this issue in Thailand and explains that in urban areas, extended family members may be far away and women working at a job in the formal sector are less likely to be able to combine work and child care. The large numbers of immigrants to Bangkok include many women who migrate without their children, leaving them in the care of relatives in rural areas. Other working women in Bangkok, even those whose children are born in the city, send them to their families in their rural home towns if they are unable to care for them. Her survey in 1991 of 1,515 women in Bangkok who were married, widowed, divorced or separated found that 10 per cent of their children were living separately from their mother. Even 7 per cent of the women who had been born in Bangkok had children living separately from them. Among women who had migrated after their first year of marriage, almost a fifth (18 per cent) were living separately from their children. More than two thirds (70 per cent) of children who were living separately from their mother lived outside Bangkok.

The family and international migration in developed countries

While the significance of individual decision-making in migration is of greater significance in developed countries than in developing countries, family influences upon the migration process are nevertheless important. Space constraints do not permit a detailed consideration of the family dimension of population movement in developed countries, but raising some aspects of the interrelationships is useful. Looking first at the case of international migration, many of the processes discussed earlier in the present chapter operate to facilitate the growing volume of South-North migration. Boyd[6] has comprehensively reviewed the research findings on the determinants and consequences of family, friendship and community networks that underlie much of the recent migration to developed countries. It is apparent from this review that family connections, family-based networks and chain migration are central to any explanation of the composition of that movement. For example, in the three traditional immigration countries of Australia, Canada and the United States, family migration has dominated the entry categories of immigrants over the last two decades. In the early postwar years, immigration policy was dominated by worker recruitment. However, in 1965 the reform of the Immigration Act in the United States made family reunification the basis of immigration policy and subsequently the overwhelming majority of immigrants entering the United States have done so under family migration provisions.

Papademetriou[56, p. 19] has summarized the situation as follows:

"Family reunification is almost universally accepted as the appropriate centrepiece for US immigration policy as it responds to and promotes a central principle of the US national ethos: family values. In a more practical vein, family reunification also responds to the recognition that families ease the sociocultural and psychological dislocations associated with immigration by serving as buffers and mediators between the individual immigrant and the host environment. Families thus become the facilitators of the immigrants' social, economic and gradually political integration."

Accordingly, for most years since the revision of the immigration law in 1965 about 9 out of 10 permanent immigrants to the United States enter under family-related policy categories. Despite changes following the 1990 Immigration Act, family migration remains overwhelmingly dominant in the intake of immigrants to the United States.

Australia and Canada, the other two traditional immigration countries, followed suit in the 1970s. Their immigration programmes were transformed from a worker-recruitment orientation to a more complex mix in which family, skill and refugee policy categories were dominant. Family linkages became one of the major bases upon which people could qualify for settlement. These major changes in immigration policy institutionalized family-based social networks as the primary vehicle for international migration into these three traditional immigration countries. Figure 12.2 shows how family migration has increased its share of the intake into Australia in recent years.

Moves have been made in all three countries at different points in the last decade to increase the significance of immigration based on qualifications and entrepreneurialism by skills and business-based migration programmes, but the essential family basis of immigrant settlement in Australia, Canada and the United States has not changed. Although the provisions of the family migration programmes in the three countries have varied over the years, families have become skilled at using them to facilitate the settlement of relatives in those countries[2 and 4].

In the Australian case, a recent study by Khoo[39] examined three aspects of families and the immigration process based on a national sample of immigrants arriving in Australia between 1971 and 1990 and made the following findings:

A   The presence of family in Australia and family sponsorship patterns: some 60 per cent of the migrants had family in Australia before they immigrated;
B   The family as a migrating unit: almost two thirds of the migrants arrived in Australia accompanied by family members;
C   Family structure and living arrangements after immigration: only 16 per cent of the immigrants had no family members to assist their adjustment to Australia, and three quarters of them had established a family unit by the time of the survey.

FIGURE 12.2. CATEGORY OF IMMIGRANTS, 1976-1993, AUSTRALIA

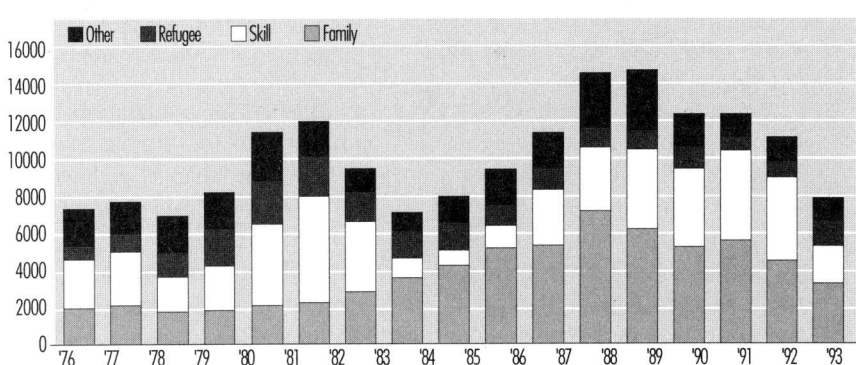

Source: Bureau of Immigration and Population Research and Department of Immigration and Ethnic Affairs, Australia, various publications.

Even in a country like Australia, where great emphasis is placed upon the Government providing services for recently arrived immigrants, the family provides the bulk of such services[52]. However, immigration also results in changes in "family structure and functioning, to new roles and relationships within families, and perhaps to changes in some of the values forming the basis of family life in the country of origin"[24, p. 19]. Hence the family may be not only a source of stability for newly arrived migrants, but also an arena of conflict as family members come under the influence of a set of new forces at the destination.

In considering internal migration within developed countries, the family again looms large. As Gober[20, p. 28] has pointed out, migration patterns result from millions of decisions by individuals and families about whether, when and where to move. In fact, when all moves are considered family- and housing-related reasons are the ones most frequently cited as reasons for moving, as shown by table 12.4 drawn from the 1991 American Housing Survey. However, the bulk of family-related reasons apply to moves over shorter distances while economic- and job-related factors dominate moves over far larger distances, as figure 12.3, using data from Australia[3], demonstrates.

In the case of the United States, Gober[20, p. 29] points out that:

"A sizeable majority of respondents reported housing or family dynamics as reasons for their move. The three most prominent reasons given were the need to establish a new household, upgrade to a larger or better unit and other family considerations (such as to be nearer to other family members, or respond to increased or decreased family size)."

Migration and the FAMILY

TABLE 12.4. REASONS FOR MOVING AMONG OWNERS AND RENTERS, UNITED STATES, 1991[a]
(Percentage of respondents citing reasons)

Reasons for moving	Total	Owners	Renters
Displacement or disaster	7	5	8
Employment-related	28	21	31
New job or job transfer	11	10	12
To be closer to work, school or other place	11	6	13
Other financial or employment	6	5	6
Housing and family-related reasons	80	96	75
Need larger or better home	26	30	24
To establish household	14	14	14
Change in marital status	8	9	8
Change from renting to owning	6	22	-
Want lower rent or maintenance	7	4	9
Change from owning to renting	1	-	1
Other reasons	18	17	19
Other or not reported	17	18	16
Number of respondents	16 753	4 363	12 391

Source: P. Gober, "Americans on the move". Population Bulletin, vol. 48, No. 3 (Washington, D.C., 1993).

[a] Totals add up to more than 100 because some respondents cited more than one reason.

FIGURE 12.3. PERSONS AGED 15+: PROPORTION WHO CHANGED USUAL RESIDENCE IN AUSTRALIA, BY REASON FOR MOVING AND TYPE OF MOVE, YEAR ENDING 31 MAY 1987

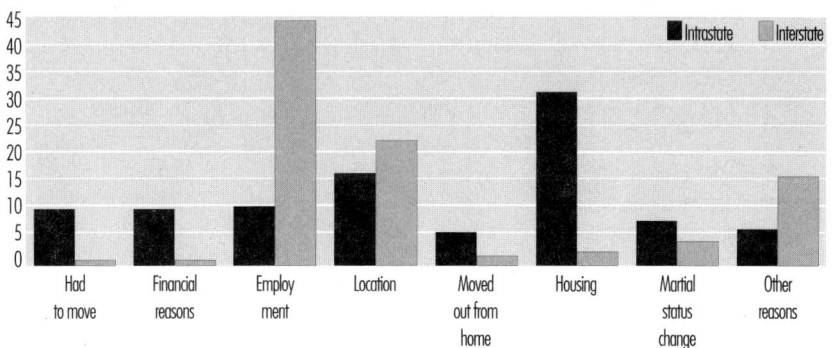

Source: Australian Bureau of Statistics, 1988.

The shifts in family structure and functioning in developed countries in recent years has had important impacts upon population movement patterns. Table 12.5 shows the extent of change in the distribution of families in Australia and the United States over the last two decades. The share of stereotypical families, i.e., two parents with children, has declined in the last two decades in developed countries while there has been a substantial growth of single-person, single-parent and couple-only families. This has had significant implications for population mobility. Increased divorce and family splitting has produced a whole new pattern of mobility for the parents and children involved. Delayed marriage, increased cohabitation before marriage and the increasing incidence of group households has not only changed the distribution of household types in developed countries but also created new patterns of population movement as well.

In the United States, a quarter of all children lived with only one parent in 1991[1, p. 8], triple the proportion in 1960. Half of the children in the United States will spend some part of their childhood in a one-parent family. In other developed countries the proportions are somewhat lower but nevertheless substantial. For example, in Australia, 14.6 per cent of families with children in 1991 were single-parent families and at least a third will spend some time in a single-parent family[37]. This pattern of a high rate of marriage breakdown is an increasing cause of mobility of the parents since at least one of them will have to move as a result of the marriage breakdown. However, it also is inducing a new type of mobility for many of the children involving them in adopting a form of "bilocality", moving on a regular basis between two homes often separated by long distances. This form of mobility and its effects and implications for the children involved has not been a major subject of research but certainly needs to be, especially for the well-being of the children involved.

TABLE 12.5.
COMPOSITION OF FAMILIES IN THE UNITED STATES AND AUSTRALIA
(Percentage)

Type of family	United States		Australia	
	1970	1990	1976	1991
Married couple with children	49.6	36.9	48.5	44.2
Married couple without children	37.1	41.7	27.9	31.6
One-parent families with children	6.4	12.0	6.5	8.8
Other families	6.9	9.4	17.1	15.4
Total	100.0	100.0	100.0	100.0
Number of families (thousands)	51,200	64,500	3,406	4,298

Source: Australian Bureau of Statistics 1976 and 1991 and D. A. Ahlburg and C. J. De Vita, "New realities of the American family", Population Bulletin, vol. 47, No. 2 (Washington, D.C., 1992), pp. 144.

A change in the representation of two-parent and couple families in developed countries has taken place, but also changes have impinged upon mobility within those types of families. Among the most important of these is the transition from a typical pattern of male-breadwinner, female-homemaker situations to dual-income families. This is illustrated in figure 12.4, which shows that over the postwar period the incidence of women working outside the home has more than quadrupled in Australia[38].

Dual-income families have gone from being the exception to being the rule in a few short decades. One of the consequences of this change has been a reduction in the level of mobility of these types of families. This is a function of the fact that any shift is going to necessitate finding a job at the proposed destination for not just one family member but two family members, influencing the extent government agencies and corporations have been able to transfer staff within and between countries as part of their traditional processes of giving experience to staff to facilitate their progression through the career cycle[73].

FIGURE 12.4. FEMALE LABOUR-FORCE PARTICIPATION RATES BY AGE AT CENSUSES CONDUCTED IN AUSTRALIA BETWEEN 1947 AND 1991

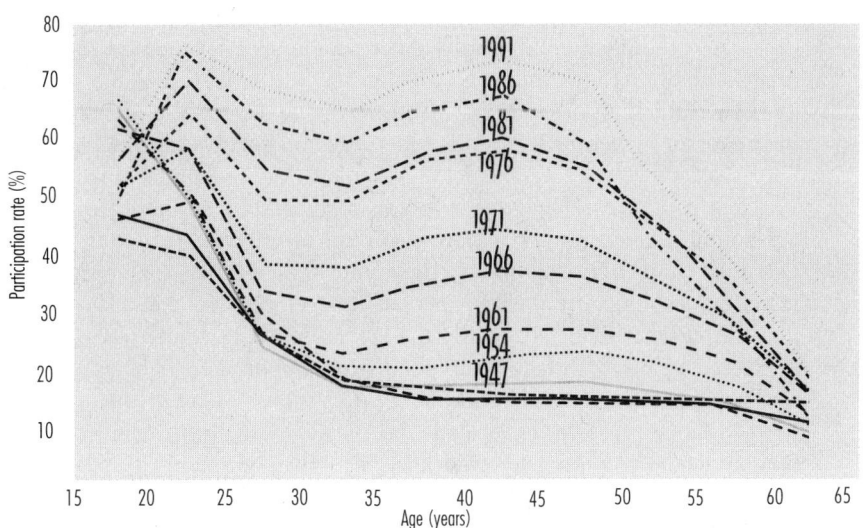

Sources: T. H. Hull, "Conflict on the home front; work, housework and the future of fertility", paper presented to a seminar on conflict and consensus held at the Research School of Social Sciences, Australian National University, 1982, and Australian Bureau of Statistics, 1986 and 1991 censuses.

Some of the most dramatic recent changes in family structure and living arrangements in developed countries have involved their elderly populations; some of these changes have had significant mobility consequences. Especially important is the fact that a greater proportion of elderly people in developed countries maintain independent living arrangements well into old age than ever has been the case. This is a function of greater longevity and better health as well as greater financial security and independence than has been the case with previous generations of elderly persons. Several new forms of mobility has engendered this independence. Some are associated mainly with recent retirees, especially in a context where early retirement is significant, as in most developed countries, although much of this is involuntary rather than voluntary early retirement.

Freed of the need to live relatively close to their workplace, many retirees seek to exercise other location options not shaped by job-related considerations. Hence substantial migrations from the frostbelt to the sunbelt in northern hemisphere countries take place among this group[5 and 64]. The movement from large cities to resort locations is significant. Increasingly, too, elderly people who do not sell their family home to migrate engage in seasonal and other short-term migration, which involves moving to more attractive ecological and climatic zones in winter[51].

In the older age groups, family-related factors are a particularly significant cause of migration. Typically older people upon widowhood or the onset of disability seek to move to live close to, if not in the same house as, their children or other family members. These motivations are evident in the reasons given by a group of older migrants surveyed in Australia[31]. Table 12.6 shows that many older people move for family-related reasons. The motivation of moving to be close to family and friends increases with age among the elderly population. Too often overlooked is the fact that extended family networks are still the cornerstone for the social, economic and physical support of elderly people in developed countries. The population mobility associated with the operation of these networks is a neglected area in both family and population mobility research.

The elderly are generally neglected in discussions of both changing patterns of family structure and population mobility. However, their growing numerical and proportional significance in developed country populations and the major changes within this subgroup in the ways they organize their lives means they should be the subject of much more research as well as attention from policy makers. Changing patterns of family size in developed countries is also having an impact upon population movement patterns. Figure 12.5 shows data[1 and 50] on the total fertility rate in two developed countries.

The pattern has been for levels of between 3 and 4 average number of births per woman in the 1950s and 1960s but declining to around 1.8 to 1.9 in the 1970s and stabilizing around those levels in the 1990s. This has meant that families are not experiencing as great a fluctuation in size between the family-formation or family-development stages of the life cycle and the pre-parent and empty nest stages of the life cycle of the family. Hence the need to make housing adjustments purely on the basis of the changing size of the family is not so great as it was in the 1950s and 1960s. This may be one of the factors contributing to a stabilizing of overall mobility levels in Australia, the United States and other developed countries over recent years[37 and 46].

The impact of economic depression in families in developed countries in recent years has been substantial. One disturbing trend is that while the bulk of people among the growing homeless populations in developed countries are individuals living alone or in non-family situations, the incidence of homelessness among families is increasing. Ahlburg and De Vita[1, p. 35], for example, observe that in recent studies of the situation in the United States, around a quarter of homeless people are in family units. This group's plight involves them in a distinctive and desperate form of mobility.

By the time they become homeless, most homeless families have spent periods in a broken circle of kith and kin networks. Or, as Burt[7] writes: "They may borrow money, leave bills unpaid, double up with other families or with friends, split up a household (for example, leaving older children with relatives), leave town to look for work ... . Even with all these strategies, however, they (were) not able to afford to stay in housing."

Thus far a few of the ways rapidly changing patterns of family structure and functioning in developed countries is impinging upon changing levels and patterns of population movement have been considered. However, as was pointed out earlier, the relationship between migration and family is complex and two-way. For instance, what is the impact of changing levels of population mobility upon the family? Are population mobility factors a significant independent variable in explaining changing family patterns in developed countries? Research here is extremely limited, and the limited writing on this issue is based more upon value-laden specialization than upon specific and focused research. Much of the literature[e.g. see 20, p. 4; 89, pp. 77-79] sees the high levels of residential mobility in the United States and other Developed countries as weakening the ties of individuals in

TABLE 12.6. REASONS FOR MOVING TO CURRENT DWELLING OF PERSONS LIVING IN PRIVATE DWELLINGS WHO HAD MOVED SINCE REACHING THE AGE OF 60, ADELAIDE AND MELBOURNE, 1981
(Percentage)

Reasons for moving to current dwelling	Age of respondent			
	60-64	65-74	75+	Total
Private dwelling				
Too large	23.5	20.4	17.8	20.2
Too costly	12.3	11.4	9.2	10.9
In poor condition	5.1	4.6	4.3	4.6
Other	16.9	18.5	11.9	16.1
Total	57.8	54.9	43.2	51.8
Environment				
To change environment	3.6	1.8	3.3	2.6
To access shops	5.1	6.8	4.3	5.7
Unsafe area	0.3	0.4	0.6	0.9
Too noisy	4.5	4.9	1.0	3.7
Disliked neighbourhood	1.5	1.4	1.2	1.4
Total	15.0	15.3	10.4	14.3
Family and friends				
To live with family	5.1	5.9	13.3	8.0
To be near friends	13.9	17.5	19.6	17.4
To live independently	2.4	3.3	5.3	3.7
Relatives, friends moved away	1.2	0.9	1.4	1.1
Total	22.6	27.6	39.6	30.2
Security				
Ill health of self/family	2.7	3.9	5.5	4.2
Old age	0.3	1.3	0.6	0.9
Total	3.0	5.2	6.1	5.1
Other				
Retirement	4.2	3.7	3.7	3.8
Bereavement	3.9	5.9	8.4	6.3
Eviction/demolition	6.9	5.7	7.0	6.3
Other	12.0	11.0	9.6	10.8
Total	27.0	26.3	28.7	27.2
Number of respondents	332	790	489	1 611

Source: G. H. Hugo, "Migration of the elderly in Australia", in Elderly Migration: An International Comparative Study. A. Rogers and W. J. Serow, eds. (Boulder, Colorado, Population Program, University of Colorado, 1988), chap. 7.

FIGURE 12.5. TOTAL FERTILITY RATES, a/ AUSTRALIA, 1921-1991 AND UNITED STATES, 1940-1989

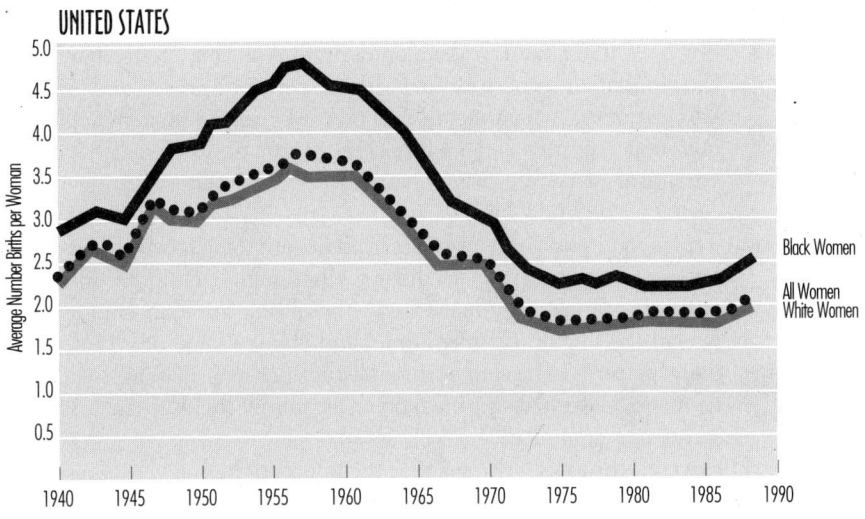

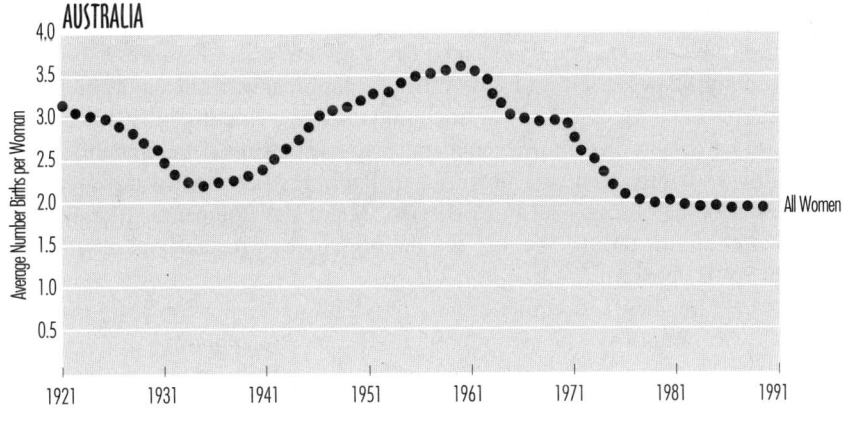

Sources: D. A. Ahlburg and C. J. De Vita, "New realities of the American family". Population Bulletin, vol. 47, No. 2 (Washington, D.C., 1992), pp. 1-44 and P. McDonald, Family trends and structure in Australia: Australian family briefings, No. 3 (Melbourne, Australian Institute of Family Studies, 1993).

a Defined as the average number of children that would be born alive to a woman (or group of women) during her lifetime if she were to pass through her childbearing years conforming to the age-specific fertility rates for a particular year.

developed countries to a place.* Breaking down people's sense of identification and commitment to their home place usually reduces the strength of ties of individuals to their family of origin. Gober[20, p. 4] summarizes the interpretations of this weakening of local ties into two broad positions as follows:

A Some see it as a positive development representing "... freedom from the familiar, one's position in society, family obligations and expected behaviours. Migrants are risk takers by seeking out new places, new opportunities and new people. Innovation emerges from the synergism of people from a variety of backgrounds sharing ideas, contacts and know how";

B The second position emphasizes the negative aspects whereby high levels of migration "... can disrupt schooling for children, interfere with one career in a dual career household, force an emotionally wrenching sale of a family home, and change some or all of life's daily patterns. The sum of these disruptions at a societal level leads to a personal isolation, breakdown in family life and the loss of a sense of community".

The overall thrust of writing about the effects of high levels of residential mobility upon the family is of negative impacts associated with separation from the wider extended family and rupturing the social bonds held by individual family members caused by the move itself. While this position undoubtedly has considerable applicability, it tells only part of the story. Moreover, it is rarely backed up by research-based evidence. Its fundamental flaw is the confusion of the geographical with the emotional separation of family members. While undoubtedly greater mobility has led to a wider dispersal of family members, at the same time developments have allowed family members not only to maintain but also to significantly enhance emotional family-based ties. These developments in transport and communication facilitate the maintenance of regular and close contact as is apparent from:

A The almost total universality of telephone ownership accompanied by a massive cheapening of long-distance telephoning;

B The associated development of other forms of communication such as computer-based systems and facsimile machines;

---

* Gober[20, p. 3] states that in the early 1990s, around 17 per cent of persons changed their usual place of residence in a single year in Australia, Canada, New Zealand and the United States; 9-15 per cent in France, Israel, Japan, Sweden, Switzerland and the United Kingdom of Great Britain and Northern Ireland, and somewhat less in Austria, Belgium, Ireland and the Netherlands.

c   The massive improvements and cheapening in all forms of long-distance transportation especially air travel and interstate highway systems.

No longer can it be maintained that geographical propinquity is a necessary condition for maintaining regular (even daily) close, personal contact between family members. The great need is to investigate these issues in depth, especially given the ageing of the population in developed countries and the need to develop systems of support for the elderly that significantly involve family members, which is the basis of most care policies for the aged in contemporary developing countries.

Return migration is a significant factor in countries such as the United States. Gober[20, p. 19] explains that a fifth of all moves made between States in the United States consist of people moving back to the State where they were born. Such a pattern is hardly consistent with an explanation of movers severing their ties with their home place.

Settles[69] has recently emphasized the centrality of family mobility in world history. The tendency has been to emphasize stability as a "moral good and characteristic of satisfactory family life in general"[69], but the reality is that movement and change in family life are more the typical experience of life than the unusual exception. As Hartley[24, p. 18] has pointed out, "movement and change is intrinsic to family life".

Conclusions

Over the last decade, population mobility in a complex variety of forms has become a major adaptive and survival strategy across a broad spectrum of groups in many developing countries. The stereotypical view of most residents of these countries as being rural-based individuals who rarely travel outside the boundaries of the ancestral community has never been fully accurate, but it certainly is not appropriate to the contemporary situation. Population movements within and between countries have expanded enormously with substantial economic, social and demographic consequences for the individuals involved and the communities out of and into which they move. Yet the understanding of these changes remains limited. Indeed in most countries the scale of population movement is not accurately known, let alone its composition, causes and implications.

More attention must be given to the conceptualization, measurement and analysis of patterns of population movement in developing countries. The attention needs to be more comprehensive in covering different types of movement since clearly many types of mobility not detected by conventional census and survey methods are economically and socially significant. These include the complex range of non-permanent mobility strategies and clandestine and undocumented movements between countries.

The outlook for the 1990s is that the trends in population movement briefly outlined at the beginning of the present chapter will accelerate. This would seem inevitable since it is difficult to foresee any diminution of the macro-forces that underpin the recent increases in scale and complexity of population movements in developing countries. The next decade will undoubtedly see an increased tempo of substitution of capital for labour in agriculture in Africa and Asia together with further moves towards the commercialization of agricultural production, the privatization and consolidation of land, an increased emphasis on markets, and mechanization, which will push many more people out of the rural areas of those regions. Increased mobility will also be facilitated by improvement in the average levels of education in the population because virtually all developing-country Governments are strongly committed to programmes to increase substantially the quantity and quality of education. The reorientation of values and attitudes wrought by education will be exacerbated to an even greater extent in the 1990s by the proliferation of mass media. Similarly the continual cheapening and increase in the accessibility, ease and speed of global and national transport systems is greatly facilitating movements of all types. The internationalization of capital also is encouraging enhanced levels of population movement, although clearly the barriers to international population movements are considerably greater than to capital flows. No doubt the growing trend towards globalization adds an important dimension to population movement.

Neo-classical economists point to interregional differences in wage rates as the fundamental cause of population movements. While the line of reasoning pursued in the present chapter suggests that this provides only a partial explanation, international or intranational differences in the supply of, and demand for, labour are probably not going to diminish in the 1990s. Indeed, at the international level these differences may well be increasing. Obviously on the demand side enormous differences exist between countries in their levels of economic growth and overall prosperity. However, countries are increasingly becoming differentiated with respect to the growth of their labour force. Those countries that began to experience a substantial fertility decline in the 1960s and early 1970s will, in the 1990s, have cohorts of diminishing size entering the labour force. When this phenomenon is combined with rapid economic growth, as it is in places such as Hong Kong, Japan, Singapore and Taiwan Province and

China, it has produced a significant labour shortage ([33] and [35]). Yet, such situations are often found next to countries where fertility decline has come much later or may not have begun at all. In these countries there tends to be a growing labour surplus. In Indonesia, for example, in the 1990s the net annual increment to the workforce will be 2.4 million persons, while 40 per cent of the existing workforce is underemployed [34]. China is said to have 200 million workers in excess of requirements [35]. Hence the potential for a substantial movement of labour between countries is present and likely to increase in the 1990s. Inequalities between areas within many developing countries are also increasing, especially between large metropolitan areas and their hinterlands. To foresee any reductions in population mobility within and out of developing countries in the 1990s is difficult, especially between rural and urban areas.

The present chapter has reasoned that any comprehensive explanation of the changes in the patterns of population mobility in developing countries must incorporate not only macroeconomic, political and social forces but also more micro-elements, especially those operating at the family and community levels. In particular, attention has been drawn to the crucial role of the family in mediating between the influence of macrostructural influences and individual migrants. It has been shown that a great deal of the population movement in developing countries results from a family's survival and adaptive strategies, which involve allocation of their labour across a variety of income-earning activities in a number of locations. Such strategies are designed to maximize family income while minimizing risk by diversifying the range of family income-generating sources. They have resulted in a wide variety of types of population movement: permanent as well as temporary moves of a diversity of periodicities, moves within and between countries, legal and clandestine moves, moves involving all gender, age, socio-economic and ethnic groups. The changing macro-context has facilitated a greater intensity of this movement and its extension across a wider spatial area and among a greater spectrum of the population than ever before.

Another important element in the family nature of much of the mobility in contemporary developing countries is the development of networks linking the communities of origin and destination. Migrant networks are "sets of interpersonal ties that link migrants, former migrants and non-migrants in origin and destination areas through the bonds of kinship, friendship, and shared community origin"[48, p. 396]. These networks play a crucial role in structuring population movement within and between countries and, once established, a process of cumulative causation is set in train so that the movement can become increasingly independent of the economic conditions that originally caused it. As Massey[48, p. 397] has pointed out: "Networks increase the likelihood of movement because they lower the costs of relocation."

These family networks must be given full consideration in any attempts at policy intervention. Where Governments are seeking to encourage movement, policies that enhance or reinforce the development of such family networks will obviously be one of the more effective levers that could be used. However, where such networks are well established, policy interventions seeking to stop movement are almost always doomed to failure because the networks operate almost totally independently of the formal institutions normally subject to policy interventions. Certainly any effective policy intervention will be dependent upon a greater understanding of how family networks operate and the identification of the key actors in those networks, especially the increasing number of agents, recruiters, lawyers, migration advisers, marriage brokers and other gatekeepers who facilitate the flow of movers through the networks.

In looking to the future, considering the rapid and far-reaching changes occurring in families in developing countries is important. Traditional, emotionally extended families where patriarchal (or matriarchal) authority is supreme are being eroded as nuclear families become predominant. In the latter case the dominant emotional and economic relationships are between partners and between parents and children. Patriarchal authority is reduced in these situations, and the ability of families to deploy their members in contradiction to the wishes of those individuals is being reduced. As the family's role as the basic unit of production is reduced, the development of nuclear family structures is encouraged. The control that patriarchal authorities can exert in such situations over the income earned by family members is also likely to be reduced, especially when they are separated by a long distance. Hence as development proceeds, the role of the family in using population mobility as a labour allocation mechanism may undergo change. Nevertheless, apparently the importance of family networks will continue to be substantial in sustaining and shaping migration flows. Indeed kinship and friendship networks are likely to become institutionalized over time with an increasing involvement of non-familial (and often profit-taking) elements.

No doubt the acceleration of population mobility witnessed in the 1980s will continue. Possibly it will continue to increase in scale, complexity and diversity. Apart from the likely continuation of the macro-forces considered in the present chapter, this burgeoning of movement will be facilitated by the huge number of people who have moved over the last decade. They have set up a myriad of new migration networks that will be increasingly activated and expanded during the 1990s.

References

[1] Ahlburg D. A. *and* C. J. De Vita. New realities of the American family. *Population Bulletin* (Washington, D.C.) 47:2:1-44, 1992.

[2] Arnold F. Unanswered questions about the immigration multiplier. *International migration review* (New York) 23:889-892, 1989.

[3] Australia. Australian Bureau of Statistics. Internal migration, Australia, 12 months ended 31 May 1987. Australian Bureau of Statistics, Canberra, 1988 (Catalogue no. 3408.0).

[4] Birrell, R. The chains that bind: family migration to Australia in the 1980s. Canberra, Australian Government Publishing Service, 1990.

[5] Bohland, J. R. *and* G. D. Rowles. The significance of elderly migration to changes in the elderly population concentration in the United States, 1960-1980. *Journal of Gerontology*, 43:5:145-152, 1988.

[6] Boyd, M. Family and personal networks in international migration: recent developments and new agendas. *International migration review* (New York) 23:3:638-670, 1989.

[7] Burt, M. R. Over the edge: the growth of homelessness in the 1980s. New York, Russell Sage Foundation, 1992.

[8] Caldwell, J. C. Toward a restatement of demographic transition theory. *Population and Development Review* (New York) 2:3-4:321-366, 1976.

[9] Carino, B. V. The Philippines and Southeast Asia, historical roots and contemporary linkages. *In* Pacific bridges, the new immigration from Asia and the Pacific Islands. J. T. Fawcett *and* B. V. Carino, *eds.* New York, Center for Migration Studies, 1987. p. 305-326.

[10] Chan, K. E. Socio-economic implications of population ageing in a developing country, the Malaysian case. Population Studies Programme, University of Malaya, 1983. Mimeographed.

[11] Chant, S., *ed.* Gender and migration in developing countries. London, Belhaven Press, 1992.

[12] Colfer, C. On circular migration: from the distaff side. *In* Labour circulation, short-term migration and the labour process. London, Groom Helou, 1985, p. 219-251.

[13] Connell, J. *and others.* Migration from rural areas; the evidence from village studies. Delhi, Oxford University Press, 1976.

[14] Corbett, Jane. Famine and household coping strategies. *World Development* (Oxford) 16:9:1099-1112, 1988.

[15] Dinerman, I. Patterns of adaptation among households of US-bound migrants from Michoacan, Mexico. *International migration review* (New York) 12:4:485-501, 1978.

[16] Fawcett, J. Networks, linkages and migration systems. *International migration review* (New York) 23:3:671-680, 1989.

[17] Frons, M. B. Jeffries *and* C. Nelson. Asia's generation gap. *Newsweek*, 22 February 1982:10-11.

[18] Fuller, T. D. *and others.* Migration and development in modern Thailand. Bangkok, Social Science Association of Thailand, Chulalongkorn University, 1983.

[19] Go, E. M. The relationship between female migration and economic activity in the Philippines. Doctoral dissertation. Australian National University, Canberra, 1992.

[20] Gober, P. Americans on the move. *Population bulletin* (Washington, D.C.) 48:3, 1993.

[21] Gonzalez, N.L.S. Family organization in five types of migratory wage labour. *American Anthropologist* (Washington, D.C.) 63:6:1264-1280, 1961.

[22] Gurak, D. T. *and* F. Caces. Migration networks and the shaping of migration systems. *In* International migration systems; a global approach. M. M. Kritz, L. L. Lim *and* H. Zlotnik, *eds.* Oxford, Oxford University Press, 1992. p.150-176.

[23] Harbison, S. F. Family structure and family strategy in migration decision making. *In* Migration decision-making; multidisciplinary approaches to microlevel studies in developed and developing countries. G. F. De Jong *and* R. W. Gardiner, *eds.* New York, Pergamon, 1981. p. 225-252.

[24] Hartley, R. Families and migration. *BIPR Bulletin* (Melbourne) 11:18-20, 1994.

[25] Hathaway, M. The migratory worker and family life. Chicago, University of Chicago Press, 1934.

[26] Hetler, C. B. Female-headed households in a circular migration village in Central Java, Indonesia. Unpublished doctoral dissertation. Department of Demography, Australian National University, Canberra, 1986.

[27] Hugo, G. J. Population mobility in West Java, Indonesia. Doctoral dissertation. Department of Demography, Australian National University, Canberra, 1975.

[28] Circular migration in Indonesia. *Population and development review* (New York) 8:1:59-84, 1982.

[29] Structural change and labour mobility in rural Java. In Labour circulation and the labour process. G. Standing, *ed*. London, Croom Helm, 1985. p. 46-88.

[30] Demographic and welfare implications of urbanization; direct and indirect effects on sending and receiving areas. *In* Urbanization and urban policies in pacific Asia. R. J. Fuchs, G. W. Jones *and* E. M. Pernia, eds. Boulder, Westview Press, 1987. p. 136-165.

[31] Migration of the elderly in Australia. *In* Elderly migration; an international comparative study. A. Rogers and W. J. Serow, eds. Boulder, Colorado, Population Program, University of Colorado, 1988. chap. 7.

[32] Population movements in Indonesia; recent developments and their implications. Paper presented to the International Conference on Migration, National University of Singapore, Singapore, 7-9 February, 1991.

[33] Recent international migration trends in Asia; some implications for Australia. *In* Immigration population and sustainable environments. J. Smith. *ed.* Adelaide, The Flinders Press, 1991. p. 118-145.

[34] Indonesian labour migration to Malaysia; trends and policy implications. Paper presented to the International Colloquium on Migration, Developments and Gender in South Asia, organized by the Population Studies Unit of the University of Malaya, Kuantan, Malaysia, 28-31 October 1992.

[35] Asia on the move; the transformation of international migration in Asia in the 1990s and its implications for Australia. Inaugural lecture, University of Adelaide, Adelaide, 23 October 1992.

[36] Manpower and employment situation in Indonesia 1992. Jakarta, Department of Manpower, 1993.

[37] Population trends. *In* The Australian urban system; trends and prospects. Canberra, Australian Housing and Urban Research Institute. Australian Government Publishing Service, 1994.

[38] Hull, T. H. Conflict on the home front; work, housework and the future of fertility. Paper presented to a seminar on conflict and consensus held at the Research School of Social Sciences, Australian National University, 1982.

[39] Khoo, S. Immigrant families and change. *BIPR Bulletin* (Melbourne), 11:15-17, 1994.

[40] Kritz, M. M., L. L. Lim *and* H. Zlotnik, eds. International systems; a global approach. Oxford, Clarendon Press, 1992.

[41] Lauby J. *and* O. Stark. Individual migration as a family strategy; young women in the Philippines. *Population studies* (London) 42:473-486, 1988.

[42] Lewis, W. A. Economic development with unlimited supplies of labour. Manchester School of Economic Studies, 22 May 1954. Mimeographed.

[43] Li, W. L. *Measurement and analysis of internal migration*. New York, University Press of America, 1983.

[44] Lineton, J. A. An Indonesian society and its universe; a study of the Bugis of South Sulawesi and their roles in a wider social and economic system. Doctoral dissertation. School of Oriental and African Studies, University of London, 1975.

[45] Lipton, M. Migration from rural areas of poor countries; the impact on rural productivity and income distribution. *World development* (Oxford) 8:1-24, 1980.

[46] Long, L. Changing residence; comparative perspectives on its relationship to age, sex and marital status, *Population studies* (London) 46:141-158, 1992.

[47] Massey, D. S. *and* others. Return to Aztlan: the social process of international migration from western Mexico. Berkeley, University of California Press, 1987.

[48] Massey, D. S. Economic development and international migration in comparative perspective. *Population and development review* (New York) 14:3:383-413, 1988.

[49] Understanding Mexican migration to the United States. Population Studies Center, Department of Sociology, University of Pennsylvania, 1990. Mimeographed.

[50] McDonald, P. Family trends and structure in Australia. Melbourne, Australian Institute of Family Studies, 1993 (Australian family briefings, no. 3).

[51] McHugh, K. E. Seasonal migration as a substitute for, or precurser to, permanent migration. *Research on ageing* (Beverly Hills, California), 12:229-245, 1990.

[52] Morrissey, M., C. Mitchell *and* A. Rutherford. The family in the settlement process. Canberra, Australian Government Publishing Service, 1991.

[53] Naim, M. Merantau: Minangkabau voluntary migration. Doctoral dissertation. University of Singapore, 1974.

[54] Ong, A. Industrial development in rural Malay households: changing strategies in reproduction. *In* Impact of development on demographic behaviour. C. Vlossof *and* B. Khuda, eds. Ottawa, International Development Research Centre, 1988.

[55] Ono, K. Coresidence of mothers and children, 1993. Mimeographed.

[56] Papademetriou, D. G. International migration in North America; issues, policies, implications. Paper prepared for the joint Economic Commission for Europe and United Nations Population Fund meetings in Geneva, 16-19 July 1991.

[57] Programa de Investigaciones Sociales Sobre Poblacion en America Latina/Centro de Investigaciones, Centro de Estudios de Poblacion, Se fue a volver; seminario sobre migraciones temporales en America Latina (Mexico, 1986).

[58] Prothero R. M. *and* M. Chapman. Circulation in the third world. London, Routledge and Kegan Paul, 1984.

[59] Rahmato Dessalegn. Famine and survival strategies; a case study from northeast Ethiopia. Addis Ababa, Institute of Development Research, Addis Ababa University, May 1987. (Food and famine monograph series, no. 1).

[60] Ranis, G. *and* J.G.H. Fei. A theory of economic development. *American economic review,* 51:533-565, 1961.

[61] Richter, K. The impact of rural-urban migration on child care and family structure in Thailand. In Proceedings of the international colloquium; migration, development and gender in the ASEAN region. J. Arrifin, ed. Kuala Lumpur, Population Studies Unit, Faculty of Economics and Administration, University of Malaya, 1993.

[62] Rodenburg, A. N. Staying behind: rural women and migration in north Tapanuli, Indonesia. Amsterdam, University of Amsterdam, 1993.

[63] Rodenburg, J. Emancipation or subordination? Consequences of female migration for migrants and their families. Paper presented to the Expert Group Meeting on the Feminization of Internal Migration, convened by the United Nations at Aguascalientes, Mexico, 22-25 October 1991.

[64] Rogers, A. and others. Elderly migration and population redistribution. London, Belhaven Press, 1992.

[65] Russell, S. S. Migration between developing countries in the African and Latin American regions and its likely future. Paper presented to the Expert Group Meeting on Population Distribution and Migration convened by the Population Division of the United Nations Secretariat, in consultation with the United Nations Population Fund, at Santa Cruz, Bolivia, 18-22 January 1993.

[66] Salt, J. High-level manpower movements in northwest Europe and the role of careers: an explanatory framework. *International migration review* (New York) 17:4:633-652, 1983.

[67] Samonte, E. Filipino migrant workers in Japan; in search of a better life - the price of a dream. *Philippine journal of labor and industrial relations.* 13:1-2, 1991.

[68] Schmink, M. Household economic strategies: review and research agenda. *Latin American research review.* 19:3:87-101, 1984.

[69] Settles, B. H. The illusion of stability in family life; the reality of change and mobility. *Marriage and family review* (Binghamton, New York) 19:1/2:5-29, 1993.

[70] Siegel, J. T. The rope of God. Berkeley, University of California Press, 1969.

[71] Skeldon, R. Migration and the population census in Asia and the Pacific: issues, questions and debate. *International migration review* (New York) 21:4:1074-1100, 1987.

[72] International migration within and from the east and southeast Asian region; a review essay. *Asian and Pacific migration journal* (Quezon City, Philippines) 1:1:19-63, 1992.

[73] Snaith, J. Migration and dual career households. *In* Labour migration; the internal geographical mobility of labour in the developed world. J. H. Johnson *and* J. Salt, eds. London, David Fulton Publishers, 1990. p. 155-171.

74 Spaan, E. Taikongs and Calos; the role of middlemen and brokers in Javanese international migration. *International migration review* (New York, forthcoming).
75 Standing G., *ed*. Labour circulation: short-term migration and the labour process. London, Croom Helm, 1985.
76 Stark, O. The migration of labour. Oxford, Basil Blackwell, 1991.
77 Todaro, M. P. International migration in developing countries. Geneva, International Labour Office, 1976.
78 Tongudai, P. Women, migration and employment; a study of migrant women in Bangkok. Unpublished doctoral dissertation. New York University, New York, 1982.
79 Torres, Amryllis T. Features of the migration of men and women in the Philippines. Paper presented to the international colloquium: migration, development and gender in the ASEAN region convened by the Population Studies Unit, University of Malaya, at Coral Beach Resort, Kuantan, Pahang, 28-31 October 1992.
80 Features of the migration of men and women in the Philippines. *In* Proceedings of the international colloquium; migration, development and gender in the ASEAN region. J. Ariffin, *ed*. Kuala Lumpur, Population Studies Unit, Faculty of Economics and Administration, University of Malaya, 1993. p. 68-114.
81 United Nations. Department of International Economic and Social Affairs. Methods of measuring international migration. Population studies no. 47. 96 p. Sales no. 70.XIII.3.
82 Department of International Economic and Social Affairs. World population monitoring 1991, with special emphasis on age structure. Population studies no. 126. 241 p. (ST/ESA/SER.A/126).Sales no. 92.XIII.2.
83 Vredenbregt, J. Bawean migrations. *Bijdragen tot de Taal-*, Land- en Volkenkunde (Dordrecht, Netherlands) 120:109-130, 1964.
84 White, J. W. Dimensions of cycles in internal migration. *In* The urban impact of internal migration. J. W. White, *ed*. Chapel Hill, Institute for Research in Social Science, University of North Carolina, 1979, p. 149-173.
85 Wildasin, D. E. Old age security and fertility. Project paper prepared for the Fertility Determinants Group, Indiana University, Bloomington [n.d.].
86 Wood, C. H. Structural changes and household strategies: a conceptual framework for the study of rural migration. *Human organization* 40:338-344, 1981.
87 Equilibrium and historical-structural perspectives on migration. *International migration review* (New York) 16:2:298-319, 1982.
88 Zelinsky, W. The hypothesis of the mobility transition. *Geographical review* (New York) 41:2:219-249, 1971.
89 The cultural geography of the United States. Englewood Cliffs, NJ, Prentice Hall, 1992.

FAMILY Leave:
Changing Needs of the World's Workers

Introduction*

"Mrs. Lentz, your approximate delivery date is November 3rd; your pregnancy appears to be normal."

"Mr. Morales, please call 776-5721. There has been an accident and your son is in City Hospital."

"I'm afraid I have some difficult news. Your mother has Alzheimer's disease ..."

"The test results are positive for the acquired immune deficiency syndrome. As you may know, AIDS ..."

Messages such as these are received by millions of people every day. The impact of birth, the ageing of parents and the onset of illness affects all realms of life, including work. With the rapidly changing demographics of the workforce, action must be taken at local, regional and national levels to accommodate the fulfilment of family responsibilities. So significant is the relationship of the family to social and economic conditions that several recommendations for national policies have been made under the auspices of the United Nations. Family leave is one of the specific solutions to assure that family responsibilities be met.

Dramatic changes have taken place in the workforce worldwide and indications are clear that such changes will continue. Women are entering the workforce in increasing numbers, often out of economic necessity. Many mothers are the sole economic providers for their children. In the last two decades, employment rates for mothers with young children have doubled in many countries. In addition, in two-parent families, both parents work outside the home in increasing numbers. Adequate support systems are needed therefore to help families cope with the effects of the increased participation in the workforce.

Balancing family responsibilities with work demands is a major challenge, especially when child care, elder care and illness are realities. As the responsibilities of a home affect employment, and employment affects home life, ways must be developed to meet the changing needs of the global workforce. In addition to changes such as more flexible hours, employer-supported child care and job-sharing, family leave is one major solution to meeting the needs of workers more appropriately.

---

* Paper prepared for the IYF secretariat by Elizabeth Beard Goldsmith, Professor, Florida State University, Tallahassee, Florida, United States of America.

Family leave is an umbrella term encompassing many policies including leave from work for the birth of a baby, the adoption of a child and the care of critically ill family members. Policy considerations include the appropriate length of leave time, whether leave should be paid or unpaid and specifications about which employees qualify for leave and which employers should offer leave. An underlying premise is that employees should not have to run the risk of losing their jobs to take care of critical family responsibilities.

The International Year of the Family (IYF) and its follow-up is an appropriate time to increase awareness of, and encourage action for, solutions to pressing problems related to the global workforce. Family leave is one solution that addresses changing family values, economic change, equity within and between families, and appropriate interventions and related policies. Family-leave policies strive to clarify the balance between how the family satisfies its own needs and those of society. Family-leave policies strengthen a family's ability to meet its members' needs; this strengthening is recognized as a social good. Everyone will benefit in the long run if each country implements family-leave policies appropriate for specific conditions.

Family leave: an overview

The term "family leave" refers to a host of issues and policies. For prospective parents who are employed, their concerns include how much time they will be allowed to be away from work before, during and after the birth of their children (leave); whether they will continue to receive pay for the time that they are away from work (wage replacement); and whether they will have a job to return to at all (job security). Similar concerns are felt by parents adopting a child. Employees can also be confronted with the critical illness of a spouse, child or parent.

Most of the research and statistics published on family-leave policies come from Europe, North America and Japan. However, family leave is a worldwide concern that will become increasingly important as more countries become industrialized and more women leave the home to enter the workforce. For example, global trends show that work for wages in an industrial setting is replacing family-based labour. According to International Labour Organization (ILO) data, the number of persons working in agriculture in developing countries in Asia and the Pacific decreased from 79.5 per cent to 66.6 per cent between 1950 and 1970, while employment in industry almost doubled.[1] Of the 828 million women estimated to be economically active worldwide in 1990, over half (56 per cent) lived in Asia, 29 per cent in the developed regions, 9 per cent in Africa and 5 per cent in Latin America and the Caribbean.[2] Traditionally, in most Asian countries, women have stayed at home to care for children and elderly relatives. Increasingly, however, they are joining the workforce in growing numbers without the societal and legislative support to help with elder and child care. Consequently, the issues of family leave and family support in general are receiving more attention than ever before in Asian countries. African, Latin American and Caribbean countries are struggling with issues of gender equality including those related to work.

At the United Nations Africa and Western Asia Preparatory Meeting for the International Year of the Family, representatives of African and Western Asian countries made recommendations concerning the removal of obstacles to women's equal and active participation in all spheres of society,[3] as did the participants in the Asian and Pacific Preparatory Meeting for the International Year of the Family.[4] In the Cartagena Declaration, participants in the Latin American and Caribbean Regional Meeting Preparatory to the International Year of the Family agreed to "reinforce programmes designed to satisfy the basic needs of families and, in particular, facilitate their access to ... employment and income generation".[5] In the Declaration of Valletta, the participants in the United Nations Europe and North America Preparatory Meeting for the International Year of the Family urged that altering conditions of work be considered to take family responsibilities into account to help family members achieve a better balance between work and family responsibilities.[6]

A historical perspective[*]

The concept of family leave, in particular maternity leave, is not new. Maternity leaves were common in many pre-industrial and preliterate societies.[7] A period of rest or isolation was granted women following childbirth both because of concern for the health of the mother and infant and because of religious beliefs and a general superstition that women were unclean and possessed by evil spirits following childbirth.[8]

The industrial revolution of the mid-nineteenth century raised new concerns related to maternity and early child care throughout Europe.

---

[*] Most of the information in the sections that follow has been adapted from Mary Benson McMullen and Elizabeth Beard Goldsmith, "Parental leave: The changing needs of the American worker", Journal of Home Economics, vol. 83, No. 4 (1991), pp. 6-21, for which permission to use has kindly been granted by the American Home Economics Association.

Women regularly worked in early industrial society, and their contributions were recognized as vital to nineteenth-century European economies; however, the workplace tended to be a dirty, hot and dangerous place where people worked long hours. Maternity leave, generally thought of as maternity protection, sought to protect women in the postpartum period from exposure to these negative conditions. Additionally, there was increasing concern about the extremely high rate of infant mortality among the babies of women who returned to work shortly after birth. Doctors became convinced that more babies would survive if women could be induced to breast-feed their babies for several months before returning to work.[7]

Germany in 1883 became the first western country where maternity protection became mandatory under national insurance legislation. In 1903, Russia enacted a national leave law followed in 1911 by France, Italy and the United Kingdom of Great Britain and Ireland. In 1919, the General Conference of ILO, convened at Washington, D.C., adopted the Convention concerning the Employment of Women before and after Childbirth (the Maternity Protection Convention). The Members of ILO recognized that a woman should have the right to take maternity leave before and after her confinement, that such leave should be paid for out of public funds or a system of insurance and that she should be allowed half an hour twice a day during working hours for the purpose of nursing her child. Subsequently, many more European countries adopted maternity protection legislation or improved their laws. Several countries altered their legislation to provide job security upon the mother's return to work. Although the United States had hosted and participated in the Conference, it did not pass or seriously consider maternity legislation at that time.

More European legislatures took action on maternity leave in the 1940s and 1950s, when many eastern European countries adopted or adapted maternity policies similar to those of the former Union of Soviet Socialist Republics. These countries desperately needed women in the workforce to help rebuild their economies after the Second World War. Furthermore, healthy babies would help much of eastern Europe to rebuild its populations.

In 1985, the more generous parental-leave policies were found in northern, western and eastern Europe. Several European countries provided leave for either parent. Sweden, Finland and France, for instance, had liberal policies that applied to either the father or the mother, allowing one or the other parent job-secured leave with partial or total wage replacement for up to two years.[9]

In October 1992, the Council of Ministers of the European Economic Community (EEC) adopted a directive on the protection of pregnant women at work, and those who had recently given birth or were breast-feeding their child. One of the provisions is an obligatory maternity leave of two weeks before, after or straddling the presumed date of delivery. In line with national legislation and practice, the actual duration of the maternity leave is set at a minimum of 124 uninterrupted weeks and the employment rights of women taking maternity leave are to be maintained. While most countries have exceeded the stipulations, some changes are still necessary to comply with the directive. An analysis of the information available reveals that 25 per cent of EEC members made significant policy changes in 1991. With the exception of Ireland, there are limitations and restrictions to the kind of work that is allowed. There is a wide variation in the number of months of job protection provided after parturition, with Belgium providing one month, Germany 36 months, and the average being 8.37 months. Eight countries have compulsory maternity-leave provisions for both pre- and post-delivery and three provide post-delivery protection. Pre-delivery leave varies from 1 to 10 weeks and post-delivery leave from 4 to 24 weeks. Two thirds of the member countries have provisions for breast-feeding. Paternity leave is increasingly provided. In Denmark, fathers are entitled to take two weeks of paternity leave in any period during the first 14 weeks after the birth of their children. The long-term impact of these provisions, however, needs to be researched over time.[10]

In the United States, not until the 1930s did the subject of married women working outside the home became a major political issue. A review of the literature reveals that most United States residents were generally opposed to married women working outside the home. During the Second World War, however, women were needed to assume positions in the workforce left by men going to war as well as to fill jobs in the new specialized war-related industries. During the war years, the Government opened and sponsored over 3,000 day-care centres for children and developed a set of guidelines benefiting pregnant and post-partum female workers.[11] Following the Second World War, however, the Government closed 2,800 of the 3,000 federally sponsored day-care centres. Many women quit their jobs and returned to home and domestic work. Data from the United States Bureau of Labor Statistics clearly indicate a substantial drop in women's employment outside the home immediately following the end of the Second World War.

Role of the United Nations

The United Nations has provided an international framework for the implementation of family-leave policies. Of particular relevance are the Convention concerning Equal Opportunities and Equal Treatment for Men and Women Workers: Workers with Family Responsibilities (No. 156) and the Recommendation concerning Equal Opportunities and Equal Treatment for Men and Women Workers: Workers with Family Responsibilities (No. 165).[12]

The Recommendation includes sections on definition, scope and means of implementation; national policy; training and employment; terms and conditions of employment; child-care and family services and facilities; social security and help in exercise of family responsibilities. The Convention and Recommendation provide for measures to be taken that promote equality of opportunity and treatment for workers who have family responsibilities including the care of dependent children, the elderly and sick family members. The Recommendation states that vocational guidance and training, to enable workers with family responsibilities to enter or re-enter the workforce, should be available. Furthermore, national conditions should be taken into account when implementing the Recommendation.

Both employers' and workers' organizations should have the right to participate in policy development. Each country should promote information and education that engender a climate of opinion conducive to overcoming the problems of workers with family responsibilities.

These instruments support the development of national policy through collaborative planning with the public and private sectors to harmonize family needs and employment responsibilities. For instance, community planning should include child-care and family services as well as facilities such as transportation.

In the Recommendation, the need for research is recognized in the provision that the competent authorities and bodies in each country should undertake or promote such research as may be necessary to provide objective information on which sound policies and measures may be based.

Family and Medical Leave Act of 1993

The Family and Medical Leave Act applies to all public agencies, including State, local and federal employers, local education agencies (schools) and private-sector employers employing 50 or more employees in 20 or more workweeks in the current or preceding calendar year within a 75-mile radius.

- Covered employers must grant an eligible employee up to a total of 12 workweeks of unpaid leave during any 12-month period for the birth or placement of a child for adoption or foster care, for the care of a seriously ill child, spouse or parent, or in the case of his or her own serious illness.
- Employers have to continue health-care coverage for the employee during the leave.
- Employers have to guarantee that employees will return to either the same job or a comparable position.
- Employers can refuse to reinstate certain highly paid "key" employees after their leave. Such employees are defined as the highest paid 10 per cent of the workforce and whose leave would cause economic harm to the employer.
- Employers can exempt employees who have not worked for at least one year and who have not worked for at least 1,250 hours, or 25 hours a week, in the previous 12 months.
- A doctor's certification has to be obtained to verify a serious illness. Employers may require a second medical opinion.
- Employers can substitute an employee's accrued paid leave (such as sick or annual leave) for any part of the 12-week period of family leave.
- Under some circumstances, employees may take the leave intermittently, by taking leave in blocks of time or reducing their normal weekly or daily work schedule.
- Employers are permitted to require an employee taking intermittent leave for planned medical treatments to transfer temporarily to an equivalent alternative position.

Family and Medical Leave Act of the United States: perseverance and progress in meeting family needs

Barriers and resistance to family-leave policies can be overcome through education and persistence, as illustrated by developments in the United States.

In the United States during the last two decades, employment rates for mothers with children under two years of age increased from 31 per cent in 1970 to 54 per cent in 1985. The employment of mothers of infants less than a year old has risen 100 per cent since 1970, up to a level of 49 per cent.[13] The percentage of working women in the United States who are in their child-bearing years (65 per cent) is particularly significant because 90 per cent of them will give birth to at least one child at some time during their employment histories.[14] Clearly there has been a need for support of family responsibilities in the United States workforce. Using documents prepared by the United Nations as backup, Representative Pat Schroeder of the United States Congress introduced the Family and Medical Leave Act bill in 1985. It called for four months of unpaid job-secured leave to care for newborn, newly adopted or seriously ill children.13 Although the bill was not passed, several States voluntarily adopted similar policies for private-sector employees who worked for large companies. This bill served as a forerunner to the Family and Medical Leave Act that President Clinton signed into law on 5 February 1993 to be put into effect on 5 August 1993. Some provisions of the Act are summarized in the box below.

While there are limitations in the Act and implementation will allow for modification based upon experience, its enactment is a historically significant step. Use of United Nations instruments and the large body of literature and experience available in the United States regarding family leave might be instructional to other countries considering the development of family-leave policies.

Why family-leave policies vary

If family leave has such a long history and is such an obvious societal good, why are national policies not more common and highly developed? This question has given rise to a variety of opinions and much speculation. One reason might be the fundamental economic and political issue of how much government intervention there should be in family life. How much should caring for family members be the responsibility of the family and how much should it be the responsibility of government? As to why

Europe developed strong family-leave policies and the United States did not until recently, one answer may lie in the differences in basic political ideology.[11] Those who subscribe to this view support the notion that the efforts of socialist parties and labour unions to improve the working conditions in early industrial Europe resulted in the adoption of social welfare policies, including maternity leave. The rationale behind the generous leave policies in the former countries of the Eastern bloc, such as the former USSR, is believed to have been to encourage an increase in birth rates to create a larger pool of workers.[9] Historically, the position of the United States has been that policies such as parental leave should not be mandated nationally, but rather should be voluntary on the part of employers and negotiated through the private sector or by agreements between labour and management.

Others theorize that the differences between Europe and the United States regarding parental leave may be rooted in the early feminist movement.[7] These theorists suggest that European women placed the emphasis of their movement on the conditions and needs of working women in order to achieve equality in pay, work status and political standing. Thus, European women focused on securing pregnancy and paternity leave and on national child-care policies. In the United States, however, feminists might have feared that making an issue out of biological differences between men and women might focus unwanted attention on the differences between the sexes, and lead to women being labelled as marginal or temporary workers, thus making it more difficult to achieve total equality in the work and political spheres.[15]

Family-leave policies are determined by political and economic theories and realities interfaced with social contexts and cultural beliefs.

Issues regarding family leave

Length of family leave

Once policy makers have decided to introduce family-leave legislation, a number of factors should be considered in setting the length of the period of family leave. A review of existing legislation at all levels and in other countries is an important first step. A review of private-sector policies is another way of determining what is appropriate. Academic research on family and medical-care matters must be examined to develop a sound understanding of the needs of families for leave and of the conditions under which a leave policy might be more likely to succeed. Essentially, a dialogue has to be established between all the parties concerned: workers, employers, legislators, family-life experts, researchers and so forth. The ultimate goals of family-leave policies are to support families in difficult circumstances, to improve family health and well-being, to strengthen the self-care ability of families and to build and maintain a healthy, productive and motivated workforce.

It is generally accepted in the research literature that individuals who are preoccupied with family health and welfare problems cannot devote their best efforts and the necessary attention to their jobs. Thus, the state of family well-being affects the functioning of workers and the work unit as a whole. In addition, while some family health or care problems can be predicted and planned for such as the arrival of a new baby, others such as the sickness of a child or the heart attack or accident of an elderly parent cannot. Policies should cover emergencies as well as planned-for events.

In regard to parental leave for the care of children, controversy exists over the appropriate length of time for such leaves. Some countries offer up to a year's leave. According to recent reports, up to 24 months of leave is available in Sweden to both men and women, most of it at 90 per cent of the salary, which may be extended to when the child reaches the age of four if the leave is taken in half-day units. Also, parents with children under 10 years of age have the right to reduce their working hours by 25 per cent.[16]

Regarding the appropriate length of leave for childbirth, most research on attachment (the time it takes to form critical relationships to significant persons in one's life, especially child and parent) and infant day care has led child development experts to support a minimum period of parental leave of three to four months as being best for both parents and child.[17] T. Berry Brazelton, a renowned American paediatrician and child development authority, advocates a leave of four months as minimal. He believes that the first 12 weeks of a baby's life is a period of major adjustment during which the baby settles into a secure routine.[18] Other experts concur and state also that consistency in caretaking during a child's early weeks is crucial.[19],[20]

Parents are likely to feel stress following the birth or adoption of a newborn baby. They must juggle the multiple roles of employee, parent, spouse and homemaker.[21] Any reduction in income because of unpaid leave or doctors' bills puts the family under additional stress. With newborn babies, lack of sleep and new scheduling patterns are also parental stressors. Stress is a relevant factor in any discussion of family leave because stress has an impact on the family and reduces a worker's effectiveness. Someone who returns to work too soon after a family health crisis, a birth or an adoption may not be able to focus adequate attention on her or his work; it would be better to take more leave from work to get family responsibilities stabilized and to be ready to return to work.

Elder care

The subject of family leave usually conjures up concerns about parental leave and child care. However, owing to the ageing of the global population, elder care has become another dilemma for workers. More and more employees are reaching the age when they also have responsibilities for the care of their parents and other older relatives.[22] In many families, elder care has become more of a long-term burden than child care.[23] Child care can be planned more easily. At the child's birth, the parent knows that the child will be ready for school within a few years and will become more independent over time. Elder care, however, can range from a few days to decades; elders usually become more dependent in the course of time. Another issue is that ageing relatives may live long distances away whereas young children usually live at home.[24] The health-care costs for ageing relatives can be astronomical in countries without federally subsidized health care. Home-based care may be the only affordable solution. In some developing countries, families are often the sole source of care for elderly persons. Middle-aged persons may find themselves maintaining two households (theirs and their parents) as well as caring for young children. In a study of full-time employees who provided elder care, it was more time-consuming and stressful for the employee to maintain two households (i.e. providing food and upkeep for two homes) than if the employed son or daughter and the elder parent lived in the same house.[25]

Workers most at risk of becoming severely stressed are those who have young children, ageing parents and teenagers.[26] The importance of the psychological condition of caregivers and care receivers cannot be underestimated. Family members are best cared for and nurtured in environments they are familiar with and that are loving and supportive. Child care has received the most attention in the press and in research, but the ageing of the population and the potential for long-range care problems of the elderly indicate that options for elder care are a necessity in family-leave policies.

Workplace policies supportive of the family

Family leave is one aspect of the larger issue of family-supportive workplace policies. The family and workplace interface is so multifaceted that policies now in place or being discussed are elemental to what is likely to come. Fernandez[24] grouped the options into three categories of specific policies and practices:

Provision of services. Under this category, the employer provides employees with information about the services available in the on-site and nearby child-care centres that some employers provide. For example, in the United States, many hospitals provide 24-hour child care in the hospital (on-site) to attract and retain staff, especially nurses.

Provision of financial assistance. The second category refers to employers' arrangements for special rates at community child-care centres and for child-care and elder-care services. In addition, cafeteria-style fringe benefits provide an opportunity for employees to select a range or variety of options that are best for themselves and their families. Options may include dental and medical health-insurance plans, child-care options or even child-care assistance by employer-contributed funds at local child-care centres reserving places for employees' children.

Provision of time for family responsibilities. This category includes maternity leave, paternity leave, the flexible use of sick days, flexitime and job-sharing.

Ideally, employees should be involved in determining the options on offer. Consistency of options within and between companies is desirable as employees change jobs and move to other locations. The benefit of having a national standard for family leave is that a worker's access to leave would be less dependent on factors such as geographic location or industry. Family leave must be considered an integral aspect of concerns related to the family and work.

Opposition to family leave

Family leave is a new or developing concept in some countries. In other countries where nationally mandated policies already exist, they will need to be constantly updated to stay abreast of societal change. John Naisbitt, author of Megatrends, states that change occurs when there is a confluence of both changing values and economic necessity.[27] Family-leave policy represents a shift in values and economics that not everyone is prepared to accept. In family-leave legislation the family and its economic contribution is valued, but the government and employers are being asked to play a more active, supportive family role, which is new to some people. This attitude is evident in titles of articles such as "Parental leave - is it the business of business?".[16] Individual managers and policy makers may not realize the strain that employees with families experience. Some have sacrificed their own families in order to succeed and may fail to see why others cannot do the same.[28] Still others consider work and family to be a women's issue, and women still lack the power needed to strive for family-friendly policies.[29] In a research study, Grover found that a significant attitudes-toward-women effect indicated that those participants who held non-traditional beliefs about women's roles in the workforce evaluated parental leave as more fair than did those holding traditional views of women.[30]

Other problems in the establishment of family leave policies include costs, scheduling difficulties, equity issues and, in some cases, union resistance.[22,31,32] Opposition to family leave comes primarily from businesses that argue that all employee benefits are costly for employers who must either absorb these expenses or pass them on to the consumers.[33] They also argue that having the flexibility to meet their individual needs, rather than having benefits prescribed by the national Government, should be allowed. Since small businesses are exempt from most national family-leave policies, this eliminates some of the hardship a small business might experience in guaranteeing a job for an employee on long-term parental or family medical-care leave. Understandably a business employing three or four persons such as an insurance office or an attorney's office would have a difficult time in functioning if one employee took an extended leave. Family-leave policies must allow for supplementary or alternative approaches in such cases including sensitizing small business employers to options they might consider (e.g. office contingency planning).

Effective legislation considers the needs of employees with families as well as the staffing problems of different-sized businesses. For example, the Family and Medical Leave Act of 1993 does exactly that because it applies only to workplaces with more than 50 employees. But family leave is far greater than a piece of single legislation; it is an ongoing issue that will continue as long as the workforce increases in diversity.

One concern of employers is that employees will abuse leave privileges. Such abuse has not been evident in recent studies conducted by the large transnational corporations of Johnson and Johnson and the American Telephone and Telegraph Company.[34] In fact, the results of the studies demonstrated that there were far more benefits than disadvantages from offering pro-family policies. Helping employees to resolve work and family conflicts boosted morale and increased productivity. For example, in the Johnson and Johnson study, absenteeism among employees who used flexitime and family leave was on average 50 per cent less than for the workforce as a whole, and 58 per cent of the employees surveyed said that such policies were "very important" in their decision to stay with the company and the number of the employees using the benefits increased to 71 per cent. As family-leave policies are implemented and research is conducted, the likelihood is greater that the needs of the family and the workplace can be fulfilled.

References

1. *The Family*, Bulletin on the International Year of the Family, 1994, No. 4, 1992, pp. 1-2.
2. International Labour Office, *Economically active population - Estimates: 1950-1980, Projections: 1985-2025* (Geneva, 1986).
3. "Report of the United Nations Africa and Western Asia Preparatory Meeting for the International Year of the Family, Tunis, 29 March-2 April 1993" (IYF/PM.1/10), p. 9.
4. Economic and Social Commission for Asian and the Pacific, "Report on the Asian and Pacific Preparatory Meeting for the International Year of the Family, Beijing, 24-28 May 1993" (SD/IYF/Rep.), pp. 11 and 14.
5. Economic Commission for Latin America and the Caribbean, "Draft Final Report of the Latin American and Caribbean Regional Meeting Preparatory to the International Year of the Family, Cartagena, Colombia, 9-14 August 1993" (DSC/1).
6. "Report of the United Nations Europe and North America Preparatory Meeting for the International Year of the Family, Valletta, 26-30 April 1993" (IYF/PM.2/9), p. 4.
7. M. Frank and R. Lipner, "History of maternity leave in Europe and the United States", *The Parental Leave Crisis: Toward a National Policy*, E. Zigler and M. Frank, eds. (New Haven, Connecticut, Yale University Press, 1988).
8. M. Jimenez and N. Newton, "Activity and work during pregnancy and the postpartum period: A cross-cultural study of 202 societies", *American Journal of Obstetrics and Gynecology*, vol. 135, No. 2 (1979), pp. 171-176.
9. L. W. Gladstone, J. Williams and R. Belous, *Maternity and Parental Leave Policies: A Comparative Analysis*, United States Government Report No. 85-148 (Washington, D.C., 1985).
10. W. Dumon, *National Family Policies in EC-Countries in 1991: European Observatory of National Family Policies* (Brussels, Commission of the European Communities, 1992), vol.I, chap. IV.
11. S. B. Kamerman, A. J. Kahn and P. Kingston, *Maternity Policies and Working Women* (New York, Columbia University Press, 1983).
12. International Labour Organisation, *International Labour Conventions and Recommendations* 1919-1981 (Geneva, International Labour Office, 1982), pp. 52-61.
13. P. Schroeder, "Parental leave: The need for a federal policy", *The Parental Leave Crisis: Toward a National Policy*, E. Zigler and M. Frank, eds. (New Haven, Connecticut, Yale University Press, 1988).
14. P. Voydanoff, *Work and Family Life* (Beverly Hills, California, Sage Publications, 1987).
15. M. Piccirillo, "The legal background of parental leave policy and its implications", *The Parental Leave Crisis": Toward a National Policy*, E. Zigler and M. Frank, eds. (New Haven, Connecticut, Yale University Press, 1988).
16. A. A. Johnson, "Parental leave - is it the business of business?", *Human Resource Planning*, vol. 13, No. 2 (1990), pp. 119-131.
17. M. B. McMullen and E. B. Goldsmith, "Parental leave: The changing needs of the American worker", *Journal of Home Economics*, vol. 83, No. 4 (1991), pp. 16-21.
18. T. Brazelton, "Issues for working parents", *The Parental Leave Crisis: Toward a National Policy*, E. Zigler and M. Frank, eds. (New Haven, Connecticut, Yale University Press, 1998).
19. E. Thoman, C. Acebo and P. Becker, "Infant crying and stability in the mother-infant relationship: A systems analysis", *Child Development*, No. 54, 1983, pp. 653-659.
20. S. Scarr, *Mothercare/Othercare* (New York, Basic Books, 1984).
21. J. Belsky and M. Rovine, "Social network contact, family support, and the transition to parenthood", *Journal of Marriage and the Family*, No. 46, 1984, pp. 455-462.
22. K. E. Christensen and G. L. Staines, "Flextime: A viable solution to work/family conflict?", *Journal of Family Issues*, vol. 11, No. 4 (1990), pp. 455-476.
23. D. Cordtz, "Hire me, hire my family", *Financial World*, vol. 159, No. 19 (18 September 1990), pp. 76-79.
24. H. C. Fernandez, "Family sensitive policies can attract employees to human service organizations", *Administration in Social Work*, vol. 14, No. 3 (1990), pp. 47-66.

[25] E. Goldsmith, "Employees' management of family, work and elder care". Proceedings of the Southeastern Regional Association of Family Economics Home Management Conference: Family Economics and Management - The Later Years, 31 January-2 February 1990, Orlando, Florida, United States of America.

[26] P. Nelson and S. Couch, "The corporate perspective on family responsive policy", *Marriage and Family Review*, vol. 15, Nos. 3-4 (1990), pp. 95-113.

[27] J. Naisbitt, *Megatrends* (New York, William Morrow, 1982).

[28] C. Lee, "Balancing work and family", *Training*, vol. 28, No. 9 (1991), pp. 23-28.

[29] J. Aldous, "Specification and speculation concerning the politics of work place family policies", *Journal of Family Issues*, vol. 11, No. 4 (1990), pp. 355-367.

[30] S. L. Grover, "Predicting the perceived fairness of parental leave policies", *Journal of Applied Psychology*, vol. 72, No. 2 (1991), pp. 247-255.

[31] E. Trzcinski and M. Finn-Stevenson, "A response to arguments against mandated parental leave: Findings from the Connecticut survey of parental leave policies", *Journal of Marriage and the Family*, vol. 53, No. 2 (1991), pp. 445-460.

[32] D. E. Friedman, "Corporate responses to family needs", *Marriage and Family Review*, vol. 15, Nos. 1-2 (1990), pp. 77-97.

[33] L. W. Gladstone, Parental leave legislation, Congressional Research Service, Order Code IB86132 (Washington, D.C., Library of Congress, 1 November 1991).

[34] M. Galen, "Work and Family", Business Week, 28 June 1993, pp. 80-88.

The Concept of FAMILY Health

Introduction[*]

The General Assembly of the United Nations, in its resolution 44/82 of 8 December 1989, proclaimed 1994 as the International Year of the Family (IYF) with its theme of "Family: resources and responsibilities in a changing world". The forty-sixth World Health Assembly, in 1993, adopted resolution WHA46.27, which inter alia urged all Member States "to give effect to the objectives of the International Year of the Family ... including the strengthening of intersectoral collaboration ... as a crucial means for meeting the health and other development needs of families". The resolution also urged the Director-General of WHO:

1. To provide coordinated support ... for research on methods for measuring and evaluating the effects of policies and programmes on the health and functioning of the family and its members, and for determining which families are at risk of not being able to provide for the basic needs of their members;
2. To examine the cost and benefits and social implications of a greater involvement of the family in health promotion, disease prevention, treatment and rehabilitation, with particular emphasis on equity and on sharing of family responsibilities."

At the ninety-third session of the Executive Board, held in 1994, particular note was taken of IYF and it was suggested that the Board should consider submitting to the World Health Assembly a resolution promoting the concept of family health as a programmatic approach at the country level. The resolution should also emphasize that the family should be regarded as the cornerstone of any population policy, and should stress the need to strengthen inter-agency and intersectoral collaboration at the country level.

Describing the family and its functions

In 1990, rather than attempting to define the concept of the family, the Human Rights Committee, in commenting on article 23 of the International Covenant on Civil and Political Rights, noted that the concept of the family might differ in some respects from State to State, and even from region to region within a State. Therefore, it was not possible to give the concept a standard definition. However, the Committee

---

[*] The present paper has been prepared for the IYF secretariat by Dr. Mark Belsey, Programme Manager of the WHO Programme of Maternal and Child Health and Family Planning; Professor Maurice Backett, formerly Professor and Chairman of the Department of Community Medicine, University of Nottingham, United Kingdom of Great Britain and Northern Ireland, and Professor A. Michael Davies, formerly Dean of the School of Public Health, Hebrew University-Hadassah Medical School, Jerusalem, Israel.

emphasized that when a group of persons was regarded as a family under the legislation and practice of a State, it must be given the protection referred to in article 23.

Regardless of its diverse forms, the family is recognized as the social unit upon which societies are built and maintained. It has been described as the natural bridge between the individual and society, and it is recognized as the proper setting for mutual love, support and companionship of spouses, as the primary determinant of the survival of the children born into it, as the first agent for the socialization of future generations, and in many societies as the only institution of support for the aged. Functions of the family include meeting the basic needs of its members for health, nutrition, shelter, physical and emotional care and personal individual development, as well as the maintenance of family morale and the customs, values and beliefs of the family's culture.

Historically, societies have evolved various patterns of family structure for social and economic functions. In pre-industrial societies a great concordance evolved between these functions, with many of the health, developmental and socialization functions taking place first within the family and then within the immediate community. Because there are so many different kinds of family, the concept of family health is often difficult to work with, to describe and for some even to accept. Yet with the decline in the prevalence of traditional family stereotypes (such as the tribe and the extended family) has come an increasing understanding of the social, psychological and biological coherence of the family and its importance. Families share a great deal more than their genes. They share their lifestyles, their intimate and extended environment, often their occupational environment, their diet and exercise patterns and nearly always their infecting and symbiotic organisms. Above all, they share their social environment, its vital roles and relationships, its pressures and pleasures, modes of conduct, value systems, sexual behaviour, mores and beliefs.

In ensuring the well-being of the family and society, both families and Governments perform interrelated tasks in the areas of health, education, income maintenance, social services, employment and housing. Poverty becomes one of the most important pervading and undermining influences on these relationships. Economic production from agriculture has been centered in the family and could accommodate other functions such as child rearing and care giving. The mobility required with the shift to urban-centred industrialized economies has put a strain on these functions, particularly on women who now bear the double burden of the demands of economic activity and caring and rearing functions. The family's responsibility has shifted to preparing individuals to be receptive to change and to value the acquisition of the knowledge and skills necessary for economic production outside the family.

The concept of community and family partnership in some family functions has recently been reviewed in the area of early child health and education [8]. Health services and parents share responsibility for the prevention and clinical management of mild childhood illnesses [12], and through programmes for early child care and education. A child's development and educational potential is more likely to be realized by a combination of day care and in-home reinforcement by transferring knowledge to, and strengthening the child-care and stimulation skills of, the parents and particularly the mother.

Childhood and adolescence are critical times for the acquisition of coping and social skills. This process is dependent on having positive attachments, the opportunity and resources to learn the skills and an absence of overwhelming stressful situations. However, the contrary also holds true. The lack of social and coping skills is too readily transmitted to the next generation, particularly where families offer low quality and inconsistent support to children; provide poor behavioural models for substance abuse; lack closeness and involvement in their children's activities; have low educational aspirations; exert weak control and discipline; and are emotionally, physically or sexually abusive of their children. One form of response has been for children to take to the streets where the other street children provide a sense of belonging to a new and often more caring replacement "family". For these young people, the street has become their habitual abode and their families are not a source of primary support. Depending on the definition used, estimates of the numbers of children and young people affected vary widely, with the majority in the developing countries. Childhope, a non-governmental organization, estimates that there are 40 million street children in Latin America, 25-30 million in Asia and 10 million in Africa.

The family life cycle

The family can be described from several analytical perspectives: the type of family; the stages of the family life cycle; and in terms of such essential demographic descriptors as size and age characteristics. Of the different dimensions used in describing the family, the family life cycle concept appears to be particularly useful in providing a framework for understanding the dynamics of how the family per se affects the health and well-being of its members and how the health and well-being of its members affect the health of the family.

Just as the health of individuals is seen against the life-cycle phases of dependency, growth, maturation, independence and, ultimately, deterioration, so too must the functions of the family be viewed in relation to the stages of its own life cycle. Several family life cycle models have been reviewed by the World Health Organization (WHO)[10]. For the purposes of research on the demography of family life cycles and their health implications, and to exploit the potential availability of cross-sectional data from census or household surveys, six phases of the nuclear family life cycle have been proposed[24]. These are described as:

A Formation;
B Extension;
C Completed extension;
D Contraction;
E Completed contraction;
F Dissolution.

To be useful in developing family health programmes, the family life-cycle model must be adapted and modified to reflect the variations both within the model and between societies. Depending on the purposes to which the model is applied, the number of stages can be either reduced or expanded. For example, additional stages or sub-stages could be inserted to reflect the age of children or other events, such as retirement. Based on the time when the oldest child is found in a particular age category, Duval provides a somewhat expanded family life-cycle model[7], which includes:

- Beginning families (married couples or couples in union without children)
- Child-bearing families (oldest child under 30 months)
- Families with children of pre-school age (oldest child 30 months to 6 years)
- Families with schoolchildren (oldest child 6 to 13 years)
- Families with teenagers (oldest child 13 to 20 years)
- Families as "launching centres" (from the time the first child leaves until the last has left)
- Families in the middle years (from "empty nest" to retirement)
- Ageing families (from retirement to the death of both spouses)[12].

The present model does not accommodate the changing family patterns of a phenomenon such as reconstituted families, those resulting from the divorce or death and the remarriage of the spouse(s); families that begin with child bearing and may not have a stable male presence, at least initially; families that for voluntary or involuntary reasons remain childless; or the extension of the family when grandparents or other older relatives are incorporated into the immediate family structure. The status of a woman will change according to the stage reached in the family life cycle. The daughter-in-law becomes a mother and, ultimately, the mother-in-law.

An example of how the concept of family life cycles can be adapted to such circumstances is found in the West Indies where the marriage patterns do not correspond to the norm found in most industrialized countries. Three types of unions are recognized in the West Indies:
- A married union (two persons living together and legally married)
- A common-law union (two persons living together but not legally married)
- The visiting union (two persons neither living together nor legally married)[9].

The passage through each phase of the family life cycle produces major family events and, at times, disturbances that are often of a severity that could affect the health of one or other family member. They are usually transitional and include episodes such as marriage, birth of the first child, retirement due to age or illness, transient diseases and bereavement. Other crises, while closely related to family life-cycle stages, do not arise from the family life-cycle stage per se. These include events such as death and handicap, divorce, chronic illness, alcoholism and other substance misuse, unemployment and the enforced institutionalization of a family member.

Failure to lay the foundation during one stage for the responsibilities and needs occurring at subsequent stages may result in stress and conflict and deterioration in the functioning of the family in subsequent stages. Lack of preparation and means for planning parenthood has an adverse multiplier effect throughout the family life cycle, affecting parents and children. The immediate consequences of unwanted pregnancies are seen in the 50-to-60-million-induced abortions each year, nearly half performed under unsafe conditions with consequent mortality and morbidity. The long-term effects of bearing an unwanted child are expressed in a wide spectrum of morbidities and even mortality, including child abuse and neglect; increased morbidity; the phenomenon of street children; impairment in socialization, language development, self-esteem and school performance; and may carry over into the next family generation with marital difficulties[4]. Even when marital harmony exists in the first life-cycle stage of formation and the pregnancy is wanted, marital harmony deteriorates in a significant number of couples within a year of the first child's birth[14].

Family structure in a changing world

The most commonly used terms to describe family structure include: the extended family, usually led by the elder male spouse and including the households of male offspring; the nuclear family, consisting of parents and their children; and other family forms that include single-parent-headed families or households, cohabitation and consensual unions. Joint and stem families are variants on the extended family, also characterized as three-generational. Concern is expressed in many societies with what is perceived as the replacement of family structures that do not reflect the perceived norm; namely, the shift from extended to nuclear, and from nuclear to single-parent-headed families and alternative family forms.

Single-parent families now account for nearly 20 to 30 per cent of all families in Africa, Latin America and the Caribbean, and for about 15 per cent in Asia and the Pacific[18]. Ninety per cent of them are headed by women and are often concentrated among the poorest and most disadvantaged sections of the population. Single-parent families also arise as a result of war, migration and hunger. In refugee and other situations of population displacement due to conflict, inadequate attention is paid both in policy and operational terms to ensuring that the integrity of the family is maintained. Studies of children's responses to extreme violence, death, abuse or hunger indicate that they are able to resist emotional stress and physical hardship as long as they remain with their families and parents[3]. Emergencies become significant as soon as separations occur and the child's primary attachments are disrupted.

As an independent unit of production, the joint or extended family provides a secure labour force and an established system for tenure and inheritance. The division of labour within traditional family structures, particularly where geographic mobility is low, is not based primarily on skill or education but according to sex, age and family status. Decision-making in the family's social and economic life is made by the male head of the household, while the private world of the home is the woman's domain.

Economic development, the demand for labour or perceptions of opportunities, and change, resulting in the mobility and migration of individuals and families, have profound effects on the structure, relationships in, and functions of, the family. On the one hand, there is a greater receptivity to change and adoption of beneficial technologies and institutions, including those of the health and education sectors, while on the other hand such change is associated with a decline in traditional community disciplines, erosion of the cultural norms, particularly among the young, and a lessening of the social and cultural bonds that help maintain community self-reliance[5].

In response to economic imperatives, changing value systems and family planning, the majority of families in most regions of the world are smaller and an increasing trend is towards nuclear families. The nuclear family is nowadays more often geographically isolated from its relatives than formerly. More children survive than die, older family members are much older and the proportion of the old and the very old is rising. Isolation and ageing are calling into question traditional roles, straining ties of affection and generally distorting family functions. While this pattern may not yet characterize many developing countries, it is becoming apparent in them, and even the assumption that the extended family model serves as the basic model for the rural areas of developing countries no longer holds true universally. The rapid social changes of both the industrial and information revolutions have changed drastically the functions of the family, particularly its older members, and have shifted many of the health, developmental and social functions to non-family institutions, from which families are often excluded or marginalized.

Gender roles are initiated within the family but are derived from and are parallel to those within the society. They determine the distribution of power and influence within both the family and society. Both within and outside the household, the system of gender relationships include sexual relations between adults, division of labour and gender socialization. These relationships affect not only health issues such as sexually transmitted diseases, including the human immunodeficiency virus/acquired immunodeficiency syndrome (HIV/AIDS) and violence against women and children, but also the division of health decision-making.

Many societies, both modern and traditional, are now paying the price of inequality in negotiating sexual relationships between male and female partners in a family, and the double standard applied to the expression of male sexuality within and outside the family. One expression of this inequity has been that the burden of, and blame for, infertility is placed on women even though up to 40 per cent of infertility may be attributed to a male factor. The term "barrenness" is applied to women, not men. It has strong negative connotations and is the basis of divorce in many traditional societies and religions[23]. Another consequence of the inequality in negotiating sexual relationships in a family has been the increasing burden that AIDS is placing on women and children. The vast majority of women with new HIV infections are monogamous and have acquired the infection from their partners. The inequity must also be measured in terms of the greater risk of HIV transmission from a man to a woman than from a woman to a man. As a consequence, the AIDS epidemic is wiping out hundreds of thousands of families, leaving even more infants and children orphaned, often in the absence of a community support system.

Public health and the advances in medical sciences have contributed to a larger portion of the population living past the age of retirement and economic productivity. In the internationalization of communications and the media, an increasing accent is on youth. This may be contributing in part to the decline in the prestige of older people as their numbers have increased. In addition, in many industrialized countries, owing to the change in lifestyles and structure of the family, be it a single-parent, divorced or reconstituted family, the reintegration of a surviving grandparent into a family may either be perceived as a burden or a benefit, with the former being the more common. The weight of such a burden depends on a number of factors, both physical and psychological: the degree of dependency of the older family member, space and privacy considerations, the psychological aspects of the need for the grandparent to exert control, or the amount of security that the younger couple has in their marriage and as parents.

The role of the elderly in the family is also undergoing considerable change in developing countries, particularly with the urban migration of young people and economically active adults. The elder members of the family and clan retain a key role even after their productive role has ended. They play a key role in the socialization and education of the young, as reservoirs of knowledge and wisdom and the providers of information on parenting and sexuality. As noted by Masamba:

"As older persons become dependent upon the adult and adolescent urban populations because of urban poverty, they ... become vulnerable to being viewed as ndoki (those who exercise witchcraft) every time relatives in the city lose their jobs or suffer from any misfortune or illness."[13]

Changing disease patterns

For several decades, a changing disease pattern, referred to as the epidemiologic transition, has become apparent in many countries as a consequence of the extension of health services, increased coverage of immunization and family planning, increased household food security and improvements in housing, water supplies and environmental sanitation. The epidemiological transition encompasses three elements:

A That common infectious diseases have begun to be replaced by noncommunicable diseases and injuries as the leading cause of death;
B That there is a shift in the peak age of morbidity and mortality from the young to the elderly;

c That a shift occurs by which there is a greater concern with morbidity and not only with mortality.

This transition is not merely a function of the control of communicable disease. It is also characterized by increased rates of the non-communicable diseases that are associated with: changes in lifestyles, especially use of tobacco, and changes in diet and physical activity; technological developments; and environmental degradation. The fragility of the positive elements of this transition and its dependence on sustained social and economic development in general and health infrastructures in particular is illustrated both in the inequity in health development in many developing countries and in the deterioration noted in many of the States of eastern and central Europe and the republics of the former Soviet Union.

In comparison to the changes in mortality and population experienced in the industrialized countries, the decline in mortality in the middle-income developing countries has taken place in a relatively short period of time. Despite the increased control over infectious diseases, they have not been fully brought under control. Furthermore, the adverse elements of the epidemiologic transition are being accelerated by the rapid increase in certain lifestyle patterns, some thought to be associated with the internationalization of the media and commercial interests, including the use of tobacco and abuse of alcohol, inappropriate use of infant formula, and increased risk-taking behaviour associated with injury and sexually transmitted diseases. Thus in many countries a process of a double burden of disease is occurring with the coexistence of the diseases of poverty and those of abundance. In several countries, both developed and developing, epidemic diseases such as tuberculosis and diphtheria, once thought to have been eradicated or controlled, have re-emerged.

Vulnerability to the burden of disease is increasingly evident throughout the life cycle. As a result of a deterioration in their economic and social circumstances, many countries are experiencing a stagnation or even reversal of what had been a pattern of increasing social involvement in health care. The major burden for care is being either shifted more to the family and community or neglected in the absence of suitable models for support to families and communities in the provision of care.

Family health

The idea that there is an entity, family health, which we strive to achieve and when achieved is at the very centre of a healthy society, is attractive and may be valuable in framing social and fiscal policy, designing services and in allocating priorities in social and medical research.

Thus, good family health is said to be recognizable when the family group itself is physically healthy, happy, productive and efficient in carrying out its tasks - particularly those of protecting, nurturing and socializing the next generation - there is a state of emotional equilibrium between the members of the family group, it serves a number of vital human needs, displays integrity in the face of adversity and resilience and the ability to cope.

Family health is more than the sum of the health of its individual members. Family health requires that the family itself is healthy, that it provides nurturing, caring and support to its members even when some family members suffer from ill health. Despite such adverse conditions of poverty, displacement and discrimination, some families have a resilience that allows them to meet the essential caring functions. These families are highly motivated, draw upon strong value systems and contribute to the health of the individual members with knowledge and skill. Much of the responsibility for such care rests on the women of the family, sometimes to the disadvantage of the girl child whose education may be terminated because of the care demands of the family. As the nuclear family becomes the norm and increasingly women assume the double roles of production and reproduction, they are at higher risks of stress and illness.

The family is one of the most important social contexts where illness occurs and is resolved, and it should serve as a primary unit in health and medical care[15]. Within the family an individual is defined as being sick and the process is initiated for seeking and utilizing care. Historically, epidemiology and public health have used the terms "family" and "household" interchangeably. While the former has generally been the unit of analysis and been adequate for characterizing the physical environment of disease transmission and acquisition of communicable diseases, it lacks the dynamic focus of the social and behavioural context that the family implies in terms of the role and position of women in the health of the family, dietary patterns and other aspects of lifestyle such as smoking and substance abuse, and the critical family function of caring. The distinction between household and family may not always be important. Yet, an important health variable such as smoking, for example, can be seen in household terms in relation to the consequences of secondary smoking risks, compounded by variables such as crowding. In family terms, smoking would be seen as a parental influence on smoking by children.

The association of mortality and morbidity with changes in the family life-cycle stages has only recently become the subject of research. The effects of life cycle are seen from the first two stages of family formation and extension, affecting such outcomes as low birth weight, and mortality and morbidity among the elderly, particularly during the last stage of family dissolution. While birth weight is closely associated with medical, anthropometric and risk behaviour factors, Ramsey and others have shown that the family function and structure account for 7 and 4.5 per cent of the known variance of birth weight[17]. Lewis has demonstrated the deterioration of marital relationship in one third of couples following the birth of the first child[14], while Berkman and others have shown an increased risk of death in the first six months following a myocardial infarction in the absence of emotional support systems[2].

The role of the home and the family, as opposed to hospitalization, as the locus of care for even serious diseases and terminal illness for the care of children and adults has been widely demonstrated in industrialized countries[1], yet most health systems remain reluctant to recognize the family as a major resource for ensuring a more acceptable and high quality of care from the perspective of the patient and the family. Such an approach, including the post-operative care following surgery, has been tested in developing countries as well, even in the environments of urban poverty [11]. Not only was the cost of care greatly reduced but also recovery, ambulation and return to normal functions significantly improved.

Indicators of family health

If a healthy family is one that carries out its functions with reasonable success within its own culture, then the functional success of the family will be the key to societal health. Yet there are few indicators of family health as distinct from the health of individual members of the family.

"Despite awareness of the importance of the family unit for personal health conditions and the health care system, the family has ... been infrequently studied from a public health view. ... To a certain extent, the lack of information is due to inadequacies in existing data collection systems, exacerbated by ambiguities in terminology and methodological problems."[20]

The duration of each stage in the family life cycle and family structure serve as two dimensions of a framework for family health indicators. Age at marriage and of first birth already provide a measure of the formation phase of the family life cycle, and provide an indirect indicator of the risks of maternal morbidity and mortality that have a profound impact on the health of other members of the family. The duration of the different stages of the life cycle in 30 countries for the period 1950 to 1970 has been studied by WHO[20]. During this 20-year period, the duration of each stage of the family life cycle increased from 3 to 6 years, mainly due to a decrease in the age of first marriage in countries with low levels of mortality, and to an increase in the duration of the penultimate life-cycle stage of completed family contraction. While these analyses have not been repeated for the period 1970 to 1990, with increasing levels of women in the workforce and their changing role, it might be expected that in some industriaized countries the first stage of family formation would be further prolonged as women delay bearing their first child. A significant shift in the number of women bearing their first child at age 35 or older would be associated with increased obstetric risks and a demand for medically assisted reproduction. Changes in the duration of family life-cycle stages would also be expected in developing countries, particularly with the changing age of marriage, changes in fertility, entry of larger numbers of women into the workforce and changes in levels of education.

A number of existing indicators of morbidity, mortality, growth and development could also serve as indicators of family health. The physical growth and psychosocial development of young children, being almost entirely dependent on the family environment and care, serves as a positive indicator of family health. With "children by choice, not chance" as a positive goal of family health, contraceptive prevalence serves as a positive indicator (see table 14.1 below). Recognizing childbearing as one of the central purposes of family formation, involuntary childlessness or infertility are also important indicators of family health.

Mortality or morbidity rates analysed according to marital status provide a measure of family health. Those who are not married, whether single, separated, widowed or divorced, experience higher mortality rates, particularly regarding cardiovascular deaths, than married people, the differential being higher for men than for women[19]. This is true for all causes of mortality together and particularly for cardiovascular deaths. Moreover, the mortality of widowers is greater than that of married men, at least for the first six months after bereavement[2].

Research is needed on methodologies and criteria for measuring and evaluating the impact of policies and programmes on the health, functioning and integrity of the family and its members; and the cost implications of a greater involvement of the family in health promotion, disease prevention, treatment and rehabilitation. Efforts have been made to develop indicators of family functioning with respect to health. An example of the family-health implications of a few existing indicators of reproductive health are provided in table 14.2 below.

TABLE 14.1. REPRODUCTIVE HEALTH INDICATORS OF FAMILY HEALTH BY GEOGRAPHIC REGION

Region	Married women who want no more children who are not using any method of contraception (Percentage)	Estimated numbers of unsafe abortion per year	Reduction of births if those not wanting more children stopped childbearing (Percentage)
Africa	77	3.3 million	17
Asia	57	10.3 million	33
Europe	-	260,000 (excluding the former republics of the USSR, which are estimated to account for 2.1 million)	-
Latin America and the Caribbean	43	4.6 million	35
Middle East	57	380 000	-

Source: "Monitoring of progress in implementation of strategies for health for all by the year 2000. Third report" (EB95/5).

As concern moves away from medical care (and considerations such as compliance) towards prevention, social care and support systems, knowledge of the family and its persona presumably becomes of even greater importance. However, few well-designed studies support these widely held views, perhaps because so many of them are deemed obvious. From what is known of the dynamics of family life it would also seem obvious that care and support of any kind will benefit the family more if all the relevant details that determine need and response are understood and if the family is treated as a single health unit.

Support needs of families and vulnerable families

Health is affected by developments in other sectors, and ill health has repercussions on many other sectors, including education, social welfare, housing, women's affairs, trade, agriculture, employment, criminal justice and the environment. What is less well appreciated is that the locus of these effects often operates within the family setting and within the fam-

TABLE 2. EXAMPLES OF INDICATORS OF FAMILIES FOR CAPACITY-BUILDING EFFORTS

Indicators of families at risk and suitable for action	Underlying factors or circumstances	Effects or family functions	Family members affected and way in which they are affected	Prevention: policies and programmes at the level of the family and community	Treatment or rehabilitation at the level of family/community
Unwanted birth	Unwanted pregnancy or ambivalence; limited education; lack of social support; lack of information and access to contraception; hostile cultural environment; legal constraints; social position of women	Increased risk of neglect; competition for food and affection within the family; impoverishment of the family; increased infant and child morbidity and mortality	Abandonment of work/education by the mother; increased risk in next pregnancy; competition for scarce household resources; child neglected, abandoned or given up for adoption	Equity in education of girls; capacity of the family for family life and sex education within the family and other institutions; availability and easy access to family planning services; freedom of choice in and diversification of reproductive health services; communication	Creation of social services and legislation to support the family; maternity and paternity leave; child-care services; support programmes for pregnant teenagers to continue school
Low birth weight (LBW)	Teenage pregnancy; substance abuse; short height; poor nutrition during pregnancy and pre-pregnancy; infection; heavy physical work. LBW serves as a more sensitive health indicator of social economic changes than infant mortality	Abandonment (particularly by single women); poor bonding; less breast-feeding; malnutrition at one year of age; increased childhood morbidity and mortality, learning and developmental disorders; increased risk of adult disease (diabetes, hypertension etc.) with increased illness, absenteeism, health-care costs etc.	Infant at increased risk of illness, malnutrition and cognitive and other impairment of development. Mother and other care-givers faced with increased care and nurturing demands. Diversion of care and attention from other children	Equity in health, education and nutrition for the girl child; "peri-conceptual" nutrition; maternity protection legislation and enforcement; increase in the age of first pregnancy	Bonding and breast-feeding: the baby-friendly hospital; mother's social support groups; crèche and early child education

ily many of the positive interventions promoting health, development and the well-being of individual family members may be most readily applied and integrated. Despite the awareness of these relationships, the family is underutilized. Communities then draw upon other institutions and resources, resulting in a greater fragmentation of responses to health and other developmental needs. All too frequently, the families in greatest need, i.e., those needing support in multiple sectors, slip through the social safety net or are recognized too late, when more costly therapeutic approaches are required. The concept of vulnerable families should be recognized and defined within the health sector and intersectorally so effective preventive action can be taken. To avoid the stigma that could be attached to labelling a family as being at risk, preferably attach the notion of risk to the particular situation making the family vulnerable and speak of families in hazardous situations.

Responses to stressful events and the ability to cope seem to be determined by the quality of relationships within the family reflected in the common patterns to be found in their robustness, their strength, their resilience or in the breakdowns that result. Gross or permanent distortion is relatively uncommon and most families achieve an equilibrium. They are more or less successful in their family relationships. One important response to stressful life events and the strain on the relationships involved can be physical illness and even specific diseases[18], but causal pathways are often unclear.

Some responses are simple and obvious; for example, the support of a sick spouse, more often of husbands by wives, is a key element in the successful control of many acute diseases. This seems to be due to the increased pressure to comply with the prescribed treatment and to provide an ordered, facilitating environment. Another example would be the need of a parent to adhere to a specific diet for a child and the consequent change in the dietary patterns of the whole supportive family. The same is true where an asthmatic child must avoid defined allergens, necessitating a change of internal environment for the whole family.

Divorce and the separation of parents, by threatening secure relationships, have profound effects on the health of the children. These effects are second only to the death of one parent. As noted in a meeting on children and family breakdown held by WHO, the consequences for children depend on their age and stage of development.

"A family separation immediately after birth can ... be critical. For example, loss of contact with the father in the first years of life can cause identification problems, particularly for boys. Although at this stage family breakdown often causes developmental and behavioural retardation resulting in lasting damage, young children have a remarkable ability to make up for lost ground and in the long term, if the crisis is managed, they will probably show no health deficiencies ... children from three to five years old can exhibit considerable distress through regression, and behavioural and psychological disorders such as aggression, fear and sleeping disorders ... between six and ten, children are more likely to react to family breakdown with sorrow and depression ... amazingly, children at this age can give emotional support to their parents, although they are also susceptible to parental manipulation."[20, 21]

Illness and the dependency of grandparents place a particular stress on the nuclear family. The need to care for elderly relatives, often living in a separate household, can also cause stress especially if associated with feelings of guilt for past neglect. Poorer families may not be able to take care of their elders, particularly if distance or limited accommodation intervene. In some cases feelings of guilt are even greater when there is pressure to seek institutional solutions.

Some families, for a variety of reasons, including the legacies of their own families, are more vulnerable than others because:

A   They are unable to meet the basic needs of their members for health, nutrition, shelter, physical and emotional care, and personal individual development;

B   They experience physical or psychological exploitation or abuse of individual members, injustice in the distribution of rights and responsibilities or distortion of the roles of their members;

C   They are subject to break-up as a consequence of external economic, social or political factors.

Large numbers of families can be considered at risk in a variety of circumstances owing to forces beyond their immediate control, particularly under circumstances of war, drought, famine, racial and ethnic violence, and economic deprivation. Labour migration provoked by poverty, single-parent families, refugee and displaced families, and those whose livelihoods have been destroyed by environmental degradation, are but a few examples of such families at risk. Identifying the characteristics of families able to provide for the basic needs of their members would be desirable in these circumstances to support and strengthen such characteristics and circumstances in other families.

Within populations of families who are providing for the basic needs of their members are individual and groups of families that, for intra-familial reasons, lack the capacity to meet the basic needs of their members. These families may manifest a variety of problems, including domestic violence, drug and alcohol dependency, sexual and child abuse, and neglect. Until such time as the full pathology of these families becomes apparent, other public or voluntary institutions, if they and the resources exist, assume a greater responsibility for the family nurturing and caring functions.

Family functioning can be described at three levels:

A   Families that function within the norms of their culture despite the stress of development and social change;
B   Families that for whatever reason are vulnerable but have not yet manifested serious dysfunction and breakdown;
C   Families in which the breakdown of function has already occurred.

In situations where this functional breakdown, affecting the health of the next generation and society at large, is already a reality, four main functions are threatened. First, the broad biological functions of protection and care. Next, the economic and social support functions of the family, then the educational and sociocultural functions concerned with the socialization of children and youth, and, finally, the psychological functions concerned with intra-family relationships and ties of affection.

The functions of the family most susceptible to disruption and most sensitive to the damaging effects of demographic, social, economic and technical change are not necessarily the most important for family survival. Thus disturbed relationships within the family, arguably of great importance in the long run, are less immediately catastrophic than are the effects of severe deprivation, inadequate economic resources, unemployment, hunger, isolation, forced displacement or serious disease. Each of these threatens the economic and protective functions of the family, which are vital to its immediate survival.

These major functions, like all those upon which family integrity and, thence in the long-term, societal integrity depends, are not distinct but are interrelated. Often the breakdown of family integrity is seen in terms of specific problems such as alcoholism or other substance abuse, mental illness, violence to women and child abuse, adolescent and unwanted pregnancies, and most recently AIDS. Strategic support from the community or State, if available, is usually problem-specific, yet to be most efficient and effective, it should be family- and system-oriented in its approach.

The consequences of functional breakdown will always be culture-specific but, at the individual level, they will have a serious effect on children and the next generation. At worst this means inadequate socialization, a loss of ties of affection, dysfunctional or damaging relationships, and delinquent, authoritarian and violent behaviour. At the community level, violence and crime feature prominently with high non-specific morbidity, all with serious implications for an unhappy, insecure and angry society in the future. But these are the crude effects of functional breakdown and it may be more accurate to assume that all aspects of the quality of family life are damaged when its normal function is much disturbed. Whatever the causal pathways are, a clustering of factors in a relatively small proportion of families renders them vulnerable to breakdown. A small proportion of vulnerable families break down and an even smaller proportion of them do so catastrophically. The effect on society of this small number of serious breakdowns is disproportionately large.

Families are vulnerable to dysfunction and breakdown for a variety of reasons; some can be predicted and prevented. The prevalence of vulnerable families in the population is rarely measured, partly because of the lack of suitable indicators and partly because of the compartmentalization of responses by individual sectors. Little is known about this type of family until such time as the problems begin to manifest themselves. If left undiagnosed and untreated, these highly vulnerable families would soon add considerably to the burden of suffering and cost to the community. If, following early diagnosis, effective intervention prevented further breakdown, the benefit would be considerable and disproportionate, all the more so if the interventions strengthened the families' capacity to deal with the immediate and subsequent problems.

Diagnosis of vulnerability to imminent breakdown presents a screening challenge. However, little is known of the accuracy (the specificity and sensitivity) of most screening tools, the predictive power of risk factors or the recovery rates with treatment. Several methods have been suggested but would require further evaluation in a variety of cultural settings. A number of research tools have been used to measure the functional capacity of families within larger population groups. Little is known, however, of the usefulness of family-oriented clinical tools to practising physicians. In one study, a large group of physicians engaged in a family practice were asked to rate the usefulness of 10 family-oriented tools. The respondents indicated a desire to develop their family counselling skills. Most family-oriented tools were reported to be useful but were used infrequently by the practising physicians[16]. These and other tools have been examined as epidemiological tools in other settings[6, 25], but rarely as clinical instruments. At present many if not most of the tools that exist require special skills in their application and interpretation. Treatment of those families deemed to be at the edge of breakdown would be dictated at first by general considerations and the family's special needs, later by the success or failure of the care provided and the resources of the family.

In Sri Lanka a nine-item field instrument has been developed for use by community health workers to identify "families at risk"[22]. The items address the age of the mother; the number of children under the age of three years; the mother's/caretaker's knowledge of the child's needs and his/her responsiveness to health messages; whether the mother/caretaker is mentally disordered or severely depressed; whether he/she is neglectful of, or shows no interest in, the well-being/development of the child; cleanliness and organization of the home; whether the father is known to be delinquent, alcoholic or otherwise mentally disordered; presence of severe marital discord; and abject poverty.

The prevalence of the dysfunctional, damaged family is relatively low but its disintegration is usually long, costly and places a great burden on a wide range of available services. Intervention is rarely successful and much suffering results. At least one generation of children is without support and the effects are serious. Resource use is prodigal and disproportionate and the benefit-to-cost ratio of treatment is low. Effective prevention is preferred to the more costly and less effective therapeutic approaches to such families. First-aid measures in some developed countries involve special housing, sheltered accommodation for threatened wives and children, substantial money grants and the re-equipping and retaining of rehoused families. Much of the time of the social services is expended on repeated breakdowns.

There have been only a few long-term cohort studies of the generation-to-generation effects of family breakdown, but these are not encouraging. Damage is reported, particularly to children's and adolescent's mental health, and to their ability to form lasting relationships. Consequently, countries that can afford it make special financial provision for long-term assistance. Once again, many sectors are involved and coordination is difficult. Legal commitments are lengthy and costly: most countries cannot afford them.

Among families subjected to almost impossible stresses such as war and extreme deprivation, a small group of survivors almost always, against considerable odds, remain with their family functions damaged but not destroyed. A study of their material, psychological and other assets, their attitudes and the sources of their resilience would be as rewarding as the studies of risk factors for breakdown.

In spite of the stresses imposed by development and social change, most families function satisfactorily within the norms of their culture. For them, the objective of health promotion is to maintain this normality through the continued transfer of existing and new knowledge and skills for healthy lifestyles and self-care. These include examples such as: the promotion of healthy food and nutrition, including breast-feeding; oral health; avoidance of substance abuse, including tobacco; responsible sexual behaviour, as well as adequate orientation about sexuality for the young; exercise; personal hygiene; safety in the home; the use of simple and safe home-based remedies such as oral rehydration salts for diarrhoeal disease; and the appropriate and timely use of health services.

New participatory educational approaches will strengthen family resources and emphasize new responsibilities for self-care and family health behaviour. At the same time, a sensitive community takes what legislative, fiscal and programmatic steps it can afford to reduce external threats and increase family security; to effect supportive food, nutrition and health policies; and to facilitate the transfer to the family of the necessary coping and other skills. Priority would be given to those activities with the highest yield in cost and benefit terms. Thus, support for women, and security of food supply, living space and employment, the care and protection of children, promotion of healthy behaviour among adolescents, safe motherhood, family planning, universal literacy and, far less tangible but nearly as important, steps to encourage family membership of supportive neighbourhood and community groups would all have a high priority. Practical attempts by the educational sector to address the issue of health promotion and protection within families require changes in school curricula. Schoolchildren can become effective agents of health education within the family.

When families have been mobilized in support of health development, be it for health promotion, protection, care and rehabilitation, the focus has been on specific problems, often approached in an ad hoc or crisis management manner. Yet many of the problems faced are interrelated and could be dealt with by using a common set of skills and knowledge transferable to families. Access to information and communication and negotiation skills within families are key ingredients in child care, optimal functioning of the elderly, support of women's needs in the family, household food security, adolescent health, family planning and the role of men.

Implications of family health for national action

International instruments, such as the Convention on the Rights of the Child (General Assembly resolution 44/25) and the Convention on the Elimination of All Forms of Discrimination against Women (General

Assembly resolution 34/180) are strongly supportive of the role and functions of the family. By ratifying such instruments, a country undertakes to meet the obligations embodied in them and must report regularly on the progress it is making in doing so. The Convention on the Elimination of All Forms of Discrimination against Women underlines the equal responsibilities of men and women in the context of family life.

The tasks in supporting families are formidable and challenging: for the individual family itself, for education, for social and fiscal policy, for local communities, for international agencies and institutions and for the health and social welfare systems. With these tasks comes the danger that attempted in isolation they will dissipate scarce resources and lose their multiplicative effect; a coordinated approach would raise both yield and understanding.

Unless the forces of change are too destructive to be resisted, families respond to challenge with surprising resilience, and the essential functions of the family often survive the most intense assaults. Thus groups of abandoned street children sometimes care for their younger members as if they were in families. Local communities spontaneously look after their elderly and sick, supporting them emotionally as well as physically. Responsibilities universally recognized as those of the family seem to be readily assumed by most human groups, later to be incorporated into the culture before passing into national social policies and sometimes becoming laws. Paradoxically, when these actions create new institutions or mechanisms for care, which may be outside the structure or value system of the family, the family's capacity for effective functioning and support may be weakened.

When this happens the State is often accused of usurping the functions of the family to the detriment of all concerned, particularly children. To avoid such pitfalls, intervention by public or voluntary agencies should be designed so as not to make the family a passive recipient of care, but an active participant with due recognition and support being accorded to the functions of the family. Economic support and legal protection are two areas that can buttress the functions of the family. The integrity of the family is so important that its protection from catastrophe should, when affordable, become a normal responsibility of the State.

Conclusion

The functions of the family have been described in relation to the six stages of the family life cycle: formation; extension; completed extension; contraction; completed contraction; and dissolution. Each phase of the family life cycle produces major family events and disturbances often of a severity that the health of one or other family member could be affected. Also altering family functions are changes in the roles and status of women: a new dynamic linked to longer education, literacy, the means to control fertility and women's changing economic value and role. Families share a great deal more than their genes; their lifestyles, their intimate and extended environment, often their occupational environment, their diet and exercise patterns and nearly always their infecting and symbiotic organisms. Above all, they share their social environment, its vital roles and relationships, its pressures and pleasures, modes of conduct, value systems, sexual behaviour, mores and beliefs. The concept of vulnerable families should be recognized and defined within the health sector and intersectorally so effective preventive action can be taken. Vulnerable families can be described as those likely to be unable to meet the basic needs of their members for health, nutrition, shelter, physical and emotional care, and personal individual development; to experience physical or psychological exploitation or abuse of individual members, injustice in the distribution of rights and responsibilities or distortion of the roles of its members; or to be subject to break-up as a consequence of external economic, social or political factors. In spite of the stresses imposed by development and social change, most families function satisfactorily within the norms of their culture. For them, the objective of health promotion is to maintain this normality through the continued transfer of existing and new knowledge and skills for healthy lifestyles and self-care.

References

1. Bergman A. B., H. Shrand *and* T. E. Oppe. A pediatric home care program in London - Ten years's experience. *Pediatrics*, 36(3):314-321, 1965.
2. Berkman L. F., L. Leo-Summers *and* R. I. Horowitz. Emotional support and survival after myocardial infarction. A prospective, population-based study of the elderly. *Annals of internal medicine*, 117(12):1003-1009, 1992.
3. Black D. Children and disaster. *British medical journal*, 285 (6347):989-990, 1982.
4. Born unwanted: developmental effects of denied abortion. By H. P. David *and others*. New York, Springer, 1988.
5. Campbell, 1990, as cited in Economic and Social Commission for Asia and the Pacific. The changing role of the family as a social institution in development in the Asia-Pacific region. United Nations, New York, 1991.
6. Chung Y. S. Analysis of factors affecting family function. *Kanho Hakhoe Chi*, 20(1):5-15, 1990.
7. Duval E. M. Family development. Philadelphia, Lippincott, 1962. As cited by L. Herberger and P.J.M. McEwan *in* The family as a unit in health studies. *In* Health and the family: Studies on the demography of family life cycles and their health implications. World Health Organization, 1978.
8. Evans J. *and* P. M. Shah. Child-care programmes for health and family support. *World Health Statistical Quarterly*, 46:214-221, 1993.
9. Germany. Federal Institute for Population Research, in collaboration with the World Health Organization. Family life cycle indicators for the West Indian family? A preliminary approach. *By* Roberts G. W. *and* S. A. Sinclair. In Health and the family life cycle: Selected studies on the interaction between mortality, the family and its life cycle, 1982.
10. Health and the family life cycle: Selected studies on the interaction between mortality, the family and its life cycle. 1982.
11. Guerrero R. Personal communications on the implementation of a controlled study of ambulatory surgery. Cali, Colombia, 1972.
12. Hardy J. B. *and* R. Streett. Family support and parenting education in the home: an effective extension of clinic-based preventive health care services for poor children. *Journal of Pediatrics*, 115(6):927-931, 1989.
13. International Federation on Ageing and the World Council of Churches, Office of Family Education. Older persons and their families in a changing village society. *By* M. Masamba. 1984.
14. Lewis J. M. The transition to parenthood: II. Stability and change in marital structure. *Family Process*, 27(3):273-283, 1988.
15. Litman T. The family as a basic unit in health and medical care: A social behavioural overview. *Social Science & Medicine*, 8:495-519, 1974.
16. Physicians' usefulness ratings of family-oriented clinical tools. By S. North *and others*. *Journal of Family Practice*, 37(1):30-34, July 1993.
17. Ramsey C. N. Jr, T. D. Abell *and* L. C. Baker. The relationship between family functioning, life events, family structure, and the outcome of pregnancy. *Journal of Family Practice*, 22(6):521-527, 1986.
18. United Nations. The world's women: trends and statistics 1970-1990. New York, 1991. Social statistics and indicators, series K, No. 8. 120 p. Sales No. E.90.XVII.3.
19. Wingard D. L. The sex differential in morbidity, mortality and lifestyle. *Annual Review of Public Health*, 5:433-458, 1984.
20. World Health Organization. Introduction. Health and the family: studies on the demography of family life cycles and their health implications. By H. Hansluwka. 1978.
21. Regional Office for Europe. Children and family breakdown. Report of a WHO Meeting: EURO reports and studies 101, 1986.
22. Report of a WHO workshop of investigators on indicators of physical growth and psychosocial development in primary health care. New Delhi, 10 to 13 September 1985, 1986. (WHO/MCH/86.2)
23. The epidemiology of infertility with particular reference to Africa. By M. A. Belsey. *Bulletin of the World Health Organization*, 54:319-341, 1976.
24. The family as a unit in health studies. *In* Health and the family: Studies on the demography of family life cycles and their health implications. By L. Herberger *and* P.J.M. McEwan. 1978.
25. Yodfat Y. The family approach in primary care: new conceptual models. *Israeli Journal of Medical Sciences*, 19(8):714-718, 1983.

FAMILY Agents and Beneficiaries of Socio-Economic Development

Introduction: Links between families and social development[*]

The Programme of Action from the World Summit for Social Development reflects the issues and consensus generated through the work of the International Year of the Family (IYF), which has underscored the manifold links between families and the development process. The opportunity provided by this conjuncture is to give substance to the assertion that families, in their various and diverse structures, are central to processes of social development, both as active participants and potential beneficiaries.

The three core issues addressed by the World Summit for Social Development: the alleviation and reduction of poverty; the expansion of productive employment; and the enhancement of social integration, are the most crucial objectives for achieving sustainable social development. This agenda encompasses the formidable task of addressing and redressing the global inequalities manifested between and within countries, and the wastage of human resources generated by the lack of productive employment, poverty and social disintegration.

The present chapter asserts that a framework placing people and their human security at the centre of the social development process must necessarily focus on the family networks. They are where most people live their lives; they account for the contexts in which individuals carry out their human functions of the care, nurture and development of children and young people, and in which intimacy and the intergenerational production of resources and their allocation takes place. People do not engage with formal economies, civil society or political systems and public policies as atomized individuals. Indeed, quite to the contrary, most people bear responsibilities for others, as part of family networks, based on reciprocity and interdependence. Furthermore, the manifestations of poverty, exclusion from productive employment and exclusion from social participation and adequate resources, which poverty entails, are not individual experiences, but are experienced by entire family networks. The failure to take a family-centric approach to social development will have the consequence of neglecting a whole sphere of potential participants, or of producing fragmented solutions likely to be ineffective in redressing inequalities or promoting social integration. This is particularly so when labour market and structural adjustment programmes, labour migration policies and development investment programmes are predicated on individuals as

---

[*] This chapter has been prepared for the IYF secretariat by Bettina Cass, Professor of Sociology and Social Policy, University of Sydney, New South Wales, and Chairperson of the Australian National Council for the International Year of the Family, and Father David Cappo, National Director of the Australian Catholic Social Welfare Commission and executive member of the Australian National Council for the International Year of the Family.

units of labour, rather than on family units and networks as the basis of primary human sociation, employment and innovation.

The observance of IYF at the international, national and regional levels has clearly demonstrated that what are often perceived only as economic policies; for example, education and training, employment generation programmes, migration programmes (both intercountry and cross-country migration), and investment in economic development, affect, and are affected by, the ties that exist within family units and the resources generated by family units. When this fact is properly understood, the dichotomy between economic policies and social policies is dissolved and it becomes evident that the only way satisfactorily to address sustainable social development is to recognize the central role that families play in community development. Furthermore, the arguments become clear for the resourcing and empowering of families as active participants in the reduction of poverty and inequality and the expansion of productive employment.

Over the past decade, awareness has been growing of the failure on the part of national economies and international transfers of finance and services in the form of traditional aid policies to progress beyond even the partial alleviation of poverty to facilitate strong and sustainable social development. Over 1 billion (approximately 25 per cent) of the world's population experience absolute material poverty.[1] As a result of such exclusion, adults, and the family members who depend upon them because of their youth or their old age, are deprived of fundamental opportunities and resources that would facilitate long-term social development and human security. These opportunities and resources include access to a reliable quality and quantity of nutrition, health care and sanitation, and elementary education; adequate remuneration for work carried out in the formal sector as well as the informal sector; and adequate social and material support for the most vulnerable groups. In addition, it is vital to consider the 120 million and more people worldwide who are officially unemployed, both in the developing countries and the industrialized countries of western and eastern Europe, and to recognize the impact of this marginalization on their families, in terms of severely reduced incomes, and loss of social participation and opportunities.

Economic growth cannot be considered outside of the context of social development; to do so would be to ignore the human participants in the processes of growth, and the social and family groupings in which their work and intimate lives are lived. The traditional concept of economic growth has placed insufficient emphasis on the provision of resources and services. However, the promotion, within the context of this narrow concept, of social development and human security so as to achieve a more equal distribution of economic welfare has, paradoxically, been detrimental to the process of economic growth itself. The emphasis on economic growth as an end in itself, without a corresponding global investment in human resources and across socio-economic groups within countries, has reinforced the barriers to the social and economic participation of those who are most disadvantaged in the distribution of income and wealth. Such omissions have also been made in respect to the whole family network, to the detriment of women and their opportunities for advancement and education. These approaches have not distributed equitably the benefits of economic growth. By not adopting a family-centric view of social and economic development, a major productive resource is overlooked because of the failure to recognize that the provision of resources to women, children and families in poverty is an investment in human security. Furthermore, such provision would yield high dividends in economic and social development beyond simply alleviating poverty, which is a necessary but short-term goal, by enriching the capacities of families to become active participants in social development.[1]

Entities such as the International Council on Social Welfare, the International Council of Voluntary Agencies and the United Nations Development Programme, with the support of national welfare and human rights organizations, have advocated overturning the false dichotomy maintained in national and international policy between the goals of economic growth and social development. These groups were active, in preparation for the World Summit for Social Development, in highlighting and seeking to redress:

A The inadequacies of short-term economic policy initiatives that have not recognized the capacity of people to contribute to sustainable social development when they have the resources to do so;

B The urgent need for private and government investment to be woven around people and their environments rather than the reverse;

C The need for long-term social development strategies to be based on community participation in regional structures, rather than on a narrowly defined welfare focus.[2,3,4,5]

Even this conceptualization of the role of people in social development does not go far enough, since it sees the actors in social development as individuals and communities. What is omitted in this configuration are the intermediary networks of family life, family-based productive systems and resource allocations, as well as families as decision makers, through which most people contribute to formal economies and the development of their communities.

A commonly accepted focus when families, economic policy and social policy are placed in the one configuration is to view families as being passively affected by the social and economic policies of countries and international institutions; as being dependent on economic and social development; and as victims of underdevelopment, economic restructuring and unemployment. These constraints on, and barriers to, families' work of care and nurture, as well as the serious reduction of their economic welfare and their capacity to contribute to economic activity and civil society must be fully appreciated if these problems are to be challenged and addressed. Families have needs that require intervention; however, this is only one side of the interactive equation.

In an interactive framework, families are seen as the central agents of social and economic development. The present chapter maintains that a series of interdependencies exist between families and formal economies, as well as between families and civil society, that need to be recognized if social development is to be effective, sustainable and equitable.

According to the Executive Summary of the Draft Declaration and Draft Programme of Action of the World Summit for Social Development: "the implementation of the proposed Programme of Action, and more generally, social progress, requires the active involvement of all actors".[6] It is a vital contribution of IYF that it is families who must be reframed as the central participants in the processes of economic and social development. Indeed, it has been stated during the course of 1994 that: "the family is a powerful agent for social, political, economic and cultural change and a potential vehicle for development".[7]

This position is succinctly summarized in the first Occasional Paper published by the IYF secretariat:

"In short, families are engines of the economic and social development process, and must be accounted for when establishing policies and priorities for economic and social development."[8]

Valuing the work of families as a contribution to social development

Families and their members are necessary contributors to the objectives of the World Summit for Social Development through their own production of goods, services and caring work and the intergenerational flow of them; through their active involvement in shaping their communities and their productive economies; and in their roles as nurturers and educators of children and young people. The corollary is that economic and social policies supportive of families' work and functions are essential if the role of families as participants in the process of social development is to be fully realized.

The term "families" is intended to encompass the diversity of family types, including two-parent families, women-headed families (about one third of the world's households), generationally extended families, families reconstituted following death, separation or divorce, and networks of kin that extend well beyond the household but that constitute the surrounding micro-economy and micro-society where most families are embedded in the industrialized as well as developing world.[9] Families must also be seen not as homogeneous entities, which can be represented by the concept of a household head, usually male, but as flexible and interactive units, composed of men and women, children, young people and the elderly, whose separate interests must be protected and supported. Protection and support must be provided, in the first instance, within the family, reinforced by other social, legal and political processes that are the subject of United Nations instruments concerned with the elaboration and protection of human rights, particularly the International Covenant on Civil and Political Rights and its Optional Protocol, the International Covenant on Economic, Social and Cultural Rights, the Convention on the Rights of the Child and the Convention on the Elimination of All Forms of Discrimination against Women. The dialectical nature of families' lives and processes makes them participants in the processes of economic and social development, and that must be the focus of the investment policies of social development.

The idea has been promulgated by some sociologists and economists that, with the increased spread and pervasiveness of industrial market economies, families have shifted from being units of production to units of consumption, except in times of economic strain.[10] The myth must be dispelled that families are no more than units of consumption, and furthermore, dependent on Governments and other institutions for support as if the flow of resources and benefits was unidirectional. Much has been said, and correctly, about the key role of supportive public policies that recognize that the work and functions of families are not private matters but generative of public goods and public benefits, in particular the public good of child care and child development.[11] But it is also crucial to emphasize the reciprocity and multidirectional nature of these resource flows: the vast production and distribution of goods and services generated within and between families, and their contribution to both economy and society.[12]

A growing body of empirical evidence, influenced strongly by feminist reinterpretations of the value of domestic and care-giving work,[13] indicates that reconceptualizing the work of families not as consumption but as the non-market production of goods and services, particularly in respect to the care of children, young people and vulnerable family members, provides a more interactive framework for identifying family members as full participants in the formal economy, civil society and the local community. Even in the highly industrial market economies of the member States of the Organization for Economic Cooperation and Development (OECD) the value of the goods and services produced within families and households is considerable.

What value has been placed on the household production of goods and services, and why should these forms of production be conceptualized as production, rather than consumption? Posing this question in the context of several highly industrialized countries in the region covered by OECD, Chadeau conceptualized the non-market production by households as: "the goods and services household members produce for their own consumption by combining their unpaid labour and the goods and services they acquire on the market".[14] The value added generated by these activities, and particularly by the work of family care, is excluded from conventional macro-economic calculations and aggregates. The systems of national accounts therefore seem to deem that the production of families and households is worth nothing, but this non-market work both increases the value of goods and services and "contributes to the formation and upkeep of human capital".[14] Estimating the volume and value of household production in Australia, France, Germany, Norway and the United States of America, using a number of methods, Chadeau found the contribution made by women to this form of production varied from two thirds to three quarters of the total time spent on household production by men and women. In addition, the value of this production varied from 60 per cent to 69 per cent of the gross national product or gross domestic product in all five countries, depending on the type of measurement used.

Furthermore, in the traditional sectors of developing countries, households are primary producers of subsistence goods and services that directly and immediately determine the survival chances of family members.[15] In these countries also, women are economically active in both the formal and informal sectors, while having major responsibility for household production.

Clearly, therefore, families, and particularly women, in their non-market work of care and in their informal work in households and extended family systems of non-market and small-scale market production, provide the infrastructure on which the formal sector of the economy depends. Social development is therefore directly linked to the active role of families, both in market employment and in the non-market production of goods and services, particularly in the provision of care and nurture. Consequently, resources allocated to social development, both through national revenues and through international development programmes, should not be conceptualized as social expenditure, but as social investment.

This recognition of the production activities of families in the formal as well as the informal sectors of the economy has direct implications for the long-term formation and development of human resources. Productive activity in the informal sector of caring and household work is greatly underestimated in its role of supporting household members, often in the extended kin network as well as in the immediate family, although such support underpins the education and training of men, women and children, and their current and future employment. Indeed, in conventional development models, such family-relevant, and thus gender-relevant considerations largely tend to be ignored. Placing family production activities in accounts under the heading of "consumption" and not providing training and investment, particularly to women through development programmes, has had detrimental impacts on national and family productivity.[15]

Investment (financial, social, education and training) directed to all family members, to women, as well as to men, children and young people, can develop both the formal and informal sectors of the economy, and both sectors contribute to raising living standards. Such investments in the informal sector may also lead to tradable activity in the formal sector, as well as to the education and vocational training of men and women better able to contribute to output, innovation and growth. A growing amount of evidence indicates that investment in human resources - in people and their capacities and opportunities - constitutes the meeting ground of economic and social policy concerned with both economic growth and the reduction of inequality. Recent economic theory has identified a correlation between social investment, human resource development, the reduction of poverty and inequality, and economic growth, and insists that the first three must be inputs to economic growth, if equitable outcomes are to ensue.[16]

This position was elaborated, in part, in the Statement of the Finnish Programme Committee to the twenty-sixth Annual Conference of the International Council for Social Welfare, held at Tampere, Finland, in July 1994. In calling for an "Integrated Social Development Strategy", the document stated:

"The World Summit for Social Development of 1995 should be made into a turning point that calls for the re-examination of the relationship between economic growth and social development. Following the United Nations Conference on Environment and Development, it is increasingly understood that there are limits to economic growth that focuses on the expansion of material consumption levels. On the other hand, it is people ... that are in the focus of development both as agents for change and as beneficiaries. Economic growth should not be seen as an end in its own right, but as a necessary but not sufficient means towards sustainable social development. In fact, a reliable social infrastructure, social security and services are necessary prerequisites for successful economic transformation and development."[17]

Acknowledging this view is not only essential but one must go well beyond it: it is not people as individual actors who are the agents and beneficiaries of social development. It is people in their intimate social connections in families and households who are central to sustainable social development and economic growth. This recognition requires a focus on investing resources in families, as well as on developing the whole range of social infrastructure. Indeed, in a range of significant ways, families are the locus of active decision-making in the growth and development of productive systems, human settlements, migration flows, the shape of modern labour markets, and the call for enhanced education and vocational training. Seeing families as key actors in social development encapsulates a future orientation that places the valuing of children and future generations as the central objective for the elimination of poverty and inequality.

One of the implications of this view is that the other key actors in the processes of social development - Governments, regional organizations, the international community, the multilateral development banks, the private sector, including employers, workers and their unions and associations, education systems, non-governmental organizations and other institutions of civil society - must put families in the centre of their policies and investment practices. Alternatively, failure to do so impairs both long-term planning and the development of human security and economic efficiency, since the importance of intergenerational relations and the implicit future orientation of such relations are not recognized; nor are the developmental roles of families exploited and strengthened.

The following two examples illustrate the paramount importance of a family-centric view of social development:
- If the processes of devising and implementing policies of social development that are aimed at reducing child mortality, maternal mortality, child malnutrition and illiteracy; providing safe water and sanitation; and extending education for girls as well as boys, do not take account of culturally diverse patterns of family life and intra-family relationships, as well as the relationships between families

and the economic system, then the initial objectives are likely to have limited success.
- In the case of unemployed workers and workers who do not earn enough to escape poverty, the most effective form of social protection includes the expansion of opportunities for remunerative work and assistance in obtaining work through active employment policies (including education, vocational training, job placement services, guaranteed employment schemes and direct employment creation). If such active employment policies do not take a family-centric view, focusing on women as well as men as potential family breadwinners, and on the opportunities for young people that their parents' employment is likely to generate, then they are no more than partial responses to the deep-seated problems of unemployment. Since experiences of unemployment tend to be concentrated in families, and their effects felt throughout families, the public policy responses must provide opportunities for the whole family of potential labour force participants to be reintegrated into the labour force.

Three principles of human security to guide social development

Three intersecting concepts of justice: integenerational equity, gender equity are used in this chapter to develop a framework concerned with the key principles underlying human security.

Intergenerational equity

The concept of intergenerational equity highlights the cross-generational flows of material, emotional and cultural resources generated by families and by their work of care and nurture in all its dimensions; for children, young people and other family members made vulnerable by age, disability or severe illness. This contribution, in the so-called private domain, is of such magnitude that it demands not only reciprocal public responses in recognition of it, but also a fundamental reconceptualization of family policies not as social expenditure but social investment. Such policies would include family payments, health and welfare services for women and children, recognition in the workplace of the family responsibilities of employees and the expansion of adequately remunerated employment for both men and women. The consequences of such a reframing would see good family policy not as a drain on national budgets, but as social investment and a key element of economic and social development. As such, the three false and misleading dichotomies of: A the public and private spheres of life and their social contribution; B independent labour force activity and the dependency of family-based carers; and C economic policy and family/social policy must be abandoned and replaced by the recognition that family-centred policies are central to social and economic development.

The recognition of the material and symbolic value of the intergenerational work of families, and their production of public goods calls forth and makes legitimate a public policy response in both national and international programmes of action and social development.

Gender equity

In recent decades, theories and practices of economic development have been challenged for failing to serve women, especially poor women, and in so doing, missing vital opportunities to invest fully and equitably in social development and the well-being of all members of the population, particularly children.[15]

The principle of gender equity is therefore intrinsic to the rationale of placing families at the heart of social development. Women are the major producers of the family-based services of care and nurture as well as the contributors to all aspects of the formal and informal sectors of the economy. Ignoring the role of families is to obscure the work largely carried out by women in their kinship and local networks and therefore to miss a fundamental human investment opportunity.

Social equity

The third of the intersecting concepts is social equity, which calls for the redistribution of income and resources to those families whose experience of inequality is greatest, and carries with it the most damaging consequences for the life chances and opportunities of their children. These include families who are unemployed, who have low incomes, who are headed by women, who are migrants and refugees, who have been displaced by war and civil strife, or those families, particularly indigenous families, who experience the deeply entrenched disadvantages of discrimination.

At a systemic level, social equity calls for measures that empower families as full participants in the processes of economic and social life. Fundamental to such empowerment are forms of social protection that would entrench the right to employment and the right to an adequate income during periods of unemployment, under-employment or withdrawal from the workforce to fulfil family caring responsibilities. The other major foundation of social protection for families is access to secure and affordable housing. Paying proper attention to social equity would also prompt action regarding economic policy to stimulate job creation and growth, to establish measures to ensure that low-income families do not bear the costs of industrial restructuring, to support women seeking to participate in employment if that is their choice, and to address gender-related wage differentials.

A more socially just distribution of resources to families, and in particular to families who are disadvantaged by social and economic processes, will occur only if strong and sustained investment is made in the provision of employment, education and training; affordable housing; redistributive family income support; good and sufficient health and welfare services for families, women and children; and services for care of the disabled and the elderly. When such investment is made as the key input to social, economic and family development, families and their individual members are enabled to be full participants in the life of employment, community, politics and civil society.

The exclusion of families from traditional economic development paradigms reveals the limitations of ignoring a whole sphere of production. If there is no recognition, or insufficient recognition of the contribution made by families to social and economic development, then there are no institutional responses that might begin to redress those inequalities in the course of life (differing levels of economic welfare at different stages of the family life cycle), and vertical inequalities (inequalities of income and wealth between families). The interactive nature of the principles of intergenerational equity, gender equity and social equity thus dissolves the distinction, indeed the dichotomy of private and public spheres of activity and responsibility, signalling that the two are intrinsically interdependent.

Domains of public policy for the implementation of principles of equity

The essential link between economic policy and social development are family policies based on the furtherance of the three principles of intergenerational equity, gender equity and social equity. These guiding principles in social development can serve as a preventive force in the fight against poverty at both national and international levels. Families may be in situations of poverty or acute disadvantage because of entrenched unemployment, under-employment and low wages, or the effects of some system of taxation or social protection that reinforces inequality. Such hardships also arise where informal systems of social protection (based on family, kinship and close community ties) are rendered less effective by the spread of market economies and wage labour and where formal systems of social protection have not yet been developed, or arise as a result of socio-political upheaval or war. In all of these circumstances, social and economic policies based on the three principles outlined previously are imperative if these families are to become agents of social development.

Some major arenas of public policy for empowering families are outlined below.

Employment, education and training

Emphasizing only families' non-market work is not sufficient without also recognizing that paid employment is essential for economic welfare. Adequate standards of living usually require participation in both the market and non-market arenas and contributions from both. In the light of this consideration, and the high rates of unemployment and long-term underemployment being experienced not only in the developing countries but also in the industrialized economies, policies promoting employment, education and training for all family members seeking to enter the labour force are an essential component of both economic growth and social development.

In fact, the high rates of unemployment, under-employment and labour force marginality, as the objectives of the World Summit for Social Development rightly identified, are one of the major sources of inequity and social exclusion. Their impacts are felt not only by individuals but also by their families, which indicates that social investments in education and labour market programmes must be family-centred and recognize all potential breadwinners including women, men and young people. The conventions of the International Labour Organization (ILO)* that recognize the family responsibilities of employees in workplace cultures and practices and the value of good quality child-care services illustrate only two, albeit major ways, in which social investment can link family-based work with market work.

Eliminating discrimination against women

The legislation and programmes that take their lead from conventions of the United Nations and ILO in embedding gender equality in the cultures and practices of countries are not only rightly seen as essential for achieving human rights and social justice, but are also a fundamental determinant of, and input to, social and economic development. Policies that provide non-discriminatory access for women to the labour market

---

* For instance, the Convention concerning Equal Opportunities and Equal Treatment for Men and Women Workers: Workers with Family Responsibilities (No. 156).

and reduce the gender gap in earnings; policies that provide flexible conditions of employment for all workers with caring responsibilities, and policies that provide family payments directly to the principal carers of children (usually women) are equity measures that produce both positive social outcomes and economic development.

It is widely accepted that increasing the educational opportunities for women also increases their labour-force participation, and their status of equality in society.[16, 18] The education and training of adult women will also have a significant impact on the educational level of families in both the transfer of knowledge and the greater awareness within family units of possibilities and opportunities for the education of girls, as well as the acceptance of education as an emancipating force for women and all family members. Research indicates that the single most important influence on the survival, health and achievement in education of boys and girls is their mother's education and command of income.[19] Fiscal outlays by Governments in the education and training of women as well as children are an investment in the social development of countries as well as a major contribution to current and future economic growth. It has been amply demonstrated that the participation of women in the social, economic and political life of a country is positively correlated with that country's well-being, not only in terms of economic contribution, but also specifically in relation to the well-being of infants.[18]

Empowerment is a critical concept in the international development debate relating to women and families. To enhance women's empowerment and, in the process, to contribute to social development requires social policies and social investments that provide literacy; education and training; maternal, ante-natal and post-natal health care; paid work; the right to adequately remunerated employment; political participation; and the equitable sharing of tasks within families and households.[15]

Supporting the care of children

Implementing the principle of intergenerational equity requires a strong focus on policies that promote the physical, social and educational development of children and young people. If social investment is to be the target of redoubled efforts, then national and international policies must focus on the benefits of investment in children which, in Theodore Schultz's words, "is in many ways akin to trees that are grown for their beauty and fruit".[20]

Bringing up children cannot be seen merely as a private matter: it is also in the interest of society and constitutes the production of a public benefit to society.[21] As such, government-transfer payments to families with children may be properly treated as an investment from the viewpoint of national budgets, because in directing resources to children and enhancing their health and welfare, inequalities are redressed that impede the life chances of children and young people.

Policies for older persons

In most cultures throughout the world, the extended family network is a critical component in the work of providing care and transmitting resources. The role of aunts, uncles, cousins and grandparents, especially grandmothers, in contributing to the care of children, particularly while parents are engaged in employment, and in redistributing resources through cross-generational flows, needs to be redefined, not only as a major contribution to family stability and well-being, but also as a social investment with significant economic outcomes. It is not appropriate to look upon intra-family resource flows as moving only in the direction of support for the elderly: the flow of resources is reciprocal.

Conversely, in many developed economies, demographic changes, particularly the projections of an ageing society, need to be addressed by Governments. The image of the aged as a homogeneous group of infirm and helpless people who are no longer able to make a contribution to society is erroneous. The majority of elderly people live in relationships of mutual interdependence with extended family, providing care for grandchildren or other forms of support for their adult offspring. Even in developed countries, only a small percentage of older family members rely on residential care.

Health and social services for older people should not be seen by Governments as items of expenditure yielding little or no return. Instead, policies should be directed to supporting the interdependence between the elderly and their extended families, as well as to acknowledging the contribution already made by the elderly to family life and labour force activity. This does not mean the responsibility for the care of the elderly should fall only or predominantly on the shoulders of their families. Rather, the principle of intergenerational equity requires that public policies properly support the elderly and their families through public pensions and health and social services, which also enhance the human dignity of older persons.

Integrating these domains

Social policies that provide resources for families with children and for the elderly; investments that expand sustainable employment, education and training; policies that enable parents to combine their employment and family responsibilities, and that embody gender equality: all of these measures create direct links to future social and economic development. Family breadwinners - both male and female - are able to be more productive in the workplace and to have more family time for their caring responsibilities when: A their education and training enable them to enter the workforce and receive adequate rates of pay for their work efforts; B they have access to health and welfare services for their families and children; and C their conditions of employment enable them to care for their children at critical stages of development, especially when the children are young or sick. Of utmost importance, children benefit from this conjuncture of policies since their care and nurture is enhanced as are their future opportunities.

Investment policies, within countries, from donor countries and through international development institutions, that invest in the productive activities of women, families and kinship networks are one of the most vital manifestations of a family-centric programme of sustainable social development, implemented at local levels. Such a family-centric programme needs to be pursued according to the principles of intergenerational equity, gender equity and social equity.

Conclusions

The contributions that families are able to make to the elimination of poverty, the growth of productive employment, the reduction of unemployment, and to social development and integration must be recognized in national and global planning. This recognition calls for a new multi-faceted role for Governments and international institutions in developing and implementing policies that empower families as full participants in the processes of economic and social development.

Future links between economic and social development and family policies could be forged around global benchmarks of human and family security. Such benchmarks might be designed with goals for the phased elimination of poverty, the improvement in levels of literacy, the provision of educational and vocational training for all family members with an emphasis on gender equality, and the reduction of unemployment and the expansion of employment, thus blending economic development with social development.

Benchmarks of family and human security could be developed around the issues of infant and child mortality, nutrition, shelter, primary health care, men's and women's literacy and numeracy, education, training and employment opportunities, basic social services for families, women and children, social security and family payments systems, family violence intervention and prevention programmes, and enhancement of the status of women and the status of children.

Such benchmarks could provide an opportunity to enforce the principles of equity in the following areas:

- Access of all families as a human and social right to the resources of human security, such as nutrition and a proper diet; appropriate, secure and affordable housing; preventive measures for health care; compulsory elementary education and access to secondary, tertiary and vocational education for girls and boys, women and men; access to affordable credit for women as well as for men; a guaranteed and adequate minimum income through market activity or the social transfer system or a combination of the two.
- Equitable redistribution of essential resources to families in a range of disadvantaged circumstances, in the form of income, goods and basic social services, public infrastructure investment and technology, and educational, training and employment opportunities. The region-specific ways in which disadvantages affecting families are created (which may include combinations of race, ethnic or gender discrimination, unequal access to income-generating activities, the lack of support for the vulnerable life-cycle stages of childhood and old age and the exigencies of disability and severe illness) must be adequately recognized and addressed in the distribution of resources.
- The access of families to information and the entitlements that Governments provide should be governed by a principle of transparency, allowing for an efficient dissemination of information that is easily understandable.
- There must be a high level of stability and certainty in the sustained provision of support structures for families. Families need to be able to engage in long-term planning, which is not possible if frequent and unpredictable changes are made to policy and support programmes.
- Families require a high level of flexibility in the economic and social policy provisions that are put in place by Governments to support them and invest in their active role in economic and social life. Such flexibility is necessary to reflect the varying needs of the range of family types and other factors such as rural/urban differences, cultural and ethnic differences, as well as the changing needs within families due to life-cycle transitions.
- Priority should be given to directing the investment in families to

carers within families, i.e. predominantly to women, as the role of caring work is the lifeblood of family life, human development and economic growth. Such caring work must also be recognized as an essential input to the economic and social development of countries.
- Investment in the status of women and children and their capacities to contribute to social, economic and political life at present and in the future is crucial to the quality of care in families, the quality of family dynamics and the degree of equality within families, as well as the strength of future families. This investment also constitutes the most vital contribution to equitable economic growth and social development.

IYF provided the opportunity and the impetus to contribute to a major set of policies necessary for the deliberations and outcome of the World Summit for Social Development. Families, as key contributors to social and economic development, put the focus on the interconnectedness of formal and informal/family economies, and on the roles of social investment in resourcing both domains. If family networks are ignored in the national and international programmes of action for social development, then the most vital and dynamic site of economic and social participation at the local levels will be absent from the social development paradigm and its practical applications. The principles of intergenerational equity, gender equity and social equity require a family-centric base for national and international social development efforts.

REFERENCES

[1] G. Ofer, "The global economy and social change at the turn of the century: The interaction between economic growth and poverty". Address to the Twenty-sixth International Conference of the International Council on Social Welfare, Tampere, Finland, 1994.

[2] H. Morales, "Civil society must claim the future", Introductory message. Asia-Pacific NGO Conference for the World Summit for Social Development, Bangkok, 1994.

[3] S. Wun'Gaeo, "Social development: Partnerships, competing interests, and regional processes", Address to Asia-Pacific NGO Conference for the World Summit for Social Development, Bangkok, 1994.

[4] International Council of Voluntary Agencies, "An ICVA approach to the World Summit for Social Development", International Council of Voluntary Agencies, Geneva, Switzerland, 1994.

[5] International Council on Social Welfare, *Some Options for the Programme of Action of the Social Development Summit*, Twenty-sixth World Conference of the International Council on Social Welfare, Tampere, Finland, 1994.

[6] United Nations, *Draft Declaration and Draft Programme of Action* (Executive Summary), Preparatory Committee for the World Summit for Social Development, second session, 22 August to 2 September 1994, New York.

[7] Vienna NGO Committee on the Family, *Guiding Principles on the Family*, United Nations, Vienna International Centre, Vienna, 1994.

[8] United Nations, "Family matters", *Occasional Papers Series*, No. 1 (1992), p. 6.

[9] United Nations, "The intersection of family, gender and economy in the developing world", *Occasional Papers Series*, No. 9 (1994).

[10] United Nations, "Family: Forms and functions", *Occasional Papers Series*, No. 2 (1992).

[11] K. J. Bieback, "Family benefits: The new legal structures of subsidising the family: A comparison of Australian, British and German social security systems". *Journal of European Social Policy*, vol. 2 (1992).

[12] A. Chadeau,, "What is households' non-market production worth?", OECD *Economic Studies* (Paris, 1992), No. 18, Spring, pp. 85-103.

[13] C. Ungerson, ed., *Gender and Caring* (Hemel Hempstead, Harvester, 1990).

[14] Chadeau, op. cit., p. 86.

[15] G. Baker and R. Balakkrishnan. "Women and families in international development", in *Families in Transition*, N. Leidenfrost, ed. (Vienna, International Federation for Home Economics, 1992), pp. 137-142.

[16] Ofer, op. cit.

[17] International Council on Social Welfare, Finnish Programme Committee for Global Welfare, "A call for an integrated social development strategy towards a society for all" (draft declaration), Twenty-sixth International Conference of the International Council on Social Welfare, Tampere, Finland, 1994, p. 3.

[18] F. Magrabi and K. Kim, "Toward Utopia: Women's participation in the socio-economic life of their countries", in *Families in Transition*, N. Leidenfrost, ed. (Vienna, International Federation for Home Economics, 1992), pp. 5-10.

[19] M. Snyder, "Comments", in *Families in Transition*, N. Leidenfrost, ed. (Vienna, International Federation for Home Economics, 1992), p. 3.

[20] T. W. Schultz, The *Economics of Being Poor* (Oxford, Basil Blackwell, 1993).

[21] "Welfare in a civil society: Report for the Conference of European Ministers Responsible for Social Affairs", European Centre for Social Welfare Policy and Research, Vienna, 1993.

BIBLIOGRAPHY

Bibliography

Anker, R. Female labour participation in developing countries. *In* International Labour Review, 122:6, 1983.

Arnold, Fred. Asia's labor pipeline; an overview. Boulder, Colorado, Westview Press, 1986.

Asis, Maruja Milagros. International migration and the changing labor force experience of women.

Paper presented at the United Nations Expert Group Meeting on International Migration Policies and the Status of Female Migrants, San Miniato, Italy, March 1990.

Between choice and circumstance; the dilemas of international labor migration. Quezon

City, University of the Philippines, 1994.

Asis, M. *and others.* Living arrangements in four Asian countries; a comparative perspective. Journal of Cross-Cultural Gerontology. 1994.

Atchley, Robert C. Social forces and ageing. Oxford, Ohio, Scripps Foundation Gerontology

Center, Miami University, 1980.

Bengtson, V., M. Rosenthal *and* L. Burton. Families and aging; diversity and heterogeneity. *In*

The handbook of aging and the social sciences. 3rd ed. New York, Van Nostrand Reinhold, 1990.

Benyaklef, M. Science, technology and society. *Institut National de Statistique et d'Economie*

Appliqué 9 (1987).

United Nations Educational, Scientific and Cultural Organization publication.

The elderly disabled and aging populations. *Bold* (Valletta, Malta), 1991.

International Institute on Ageing publication, 1991.

Socio-economic statistics of population ageing. *In* International conference onpopulation ageing. San Diego, California, San Diego University, 1992.

Bernardo, F. Social adaptation to widowhood among a rural-urban aged population. Washington Agricultural Experimental Station Bulletin 689.

Reprinted in: Ageing, the individual and society; readings in social gerontology. New York, St. Martin's Press, 1967.

Bezrukov, V. V. Self-care ability and institutional/non-institutional care of the elderly. *Journal of cross-cultural gerontology* 8:349-360, 1993.

Bezrukov, V. V. *and* N. N. Sachuk. USSR nations. *In* Developments and research on aging;

international handbook. E. B. Palmore, ed. Westport, Connecticut, Greenwood Press, 1993.

Blay, S., J. J. Mari and L. R. Ramos. Validity of a Brazilian version of the older Americans resources and services mental health screening questionnaire. *Journal of the American Geriatrics Society* 36:687-692, 1988.

Bock, W. Aging and suicide; the significance of marital, kinship, and alternative relations. *The family coordinator* 21:1, 1972.

Bulgaria. Public health statistics annual, Sofia, 1991.

Chamie, M. Aging, disabilities and gender. *Bold* (Valletta, Malta), 1991.

International Institute on Ageing publication.

Chebotarev, D., N. Sachuk and N. Verzhikovskaya. Problems of health and position of the elderly in socialist countries of Eastern Europe. *Zeitschrift für Alternsforschung* 36:6:437-472, 1981.

Chen, Ai Ju *and* Paul P. L. Cheung. The elderly in Singapore; Singapore country report; Socioeconomic consequences of the ageing of the population, 1988. Prepared for the Phase III ASEAN Population Project.

Chen, Ai Ju *and* Gavin Jones. Aging in ASEAN; its socio-economic consequences. Singapore, Institute of South-East Asian Studies, 1989.

Cheng, Shanzhe. The income security of the aged in China, 1989.

Prepared for the Japan-China Workshop on Population Aging, Japanese Organization for International Cooperation in Family Planning, Tokyo.

Coleman, D. A. Contrasting age structures of Western Europe and of Eastern Europe and theformer Soviet Union; demographic curiosity or labor resource? *Population and development review* 19:3, 1993.

Cowgill, Donald O. *and* Lowell D. Holmes, eds. Aging and modernization. New York, Meredith Corporation, 1972.

The demography of ageing. Springfield, Illinois, Charles C. Thomas, 1970.

Domingo, L. Government and non-government response to the issue of aging in the Philippines. Paper presented at the Round Table on the Ageing of Asian Population sponsored by the Economic and Social Commission for Asia and the Pacific in collaboration with San Diego State University, Bangkok, 1992.

Domingo, L. *and* J. Casterline. Living arrangement of the Filipino elderly. *Asia-Pacific population journal* 7:3:63-88, 1992.

Domingo, L. *and* M. Asis. Living arrangements and the flow of support between generations. *Journal of cross-cultural gerontology*, 1994.

Domingo, L. *and others.* Socio-economic consequences of the aging population; insights from the Philippines experience. Manila, Demographic Research and Development Foundation, 1990.

Dooghe, G. *and* J. Helander. Family life in old age. The Hague, Martinus Nijhoff Publishers,1979.

Ealans, F. Sri Lankan women in the Middle East.

Paper presented at the United Nations Expert Group Meeting on International Migration Policies and the Status of Female Migrants, San Miniato, Italy, March 1990.

Fratczak, E. Living arrangements of the elderly in Poland; evidence from Polish retrospective survey 1988.

Paper presented at the European Population Conference, Paris, October 1988.

Fratczak, E. Population aging in Poland; selected aspects. Valletta, Malta, Comité International de Coopération dans les Recherches Nationales en Démographie, 1993.

Garrett, M. International conference on population and development, UN Expert.

Paper presented at the United Nations Expert Group Meeting on Population Growth and Demographic Structure, Paris, November 1992.

Gatz, M., V. L. Bengston and M. J. Blum. Caregiving Families. *In* J. Birnen *and* W. Schile, *eds.*

Handbook of the psychology of the ageing. 3rd ed. New York, Academic Press, 1990.

Gaude, J. Phénomène migratoire et politique associée dans le contexte africain; études de cas en Algérie, Burundi, Cameroun, Haute-Volta. Geneva, International Labour Organisation, 1983.

Habib, J. The aging process and its implications in Europe and the USSR. *European Journal of Gerontology* 1:3, 1992.

Hendricks, Jon *and* C. Davis Hendricks. Aging in mass society, myths and realities. Cambridge, Massachusetts, Winthrop Publishers, 1981.

Hluchanova, R. Mezigeneracní vztahy. *Demographia* 3:211-220, 1985.

Hugo, G. Population mobility in West Java. Yogyakarta, Indonesia Gadjah Mada University Press, 1978.

Review of the population aging situation and major aging issues at local levels. New York, 1993. (Asian population studies)

Hulkko, J. Europe and the European family in the turn of the century. Helsinki, Population Research Institute, 1982.

Kalache, A., R. P. Veras *and* L. R. Ramos. Ageing of the world population; a new challenge.

Revista de Saude Publication 21:3, 1987.

Kinsella, Kevin. Aging in the Third World. Washington, D.C., U.S. Department of Commerce, Bureau of the Census, 1988.

Living arrangements of the elderly; a cross national data comparison.

Paper given at the International Conference on Population Aging, San Diego, California, 1993.

Kinsella, Kevin *and* C. M. Taeuber. An aging world II. Washington, D.C., U.S. Department of Commerce, Bureau of the Census, 1993.

Knodel, J., Chayovan Napaporn and Siriboon Siriwan. The familial support system of Thai elderly; an overview. *Asia-Pacific population journal* 7:3, 1992.

Knodel, J., Saengtienchai Chanpen and Sittitrai Werasit. The living arrangements of Thai elderly; views of the populace, Journal of cross-cultural gerontology, 1944.

Laczko, F. Older people in Eastern and Central Europe; the price of transition to a market economy. K. Payne, ed. London, 1993.

Lakiza-Sachuk, N. Family breaks in Ukraine in the conditions of socio-economic crisis.

Paper presented at the World NGO Forum Launching the International Year of the Family, Valletta, Malta, 28 November-2 December 1993.

Laslett, P. Family life and illicit love in early generations. Cambridge, Cambridge University Press, 1977. Lopez, M. The Filipino family as home for the aged. Ann Arbor, Population Studies Center, University of Michigan, 1991. (Comparative study of the elderly in Asia, report, 91-7)

Martin, L. Living arrangements of the elderly in Fiji, Korea, Malaysia and the Philippines. *Demography* 26:4, 1989.

Mason, K. Family changes and support of the elderly in Asia. *Asia-Pacific population journal* 7:13-32, 1992.

Mehta, K. Women's role in family support system.

Paper presented at the Workshop on Population Aging, National University of Singapore, sponsored by the Japanese Organization for International Cooperation in Family Planning, March 1994.

Mehta, K. *and* others. Living arrangements of the elderly in Singapore; cultural norms in transition. *Journal of cross-cultural gerontology*, 1994.

National economy of Ukraine in 1992. Kiev, Tekhnika, 1993.

Neysmith, S. M. *and* J. Edwardh. Economic dependency in the 1980s; its impact on Third World elderly. Ageing and society 4:1:21-44, 1984.

Parming, T. Long-term trends in family structure in Soviet Republics. *Sociology and social research* 63:3, 1979.

Pedich, W. Living conditions. In The elderly in eleven countries; a sociomedical survey.

E. Heikkinen, W. E. Waters and Z. J. Brzezinski, eds. Copenhagen, World Health Organization, 1985.

Peek, P. *and* P. Antolines. Labour migration in the sierra of Ecuador; causes and incidence.

Geneva, International Labour Organisation, 1980.

Perera, P. Aging of Sri Lanka population.

Paper presented at the Round Table on the Ageing of Asian Population sponsored by the Economic and Social Commission for Asia and the Pacific in collaboration with San Diego State University, Bangkok, 1992.

Population of Ukraine, 1992; demographic yearbook. Kiev, Tekhnika, 1993.

Quadaguo, Jills S. Aging, the individual and society. Lawrence, Kansas, University of Kansas, 1980.

Ramos, L. R. Growing old in São Paulo, Brazil. London, University of London, 1987.

Family support for the elderly in São Paulo, Brazil. *In* Family support for the elderly; the international experience. Oxford, Oxford University Press, 1992. (World Health Organization monograph)

Brazil. *In* Developments and research on aging; an international handbook. Westport, Connecticut, Greenwood Publishing, 1993.

Ramos, L. R., R. P. Veras and A. Kalache. Population ageing; a Brazilian reality. *Revista de Saude Publication* 21:3:211-224, 1987.

Ramos, L. R. *and* S. Goihman. Geographic stratification by socio-economic status. *Revista de Saude Publication* 23:6:478-492, 1989.

Ramos L. R. *and* P. Saad. Morbidity among the aged. In SEADE-Fundacão Sistema Estadual de Analise de Dados. São Paulo, SEADE, 1990.

Sachuk, N. The connection between health state of elderly people and their family status investigation. Moscow, Zdravoohranenie Rossijskoj Federatsii, 1984.

Singh, R. D. Labour migration and its impact on employment and income in a small farm economy. Geneva, International Labour Organisation, 1983.

Smith, P., Khoo Siew-Ean and P. Stella. The migration of women to cities; a comparative perspective. *In* Women in the cities of Asia. Boulder, Colorado, Westview Press, 1984.

Stoller, E. P. Males as helpers; the role of sons, relatives and friends. *Gerontologist* (Washington, D.C.) 30:2:228-235.

Sussman, M. B. The family life of old people. *In* Handbook of aging and the social sciences. New York, Van Nostrand Reinhold, 1985.

Tibbitts, Clark. Handbook of social gerontology; social aspects of aging. Chicago, University of Chicago Press, 1960.

Treas, J. Aging and the family. *In* Scientific perspectives and social issues. J. E. Birren and

R.B. Sloane, eds. Eaglewood Cliffs, New Jersey, Prentice-Hall, 1975.

Tryfan, B. Family support to elderly people in Poland. *In* Family support for the elderly; the international experience. H. Kendig, A. Hashimoto and L. C. Coppard, eds. Oxford, Oxford University Press, 1992.

Union of Soviet Socialist Republics. Demographic yearbook of the USSR. Moscow, Finansy i Statistika, 1990.

Itogi vsesoyuznoj perepisi naselenija 1979 goda. Moscow, Central Statistical Office, 1983.

USSR population in 1987. Moscow. Finansy i statistika 1988.

United Nations. Report of the World Assembly on Ageing, Vienna, 26 July to 6 August 1982. September 1982. 101 p. (A/CONF.113/31) Sales no.: 82.I.16.

Department of International Economic and Social Affairs. Ageing and urbanization; proceedings of the United Nations International Conference on Ageing Populations in the context of urbanization, Sendai, Japan, 12-16 September 1988. July 1991. 461 p. (ST/ESA/SER.R/109) Sales no.: 91.XIII.12.

The prospects of world urbanization, revised as of 1984-85. May 1987. 268 p. (ST/ESA/SER.A/101: Population studies no. 101). Sales no.: 87.XIII.3.

Department of International Economic and Social Affairs. The world aging situation; strategies and policies. August 1985. 301 p. (ST/ESA/150) Sales no.: 85.IV.5.

World population prospects, 1990. February 1991. 605 p. (ST/ESA/SER.A/120: Population studies no. 120) Sales no.: 91.XIII.4.

World population monitoring, 1990, with special emphasis on age structure. 1990. p. (ST/ESA/SER.A/126: Population studies no. 126) Sales no.: 92.XIII.2.

United Nations. Economic and Social Commission for Asia and the Pacific. Population Ageing; review of national policies and programmes in Asia and the Pacific. New York, 1992. (Asian population studies series, no. 109)

United Nations. International Research and Training Institute for the Advancement of Women. The situation of elderly women. 1993. Sales no.: 94.XVIII.3.

United Nations. Statistical Office. Statistical chart on world families. 1993. (ST/ESA/STAT/SER.Y/7) Sales no.: 93.XVII.9.

United Nations Children's Fund. Central and Eastern Europe in transition, 1993; public policy and social conditions. November 1993. (Regional monitoring report, 1)

United States of America Department of Commerce. Population and health transitions. Washington, D.C., 1992. (International population reports)

Veras, R. P., L. R. Ramos and A. Kalache. Growth of the elderly population in Brazil; changes and consequences for society, *Revista de Saude Publication* 21:3:225-233, 1987.

Woodruff, Diana and James E. Birren, eds. Aging; scientific perspectives and social issues. New York, D. Van Nostrand, 1975.

Wu, C. Aging process and income security of elderly under reform in China. Paper presented at the Round Table on the Ageing of Asian Population sponsored by the Economic and Social Commission for Asia and the Pacific in collaboration with San Diego State University, Bangkok, 1992.

Yatim, M. Population aging in Malaysia. Paper presented at the Workshop on Population Aging, National University of Singapore, sponsored by the Japanese Organization for International Cooperation in Family Planning, March 1994.